Dickinson's Fascicles

# Dickinson's Fascicles
## A Spectrum of Possibilities

*Edited by*
**Paul Crumbley** *and*
**Eleanor Elson Heginbotham**

THE OHIO STATE UNIVERSITY PRESS
COLUMBUS

Copyright © 2014 by The Ohio State University.
All rights reserved.

Library of Congress Cataloging-in-Publication Data
Dickinson's fascicles : a spectrum of possibilities / edited by Paul Crumbley and Eleanor Elson Heginbotham.
　　pages cm
　Summary: "In this volume, a number of senior and emerging Dickinson scholars raise their disparate voices with a particular set of theoretical premises, each selecting specific fascicles for close inspection. The result is the first practical, balanced, common ground for studying Dickinson's poetry in her own context"— Provided by publisher.
　Includes bibliographical references and index.
　　ISBN 978-0-8142-1259-2 (hardback) — ISBN 0-8142-1259-X (cloth) — ISBN 978-0-8142-9363-8 (cd-rom)
　1. Dickinson, Emily, 1830–1886—Criticism, Textual. 2. Dickinson, Emily, 1830–1886—Technique. 3. Dickinson, Emily, 1830–1886—Manuscripts. I. Crumbley, Paul, 1952– editor of compilation. II. Heginbotham, Eleanor Elson, editor of compilation.
　PS1541.Z5D495 2014
　811'.4—dc23
　　　　　　　　　　　　2013049757

Cover design by Janna Thompson-Chordas
Text design by Juliet Williams
Type set in Adobe Garamond

∞ The paper used in this publication meets the minimum requirements of the American National Standard for Information Sciences—Permanence of Paper for Printed Library Materials. ANSI Z39.48-1992.

9  8  7  6  5  4  3  2  1

# CONTENTS

*List of Illustrations*   vii
*List of Abbreviations*   ix
*Acknowledgments*   xi

**Introduction**  "The Prism never held the Hues": (Fr1664)   1

**Chapter 1**  Dickinson's Fascicles
        SHARON CAMERON   12

**Chapter 2**  The Word Made Flesh: Dickinson's Variants and the Life of Language
        MELANIE HUBBARD   33

**Chapter 3**  Magical Transformations: "Necromancy Sweet," Texts, and Identity in Fascicle 8
        ELEANOR ELSON HEGINBOTHAM   63

**Chapter 4**  The Precincts of Play: Fascicle 22
        DOMHNALL MITCHELL   86

**Chapter 5**  "Looking at Death, is Dying": Fascicle 16 in a Civil War Context
        PAULA BERNAT BENNETT   106

**Chapter 6**  Civil War(s) and Dickinson Manuscript Book Reconstructions, Deconstructed
        MARTHA NELL SMITH   130

| | | |
|---|---|---|
| **Chapter 7** | Managing Multiple Contexts: Dickinson, Genre, and the Circulation of Fascicle 1 | |
| | ALEXANDRA SOCARIDES | 150 |
| **Chapter 8** | Manuscript Study, Fascicle Study: Appreciating Dickinson's Prosody | |
| | ELLEN LOUISE HART | 169 |
| **Chapter 9** | "This – was my finallest / Occasion – ": Fascicle 40 and Dickinson's Aesthetic of Intrinsic Renown | |
| | PAUL CRUMBLEY | 191 |
| **Chapter 10** | Coda from *My Emily Dickinson* | |
| | SUSAN HOWE | 217 |

| | |
|---|---|
| *Notes* | *219* |
| *Works Cited* | *252* |
| *Contributors* | *265* |
| *Index of First Lines* | *267* |
| *Index to Letters (including poems cited as letters)* | *273* |
| *General Index* | *274* |

## LIST OF ILLUSTRATIONS

| | | |
|---|---|---|
| **Figure 1** | Fascicle 13, "Of bronze and blaze." By permission of The Houghton Library, Harvard University. (MS Am 1118, 3 [74]). © The President and Fellows of Harvard College. | 29 |
| **Figure 2** | Fascicle 13, "There's a certain slant of light." By permission of The Houghton Library, Harvard University. (MS Am 1118, 3 [74]). © The President and Fellows of Harvard College. | 30 |
| **Figure 3** | MS 0778 Josephine Kingsley Hardy Papers. Series 2, "Casket of Gems," essay 7; Series 2, "What Employment Brings the Most Happiness" composition. Mount Holyoke College Archives and Special Collections. | 41 |
| **Figure 4** | "John Milton as a Politician." Amherst College, Archives and Special Collections. | 44–5 |
| **Figure 5** | Fascicle 33 MSS Boxes "K." Charles Baker Kittredge. Courtesy of the American Antiquarian Society. | 48–9 |
| **Figure 6** | Fascicle 8, "Ah, Necromancy Sweet!" By permission of The Houghton Library, Harvard University. (MS Am 1119.3 [16d]) © The President and Fellows of Harvard College. | 64 |
| **Figure 7** | Fascicle 2 (80–1), "There is a word." Amherst College Archives and Special Collections. | 140 |

| | | |
|---|---|---|
| **Figure 8** | Fascicle 2 (80–9), part of inked out "One Sister have I in the house." Amherst College Archives and Special Collections. | 141 |
| **Figure 9** | Fascicle 2 (80–6 verso facing 80–7), "Once more, my now bewildered Dove." Amherst College Archives and Special Collections. | 144 |
| **Figure 10** | Fascicle 19 (80–7 recto), "The Face I carry with me – last –" Amherst College Archives and Special Collections. | 145 |
| **Figure 11** | Fascicle 2 (80–8 recto), "Bless God, he went as soldiers." Amherst College Archives and Special Collections. | 146 |
| **Figure 12** | Fascicle 2 (80–8a), inked-over manuscripts. Amherst College Archives and Special Collections. | 147 |
| **Figure 13** | Fascicle 2, canceled out with pencil, transcription by Todd of second stanza of "To venerate the simple days." Amherst College Archives and Special Collections. | 149 |
| **Figure 14** | Fascicle 1, "As if I asked a common alms –" Amherst College Archives and Special Collections. | 158–9 |
| **Figure 15** | Pre-fascicle draft of "If those I loved were lost." Amherst College Archives and Special Collections. | 165 |

## LIST OF ABBREVIATIONS

L = *The Letters* number

Fr = Franklin poem number

F = Fascicle number

*MB* = *Manuscript Books* page number

## ACKNOWLEDGMENTS

For a volume such as this, one that represents the dedication and scholarship of numerous contributors, it is impossible to trace a single path that neatly leads from first conception to final completion. The book began when, after a particularly lively meeting of the Emily Dickinson Society, in a restaurant in Amherst, Massachusetts, in the summer of 2003, we (Eleanor Heginbotham and Paul Crumbley) talked of the need for thoughtful, informed responses to the still-new and already somewhat contentious subject of Dickinson's fascicles. There and then we decided to co-edit a volume of essays. We agreed that it would be a daunting but timely project, one that would require the best minds in the field, so we immediately assembled a dream list of contributors, sent out invitations, and then asked everyone to be patient. We had to be patient because the work was hard and most of us didn't know where we would wind up once we got started. We did know that we would have to be flexible and allow the work to take shape over time; even the fastest among us understood that. As a consequence, the people we most want to thank are our contributors, the wonderful scholars who stuck with us over the years and so generously granted each other the time to let their thoughts mature. From the very beginning of our work, influential early scholars of the manuscripts, Sharon Cameron and Susan Howe, also encouraged our project and contributed greatly to it through their significant books and by allowing us to use portions of their groundbreaking work to frame our current collection. We hope all of you will agree that the highest expression of our gratitude to you is the book itself and the opportunity it affords all of us to make this important work available to the public.

Second only to the contributors, we want to thank the patient and expert editing wisdom of the team at The Ohio State University Press: Malcolm Litchfield, Director; Eugene O'Connor, copyediting coordinator; Juliet Williams, tyepesetter; Lindsay Martin, acquisitions editor, and Kristen Ebert, our copyeditor. Special thanks, too, to the press's former Senior Editor, Sandy Crooms, for her indefatigable wisdom and encouragement through the long gestation of this project. As work on the book progressed, we became greatly indebted to the peer reviewers, whose suggestions for organization, particularly, helped us to shape the book into its present form and whose questions and suggestions sharpened the work. We also thank our cohorts in the Emily Dickinson International Society for their promotion of Dickinson scholarship and the support they have provided to all the contributors to this volume. We have all benefitted from annual meetings, international conferences, and the dissemination of scholarship through the *Emily Dickinson Journal* and the *Emily Dickinson International Society Bulletin.*

Paul personally wants to thank the Utah State University English department for the encouragement and generous support they have provided over the duration of this project. Eleanor listed her mentors in her first book for The Ohio State University Press; she has only increased her gratitude for those at the University of Maryland and at Concordia University Saint Paul in subsequent years. Both editors thank their families for *their* support and encouragement as well.

We gratefully acknowledge the following presses and institutions for granting us permission to reproduce the materials that appear below.

Emily Dickinson's manuscripts are quoted by permission of the Trustees of Amherst College and the Houghton Library of Harvard University. The poems of Emily Dickinson are reprinted by permission of the publishers and the Trustees of Amherst College from *The Poems of Emily Dickinson: Variorum Edition,* ed. Ralph W. Franklin, Cambridge, MA: Belknap Press of Harvard University Press, Copyright © 1998, 1999 by the President and Fellows of Harvard College. Copyright © 1951, 1955, 1979, 1983 by the President and Fellows of Harvard College. The Dickinson letters are reprinted by permission of the publishers from *The Letters of Emily Dickinson,* ed. Thomas H. Johnson, Cambridge, MA: Belknap Press of Harvard University Press, Copyright © 1958, 1986 by the President and Fellows of Harvard college; 1914, 1924, 1932, 1942 by Martha Dickinson Bianchi; 1952 by Alfred Leete Hampson; 1960 by Mary L. Hampson.

"Dickinson's Fascicles" by Sharon Cameron is an adaptation of portions of the introductory chapter to *Choosing Not Choosing,* by Sharon Cameron © 1992 by the University of Chicago Press. All rights reserved. The adaptation was first published in *The Emily Dickinson Handbook,* edited by Gudrun Grabher, Roland Hagenbüchle, and Cristanne Miller (Amherst: University of Massachusetts Press, 1998).

The "Coda" contribution from Susan Howe that ends our book is from *My Emily Dickinson,* copyright © 1985 by Susan Howe. Reprinted by permission of New Directions Publishing Corp.

A WORD about what readers will see as misspellings in some of the poems, letters, and scraps of Emily Dickinson: we have not applied the "sic" label to such words as "opon," "exhilirates," and "it's" as a possessive pronoun. Readers unfamiliar with the Manuscript Books of Emily Dickinson and other studies of her handwritten texts will note that some essays include her vairant, signaled with this sign: +. Along with the dash, it is all part of the challenge and rewaqrd of reading her face to face in these poems.

INTRODUCTION

# "The Prism never held the Hues"
## (Fr1664)

The phrase "spectrum of possibilities" that appears in the title of this volume quite literally refers to the diversity of interpretive stances presented in these pages. This collection of essays does not aspire to consistency in the approaches of its contributors; instead, it gathers a range of scholarly perspectives on Emily Dickinson's forty handcrafted manuscript "books"—generally referred to as fascicles, the term one of her first editors, Mabel Loomis Todd, used to describe them—in order to express the state of fascicle scholarship at this time. In putting together this first collection of scholarly essays ever dedicated exclusively to the fascicles, we thought it important to offer an honest overview of current research as now practiced by leading Dickinson scholars, most of whom are already well known for their published work on Dickinson and her manuscripts. Differences of opinion regarding approaches to fascicle reading, including the benefits of such reading, are consistent with Dickinson criticism in general, characterized as it is by conflicting assumptions about where best to ground textual analysis. Dickinson's extensive holographic record and its varied print manifestations have provided multiple pathways into the poems and letters, and the tendency among scholars has been to favor one over the others. For this reason, our title phrase, "spectrum of possibilities," also performs the metaphorical function of acknowledging that for Dickinson, especially, the word spectrum extends to the color spectrum revealed when a beam of light passes through a prism, yielding an array of colors, each of which can become a particular source of fascination.

When Dickinson writes that "The Prism never held the Hues," her speaker might well be acknowledging the fact that poetry itself performs as a prism that reveals an array of colors, among which each reader selects according to the light of his or her own individual intelligence. Disagreement, therefore, especially spirited disagreement, is celebrated in these pages as registering the vitality of Dickinson's literary art. Even so, our arrangement of the essays is designed to assist readers as they make their way through divergent lines of enquiry. We deliberately open this volume with "Dickinson's Fascicles," an adaptation of the first chapter of Sharon Cameron's influential 1992 book *Choosing Not Choosing: Dickinson's Fascicles*, because this work has proven so influential in establishing the terms for succeeding fascicle scholarship. Most notably, Cameron's was the first study of the fascicles that challenged readers to examine carefully the nonnarrative, indeterminate, and highly disruptive attributes of fascicle poems. While Cameron was not the only scholar to wrestle with the manuscript complexities that became so much more available for scholarly consideration after the 1981 publication of Ralph W. Franklin's *The Manuscript Books of Emily Dickinson*, hers was the first book-length effort to propose an organizational principle grounded in indeterminacy rather than some form of linear coherence.

Cameron spoke for many in the world of Dickinson studies when she declared, "one of the reasons that the few existing theories about the fascicles have been so unsatisfying is that they variously attempt to account for the fascicles as if they had a single discernible principle of order—for example, a love story" (16). The love story reference applies most directly to William H. Shurr's 1983 *The Marriage of Emily Dickinson: A Study of the Fascicles*, one of the important early efforts to make sense of the fascicles that unearthed a master narrative of one sort or another. Other early attempts to grapple with the implications of Dickinson's fascicle project include Ruth Miller's 1968 *The Poetry of Emily Dickinson*, based on a pre-Franklin ordering, which called the books "long link poems" (239); M. L. Rosenthal and Sally M. Gall's 1983 *The Modern Poetic Sequence: The Genius of Modern Poetry*, which placed Dickinson's fascicle poems in the context of books by Housman, Hardy, Eliot, and Pound; and Dorothy Huff Oberhaus's 1995 *Emily Dickinson's Fascicles: Meaning and Method*, which focuses on Fascicle 40 as a "conversion narrative." These works and others, including books by the co-editors of this volume, make important contributions to our understanding of what the fascicles are and how to read them, but some of them aspire to a degree of resolution and coherence that Cameron presents as inconsistent with the holograph record. For the writers who appear in this collection, Cameron's statement has served as a turning point in fascicle scholarship that now finds value in charting multiple sources of meaning rather than articulating a single overarching order.

Cameron's observation that "unity is not produced by reading Dickinson's lyrics in the fascicle context" (4) has provided a powerfully generative stimulus for the wide range of scholarly approaches to fascicle analysis that appear here. This is not to say, however, that scholarship after Cameron has simply elaborated the many implications of her argument; far from it. As the following essays demonstrate, critics take issue with many of Cameron's most daring assertions: that "variants extend the text's identity in ways that make it seem potentially limitless" (6), that "the material placement of the poem is essential to discerning its identity" (6), that the fascicles ought to be regarded "as definitive, if privately published, texts" (8), that "the unit of sense is not the individual poem but rather the fascicle book" (15), are just a few. The enduring influence of Cameron's study rests on the sweeping implications of her core argument that Dickinson is a poet of "not choosing" whose precise attention to manuscript construction forms part of an audacious poetic project founded on the interrelationship between indeterminacy and identity.

Unlike most of the writers gathered here, Cameron does see evidence of a conceptual scheme in Dickinson's fascicle arrangements, though she is quick to point out that "the question of the author's intention is always undecidable" (18). With this fundamental qualification in place, she then proposes that the poet's deliberate copying of poems into the fascicles is evidence that "Dickinson intended something"; the issue for the critic, then, is "what did [Dickinson] intend?" Cameron's avowedly speculative answer to this question is that "Dickinson's intention was to be indeterminate with respect to the relation among the poems. . . ." For Cameron, understanding the way Dickinson's use of indeterminacy bears on identity requires close examination of the fascicle context. The scholars who appear in this volume follow Cameron's lead by eschewing the quest for a master narrative in favor of providing speculative answers to the question of what it was Dickinson intended, but they do not all agree that the fascicle context is primary or even useful as a conceptual or aesthetic structure.

A central benefit of a collection such as this—that does not offer a consensus view of how best to read the fascicles—is that it further demonstrates the versatility and depth of Dickinson's body of work, making clear the fact that there are many points of entry to this extensive and largely unexplored feature of Dickinson's literary landscape. Such a diverse array of approaches helps to crystallize key points of contention, as well as emerging areas of agreement that distinguish the ways Dickinson scholars view the fascicles and develop productive strategies for reading. Our sequence of contributions aims to clarify significant developments in fascicle scholarship that we think are made evident for the first time in this volume. To this end, we chose to follow Cameron's chapter with Melanie Hubbard's essay because Hubbard so directly challenges Cameron's view of Dickinson's variants and the conceptual structure of fascicle gatherings. This sequence of arguments immediately identifies a central debate over the coherence of the fascicle unit that other contributors engage with directly or indirectly and that will play a key role in future fascicle scholarship. An important feature of Hubbard's essay that may point to an emerging consensus within fascicle study is her effort to situate the works within a distinct historical context that in her case includes linguistic theory and rhetorical practice.

The next two essays, those by Domhnall Mitchell and Eleanor Heginbotham, also read fascicle poems as corresponding to contemporary historical events, although for them the associations are literary and religious. An important difference between the approaches of these two scholars is that Heginbotham concentrates on poems within a single fascicle while Mitchell draws from multiple fascicles and in doing so joins Hubbard in questioning the value of the fascicle unit. Paula Bennett and Martha Nell Smith, whose contributions form the next pair of essays, consider the Civil War as a significant historical influence on fascicle poems. Bennett, like Heginbotham, limits her comments to a single fascicle, while Smith, like Mitchell, reads across fascicle divisions. The final grouping of essays is based on a shared interest in the way fascicle poems mark a phase in Dickinson's artistic development. Alexandra Socarides, whose essay is the first of the final three, describes fascicle poems as part of Dickinson's ongoing experimentation with literary genre that Socarides traces through the fascicles to correspondence and late poems. Ellen Louise Hart focuses on changes in Dickinson's visual prosody that she tracks through numerous fascicles and also connects to later poems. Paul Crumbley explores Dickinson's developing understanding of literary fame and is the only scholar in this final group who centers discussion on a single fascicle, though he also draws on documents that lie outside the fascicle confines.

Hubbard's essay, "The Word Made Flesh: Dickinson's Variants and the Life of Language," presents Dickinson's fascicle gatherings and her inclusion of variants as consistent with widespread nineteenth-century compositional practices. Through a careful examination of these methods and their relationship to linguistic theories advanced by the rhetorical texts Dickinson studied, Hubbard argues that the fascicles do not function as coherent units of meaning that reflect authorial intent or achieve the metaphysical status of books. Challenging Cameron's view that Dickinson's variants uniformly promote "not choosing" and therefore resist the limitations of time, Hubbard proposes instead that the variants record a range of thought processes and consequently perform multiple functions, some of which are consistent with Cameron's analysis. Hubbard describes Dickinson's thought as emerging through poems poised between the timeless fictive world of linguistic embodiment and the inevitability of physical death. Dickinson's contemplation of possibilities from within this perspective reflects a deep investment in the life of language that Hubbard presents as fraught with peril due to the likelihood that future readers will misread and incorrectly interpret the poetic record. Hubbard demonstrates that "Shall I take thee, the Poet said" (Fr1243) supports Cameron's theory of "not choosing," while "My life had stood – a Loaded Gun –" (Fr764) does not. The poem "A Word made Flesh" (Fr1715) explores yet another possibility; in this case, the "Word" reflects a "collective self" that simultaneously exists in the time-bound body and the ongoing life of language.

Heginbotham's essay, "Magical Transformations: 'Necromancy Sweet,' Texts, and Identity in Fascicle 8," looks closely at the physical placement of the twenty poems in this fascicle as they play off one another visually and thematically. Heginbotham approaches the individual poems as lyrics that function collectively as a "long-link poem" that has its own "thumbprint": "its sworl of images or themes or concerns that sets it apart from the other [fascicles]." In this fascicle, the core concern, or hub, is necromancy, the artistic power to reach across the divide between past and present, life and death, to transform poet and reader. As background to her discussion of the fascicle, Heginbotham situates Dickinson's reference to necromancy in the context of nineteenth-century Spiritualism, a popular religious movement that believed in the possibility of communication with the spirits of the dead. Accordingly, Dickinson's readers in effect act as mediums who channel the latent potential of the poems, interpreting for their own purposes the many inferences suggested by repeated images, symbols, and juxtapositions. A distinctive feature of Heginbotham's approach is her insistence that fascicle reading is itself a playful process of discovery that discloses Dickinson's wit, embrace of serendipity, and intellectual intensity.

"The Precincts of Play: Fascicle 22" shares Heginbotham's emphasis on playfulness as a core feature of fascicle reading, but Mitchell extends the range of playful associations beyond the bounds of Fascicle 22. His approach to reading builds on two primary perceptions: that fascicles are not structured as narratives and that poems that appear in the fascicle context can be productively interpreted though associations with biography, literary history, current history, and contemporary writers, all of which lead reading away from the fascicle setting. Mitchell structures his essay as an effort to determine what kind of reading best fulfills the critic's obligation to provide readers with the "richest interpretations available" (87). He concludes that while fascicle gatherings that he refers to as "anthologies" will always be valuable resources for Dickinson study, they should not be viewed as "autonomous aesthetic objects" (105). As Bennett does in her essay, Mitchell identifies the way fascicle poems incorporate images and themes that link her work to other writers. In his case this includes Shakespeare, Donne, Wordsworth, and Byron. Byron's "The Prisoner of Chillon," for instance, provides a wealth of parallels with Dickinson's "A Prison gets to be a friend –" (Fr456) that Mitchell explores at some length. He also examines "He fumbles at your Soul" (Fr477B) in light of sermon influences and print documents by contemporary theologians, most notably accounts of Charles Wadsworth's preaching style and published work by Amasa Park.

Bennett contributes to the growing subfield of Dickinson's Civil War poetry in her essay titled "'Looking at Death, is Dying': Fascicle 16 in a Civil War Context." Drawing on her extensive knowledge of nineteenth-century poetry in England and the United States, Bennett describes the poems that appear in this fascicle as contributing to a category of poems she defines as "dramatic lyrics." These hybrid poems incorporate elements of drama and lyric that Dickinson utilizes in her presentation of speakers who do not serve as surrogates for her own subjectivity but rather represent personalities from quite different walks of life. Speakers that appear in Fascicle 16 include a New England farm boy, a battle-hardened veteran, a soldier wrestling with religious faith, and a soldier who has abandoned hope, among others. Bennett links Dickinson's dramatic lyrics to the work of Robert Browning and Sarah Piatt in particular, but many other contemporaries as well, especially those whose published Civil War poems Dickinson would have encountered. In her reading of the fascicle, Bennett links poems in pairs that clarify the multiple and varied perspectives on the Civil War that Dickinson explores. Her procedure is based on her belief that these fascicle poems reflect the imprint of the war but do not appear as part of a narrative or any other overarching principle of order. Dickinson's response to the death of Frazar Stearns informs a number of Bennett's readings.

Smith acknowledges Fascicle 24's connection to the Civil War, adding to the sort of analysis put forward by Bennett, but Smith also directs attention to the very different civil war waged around Austin Dickinson's affair with Mabel Loomis Todd and the mutilation of fascicle sheets in an effort to remove evidence of Sue Dickinson's prominence. This deliberate alteration contributes significantly to the editorial history of fascicle construction that raises questions about the authenticity of fascicle gatherings as established by Franklin. "Civil War(s) and Dickinson Manuscript Book Reconstructions, Deconstructed" urges readers to consider the different ways fascicles have been arranged by editors and to contemplate the influence this may have on interpretation. Acknowledging that poems in Fascicle 24 present a strong seasonal orientation that begins with winter and cycles backward to spring, and that prominent references to the colors blue and grey combine with frequent references to blood suggestive of the Civil War, Smith cautions against attributing any specific set of meanings to Dickinson. Instead, Smith examines the crucial role audiences play as readers and editors who project their own stories on the manuscript remnants left by the poet. Smith is quick to point out that the arbitrary nature of such readings does not invalidate them but rather opens the study of fascicle meaning and construction to theoretical investigation bearing on questions of representation, intention, and reception.

In "Managing Multiple Contexts: Dickinson, Genre, and the Circulation of Fascicle 1," Socarides looks closely at a narrow selection of poems from this fascicle to illustrate Dickinson's practice of circulating fascicle poems through letters and revising them in later compositions. Socarides explains that this multiplication of poem settings represents Dickinson's interest in violating the boundaries that separate literary genre. Drawing on Virginia Jackson's observation that the circulation history of Dickinson compositions militates against the tendency to treat them exclusively as lyric poems, Socarides argues that poems included in the first fascicle must be understood as participating in ongoing compositional processes consistent with highly flexible verbal constructions. Such a view contests the assumption that fascicles groupings act as enclosed poetic spaces. Her point is that Dickinson returned even to the poems that appear in the first fascicle and continued to experiment with them throughout her writing life, mixing poetic and prose genres rather than shifting from one to the other. As a consequence, fascicle poems are best thought of as one stage in an ongoing history of textual reformulation rather than as fixed lyrics.

In "Manuscript Study, Fascicle Study: Appreciating Dickinson's Prosody," Hart argues that Fascicle 10 represents a stage in Dickinson's prosodic development that is best understood through a systematic combination of manuscript scholarship and fascicle study. Features of Fascicle

10 that most interest Hart include Dickinson's use of underlined words and phrases, her line division, and her dedication to alliteration. Most specifically, Hart argues that Dickinson's experimentation with visual techniques such as line division and underlining reinforces her dedication to the aural dimension of poems, a dedication that Hart links to the poet's ongoing concern with alliteration. Hart notes that in Fascicles 9 and 10 Dickinson moves her dashes from the ends to the middles of lines while also using underlining and the division of metrical lines to emphasize midline content. Underlining that achieves the highest frequency in Fascicle 10 gives way to the short-line format in later fascicles and sets that Hart presents as a shift in prosodic technique designed to control reading speed and magnify discrete aural and semantic effects. Along with this change, Hart identifies a move away from the dash that Dickinson increasingly replaces with line breaks and the later introduction of inline spacing to emphasize interior rhyme, assonance, and alliteration. The essay concentrates primarily on Hart's diplomatic transcriptions of two poems, one from Fascicle 10 and one from Set 10, transcribed by Franklin as "Safe in their Alabaster Chambers –" (Fr124) and "To disappear enhances –" (Fr1239B).

Crumbley's approach to fascicle reading in "'This – was my finallest / Occasion –': Fascicle 40 and Dickinson's Aesthetic of Intrinsic Renown" links the poems to nineteenth-century debates over copyright and Dickinson's ongoing reflections on the nature of literary fame. He sees the twenty-one poems of the fascicle as organized in groupings that achieve greatest coherence by virtue of their placement on six individual fascicle sheets or bifolia. Like Bennett, Crumbley presents the fascicle as a grouping of poems that approach a central issue from a multitude of points of view; however, in the case of Fascicle 40 the core concern is the poet's relationship to the creative process and the life poetry enters once it is released into the world. Crumbley points out that 1864, the year the poems of Fascicle 40 were copied into the fascicle, was momentous for several reasons that may have contributed to Dickinson's reflections on the future of her work. Most notably, it was the year when more Dickinson poems appeared in print than at any other time; the year when she received the most extended treatment for eye problems; the year when the total number of poems or letter-poems sent out in correspondence reached at least 251; the year when she ceased binding her fascicle sheets. Crumbley connects the poems of this fascicle to "Publication – is the Auction" (Fr788) and to an 1877 letter to Thomas Wentworth Higginson in which Dickinson responds to his poem titled "Decoration."

DESPITE THE diversity of approaches just outlined, there are a number of valuable observations regarding shared perceptions that herald scholarship to come. Of these, the most broadly accepted is the view that fascicles do not show evidence of narrative continuity or linear sequence as a source of individual or collective coherence. For several of the contributors, this perception derives from Dickinson's practice of stacking sheets of paper that were prefolded at the time of purchase and then stab-binding them with thread or string. Her decision to stack rather than nest the sheets inside one another points to the single folded sheet, or four-page bifolium, as the primary unit of meaning, not the fascicle. Had Dickinson composed poems so that they consistently ran from one bifolium to another, this could be viewed as evidence that she understood the sheets as significantly connected. In the absence of such evidence and the lack of clearly discernible patterns of continuity, the existence of a governing rationale for binding the fascicles remains a matter of debate. The persistent uncertainty regarding a universally observable organizational scheme contributes to the agreement among contributors that it is simply not possible to identify authorial intent. As a consequence, the readings offered by scholars are presented as speculative, or as reflecting varying approaches to the reading of poems that could also support alternative interpretations. The outcome is a general tendency to present individual fascicle readings as nonexclusive interpretations that do not pretend to exhaust the meaning potential of the poems they consider.

Widespread agreement that the fascicles support multiple approaches to reading has quite understandably contributed to increased scholarly interest in historical and biographical context. One explanation for this is that the critical shift away from authorial intent and correlative searches for linear orderings has diminished emphasis on Dickinson as isolated creator and given rise to the view that Dickinson's literary art very much bears the imprint of the world around her. Hubbard's argument that the material construction of fascicle gatherings is not unique to Dickinson and is in fact consistent with the records left by her contemporaries is a prime example of this. Similarly, Bennett's observations about the origins of specific speakers in Dickinson's Civil War poems has led her to conclude that Dickinson incorporated stories from the front within a specialized lyric form that Bennett refers to as the dramatic lyric. Several other essays, notably Heginbotham's and Crumbley's, place fascicle poems in conversation with contemporaneous events, such as the Spiritualist movement and copyright debates. That Bennett, Heginbotham, and Crumbley also concentrate primarily on single fascicles as the basis for their discussions may indicate that fascicle study most directly concerned with historical context is best pursued when analysis is limited to poems bound together at the same time. For this reason, further clarification of the process by which Dickinson gathered fascicle poems and additional verification of the dates she bound them may well prove crucial to this trend in fascicle study. If, as Franklin, Socarides, and others have argued, the basic unit of meaning is the individual sheet and not the stacks of sheets bound to form fascicles, dating of individual sheets may prove more critical than determining when Dickinson bound them together. Even so, a precise history of the editorial disassembly and reconstruction of the fascicles that Smith calls for in her contribution will be essential to our understanding of Dickinson's groupings.

    A last consideration for future scholarship suggested by this collection has to do with the big question of what a Dickinson poem is. If, as many of the writers in this volume suggest, the fascicle format is not Dickinson's preferred setting for her poems and therefore not the closest we can get to an author-approved manuscript edition, the fascicle project—or whatever Dickinson may have called it—must be taken seriously as one of multiple arrangements Dickinson used. Such an understanding challenges the tendency to treat fascicle poems as components of internally coherent self-enclosed books sealed off from the surrounding world. At the same time, however, such a view acknowledges that fascicle arrangements may be significant as part of an ongoing artistic or cultural dialogue that does not aspire to closure. Even Mitchell, who argues that fascicle units do not provide the most productive critical contexts for literary interpretation, does not deny the value of the fascicle gatherings he refers to as Dickinson's anthologies. Viewed as but one setting that stands alongside others, such as letter-poems, poems enclosed in letters, and other fair copy drafts, the fascicles become valuable precisely because they indicate that Dickinson was not hierarchical and did not perceive new formats as displacing those that preceded them. The fact that Dickinson chose to preserve the fascicles even though she meticulously destroyed rough drafts of poems suggests they were important to her for reasons that may be connected to literary form. This is the position Socarides advances in her essay where she argues that reading Dickinson poems as they appear in multiple contexts, including fascicles, provokes reconsideration of their status as lyric poems. Her proposal that they express Dickinson's ongoing experimentation with literary form is both provocative and reasonable. Bennett's attention to Dickinson's use of the dramatic lyric is less provocative but similar in that she represents a departure from the more traditional lyric frame while also linking her examination of genre to fascicle context. Hart's analysis of Dickinson's prosody shares Socarides's view that fascicle gatherings reflect changes in Dickinson's understanding of poetic form, though she does not associate these changes with experimental departures from the lyric tradition. The freshness and vigor of these approaches indicate that there is much more to be said about the influence context has on form and genre.

Even though there are undeniable points of convergence and hints of emerging trends that unite some or all of the essays, what is most distinctive about this collection is its spectrum of scholarly approaches. Writers included here embrace extremes that extend from confidence in the benefits of fascicle investigation to skepticism regarding the productivity of such an undertaking. This diversity is welcomed in large part because we are convinced that scholarly study of Dickinson's fascicles is only now entering its infancy, and that a rich and exciting new field of enquiry is just opening. We take this position because we and most of the contributors to this collection have overcome our own skepticism to discover reaches of meaning where we had not expected to find them. More to the point, even, we believe that the fascicles are simply too extensive and too important a part of the poet's manuscript record to be ignored any longer. Nevertheless, skepticism is healthy in any serious intellectual endeavor, and one of our primary objectives is to ensure that all persons seeking to engage in future fascicle study do so with their eyes open. We look forward to the future illumination of "possibilities" that is sure to follow as more scholars read Dickinson in the context of the forty gatherings she bound between 1858 and 1864, at the time of her greatest productivity.

# Dickinson's Fascicles

SHARON CAMERON

### The Subject of Context

To look at the history of Dickinson criticism is to see that what is memorialized are her ellipses, her canceled connections, the "revoked . . . referentiality" of the poetry. The phrase is from Geoffrey Hartman's *Criticism in the Wilderness* (129), but one thinks also of Jay Leyda's description of Dickinson as writing "riddle[s]," poems of the "omitted center" (1:xxi); of Robert Weisbuch's characterization of this poetry as "sceneless," producing "analogical language which exists in parallel to a world of experience, as its definition" (*Poetry* 19); of David Porter's assessment that "here is the verbal equivalent of *sfumato*, the technique in expressionistic painting whereby information . . . on a canvas is given only piecemeal and thereby necessarily stimulates the imaginative projection of the viewer, who, out of his own experience, supplies the missing . . . context" (*Early Poetry* 99); of an earlier claim of my own that the poems "excavate the territory that lies past the range of all phenomenal sense" (*Lyric Time* 9). Or, to allow Hartman to make the point one more time: Dickinson, the "dangerous" purifier, italicizes "leanness," more than leanness even—the "zero" meaning of the hyphen that punctuates the poetry (130–31). In Hartman's discussion, the hyphen becomes emblematic. "Perhaps because it both joins and divides, [it is like] a hymen. . . . That hyphen-hymen persephonates Emily" (126).

But does it?[1] What if this way of reading her poetry belies the way it was written, or, once written, put together (both internally structured and also made contiguous)? What if these poems are less alien than we had supposed? Or not alien in the way we had supposed? What if they are not quite as sceneless or cryptic (even apparently subjectless) as the characterizations insist? Or what if the scenes and subjects can be said to unfold between and among the poems as well as within them?

To consider poems as individual lyrics is to suppose boundedness. To consider poems as related—as, say, a sequence would relate them—is differently to suppose boundedness, in that poems which are seen to be connected must first be seen to be discrete. To consider poems as not discrete but also as not related is to complicate the negotiations between interior and exterior. This Dickinson does by raising questions about the identity of the text. With respect to Dickinson's fascicles—to anticipate my argument—the variant is a way of getting at what the text "is." That is, in Dickinson's poems, variant words (and poems which we come to see as variants of each other) raise the question of what counts as the identity of the text in question. The question raised is: if this word—or this second poem—conventionally understood to be *outside* the poem is rather *integral* to the poem, how is the poem delimited? What *is* the poem? I shall argue that words that are variants are part of the poem outside of which they ostensibly lie, as poems in the same fascicle may sometimes be seen as variants of each other. In Dickinson's fascicles—where "variants" are more than the editorial term for discrete delimited choices—variants indicate both the desire for limit and the difficulty in enforcing it. The difficulty in enforcing a limit to the poems turns into a kind of limitlessness, for, as I shall demonstrate, it is impossible to say where the text ends because the variants extend the text's identity in ways that make it seem potentially limitless.[2]

Initially, however, my aim is to ask how the situation for understanding Dickinson's poems changes when we consider that they are at once isolated lyrics, as Thomas H. Johnson presented them in *The Complete Poems* (and in his variorum text), and poems that have the appearance of a sequence, as R. W. Franklin presented them when he published *The Manuscript Books of Emily Dickinson*, a volume crucial for our reassessment of this poetry, about which I shall therefore say a few words before proceeding.[3] First, the assertion that Franklin presents Dickinson's poems in sequences is one he would not accept. Dickinson organized most of her nearly eighteen hundred poems into her own form of bookmaking: selected poems copied in ink onto bifolia, "sheets of letter paper already folded by the manufacturer to produce two leaves" (Franklin, *MB* xi). Then she stabbed them and bound them with string. Franklin has argued that no aesthetic principle governs their binding. It was, nevertheless, Franklin's goal to reproduce in facsimile the manuscripts that Dickinson bound with string into forty fascicles from about 1858 to 1864 and the fifteen "sets"—poems which, primarily after 1864, she copied but never bound.[4]

Second, Franklin claims the binding was a means of keeping order among her poems. But an alternative speculation is that the fascicles were a form of private publication.[5] Franklin's assumption that they were a means of keeping order among her poems begs the question of what such an order would be. The alternative, that the fascicles were a form of private publication—halfheartedly endorsed by Franklin in the introduction to the facsimile, and (as I shall explain) contested by him elsewhere—has its plausibility heightened by reference to "New Poetry," an essay of Emerson's printed in *The Dial* in 1840, in which he advised authors, in distinction to the dominant strain of poetic tradition, to collect album poetry, for, Emerson writes, a "revolution in literature is now giving importance to the portfolio over the book" (1169). In making her lyrics into manuscript books—in effect, constituting manuscripts as if they were books—Dickinson may have been responding to a revolution like the one predicated by Emerson. Indeed, once Dickinson had copied poems into fascicles she usually destroyed her worksheets. Such a practice invites us to regard the poems copied in the fascicles in the same way that her manner of collecting them suggests she might herself have regarded them: as definitive, if privately published, texts. The copying and binding, and the destruction of the worksheets, insist that this is the fascicles' status, despite the fact that Dickinson subsequently adopted variants from the fascicle sheets in the "text" she sent to friends, and despite the fact that it is one of the characteristics of the fascicle texts, especially after 1861, that variants to words also exist in fair copy, indeed exist as *part* of the text of the last thirty fascicles.[6]

When Franklin writes that the fascicles were a means of keeping order among Dickinson's poems, he means that they literally helped her to tidy up: "The disorder that fascicle sheets forestalled may be seen in the 'scraps' of the later years. When she did not copy such sheets and destroy the previous versions, her poems are found on hundreds of odds and ends—brown paper bags, magazine clippings, discarded envelopes and letters, the backs of recipes" ("Fascicles" 16). Thus Franklin imagines Dickinson's keeping order as her means of making the poems consistent with respect to their physical appearance, rather than as her means of organizing them. According to his explanation, the poems are not "artistic gatherings" at all but rather "private documents with practical uses, gatherings of convenience for poems finished or unfinished" (17).

When Franklin speculates that the fascicles are meant to order (tidy up) rather than to arrange (make significant), as evidence of this he cites the fact that Dickinson may have had a backlog of poems written before they were copied and bound. This was probably the case in 1862 when, Franklin writes, "Emily Dickinson could have had a significant number of poems in her pool and, in that year, perhaps spurred on by the correspondence with Higginson, set in vigorously to organizing them, now letting poems enter the fascicles trailing many alternates" ("Fascicles" 15). An opposite assumption is that Dickinson was saving these poems to see *how* they would go together, allowing single lyrics, or several lyrics copied onto one bifolium, to remain temporarily separate or piecemeal so that she could ultimately stitch them into the different comprehensive entity that the fascicle gathering made of them. And if it is more probable to suppose (as Franklin also does; see "Fascicles" 13) that the poems in twenty of Dickinson's forty fascicles were *copied* rather than all (necessarily) written in 1862, then whether Dickinson saved her poems with the idea of eventually organizing them or whether in 1862 she came to group and identify poems previously seen as discrete—identifications marked by the copying and the fascicle binding—is in a sense less significant than that we consider what the gatherings made of these poems. It is important that we consider, as the copying most dramatically in that year instructs us to do, whether structures are being created out of ostensibly discrete entities. Sometimes sheets were copied in different years and only subsequently bound. Of these Franklin writes: "Binding followed copying, sometimes years later mixing sheets from different years. That such sheets were copied in different years suggests that no fascicle-level order governed their preparation" (17). Yet sheets copied in different years and only subsequently bound rather suggest to me sheets over which a high degree of order has been exercised, suggest that, in the delay between the copying and the binding, what is precisely being governed, made visible, and materially determined is the preparation of an entity.

Whatever his suppositions about Dickinson's texts, Ralph Franklin's reestablishment of the order in which the sheets in each fascicle were bound is of inestimable value to all readers of Dickinson, and in fact to all readers of poetry. Indeed, Franklin's restoration of the internal sequence of the fascicles—no internal order could be established for the sets since they were never bound—in *The Manuscript Books of Emily Dickinson* has immediate practical consequences for Dickinson's reader, for reading Franklin's text of the poems is different from reading Johnson's text of the poems. This is the case even when Franklin and Johnson ascribe identical dates to the poems so that there is the same consecutive relation among several poems in both editions. In the Johnson edition the unit of sense is the individual poem; beyond that, it is whatever arbitrary place the reader decides to close the book. In fact, although Johnson arranges the poems chronologically, that arrangement of poems gives the reader the impression of no arrangement at all, because in a year like 1862 there are over three hundred poems. In the facsimile, these poems do not follow on the page as they do in the Johnson variorum. Rather, as I hope to show, in Franklin they exist in groups with internal sequences.[7] Thus, in the Franklin edition, the unit of sense is not the individual poem but rather the fascicle book, and one wonders about the relation among the fascicles as well as about the relation between the fascicles and the sets—or at least the question of such relations is raised by the contiguity of these units.[8]

That Dickinson ordered her poems is argued by other evidence of the manuscripts: by the fact that, for example, on the first leaf of Fascicle 9 (dated by Franklin and Johnson as copied in 1860) Dickinson added "Bound – a trouble –" (Fr240A, dated as added about 1861), although there would have been room to add this poem elsewhere in the same fascicle (on the second side of the next leaf), and by the fact that in Fascicles 12 and 14 poems from different years—from 1860 and 1861, in the case of 12, and from 1861, 1858, and 1862, in the case of 14—are bound together, although in each of these years Dickinson wrote numerous poems and in other fascicles she characteristically bound poems from the same year together. It is further argued by the example of Fascicle 8, in which a poem (Fr174) is copied twice in different places in the fascicle with variant first lines ("Portraits are to daily faces" [*MB* 136] becomes in the second instance of copying "Pictures are to daily faces" [*MB* 145]), as if each were a separate poem. Since the repeated poems are separated by several leaves and by nine intervening poems, and since there is space earlier in the fascicle to have copied "Pictures are to daily faces," Dickinson may have been structuring the fascicle by her disparate placements of the so-called same poem. This arrangement of poems—perceptible in Dickinson's copying practices; in her adding to a "completed" fascicle; in her repeating a poem within a fascicle; in her copying on matching leaves poems she then placed in separate fascicles; in her composing a fascicle with poems from different years—suggests a conceptual scheme, although Fascicle 9, the same fascicle that suggests that scheme by virtue of the added poem, also leaves the reader uncertain how the scheme is to be understood, because it is not clear to what the poem is "added" (the immediate sequence of poems? the specific poem preceding it? the whole fascicle?).

Here one could equivocate about questions of order by saying that whether Dickinson produced the order or whether the reader produces the order of the fascicles by registering the poems' juxtaposition there is immaterial, since the question of the author's intention is always undecidable. But the question of intention, at least at one level, is not undecidable—because we know that Dickinson intended something. After all, she copied the poems into the fascicles. The question then is, in doing so, what did she intend? Looking at the fascicles it might even appear that Dickinson's intention was to be indeterminate with respect to the relation among these poems, since lyric structures whose boundaries are conventionally left intact are in the fascicles characteristically punctured by the "outside" (which I shall argue is not an "outside") composed of variants and other poems. Or, to explain the situation in positive terms: it seems that given such violations of boundaries it might differently appear that Dickinson intended to redetermine our very understanding of how the identity of a poetic structure is to be construed. With respect to the binding, we do know, however minimal this knowledge may initially be deemed to be, that Dickinson intended to associate these poems with each other. Thus the question is not whether intentions are relevant. The question is rather how to understand the extraordinarily complex, perhaps even conflicted, set of intentions, beliefs, desires that are registered when Dickinson's poems are read in the fascicles in which she copied them. For to read the poems in the fascicles is to see that the contextual sense of Dickinson is not the canonical sense of Dickinson.

The point, then, is to examine what kinds of connections among poems are apparent when they are read in the fascicles, and perhaps even on what principle the "apparent" will be produced. Connections, while not possible to illustrate in all of the poems in a given fascicle, are demonstrable in a sufficient number of the poems to give the fascicle as a whole the appearance of a structure. This apparent structure consequently affects our understanding of the subjects of the poems. Specifically, as I shall explain, it affects our understanding of what subjects are. By "subjects" I do not here mean the first-person speaker, but I also do not mean the conventionally defined headings that Johnson produces in his "Subject Index," which designate rhetorical and wholly unproblematic topics or themes. In fact, while the poem I shall consider at the beginning of the next section of this essay confirms the standard notion that a lyric of Dickinson's is devoid of a subject, when one returns that lyric to the fascicle context the question of the subject comes back in a different way as a question about the nature of poetic subjects.

To sum up, then, I mean to ask how reading a lyric in a sequence is different from reading the lyric as independent, for to do the latter is to suppress the context and the relations that govern the lyric in context—a suppression generating that understanding of Dickinson's poems as enigmatic, isolated, culturally incomprehensible phenomena which has dominated most Dickinson criticism, including my own. At issue in the following examination is the question of what happens when context—when the sequence—is not suppressed.

THE FASCICLES invite us to read Dickinson's poems in the context of other sequences—Herbert's *The Temple,* Barrett Browning's sonnets, Tennyson's *In Memoriam,* Shakespeare's sonnets—which we can presume Dickinson had read.[9] Yet to place Dickinson's poems in the context of other lyric sequences does not imply that we should read her poems only in sequence, or even mainly in sequence, rather than as isolated lyrics. Therefore, demonstrating that the poems can be read in sequence, and demonstrating the multiple ways in which sequences can be read (as I shall in Fascicle 15), does not clarify whether the poems are to be read in sequence or isolation. But the reason it does not illuminate this, I shall argue, is that Dickinson herself was uncertain about how her poems should be read, an uncertainty demonstrated by the fact that she both sent her poems to friends as individual lyrics and copied them in the fascicles in sequences. Or, to formulate the point more strongly, it is not merely that Dickinson was uncertain, but that she refused to make up her mind about how her poems should be read. This refusal—another aspect of what I call choosing not to choose—is crucial to the problematic of reading her poetry.

Multiple ways of reading Dickinson's poems are consonant with the multiple variants in those poems; I have touched on this topic earlier. Interestingly, the variants have characteristically been understood as a nuisance by her readers. In 1890 Dickinson's first editors, T. W. Higginson and Mabel Loomis Todd, eliminated all variants when they made other substantive textual changes. In 1960 Thomas Johnson did the equivalent, as he chose among the variants he had recorded to make a reader's edition. But what if we are to see the variants interlineated in a poem as posing alternatives to given words, which—this is crucial—are part of the poem? What if what Dickinson has to teach us is the multiplicity of meanings that, properly understood, resist exclusion? In other words, Dickinson appears to be understanding variants as non-exclusive alternatives—a phenomenon that would have analogues in Christopher Ricks's description of the anti-pun in which a poet "creates meanings which take into account those absent senses of a word which his verse is aware of fending off" (99). In Ricks's discussion of anti-puns, though, these senses are absent in the sense of being implied while also being precluded. They are incorporated, for instance, in the second sense of a word which is implicitly ruled out. In Dickinson's poems alternative senses are displaced but not decisively so because they remain ambiguously counterpointed to the word to which they stand in explicit juxtaposition, and to which they often stand in direct proximity on the manuscript page. Thus, whereas in Ricks's notion of the anti-pun a second sense is entertained and then dismissed, in Dickinson's poems alternative words collide without particular words being clearly made secondary or subordinate. For alternatives to various words are not treated in Dickinson's text as *other* than those words.

One way of understanding variants is that a reader is required to choose between them and there is even evidence for both choices. Preliminary dilemmas aside, one is supposed to choose, and, indeed, if one had the right evidence, one could make the right choice. There is nothing ontologically tricky about such a situation.

A second way of understanding the problem of two entities that look like variants is that while they look as if they require to be chosen between, they do not so require because both are clearly part of the poem or of the single entity, as the following examples from Whitman's and Yeats's poetry clarify. Thus, for instance, in section 6 of *Song of Myself* where we are told of the grass, "I guess it must be the flag of my disposition . . . / Or I guess it is the handkerchief of the Lord, / . . . / Or I guess the grass is itself a child . . . " we are not meant to choose among these possibilities. Similarly, in the last stanza of Yeats's "Among School Children," where "nor" in effect means "or," when we are told that "Labour is blossoming or dancing where / The body is not bruised to pleasure soul, / Nor beauty born out of its own despair, / Nor blear-eyed wisdom out of midnight oil" we are not meant to choose among the possibilities. Not only is no choice required, but a choice would in fact be a mistake.

A third way of understanding variants—a way of understanding them necessitated by reading Dickinson's fascicles—is that they are meant to be experienced *as* variants, and so one is also meant to be experiencing the necessity of choosing between them. Thus the situation exemplified by Dickinson's variants is more like the first case than it is like the second. But it is different from the first case because there are no possible criteria that could enable one to choose. So, in this third case, the reader experiences the necessity for choosing, without access to the criteria by which she could make a choice. In other words, the problem is not solved by having more evidence, because the problem is not raised as a question of evidence. And in fact, as I have argued elsewhere, there is no way that the problem posed by the imperative to choose countered by the prohibition against choosing could be simplified or solved.[10]

One implication of not being able to choose among the variants is that we would have only one adequate text of Dickinson's poems—that of the facsimile—an unsatisfactory solution because in effect no one reads this text. That problem would seem to be solved if the decision were made to print a transcript of the fascicle texts, for then people would read them. Yet even if a transcript of the fascicle texts were printed, such publication would not address what I take to be the real problem: the nature of the relation between poem and text. That is, there is the "text" that is the document; there is the "text" that is the poem as the published or, in Dickinson's case, publishable entity; and there is the more contemporary sense of "text," which is what the poem becomes as "read." In Dickinson's case the contemporary or semiotic nature of "text" depends on the text as document. It specifically depends on the felt ladenness of the document's *alternatives* in some exacerbated way.

What is central here is the question of form. What the fascicles raise is precisely a question about the relation between text and poem (about the non-identity of text and poem), a relation shown to be problematic by the fact that our difficulty of reading is not solved once one has chosen which text (Johnson's, Franklin's variorum edition, or *The Manuscript Books*) one is going to read. For once a text has been chosen, if there are variants to that text, one has still not cleared up the question of how to read the variants. The metrics of the poem insist we choose only one of the variants. But the presence of the variants insists on the impossibility of doing so. Another way to describe the dilemma is that, since Dickinson refuses to choose among the variants, she disallows us from doing so. The conventional interpretation of this situation is that there are as many poems as there are variants. This is precisely the wrong way to understand how words work in poems. The variants exert pressure against each other in a *particular* poem and at particular places *within* that poem.

DICKINSON'S not choosing among the variants opens onto other aspects of not choosing in her poetry. I enumerate, albeit briefly, other aspects of doubleness—of choosing not to choose—in Dickinson's poetry that the examination of the textual situation helps to enlarge.

1. First, it is a commonplace that at the level of syntax Dickinson is characteristically choosing not to choose. It is not, for instance, clear whether "Slow Gold – but Everlasting –" in "Some – Work for Immortality – / The Chiefer part, for Time –" (Fr536) refers to the compensations of "Time" or those of "Immortality." By association with the previous line the tenor of the metaphor would be "Immortality," not "Time," but in light of the following line it would be "Time" rather than "Immortality." Nothing will produce a resolution to the question about reference, since the syntax is unresolved, and definitively so, for according to the indeterminacy conveyed by the dashes the line cannot but be read in opposite directions and this simultaneously. Such doubleness, both syntactical and semantic, is less complicated in "At least – to pray – is left – is left –" (Fr377). But it is quite complicated in the last stanza of "Rehearsal to Ourselves" (Fr664): "We will not drop the Dirk – / Because We love the Wound / The Dirk Commemorate – Itself / Remind Us that We died." In these lines there is a choice between reading "Itself" as allied with "Dirk," with the reflexivity applied to the instrument, and reading "Itself" as applied to the wound inflicted by the dirk. In the second interpretation of the syntax the recollection is still fatal, but it is not, as in the first, futile. Since the fatality is caused by the loss—rather than by the recollection of the loss—it is compensated by being also caused by the "Bliss" associated with the loss, and inevitably recollected at the same time. And this choice is unresolvable since no amount of parsing will convert the syntax into conventionally punctuated lines that indicate which noun is underscored as object of the self-reflexive action. The dashes permit, even insist on, these overlapping, disparate meanings, suggesting both the futility of recollection and its compensations.

2. But if Dickinson characteristically does not choose syntactically, she also characteristically does not choose between the story ostensibly being told and the story actually being told. In "I cannot live with You –" (Fr706), for instance, choosing not to be with a lover rather means choosing the grounds on which to meet him: it means equating him with the God for whom he has ostensibly been given up. Often apparent in the difficulty of this poetry is the fact that two conflicting stories are told simultaneously (see Cameron, *Lyric Time* chap. 2). While the disruption caused by the doubleness punctuates the experience of reading the poems, it is also

a characteristic of these poems not to acknowledge the existence of double stories, hence not to establish alliances with one or the other of the stories, and thus to predicate a seamlessness belied by what is being voiced. So voice is at odds with itself in these poems, so much so that the proper term for the disagreement is in fact heteroglossia.

3. Dickinson is also choosing not to choose between the suggestion that certain experiences can be mapped—can be made comprehensible in terms of geographies and exteriors—and the suggestion made by the same poems that such experiences cannot be. Thus, for example, in a poem like "Bereaved of all, I went abroad –" (Fr886) a speaker attempts to reside elsewhere than where the loss is, literally to place herself at a geographic distance from loss, although the speaker is more explicit about the futility of such efforts than elsewhere. Such poems, in search of correlatives for interior experience, often resort to the language of measurement in order to insist on the impossibility of it (as in "A nearness to Tremendousness –" [Fr824]). Or they raise questions about what it means to define experience in terms of categories without content ("I stepped from Plank to Plank" [Fr926]). These poems might be described as sceneless, but in fact they avail themselves of quite elaborate maps, geographies, scenes, and coordinates ("Behind Me – dips Eternity – / Before Me – Immortality – / Myself – the Term between –" [Fr743]), even if the claim made by the elaborate representations is countered by the categorical emptiness of the same representations, by the fact that what is being mapped is only technically or terminologically coherent. In the poems Dickinson is choosing not to choose whether certain experiences *can* be mapped—whether something that is only categorically comprehensible is comprehensible or not. She is choosing not to choose what the coordinates of an experience are, choosing not to choose whether internal scenes can have external coordinates. And she is choosing not to choose whether certain exteriorizations ("a Funeral, in my Brain" [Fr340]) fulfill the task assigned to them—here to make a conceit of repression—or whether, in not forestalling the repression, the exteriorization fails to fulfill the task assigned to it. In fact, this exteriorization is itself equivocal: it gives literal, external form to an inner event but immediately relocates it within ("in my Brain").

4. Dickinson is also not choosing how particular words are to be read. Consider "None may teach it – Any –" in "There's a certain Slant of light" (Fr320) where what is implied is "None may teach it – [not] Any[one] –"; "None may teach it – Any[thing] –" (it is not subject to alteration); and "None may teach it – [to] Any[one else] –." In "I felt a Funeral, in my Brain," consider the poem's last line: "And Finished knowing – then –,"

where it is ambiguous whether knowing is finished or whether the experience which prevents knowing is finished. And consider the last line of "After great pain, a formal feeling comes –" (Fr372), "First – Chill – then Stupor – then the letting go –" with its ambiguity about whether what "letting go" implies is the ability to feel, which would reverse the "Chill" and "Stupor" that have preceded it, or whether what is oppositely implied by the whole series of nouns are the final stages of the inability to feel that terminate in death.

5. The refusal to choose—choosing not to choose—how syntax is to be read, how double voices and sometimes contradictory stories are related to each other, how lines which *can* be read in antithetical ways *should* in fact be read, is reiterated in the question mark with which so many of Dickinson's poems conclude: "Which Anguish was the utterest – then – / To perish, or to live?" (Fr425), "Could it be Madness – this?" (Fr423), "And could I further 'No'?" (Fr346B), "Say, Jesus Christ of Nazareth – / Hast thou no arm for Me?" (Fr377), "'My Husband' – women say – / Stroking the Melody – / Is *this* – the way?" (Fr194A), and so on.

6. Finally, Dickinson's choosing not to choose is dramatically reiterated in the questions raised by the discrepancy between the boundedness implied by the quatrain form and the apparent boundlessness implied by the variant. Not choosing in Dickinson's poetry thus results in a heteroglossia whose manifestations inform every aspect of the poetry.

## Excess

In an atypical but logically first example of what we might expect from consideration of a poem in its fascicle placement, recourse to the fascicle context can prove simply clarifying. Consider the following poem (Fr633) as an isolated lyric:

> I saw no Way – The Heavens were stitched –
> I felt the Columns close –
> The Earth reversed her Hemispheres –
> I touched the Universe –
>
> And back it slid – and I alone –
> A Speck upon a Ball –
> Went out upon Circumference –
> Beyond the Dip of Bell –

Read thus—as an isolated lyric—the poem seems like an exercise in solecism, as well as solipsism, having not only no referent but also no context: barely comprehensible.

But to read the poem differently in the context of the poem that precedes it on the same bifolium in Fascicle 31 is to see that there could be a referent for the experience. For the first line of the previous poem, copied on the other side of the page of "I saw no Way" is "To lose one's faith – surpass / The loss of an Estate –" (Fr632), and this proximity, however loosely, establishes the poems in a relation to each other, suggesting that the cause of the disorientation might not be mysterious at all, but rather loss of faith. Moreover, to read "I saw no Way" in relation to yet a different poem, the first in the same bifolium, "The Soul's Superior instants" (Fr630), is to see that it too represents a geography in which recognizable features of a scene are abolished, the speaker in "The Soul's Superior instants" being said to have "ascended / To too remote a Hight / For lower Recognition"—to have ascended, in other words, to a sphere in which what occurs is called "Mortal Abolition," the abolition of the mortal world which is then replaced by an apparitional world not dissimilar to that in "I saw no Way."

Yet to establish a relation between and among poems is not yet to clarify it. Would, for instance, the epithet "Superior," which characterizes the moments of dissociation from the earthly world in "The Soul's Superior instants," equally apply to similar moments in "I saw no Way"? Or would it rather be the case that the exaltation and the despair of such alien moments were, in the two poems, being counterpointed to each other? Ultimately, in the second of the poems in the same bifolium ("Me prove it now – Whoever doubt" [Fr631]), what is represented simultaneously is the imminence of a *speaker's* death and the recollection of her lover's death. As "Me prove it now" precedes "To lose one's faith – surpass / The loss of an Estate –," would the lover's death in one poem be the cause of the loss of faith in the next, a loss of faith whose *consequences,* one could say, are demonstrated in the apocalyptic imagery of the poem "I saw no Way – the Heavens were stitched –" with which we began? To ask these questions, as the poem read in the fascicle context makes it inevitable that we do, is not to arrive at a more stable interpretive situation, but it is to arrive at a different interpretive situation than that in which the poem is read elliptically as a decontextualized utterance. It is to be confronted by a different interpretive situation just to the extent that there are relations among poems that we cannot disregard and, as much to the point, that we do not precisely know how to comprehend.

To see a poem contextualized by a fascicle is sometimes to see that it has an altogether different, rather than only a relationally more complex, meaning when it is read in sequence rather than as an isolated lyric. For example, to read "Because I could not stop for Death –" (Fr479) with reference to other fascicles and to other poems in Fascicle 23 is to see that the speaker's journey may not be solitary, not because she is accompanied by the abstract figures of death and immortality but perhaps rather because she is accompanied by a lost lover here personified as death. This way of understanding the poem would be consonant with the many poems in the other fascicles and some of the poems in this one, poems in which a lover has died, and it would explain why in "Because I could not stop for Death –" death is figured as a lover or in any case as a suitor. Such a contextualization changes the sense of the poem. It changes it since the speaker's inability to imagine an end to the journey because death cannot be imagined (the conventional reading of the poem) is different from her inability to imagine death's end because she is not in fact dead. Reread in the context of the fascicles, "Because I could not stop for Death –" proposes a haunted relation to a death, which, though always there in memory, *cannot* deliver passage to eternity since, though death is always present, it is never, in fact, one's own.[11]

Yet if to read a poem in the fascicle context is potentially to domesticate it—to make it less uncanny than the conventional interpretation does—in other instances, poems read in the fascicle context call such a domestication into question. Thus in Fascicle 24 "This is my letter to the World / That never wrote to Me – / The simple News that Nature told – / With tender Majesty" (Fr519)—that poem anthologized in high school textbooks to epitomize Dickinson at her most saccharine—is not necessarily a poem about a benign telling of nature's secret. Rather, at least with reference to surrounding poems in the fascicle, the secret being told is ominous. One poem in the same fascicle, for example, describes the earth as "A Pit – but Heaven over it –" (Fr508); in others, life extends without significance or value, one speaker explaining: "Therefore – we do life's labor – / Though life's Reward – be done – / With scrupulous exactness – / To hold our Senses – on –" (Fr522). In still another poem, "It sifts from Leaden Sieves –" (Fr291B), nature in the form of a snowstorm obfuscates the visible, making it unrecognizable, as negation makes things unrecognizable. In "This is my letter to the World," the telling of nature's story is not benign but rather informed by sinister aspects of the fascicle's other poems. For the letter to the world, its delivery to our "Hands," to hands the speaker "cannot see," is inescapably to be read as analogous to those stern communications the speaker has herself received.

But if reading poems in the fascicle context specifies subjects for poems and even in some cases their antecedents, it also raises problems about how the very groupings that contextualize poems are related to each other within the fascicles. I want now to sketch out these problems with respect to two issues raised in Fascicle 15: the way in which the pairings of poems within a fascicle govern lyrics not implicated in the pairing; and conversely, the way in which a central poem in a fascicle can be seen to govern poems that appear paired or clustered.

By "paired" I mean the following: In several of the fascicles the first and last poems are either complementary or antithetical, or the poems are complementary *and* antithetical. In Fascicle 28, for instance, the first poem ("My period had come for Prayer –" [Fr525]) and the last ("I prayed, at first, a little Girl" [Fr546]) refute each other, in that while one suggests that prayer is transcended by worship, the other suggests that prayer is deflected by the impossibility of worship. In Fascicle 34 the first poem ("Bereavement in their death to feel" [Fr756]) represents a speaker's experience of a death for which there is no recompense, while the last poem ("Essential Oils – are wrung –" [Fr772]) represents consolation for death in the essence that survives it: "this" ["The Attar from the Rose"] "Make Summer – When the Lady lie / In Ceaseless Rosemary –." In Fascicle 40, the last of the fascicles, the first and last poems ("The Only News I know / Is Bulletins all Day / From Immortality" [Fr820] and "Unfulfilled to Observation –" [Fr839]) represent speakers who perceive immortality and who, oppositely, are unable to do so. Thus the first and last poems of many of the fascicles, while differently related to each other, are undeniably linked, often by the reversal or countering of the idea in the initial poem. While outside of the fascicle context to see the same theme treated differently in disparate poems can seem an accident resulting from arbitrarily placing these poems in proximity, within a fascicle context, in the instances I have described, it is impossible to see such conjunctions as arbitrary, since, placed by Dickinson at the beginning and end, they in effect frame what lies between them.

Fascicle 15 exemplifies the terms in which the phenomenon of pairing—and the heteroglossia made manifest in the pairing—is significant. Fascicle 15 contains paired poems governed by three sets of antithetical assertions: first, that madness can't be stopped ("The first Day's Night had come –" [Fr423]) and that it *can* be ("We grow accustomed to the Dark –" [Fr428]); second, that losing a lover—and therefore only having him speculatively—is unbearable ("It is dead – Find it –" [Fr434]) and, conversely, that having him only speculatively is entirely bearable ("Not in this World to see his face –" [Fr435] and "If I may have it, when it's dead" [Fr431]);

third, that direct knowledge is desired ("You'll know it – as you know 'tis Noon –" [Fr429]) and, conversely, that oblique knowledge is superior ("A Charm invests a face / Imperfectly beheld –" [Fr430]). Moreover, these three apparently unrelated topics may be seen to be connected because, in the fascicle context, through the proximity of the poems, antithetical attitudes toward madness and toward knowing are generated by the specific subjects of not knowing—and of not having—the lover. Therefore a narrative not suggested by any of the poems read singly is suggested by the poems read in relation, though not in chronological relation.

In Fascicle 15, as noted, the connections among paired poems also affect a reader's understanding of poems not implicated in the pairing. More, poems that are not part of a pair, and not apparently implicated in the concerns of any of the pairs, may seem to govern all of the pairs by applying, if only indeterminately, to even one of the three concerns they manifest. This is the case with "I found the words to every thought / I ever had – but One –" (Fr436), because which *one*—which thought—seems to refer to one of the fascicle's three central topics (not having the lover, not knowing [the lover], madness [because of not knowing or not having the lover]) without being definitively identified with any one of these. The indeterminacy has the effect of retaining the ambiguity of the one subject for which words cannot be found. Indeed, it has the effect of heightening the tension around the poem's ambiguity since the possibilities are narrowed to three without being reduced to one. Similarly, "I had been hungry, all the Years –" (Fr439), that poem which, even read singly, presents hunger as a conventional metaphor for desire, addresses, by changing the terms of, the three topics that dominate the fascicle. It does so because, as this is the last poem in the fascicle, "I had been hungry, all the Years –" would seem to advocate *not* having, *not* knowing, *not wanting,* except speculatively, the lover of whose presence the speaker had—in the paired antitheses—earlier been *deprived.* Thus the final poem in the fascicle, which in effect specifies a complicated connection between having and desiring, itself exists in opposition to the attitude toward desire expressed by the poems that have preceded it. They adopt various stances toward what the speaker desires but does not have. The final poem oppositely defines having as itself antithetical to desire.

That a fascicle's various paired antitheses should, by proximity or contiguity, be associated with each other; that poems unimplicated in any of the fascicle's antithetically paired poems should nevertheless seem to refer to them (as "I found the words to every thought / I ever had – but One –" does); that a single poem should come into definitive antithetical relation to the series of paired opposites against which that single poem chronologically positions itself (as "I had been hungry, all the Years –" does)—in other words, that patterns discernible in some of the poems should inevitably affect a reader's perception of other poems ostensibly outside of that pattern—reveals yet another order a fascicle imposes on the poems within it. The order not of a narrative, and not of a single structure, it is, in the case of Fascicle 15, the order of antithetical perspectives that come to seem complementary, come even to seem unified when they are read in opposition to a poem—the last in the fascicle—whose assertions assault the supposition on which the oppositions are founded. It is the order of poems whose allegiances shift, and can be seen to do so.

To exemplify, one last time, the differences between reading in the fascicles and reading lyrics singly, consider the relationship between two celebrated poems, "Of Bronze – and Blaze –" (Fr319) and "There's a certain Slant of light" (Fr320), that follow each other in Fascicle 13 (figs. 1–2), a juxtaposition which is fascinating for the disparate stances it offers toward the attempt to take loss impersonally, to reconstrue nature's manifestations of indifference to persons as benign. In "Of Bronze – and Blaze –" nature's indifference to the self is what we are to cultivate in relation to ourselves. But if "Of Bronze – and Blaze –" records the indifference to the self that the self should and does adopt, "There's a certain Slant of light" cannot do this, the speaker there rather internalizing indifference as the difference that is betrayal—as a sign of despair and death. Fascicle 13 records a series of connected attempts to understand loss as natural, as a mere conversion, say, of day into night. To the extent that the speakers accept the impersonality of such a metaphor (as "Of Bronze – and Blaze –" does), loss is inconsequential; to the extent that loss seems only alien, the speaker is afflicted by the difference that registers as internal ("Where the Meanings, are"). For with respect to the shifting light that "comes," that "goes," this shifting, when internalized, when taken in or taken personally, turns to despair. "Of Bronze – and Blaze –" does not, then, simply contextualize "There's a certain Slant of light"; it also changes its meaning, for when the two poems are read as retorts to each other, the second becomes a denial of the neutral perspective advanced as natural in the poem that precedes it. Or rather the second poem makes clear that the *natural* perspective is not the *person's* perspective and cannot be made so.

In my discussion of Dickinson's fascicles in general and of Fascicle 15 in particular, I have raised questions rather than answering them: What is the difference between reading a poem in a fascicle context and reading it as an isolated lyric? What are the distinct ways in which poems are

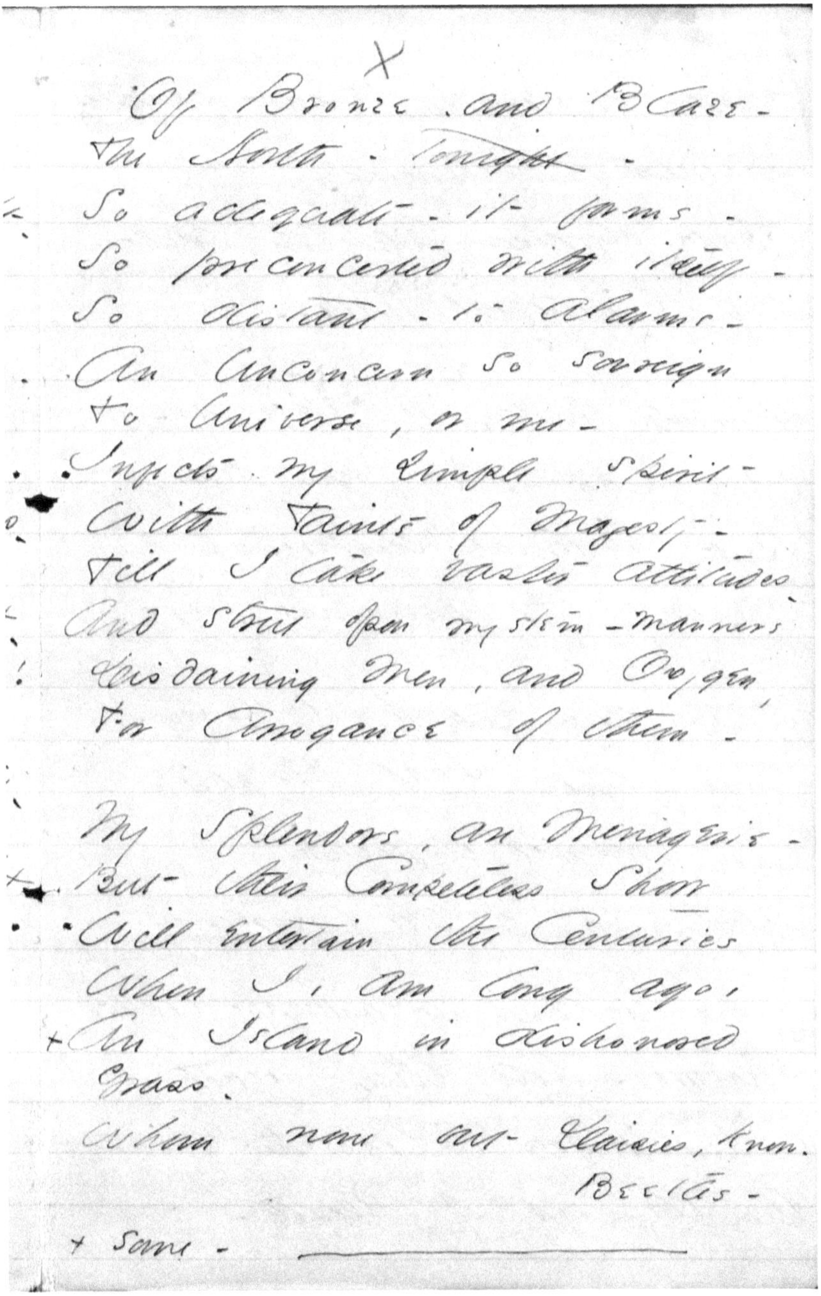

"Of Bronze – and Blaze –
The North – Tonight –
So adequate – it forms –
So preconcerted with itself –
So distant – to alarms –
An Unconcern so sovereign
To Universe, or me –
Infects my simple spirit
With Taints of Majesty –
Till I take vaster attitudes –
And strut upon my stem –
Disdaining Men, and Oxygen,
For Arrogance of them –

My Splendors, are Menagerie –
But their Competeless Show
Will entertain the Centuries
When I, am long ago,
An Island in dishonored
Grass –
Whom none but Daisies, know.
Beetles –
+ Save –

*Figure 1.* Fascicle 13, bifolium 3, second recto, "Of bronze and blaze."

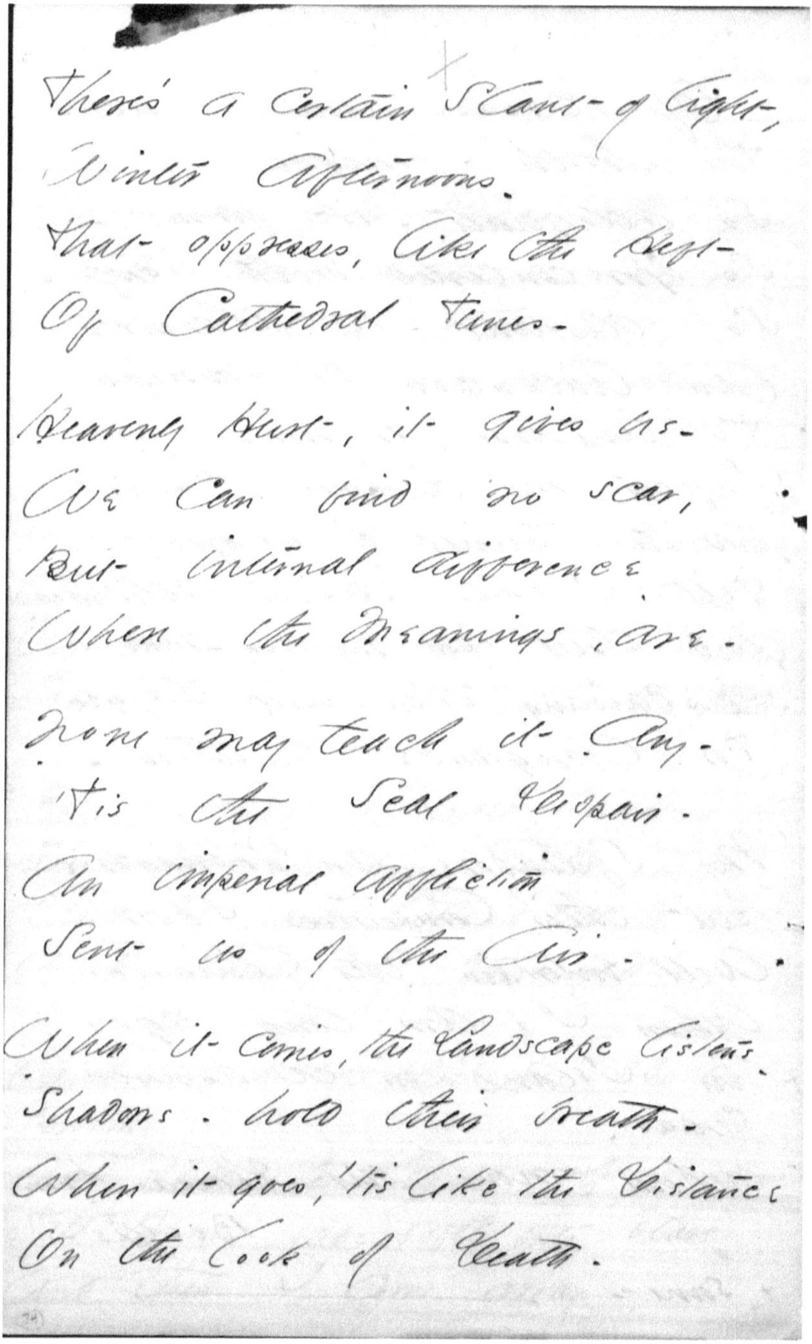

There's a certain Slant of light,
Winter Afternoons —
That oppresses, like the Heft
Of Cathedral Tunes —

Heavenly Hurt, it gives us —
We can find no scar,
But internal difference,
Where the Meanings, are —

None may teach it — Any —
'Tis the Seal Despair —
An imperial affliction
Sent us of the Air —

When it comes, the Landscape listens —
Shadows — hold their breath —
When it goes, 'tis like the Distance
On the look of Death —

*Figure 2.* Fascicle 13, bifolium 3, second verso, "There's a certain slant of light."

related in a fascicle? How do poems which seem grouped in clusters or pairs affect poems not ostensibly implicated in that grouping? How do single poems become central poems in the fascicle context? Finally, I would want to ask why these are not merely formal questions. Or in what way do formal questions have theoretical implications for rethinking the very nature and limits of form? I conclude this essay by briefly taking up the last of these questions.

BLAKE systematized meaning. Spenser allegorized it. Whitman eroticized it. More than any other poet Dickinson economizes it: makes the question of its economy (how much or little) and the question of its relativity, its in(ter)determinacy (how much and how little in relation to what) central to the poetry. For while a first, cursory understanding of economy would endorse the ideology of leanness as an absolute condition of Dickinson's poems and of their meaning, in fact what Dickinson is ultimately always questioning is the economy according to which poems are written, as she is also always questioning the economies within them, endlessly raising questions of relation and magnitude. It is as if sense for Dickinson were defined in the tension between too little and too much—specifically the tension occasioned by how subjects are construed, given delimited boundaries and related—that imperfectly regulates the experience of her poems. This too little or too much is easily recognizable in the thematics of her poetry, as in the disequilibrium of the "one Draught of Life –" paid for by "existence –" (Fr396) or the temporal disequilibrium of "Transporting must the moment be – / Brewed from decades of Agony!" (Fr199). And there are other examples: "Because You saturated Sight – / And I had no more eyes / For sordid excellence / As Paradise" (Fr706A); "Why Floods be served to Us – in Bowls – / I speculate no more –" (Fr767); "I had not minded – Walls – / Were Universe – one Rock . . . But 'tis a single Hair – / A filament – a law – / A Cobweb – wove in Adamant – / A Battlement – of Straw –" (Fr554). But this too little or too much is also recognizable in the disequilibrium of excess—words crowding each other out in the displacements of variants that don't in fact displace each other, in alternative ways of reading that are not really alternative.

As this description implies, if Dickinson's poems economize meaning, in so doing they make it problematically relational, illuminating what could be described as a central discovery of Dickinson's poems, perhaps even the thing they most have to teach us: how relations specify subjects by obliquity and juxtaposition, and indeed specify subjects in the process of either evolving or shifting. I have now indicated preliminarily how this works in a fascicle context where poems are paired in ways that are both antithetical and fluid. In conclusion I touch on how meaning is made relational in a single instance. For although one manifestation of Dickinson's presumed intention may be seen to confine the reading of poems to the fascicle, when lyrics are nevertheless read outside this context, the poems may newly be seen to reveal, perhaps by virtue of the fascicle reading, what the boundaries of their subjects are and how those boundaries must be seen to shift. Or perhaps it is the case that the multiple shifts that we see in the fascicles suddenly make sense of—even actually make visible—shifts that have always, albeit unaccountably, marked aspects of our reading of the poems considered singly.

At the end of "Because I could not stop for Death –" (Fr479), the "Horses' Heads" loom over the edge of the poem, claiming our attention, for these heads, which are regarded from the vantage of the carriage, block or obstruct. The "Horses' Heads" are not, then, only a synecdoche for the horses; they are also, more precisely, a way of delineating that impediment to the speaker's vision: they are all she can see, or what she cannot see beyond. What I mean to emphasize in this familiar instance is the way in which the subject is made to change as the part subsumes the whole, or potentially does so—synecdoche being a governing as well as a topical issue—even while its unspecified relation to that whole remains insisted on, in the vision of the "Horses' Heads" that replaces the vision of "Death." The formal concerns raised by the fascicles duplicate the formal concerns raised by single lyrics, occasioning, not incidentally, questions that are not formal.

What is a subject? How is it bounded? What are the boundaries around what something is? Dickinson raises these questions because she writes into being subjects (in the sense of topics) that are conventionally written out of it. But she also raises these questions by reconstructing the subject as something that is at once economized and relational; by insistently treating the subject as something not given and also not single (one specific relation in question being that of part to whole); by amplifying the idea of a subject to include its variants as well as variant ways of conceiving it. Finally, Dickinson raises these questions by producing utterances that are extrageneric, even unclassifiable, and (for that reason, in a way that it seems to me no one yet has quite explained) untitled.

# The Word Made Flesh
Dickinson's Variants and the Life of Language

Melanie Hubbard

When read in their historical and philosophical contexts, Dickinson's fascicles prove to be neither coherent artistic structures nor especially deviant from what others of her time and place were doing. As I will demonstrate, many people made little bound gatherings of their writings, and many generated and preserved variants. Dickinson and her peers generated variants in a thriving manuscript culture because of a complex education in rhetoric that ultimately stressed the importance of word choice and style, an emphasis derived from the skeptical semiotic theories of Locke and Hume. These facts cast doubt on the metaphysical interpretation Sharon Cameron advances for the fascicles. In a reading of several of Dickinson's poems reflecting upon the composition process, I demonstrate both the presence of these rhetorical theories and their consequences in repeatedly staged crises of reference and articulation. The variants can be seen to be not a compositional strategy but the evidence of an ongoing struggle. My attention to the philosophical (or rhetorical-theoretical) origins of Dickinson's composition practices, and the historical norms of her variant-generation and fascicle-binding project, ultimately objects to Sharon Cameron's masterful, beautiful, and persuasive argument that the fascicles are a Transcendental structure in which poems, varying from themselves and each other, break the boundaries of identity and therefore, by dissolving a unitary consciousness, achieve a collective consciousness which defeats time, space, and death. Instead, I show that Dickinson understands language itself to be a generative collective consciousness very much subject to limit, failure, and death.

Sharon Cameron's *Choosing Not Choosing* argues that Dickinson's fascicles have to do with the lyric speaker's response to death, that the fascicles are a structure mounted, like a defense, to render death fictive. First, though she calls it a "speculation,"[1] she takes the fascicles to be intentionally composed by Dickinson as formal units with, therefore, formally significant structure. She then argues that because of the variants within individual poems, and the variant structure of poems-addressing-each-other-within-fascicles, meaning and closure, choice and limit are eternally deferred. Ultimately, distinctions between the living and the dead, inside and outside, are rendered irrelevant in and through language. "Put in different terms, what these poems make available is interiority itself—interiority without either origin or outside" (Cameron, *Choosing* 187). They accomplish what in Alan Grossman's terms is called "aperture" (which he identifies with Whitman), the speaker's identification with (and emptying out toward) Being.

In her earlier book about Dickinson, *Lyric Time,* Cameron argues that lyrics, in their singular cry, allow the speaker to stay or escape from the flow of time. Lyric protest, the poet's rage against death, takes place in the arrangement (or array) of language; the poem provides the prospect of wresting insight from experience, of ordering the ceaseless flow of time (toward our annihilation) through meter and rhythm—and that is what makes death or boundedness tolerable. Grossman terms such condensation "closure," and he cites Dickinson more than once as its chief exemplar.

But in the interim between the earlier *Lyric Time* and the later *Choosing Not Choosing,* Cameron has changed her mind about what sort of poet Dickinson is, chiefly because the publication of the *Manuscript Books,* edited by Ralph Franklin, presents the poems not as singularities but as series, not as wholes but as processes. By the perhaps tellingly Germanic end of *Choosing Not Choosing* (with its recourse to Rilke and Heidegger), Cameron lands Dickinson firmly in the field of aperture, almost to the exclusion of any notion of limit or even bodily being. When she observes that Dickinson's speaker is "inhuman,"[2] it is because the speaker is suspended above all possibilities, partially identified with each and with Being; she is invulnerable, or reserving an invulnerability. Unfortunately the variants, in this account, can be read as a kind of proliferating, obsessive, disembodying hysteria. Cameron wishes to place Dickinson as a poet of possibility and imagination, one who heroically dissolves what separates us from one another, and from pure Being. The problem is that the identification of the speaker with Being in effect anticipates or pre-empts—or costs—the death of the self as an individual in time. Cameron's ultimately Emersonian (and Whitmanian) vision of Dickinson's approach to ontological threat, then, swings so far away from time-bound, individually embodied lyric protest that I find it inconceivable that the Dickinson who chose Earth over Heaven would have pursued it. If Cameron were right about the fascicles as a whole, such a theoretical disembodiment of the speaker would have been reason enough to abandon them. But it is not necessary to see the fascicles as organized, not to say overdetermined, formal structures in order to conceive of Dickinson's theorizations of identity as immensely complex. Cameron's delicious finale, a reading of "The Brain – is wider than the Sky –" (Fr598, F26) does not depend upon the variant to rebalance identity, language, and self precisely on the cusp of limit and limitlessness, "Syllable" and "Sound."

While Cameron's argument depends upon our taking the fascicles to be artistic structures, many of the fascicles cannot plausibly be made to cohere. Cameron admits as much, in a torturous passage establishing the fact that individual poems cannot be conceived to be "parts" of the "whole" which is the fascicle—because the fascicle, as a jumble of competing energies, displays no wholeness (and therefore escapes limit) (178–79). I (and my students) have certainly tried to shoehorn recalcitrant stray poems into strained thematic readings over an array of sixteen or twenty-two lyrics, but no matter how ingeniously conducted, such attempts merely make clear the limits of the straightforward, literal approach. And yet the fascicles seem as if they might make sense. They seem to present themselves as artistic units, poetic sequences—and there are quite promising runs of poetic colloquy among them. So what aesthetic determines them? Why do some fascicles seem to mean so much, while others just baffle us?[3]

I believe that since Cameron's argument rests on an admitted speculation that the fascicles are a coherent, intentionally artistic or composed structure, it is precisely this speculation that needs to be investigated. My finding is that the fascicles are simply, as Bruce Clary argues in his dissertation, "Emily Dickinson's Menagerie," bookkeeping structures like scrapbooks. The fascicles are not print culture structures, though they look like little books ready for print, and they arise within a culture eagerly embracing print. It has been easy enough to take them as the author's final intention toward her work, and to attempt to read them as intentional poetic sequences. One problem at the outset is that we do not and cannot know Dickinson's "final intention" toward her work; a corollary is that "final intention" is a concept generated within the editorial theory of printed works. As Jerome McGann makes clear in *A Critique of Modern Textual Criticism,* only the process of going into print, and the negotiations with editor and publisher, can be regarded as definitively intentional toward the printed work—and even then, the process is social rather than pure. Dickinson's eschewal of print suspends the entire question.[4] Margaret Ezell, in *Social Authorship and the Advent of Print,* makes a number of important points about manuscript culture and authorship outside of print norms which are helpful when considering just what sort of work Dickinson took herself to be doing. Perhaps the most important point is simply that print (and the model of the printed book) is not in most circumstances the historical norm. Manuscript culture—and social authorship—must be taken on its own terms.

> As Roland Barthes long ago observed, modern criticism is obsessed with the figure of the author as the source of explanation, and we who work in literary history have concentrated on reimagining that individual's desires as an explanation for authorial choices to the extent of denying that that individual was part of a culture whose reading and writing practices are quite different from our own. (Ezell 18–19)

Instead of focusing on Dickinson's intentions as an author—or attempting to peer through the manuscript evidence to the "thought" of Emily Dickinson—my approach takes the parameters of Dickinson's milieu seriously as determinants of what structures were, in fact, available to her. My argument that the fascicles are simply gatherings much like everyone else's, then, is historical or even circumstantial; and Bruce Clary's formalist analysis of how Dickinson actually put the fascicles together, sheet by sheet, confirms their mundanity. Dickinson's fascicles are physical objects with historical determinants; they tend to affirm boundaries—the boundary of the sheet—and they are time-bound by virtue of their successive making.

Ralph Franklin, editor of the *Manuscript Books,* has contended that Dickinson's unit of composition within the fascicles is the sheet.[5] That is, they are not composed as wholes, from the beginning to the end of a fascicle. Rather, they are put together in runs of two or three or four, according to space available. Bruce Clary has clarified and illustrated, through an analysis of the physical evidence represented in the *Manuscript Books,* that the fascicles are best understood using a scrapbook model. That is, given the confines of a particular form, in this case a collection of from 4 to 6 bifolded sheets, the content will respond to the constraints of the form, just as a scrapbooker arranges items of interest using the space of a scrapbook page as the boundary.[6]

Space considerations will predominate as the poet seeks to arrange poems on each of the four sides of the folded sheet. If the first page's poem is carried over onto the second page (the verso), and perhaps finishes somewhere near the top with one stanza, the poet habitually draws a line after the finished poem and begins another a little bit lower down. That poem may fit the page or be carried over, and so on. The final poem almost never exceeds the bottom of the last page; that is to say, it remains confined to the sheet. Clary argues that if Dickinson is fitting poems to pages, she is not necessarily—or solely—ordering poems according to thematic or meaningful resonances. And if the sheet is the unit of composition, the fascicle is merely a collection of a set number of sheets, sheets which may have little or no thematic relationship to one another, especially given the fact that poems do not run over from one sheet to the next (which would imply a preconceived sequence). As he puts it,

> There are 218 folio sheets in the fascicles. Dickinson ran the text of poems over from the last page of a sheet to the first page of the following sheet two times. Ten other times, she inserted a slip or single leaf to capture the overflow. Thus, Dickinson overran her sheet about five percent of the time. If the fascicles were gatherings of poems in which aesthetic considerations uniformly outweighed space considerations, texts would surely have violated the artificial boundaries of the sheet more frequently. (Clary 109–10)

Clary mounts a variety of arguments I find convincing, not least of which are the facts that Dickinson seems to have used up all the poems she had at hand, and that the number of sheets in a fascicle is set by habit. A poet ordering poems in any sort of series (such as sections of a book) conceived to be meaningful will have left poems out; and if the sequence is one of thought and feeling, surely an organic structuration of such waves will have taken, in different sequences, sometimes more and sometimes fewer sheets to accommodate.

This is not to say that there is no aesthetic at work; just that it is constrained, and if a short flower-gift-poem fits the bottom three-quarters of a page, it will interrupt an otherwise thematically unified sequence and frustrate our attempts to read coherence. I also agree with Clary—and Cameron notes this, too (*Choosing* 34)—that the poet quite often works in thematic clusters of two or three. The fact that any one of us could "compose" a fascicle by choosing almost randomly from Dickinson's extraordinarily intense lyrics should give us pause, just as it is possible to "compose" a reading which unifies a great variety of poems.[7] It is important to generate a picture of the poet dealing with a physical form because I think it can help to undo what seems like the necessity of Cameron's "speculation." If we can conceive of the poet as less bound by the notion of artistic sequence (and the book) than we are, I think we can retain much of Cameron's argument without making a metaphysic of the complex relations among the poems.

Dickinson was part of a culture of manuscript manufacture, and her fascicle-making came with the territory of widespread educational practices around composition, declamation, and manuscript circulation.[8] When Dickinson pulled together her drafts, copying as neatly as possible onto sheets sewn into booklets, such as she must have made at Amherst Academy and Mt. Holyoke Female Seminary, she was doing what nearly every educated young person in the vicinity did for at least the first three-quarters of the nineteenth century. I do not limit the frame of reference to just those years Dickinson herself was in school, and by taking in Amherst College, I consider her milieu—and that of her brother—as indicative of experiences quite close to her. Further, I see the practices of pastors and seminary students to be of-a-piece with the undergraduate and high school academy experience of declamation of one's writings. In fact, many colleges such as Amherst were expressly founded to provide the training necessary for young men to go on into the professions most dependent upon compositional skills and oratory—preaching, missionary work, teaching, jurisprudence, and politics. Mt. Holyoke Female Seminary harbored for its students similar aspirations.

In this brief survey of contemporary composition practices I wish to establish that others hand-bound their writings and generated and saved variants as a matter of course, and thus that Dickinson's work should not be read apart from these generative contexts. At midcentury, weekly exercises were turned in at Mt. Holyoke on one or more bifolded sheets, folded in thirds, and addressed to the teacher on the blank back middle, like a letter.[9] Compositions were declaimed weekly there, just as they were at Amherst College among the debating societies and clubs. Lucy Goodale's letter is perhaps a typical indication of the reality, though she attended the seminary ten years earlier than Dickinson did. "If you want to pity me, you may next Thursday for I am to read a composition before an assemblage of ladies. And besides all this I am behind in composition as are both my roommates, and have yet very many hours to write. However we get off from composition troubles pretty well and now we are through Chem we have more time" (Letter July 13, 1838).

Though composition was a chore for many, others couldn't write enough. Approximately ten years later than Dickinson's matriculation, Josephine Kingsley Hardy is among the many young women producing "commonplaces" (Mt. Holyoke's rather deceptive term for amateur newspapers). Usually edited by more than one girl, some have been bound at the spine with thread or ribbon. *The Mountain Echo*, edited by Josephine Kingsley and Francis E. Tower, is nicely done on blue legal-sized lined paper, further ruled into a head and columns, and bound with yellow-bordered red ribbon. This is the sort of thing that *Forest Leaves*, edited by Emily Fowler Ford and Dickinson,[10] would have been, although that was an Amherst Academy production. Obviously the girls were well acquainted with the idea of writing down, sewing up, and circulating items of interest in what was a vibrant manuscript culture both in and out of the curriculum.

THE BOYS at Amherst College were equally under the onus of producing weekly compositions, both for evaluation by the tutors and for declamation before their peers in the college clubs, whose members competed for academic rank, leadership positions, and club reputation. The papers of Robert Henry Davis, Class of 1868, Amherst College, collected in his scrapbook, are particularly instructive. Among other items of interest is a string-bound signature of three bifolia (12 pages), inserted one inside another. It is very neatly done, with two spinal stitches and a string pulled taut down the center page. Called "Lincoln City," Davis notes in pencil, "Read for my first Comp before the Athenae. Oct 25, 1865." It is written straight through, so that the order of writing was from one page to the next, inserted in place. Thus the pages must have been in place first. (The last three pages are written on the right-hand rectos only.) Another composition, "Socrates as a Teacher," is on one bifolium with a half sheet inserted and pasted into the middle (for a total of 6 pages). Again, the bookmaking must have preceded the copying, for he anticipated needing two extra pages. (It is very likely that he was working from a penciled, and variant-riddled, draft, as appears to have been the custom of Benjamin Kendall Emerson, AC 1865.) The note in pencil says "Examined R. H. M." and the pen date is March 25, 1865. It's been folded lengthwise, as if placed into a pocket on the way to the tutor's rooms. Another, "Extracts from Address . . . On Decision of Character" consists of two (inserted) bifolia stitched tautly and neatly with string (8 pages in ink), dated Feb 14, 1866. These examples bespeak both an element of improvisation or homemade-ness and an element of professional, perhaps female, assistance.

Another example is quite clearly like a Dickinson fascicle and more obviously made by the writer himself. It consists of four bifolia stacked one upon the other and stitched not too handily at the spine (though well enough) with dark brown thread using seven holes. Signed R. H. Davis. 31 S. C. Oct 17, 1867, it is called "Rise of the East India Company." It is labeled "I" in the top left-hand corner; the next bifolium is labeled "II" in upper left, and the next, III, and the next, IV. The blue-lined paper has no embossment, unlike the others, further suggesting homemade status. The numbered sheets suggest that he must have written them out loose, then needed to know the order in which to bind them correctly. Though Dickinson did not number her sheets, the fact that they are stacked rather than inserted—and that she takes care not to overrun the sheet—suggests that the order of the poems, especially beyond the sheet, was neither fixed nor premeditated. It is well to bear in mind, too, that the "order" of the fascicles we have in the Franklin edition is strictly a matter of paper date—that is, a copying chronology.

Binding composition booklets, manuscript miscellany "newspapers," and other material is obviously a widespread practice cultured in the high schools and colleges of the period, but less obvious perhaps is the presence of variants in ostensibly "finished"—or even "published"—material. But they are everywhere. One young woman at Mt. Holyoke Female Seminary, "Ella," a writer for "The Casket of Gems" Volume 1, part 3, uses variants on two occasions, both times mentioning the need for a "composition":

> The teacher says that we must have a declamation or composition for Saturday, but as a declamation is out of the question, I shall write a few words which I shall call a composition. I propose to give you a brief description of Lapland. . . . Their riches consist of large herds of [cattle] reindeer which they train to draw them over the snow in sledges.

Next is, "Compositions. I have set down and am now [trying] going to try to write a composition although I do not think it is a very pleasant thing[.]" Apparently she would rather write about writing a composition than actually concentrate on the assigned task. And she produces an ostensibly published, circulating, fair copy newspaper with variants self-consciously bracketed. The variants provide a sort of curious in-joke: compositions are funnily about generating variants, the laborious task of

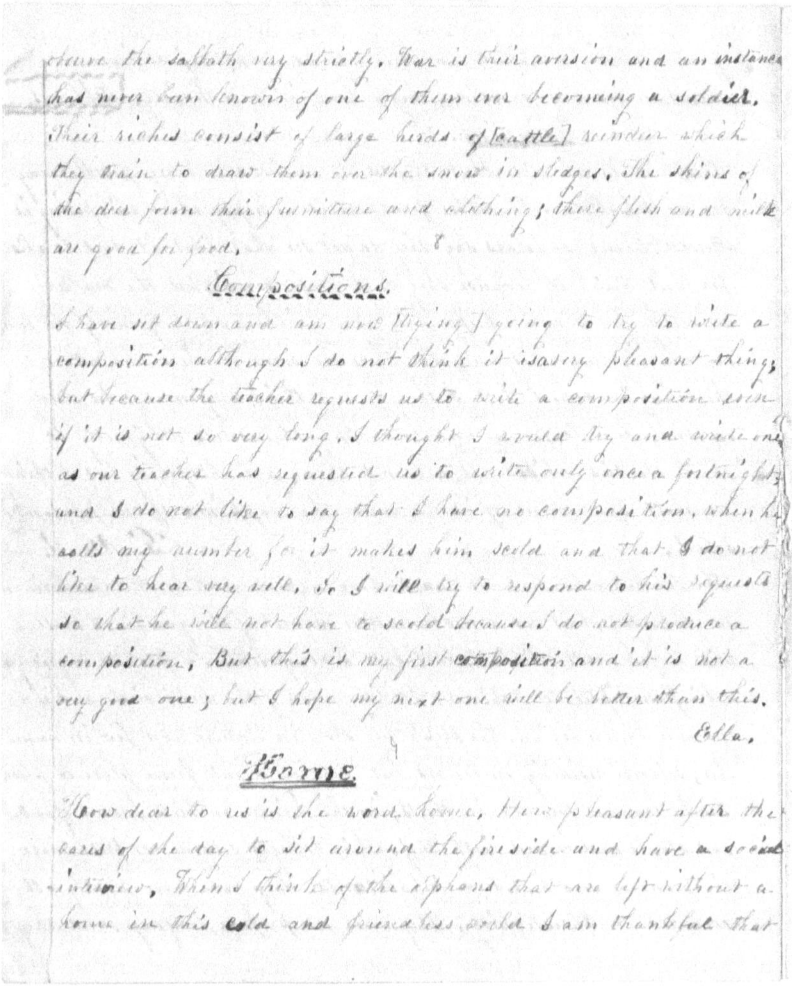
observe the sabbath very strictly. War is their aversion and an instance has never been known of one of them ever becoming a soldier. Their riches consist of large herds of [cattle] reindeer which they train to draw them over the snow in sledges. The skins of the deer form their furniture and clothing; their flesh and milk are good for food.

Compositions.

I have sit down and am now [trying] going to try to write a composition although I do not think it is a very pleasant thing; but because the teacher requests us to write a composition even if it is not so very long. I thought I would try and write one as our teacher has requested us to write only once a fortnight and I do not like to say that I have no composition, when he calls my number for it makes him scold and that I do not like to hear very well. So I will try to respond to his requests so that he will not have to scold because I do not produce a composition. But this is my first composition and it is not a very good one; but I hope my next one will be better than this.

Ella.

Home.

How dear to us is the word home, How pleasant after the cares of the day to sit around the fireside and have a social interview, When I think of the orphans that are left without a home in this cold and friendless world I am thankful that

***Figure 3.*** MS 0778 Josephine Kingsley Hardy Papers. Series 2, "Casket of Gems," essay 7; Series 2, "What Employment Brings the Most Happiness" composition.

finding the right word. (Why this should be the case will be discussed later.)

In Josephine Hardy's composition, "What employment brings most happiness," we find the sentence, "I wandered far from the crowded city, and found nestled (beneath) among the trees a lowly cottage." The use of brackets or parentheses, or sometimes both, to indicate variants seems to have been the common practice, and in both cases, the composition is labeled, folded, and signed—as if it were a fair copy given for normal presentation to the teacher. There seems, then, for at least some students to have been a tolerance of variants, and a habit of retaining them, in the "finished" product; perhaps the student was inviting the teacher to help her choose the best expression.

This makes a sort of sense, since the practice of using "fill-in-the-blank" exercises at the elementary and secondary levels[11] would have ingrained both the necessity of choosing fitting grammatical expressions, and the teacher's superior authority to determine their fitness. For example, in Eliza Washburn's high school papers from the 1840s (AAS), there is a paper simply titled "Composition" with a few exercise sentences on it in which the student was to fill in the blanks:

> No pleasure can be—unless we are willing to—the full—for their enjoyment.
>
> No pleasure can be enjoyed unless we are willing to sacrifice the full worth of them for their enjoyment.
>
> Virtue and—will secure all the—of this life. Religion will—us under the—of the world and—us for that which is—.
>
> Virtue and ~~industry~~ Religion will secure all the happiness of this life. Religion will put us under the reproach of the world and prepare us for that which is usful [*sic*].

What is interesting is that such popular and prevalent exercises, called "ellipticals," emphasize the "slots" to be filled, the potential to fill the slots differently, and the deviance, corrected by the teacher, of even the most innocently appropriate alternatives (such as "industry" instead of "Religion"). As Ian Michael notes in *The Teaching of English,*

> The value of works such as this depended on the teacher's linguistic sensitivity. If, as most of the eighteenth-century teachers taught, there was only one word that could correctly fill a blank, the exercise merely reinforced stereotyped expressions and did more harm than good. If the pupil felt free to suggest one or more words that might fit the blank, a number of useful questions arose. Did the suggested word fit the structure of the sentence? Did the resultant meaning fit the context? If more than one word could be inserted were there grounds for preferring one to another? These possibilities were seldom realized, even in the twentieth century. A potentially

valuable method of training inferential skill and of enlarging vocabulary was restricted to the endorsement of banality. (354)

But I suspect that in the case of Dickinson's education, especially at Amherst Academy and Mount Holyoke, and given Richard Parker's and Samuel Newman's pervasive emphasis on linguistic control, these exercises were in fact used to encourage making fine distinctions in diction and sentence structure.[12] Suppleness, clarity, and precision were announced values, and in a good school, teachers—and students—would have welcomed the chance to discuss the finer points.[13]

The generation of variants is equally apparent at Amherst College. Though Robert Davis's compositions do not retain variants, his oral declamations do, and they are on much larger paper, quite obviously handbound for the occasion. "Our Relation to China" is on a legal-sized bifolium; that is, each page is legal-sized; the entire sheet is twice legal size and lined, back and front. The speech contains penciled corrections, cross-hatchings, carets—and alternate readings, either written above the syntax in question or indicated by parentheses. Often part of a sentence is crossed out and the rest of the sentence made to adjust with the use of carets and interlineated prose; but sometimes the correction itself is crossed out, or only the parenthetical elements have been retained in the clear, and those are to be read as variants. But other times he eschews parentheses: "More friendly and fraternal feelings will be engendered and cherished over/between all the earth/nations and races of mankind." In this case, the variant appears above the word or phrase it may replace. The variants are inserted in pen in a sloppier hand (but still Davis's); and certain insertions throughout the speech appear careted and interlineated in pencil, perhaps still later. This sort of inconsistency about how to record or place variants is similar to what goes on in Dickinson's sheets.

A speech on "John Milton as a Politician" (on 7 sheets, or 14 large pages) has numerous cross-outs, parenthetical options, and not a few alternate readings. These are written above the epithet in question, which has been put in parentheses, like this: "(ecclesiastical) /church" and "(earthly) / terrestrial." Or parentheses may be left out: Milton's "firm adherence to" has penciled above it "attachment to the Republicanism" with neither cancelled nor affirmed. There are cancellations when a reading is clearly preferred, as in "allowed," which has been crossed through, with "advocated" written in pencil above it. These are obviously clean enough copies to speak from—and given the arduous nature of rewriting a thing in pen, they are understandably retained.

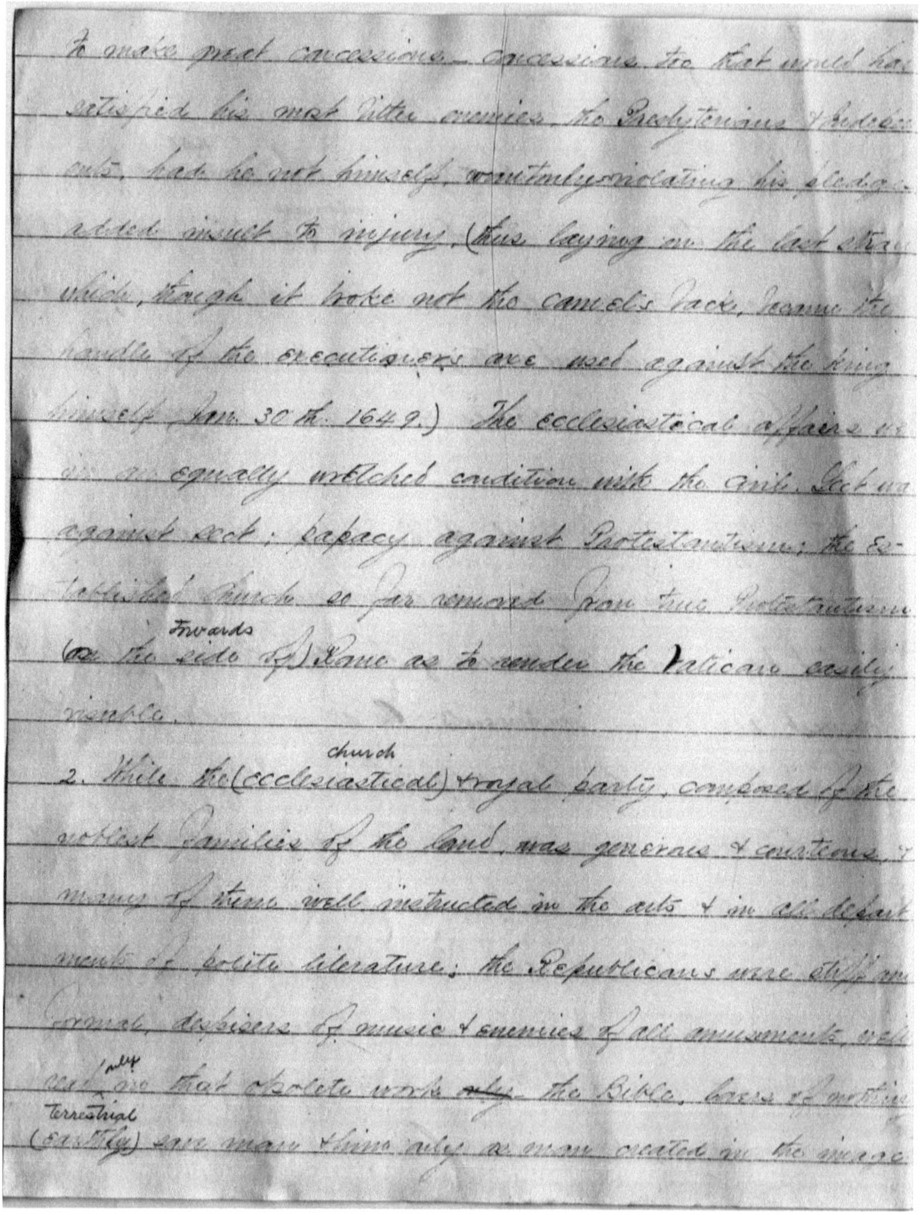

to make great concessions— concessions too that would have satisfied his most bitter enemies, the Presbyterians & Independents, had he not himself wantonly violating his pledge added insult to injury. (Thus laying on the last straw which, though it broke not the camel's back, became the handle of the executioners axe used against the King himself Jan. 30th 1649.) The ecclesiastical affairs were in an equally wretched condition with the civil. Sect was against sect; papacy against Protestantism; the Established Church so far removed from true Protestantism (on the side of) towards Rome as to render the Vatican easily visible.

2. While the (ecclesiastical) church & royal party, composed of the noblest families of the land, was generous & courteous, & many of them well instructed in the arts & in all departments of polite literature; the Republicans were stiff in formal, despisers of music & enemies of all amusements, well called only terrestrial (earthly) that obsolete work only the Bible, cares of nothing save mean things only as man created in the image

*Figure 4.* Robert Davis, "John Milton as a Politician."

and likeness of God, in fine they respected no vain titles and kingly prerogatives, and feared only the displeasure of the King of Kings. But Milton, well-trained from youth, & a graduate of Cambridge where he had become an excellent scholar in all departments, was an ardent lover of every species of legitimate amusement, was frank & generous, seemingly gifted by nature as well as by culture and taste for poetry, and cordial sympathy with the royalists. That he othered, to nay rather went far ahead of his father's sentiments, in his plans for an independent church and a free government, is indeed ~~becoming~~ strange. For had he been led by his qualifications and disposition to join the royal party it would have appeared quite natural.

To give the reasons then for his ~~firm adherence~~ "attachment * the Republicanism" to and nerve his leadership of the reform measures is to give the principle of his political life.

In the early part of his controversial writings he says he felt himself no better armed for ~~a cross~~ "contests" than

In Davis's case, declamations appear to have been presented multiple times, and perhaps this process, and the fact that they are written to be performed rather than perused, generates variants and a tolerance for retaining variants. The Davis scrapbook indicates both the use of variants in orally delivered compositions and the use of hand-bound bifolia to keep one's compositions intact. The most exciting find is obviously the stacked four-bifolia inexpertly stitched booklet because it is exactly the technique Dickinson uses to maintain a little order as she gathers poems.

There are further examples in the Davis scrapbook—a credo to be pronounced before a church, a penciled sermon draft full of alternate expressions—and further examples in the Amherst College archives—but I will leave them in order to introduce the extraordinary example of one more writer, Charles Baker Kittredge.

Kittredge (1806–84) graduated from Andover Theological Seminary in 1832 and preached as a Presbyterian minister in Monson, near Amherst, as well as all over Massachusetts, from about 1833 to about 1859. His papers at the American Antiquarian Society contain 84 numbered sermons, many of which were delivered on numerous occasions.[14] What is useful about his example is that his manuscript practices regarding the recording and preservation of his sermons remain consistent over time—and they are very much like Dickinson's. His booklets are obviously handmade; he stacks his bifolia (usually 8 to 10 sheets) and stitches them on the top left margin with plain cotton string through two holes; they are final copies in ink, and he records variants in pencil interlineated above the syntax in question, or he circles the syntax within a sentence in pencil, which means he can say the encircled part or not, as the occasion suits—or he does both, boxing the fair ink within the sentence, then providing a penciled variant above it. He also, very helpfully, records on the last page (or the back) the date and place of every time he preached the sermon.

Just a few examples will suffice to indicate his practices. Sermon 33, "Moral perfection of God," or, 1 Sam. 6:20. "Who is able to stand before this holy Lord God?" is in brown ink, on nine stacked bifolia bound with string on the front margin through two holes. This fair copy has no ink cross-throughs, but does have penciled brackets and cross-throughs for deleted paragraphs (the light pencil mark may indicate neatness or non-finality); there are penciled boxes for variant expressions like "remove this ark [of G.] from" as well as penciled variants above boxed ink fair copy, such as "honors his [command] ordinance [ . . . ] & at the same time [bears convincing] spreads dismay & woe [upon] (*illegible*) the spirits of the lost." "Spreads" and "(*illegible*)" are in pencil above boxed ink fair copy (indicated by my brackets). In a nearby sentence, "holiness" sits in pencil above "[moral purity, unspotted and divine]," which is boxed in pencil. Another example has "setting sin & holiness in contrast, [flashing shame upon] disclosing the deformity of the one, & [shedding a benign complacency upon] ^the beauty of the other," where "disclosing" is written above the boxed ink fair "[flashing shame upon]" and "the beauty of" is interlineated with a caret above "the other." No syntax is crossed through, and both choices remain live options at the moment of speech. This sermon was first delivered in Groton, December 1833; in all, there are thirteen recorded occasions of delivery.

Sermon 35 says "Rewritten," but this designated fair copy has the usual penciled boxes and variants interlineated above. Sermon 37 is very clean-looking, with just a few ink cross-throughs and insertions, and no penciled marks. There is no note on delivery. Sermon 37B has penciled variants and boxes, plus slips of paper tipped (with sealing wax) into the margin (with penciled notes). The sermon uses the same verse as 37, and though it looks like it may be a draft of 37, it is actually an entirely different set of thoughts. So we have versions of a sermon, each its own entity and unity, but each also related through the base text. Dickinson is not the only one who returns over and over again to the same subject.

Now, clearly not everyone writing at the time retained variants in fair copy manuscripts, and those who did may well be the exceptions; it seems likely, however, from the evidence that nearly everyone generated variants in at least their penciled drafts because of a peculiar emphasis in the rhetorical theory and practices of the time on style, and in particular on diction. But some writers clearly took the task to a level in fair copy ink for which they had to devise *systems*. Such codification or regularization of method—the habit not only of retaining variants but clearly indicating to oneself their status—is unusual, apparently somewhat prevalent, and in need of explanation. What would writers of the time have understood themselves to be doing? It seems unlikely that, in the midst of collecting their compositions into little booklets, they were self-consciously troubling notions of identity and closure.

The contents of one sermon are of interest because they begin to explain why a pastor—and perhaps even a poet—would have taken such perhaps obsessive care with composition. On the first page of sermon 78 a penciled note reads, "Never to be preached again—." The verse is 2 Cor. 2:16: "To the one we are the savor of death unto death; and to the other the Savor of life unto life: and who is sufficient for these things?" Amid boxes in pen and pencil, interlineated variants, and even a bit of inserted stationery, wards permitted to see, upon [the same] throne high & lifted up, with a dazzling coronet, formed of [rays] of moral purity, like a rainbow about [throne].

But there are, to us other revela[tions] of [His] perfect & infinite holiness, no less incontestable than [visions] of his face. And these revela[tions] are throw[n] their light in all our path; setting sin & holiness in contrast, [flashing] disclosing them upon [the] deformity of [one], & shedding a benign complacency upon [beauty of] [other]; & just in propor[tion] as men come to this light, darting convic[tion] upon [the wicked], & drawing forth [the love] of [the good]; but who, if duly pondered

brethren — not of the rod in his hand
& keys of life & death — but / exhibition
of his holiness, his hatred of sin, &
his jealousy for / honor of his command. This is / attribute in his char.
wh. makes him / object of love to holy
beings, & of hate to / wicked. It is this
wh fills heaven with light & joy — &
at / same time spreads dismay
woe and / spirits of / lost. "G's. bright-
est glory is his moral glory; his
highest
purity his moral purity. His
holiness It is
moral purity, unspotted & divine, (?)
It is holiness wh —
pervades all his other attributes, & gives
character
beauty & symmetry to / whole. It was
a vision of this moral purity shining
out

Kittredge reflects on his own responsibility to preach the word of God with care—with eternal vigilance.

> The responsibilities connected with preaching of the gospel were in view of the Apost. Truly appalling [ . . . ] And when his mind turned to the influence he was destined to exert in discharging the functions of his holy office; when he remembered that he was set to watch for souls as one that must give account; that if thru his unfaithfulness they were lost, their blood w. be repaired at the watchman's hour;[ . . . ] Who can stand as the messenger of God and look upon a congregation of immortal beings, with the appalling certainty that every word he utters will be made by those who hear to work out their everlasting destruction or salvation!

One need only recall Dickinson's remark in "A Word dropped careless on a Page" (Fr1268), that "Infection in the sentence breeds / And we inhale Despair," to see that she shared this vision of the seriousness of putting words to thoughts. And yet, there is a still more troubling idea revealed in these few words: that the Divine Being must appear in or act through human words, must be represented and understood through "every word he utters." What is the difference between human words and the Divine Word? Are they ever the same, coinciding? Or are they ever separate, the words unwieldy counters, always mismatched against an unknowable ideal? What if Kittredge's "unfaithfulness" is not a matter of intention but a failure of language itself? No wonder he takes such care.

The peculiar emphasis on generating variants as a compositional stratagem (whether they are retained or not) can be attributed to the widespread influence of the rhetorics of Richard Whately, Samuel Newman, and George Campbell. George Campbell's *Philosophy of Rhetoric* (1776), inheriting Hume, explicitly divorced words from any necessary correspondence with things, thus deepening an anxiety already provoked by Locke. Language was simply customary, based on usage and association, and there was a constant slippage between words and the reality they were taken to refer to. Furthermore, where Locke had maintained a skeptical gap between words and the "ideas" they referred to, Campbell, a "nominalist," held that words and ideas were practically the same thing; he therefore emphasized style as the very medium of thought. Dropping entirely the project of reference or truth-to-Being, composition became almost entirely taken up with word choice, usage, and tropes, not only as a matter of articulation but also as a matter of forcefully reaching one's audience.

James A. Berlin, in *Writing Instruction in Nineteenth-Century American Colleges,* lays out the idea that compositional practices stem from particular philosophical assumptions:

> Every rhetoric [ . . . ] has at its base a conception of reality, of human nature, and of language. In other terms, it is grounded in a noetic field: a closed system defining what can, and cannot, be known; the nature of the knower; the nature of the relationship between the knower, the known, and the audience; and the nature of language. Rhetoric is thus ultimately implicated in all a society attempts. It is at the center of a culture's activities (2).

George Campbell was the fountainhead in 1776 of what came to be called the New Rhetoric, which derived from the skeptical philosophy of David Hume and was broadly allied with the Scottish Common Sense movement embraced by Dickinson's culture. Since knowledge resulted from the direct, sensory experience of the individual, it could only be conveyed by activating, in language, the receptive percipient faculties of the audience. As Campbell himself puts it, "If he purposes to work upon the passions, his very diction, as well as his sentiments, must be animated. Thus language and thought, like body and soul, are made to correspond, and the qualities of the one exactly to cooperate with those of the other" (215).[15] The question of correspondence or truth-value invisibly subsides, and arrangement and persuasion—the organization and deployment of forcible or convincing sensation—becomes the chief object of study. The shared experience of language is paramount, as is the calibration of the speaker–listener relationship through language designed to be literally sensational. Style becomes the main determinant of rhetorical success.[16]

Dickinson inherited Campbell through Samuel P. Newman (1827) and Richard Whately (1828);[17] they were required at Amherst Academy and Mt. Holyoke Female Seminary, respectively; and Richard Whately's *Elements of Rhetoric* in the 1834 edition was in the family library.[18] These two rhetoricians neatly limn two sides of the question about language's relation to thought, though both reject the idea of a connection between language and reality, as, in fact, had Locke. As Campbell puts it,

> One thing, indeed, every smatterer in philosophy will tell us, that there can be no natural connection between the sounds of any language, and the things signified, or between the modes of inflection and combination and the relations they are intended to express. (140)

Indeed, Newman, paraphrasing Campbell's ideas with his own illustrations, sounds like Saussure and even Todorov as he lays out for his students the prevailing Lockean linguistic theory. Using the example of the Spanish *entrada* and the fact that pictures of the conquistadors were brought to Montezuma, he remarks, "Hence we infer, *that words answer the same purpose as pictures; they bring up to the mind subjects and thoughts which they are designed to represent*" (115; emphasis in original). Further clarifying that the Spaniards and the English use different languages (and therefore a different word) to refer to the same object, he remarks, "Hence we infer, *that there is no natural connexion between words and the objects which they represent*" (115; emphasis in original). It bears repeating that even Newman's pictorial theory emphasizes that a picture or words *represent* "thoughts"; they are not natural images of them. In conclusion, he notes that even within a language, change means that "at different periods different words are used in the same language, as the symbols of the same object. [ . . . ] If words, like pictures, were the exact representatives of objects, or the same word always, in every period in the history of a language, and whenever used, had the same thought attached to it by all who speak or write the language, there would evidently be no necessity for verbal criticism" (116). Hence not only the necessity to focus on very fine shades of meaning to depict very fine shades of emotion (or other experience—but a sensationalist rhetoric can quickly become a sentimental one), but also an increasing need for what was called philology—linguistics, lexicography, and the study of vernacular literatures. Berlin sums up Newman, whose *Practical System* was intended more as a textbook than as a philosophical treatise: "Language is regarded as a mechanical sign system, separate from thought, throughout" (38). Newman's project is to regulate or at least keep up with both linguistic tokens and their users by inculcating a supple literacy.

Richard Whately equally maintains that words have no motivated relation to reality, but he differs from Newman regarding the relation of words to thoughts. More closely hewing to Campbell's nominalism, he regards a word to be not simply a token for an idea, but an idea's medium.

> There are still [ . . . ] many [ . . . ] who, if questioned on the subject, would answer that the use of Language is to *communicate* our thoughts to each other; and that it is peculiar to Man; the truth being that *that* use of Language is *not* peculiar to Man, though enjoyed by him in a much higher degree than by the Brutes; while that which does distinguish Man from Brute, is another, and quite distinct, use of Language, viz. *as an instrument of thought*,—a system of General-Signs, without which the Reasoning-

> process could not be conducted. The full importance, consequently, of Language, and of precise technical Language,—of having accurate and well-defined "names for one's tools,"—can never be duly appreciated by those who still cling to the theory of "Ideas"; those imaginary objects of thought in the mind, of which "Common-terms" are merely the names, and by means of which we are supposed to be able to do what I am convinced is impossible; to carry on a train of Reasoning without the use of Language, or of any General-Signs whatever. (Whately 20)

Thus Whately's readers are to understand that language is not simply a representation of thought—it is the medium of thought. As Campbell puts it, "Now, beyond particular truths or individual facts, first perceived and then remembered, we should never be able to proceed one single step in thinking, any more than in conversing, without the use of signs" (260). Style is therefore not simply ornament, but argument. Campbell devotes fully a third of his magnum opus to word choice, and Newman and Whately, after briefer philosophical forays, spend most of their time adjudicating usage. Campbell is a harbinger of the Romantic insistence that style—the way one puts something—is constitutive:

> Having now discussed what was proposed here concerning tropes, I shall conclude with observing that in this discussion there hath been occasion, as it were, incidentally to discover,—that they are so far from being the inventions of art, that, on the contrary, they result from the original and essential principles of the human mind. (316)

Whately, following Campbell, hits very close to Emerson when he remarks that metaphor and synecdoche, far from obscuring or cluttering thought, are often the clearest medium for it:

> indeed Metaphor, which is among the principal of them [ornaments], is, in many cases, the clearest mode of expression that can be adopted; it being usually much easier for uncultivated minds to comprehend a similitude or analogy, than an abstract term. And hence the language of savages, as has often been remarked, is highly metaphorical; and such appears to have been the case with all languages in their earlier, and consequently ruder and more savage state. (174)

The tropes are "clearest" and "earlier" because they reflect the imagination's primary processing of the world. But Whately is clear that it is a mistake to imagine that words or tropes—especially analogy—somehow partake of or "carry" with them the reality to which they refer (as Symbolism will soon enough suggest). Though many words possess an "analogical aptitude" (204), somewhat resembling what they describe, Whately paraphrases the Common Sense philosopher Dugald Stewart at length, who suggests

> that it is well for the understanding, though it may be a loss to the fancy, when a metaphorical word has lost its pedigree—that is, when it no longer excites the primary idea denoted by it, and is reduced by custom to a plain and direct appellation in its secondary sense. He suggests also with equal ingenuity, in cases where words have not yet been worn down to this use, the expedient of *varying* our metaphor when speaking of the same subject, as a preservative against this dangerous and encroaching error [ . . . ] I think it may be regarded as an advantage of the same kind, that the parables of the New Testament are drawn from such a great diversity of objects, as to check the propensity in man, especially in matters of religion, to attach some mystical character to the images so employed, and to look upon them as emblems possessing an intrinsic virtue, or at least a secret affinity with those spiritual truths, to the illustration of which they are made subservient. (Whately 312–13)[19]

Words may begin as metaphors, but metaphors are submerged analogies, and they do not hold; words are not symbols of natural facts, à la Emerson; they do not have a motivated relation to reality—but they are the medium of thought. If Dickinson does not buy Emerson (as many, including Hagenbüchle and McIntosh, contend[20]), and is constrained between Whately and Newman, what is she left with? A sensationalist rhetoric unanchored in anything beyond private experience and shared linguistic history. But that shared linguistic history is key. It means that human knowing is as collective as it is private.

It should be clear now that Dickinson's consistent generation of variants in the throes of composition stems from the urgent impetus of the rhetorical theories she and her peers imbibed. And though Locke was not the first to declare signs arbitrarily related to the "real," the rhetorics that followed powerfully replaced language's reference to the real with the tightly bound identification of language with the workings of the human mind. The composition process itself was understood to be the moment or advent of knowledge. Dickinson's variants record the processes of thought, its dialectical turns and paradoxes, its substitutions and failures to translate, its reaching as much as its arriving.

Seeing their origin, and the origin of the variants of others, as deriving from a variety of related rhetorics emphasizing diction and style—emphasizing, in fact, choosing in the face of the philosophical impossibility of choosing correctly—should serve to historicize Dickinson's practice by locating its deep philosophical roots and aims. In fact, this brief survey of nineteenth-century rhetorical theories and historical practices should suggest that there are at least four competing rhetorics to be found in Dickinson's poetry: 1) language as the "dress" of thought (the "mechanical sign system" of Newman), 2) language as its "body" (following Whately and Campbell),[21] 3) the original trauma of Locke's divorce of words from things, and 4) Emerson's haunting intimation that words *are* symbols and *do* correspond to the real. It might be expected, therefore, that Dickinson's "rhetoric" is liable to be inconsistent, and that her variants might signify differently over a range of rhetorical possibilities. Some may register an anxiety over the fit between word and world; others seem simply to exchange one token for another. Some of Dickinson's variants are humdrum, implying that a choice has simply been deferred to perhaps the moment of presentation to a recipient, while others record an explosive dialectical tension in which no choice is possible because each term expresses through the other the coming-into-being of the conflict at the heart of the poem. I want to suggest that such a gamut of variant types emerge *because* of these competing, and sometimes complementary, rhetorics. I also want to insist that all these rhetorics (except Emerson's) are explicitly anti-metaphysical.

By examining a few poems about the composition process, I want to demonstrate the range of Dickinson's thinking about choosing and not choosing to communicate in words, and further to shake up Cameron's argument that the variants always trouble identity in a way that ultimately triumphs over our human boundedness. We can grant that ultimately the collective and conservative nature of language itself may override the limits of time and space, allowing one person to communicate with another through writing or recording; and ultimately, therefore, that the self in its consciousness (in a language) is collective as much as private. However, Dickinson's awareness of the possibility of failure, misrepresentation, and sacrifice posed by language use subject to history is at least as present to her as the possibility of achieving a fundamental if perhaps momentary fit between words and their users (if not between words and the world).

Ultimately it is boundedness, not boundlessness, which allows both humans and words to live—and to die. It is well to remember that when Dickinson gave her poems to the world in her letters and notes, she chose among variants and committed to the possibility of failure; but she didn't necessarily choose the same variants every time she sent out a poem. The rhetorical theories available to her were transactional, concerned with a word's effect on another—in a particular language, in a particular time. Therefore the fascicles, and the sets thereafter, gathering drafts with variants, should be read as a collection of the "Possibilities" Dickinson dwelt in rather than the final statement of the "author" of a "book."

Fr1243, which Franklin dates to 1872, and which is outside of the fascicle context, directly discusses the composition process, variants and all.

> Shall I take thee, the Poet said
> To the propounded word?
> Be stationed with the Candidates
> Till I have +finer tried –
>
> The Poet +searched Philology
> And +was about to ring
> for the suspended Candidate
> +There came unsummoned in –
> That portion of the Vision
> The Word applied to fill
> Not unto nomination
> The Cherubim reveal –
>
>    +vainer +further +just +when
>    +probed       +Advanced[22]

The poem registers the presence of variants even as it thematizes the impossibility of choosing among them. Variants may proliferate in such a way as to suggest the failure of language to contain a "Vision" which escapes representation entirely. To choose a word would be to be satisfied with an equivalence of word for Being, and that tacit acceptance of substitutability would impose finitude upon the "Vision." As Cameron puts it in *Choosing Not Choosing,*

> Choosing, then, empowers by establishing or demarcating identity—and, not incidentally, by supplementing the sense of what such an identity might be. But *not* choosing empowers in an entirely different way. For if everything is inconclusive, if nothing is absolute, then, also, nothing is excluded. Thus choosing and not choosing suppose different understand-

ings of totality: one predicated on substitution and discrete identity, the other predicated on identity that is inclusive, even illusorily infinite—a conclusion pertinent to a possible way of understanding the advantages implicit in Dickinson's not publishing. (153–54)

Interestingly, this is not a fascicle poem, yet it adopts the fascicle-strategy Cameron defines. Though Cameron advances this argument for the structure of the fascicles as a whole, I want to suggest that this argument holds only for certain poems, those predicated on an understanding of language as referential to Being. While this is certainly the logic at work in this poem, Dickinson saw that it was problematic: articulation, and even reference, can only be a betrayal of the "Vision." A correspondence theory of language is bound to fail. As Cameron puts it in *Lyric Time,* "for all poems [ . . . ] are not so much past or present as they are referential in tense, and what they refer to is no longer there"(187).

One of the most famous, and knotted, poems in the entire Dickinson oeuvre murderously works to assuage—or inhabit—that guilt by imagining the perfect empowerment of the speaker (language!) in the reflective reference of word and world.

> My Life had stood – a Loaded Gun –
> In Corners – til a Day
> The Owner passed – identified–
> And carried Me away –
>
> And now We roam +in Sovreign Woods –
> And now We hunt the Doe –
> And every time I speak for Him
> The Mountains straight reply –
>
> And do I smile, such cordial light
> Opon the Valley glow –
> It is as a Vesuvian face
> Had let it's pleasure through –
>
> And when at Night – Our good Day done –
> I guard My Master's Head –
> 'Tis better than the Eider-Duck's
> +Deep Pillow – to have shared –

> To foe of His – I'm deadly foe –
> None +stir the second time –
> On whom I lay a Yellow Eye –
> Or an emphatic Thumb –
>
> Though I than He – may longer live
> He longer must – than I.
> For I have but the +power to kill,
> Without – the power to die –
>
>   +the – +low +harm +art
> [Fr764, F34, 1863]

Cameron, who in *Lyric Time* explicitly doubts that this poem is about language, nevertheless brilliantly articulates its logic toward the end of her analysis of lyric:

> The reification of the word, the breathing of life into it, and with life, design, and with design, designation apart from the desire that worded it, is predicated on the detachment of word from life not so that the word might create or mirror life (our usual conception of what mimetic art does) but rather that it might survive life. For the other side of language viewed as the loss of being is an immortality of the word that specifies being's death as its first, most urgent requirement. (188)

This poem presents language speaking itself and the problem of its appearance in the formerly undifferentiated world. Language institutes both objects and persons; it kills process, possibility, and immediacy, and it produces individuated consciousness identified in relation to the objects it knows by killing them. Language is allowed to operate at all—its institution of loss is accepted—as long as it is understood to refer to something apparently real, nonlinguistic: Being, the object of desire. "And now We hunt the Doe."

"And every time I speak for Him – / The Mountains straight reply –" has Nature (or formerly undifferentiated Being) abject before the gun, uttering not a sharp cry, but an automatic report. The privilege of an original gaze, the "Yellow Eye," is distinctly antisocial and suspiciously like Emerson's "Transparent eyeball," here demonized, aggrandizing, reaching only to master "foes" with an "emphatic Thumb." The dream of perfect concord between word and world subsumes the human user; master and slave trade places, and the linguistic artifact takes on the consciousness it has alienated through its "power" or "art." Such "art" seems to ensure eternal or invulnerable existence, and yet this utterly inhuman speaker longs, like a Pinocchio or even a Christ, for a human—and humane—existence. Lyric rage, in short, will never really do.

If, in the "Vision" poem, no variant adequately refers to Being, and if, in the "Loaded Gun" poem, variants are rather like interchangeable parts in a murderous artifact, then one poem represents "not choosing" and the other represents "choosing." Dickinson thought through the problem yet again: perhaps she could use the variants as a way to represent the tension, not just between choosing and not choosing, but between the linguistic theories available to her. Whately had given her recourse to the identification of language and thought, but not word and world (or Being).[23] The following poem (Fr404, F20) mediates between—or can't decide between—the two linguistic theories.

> To put this World down, like a Bundle –
> And walk steady, away,
> Requires Energy – possibly Agony –
> 'Tis the Scarlet way
>
> Trodden with straight renunciation
> By the Son of God –
> Later, his faint Confederates
> Justify the Road –
>
> Flavors of that old Crucifixion –
> Filaments of Bloom, Pontius Pilate sowed –
> Strong Clusters, from Barabbas' Tomb –
>     +indorsed
> Sacrament, Saints +partook before us –
> Patent, every drop,
>     +stamp
> With the +Brand of the Gentile Drinker
>     +Enforced
> Who +indorsed the Cup –

The poem discusses "renunciation"—the acceptance of a substitute for union with Being—(that is, the necessity to live within the limits of a human body) in terms of death and martyrdom: Christ was the first "to put this World down," and his disciples followed suit. The problem in the poem is whether dying (or being subject to death) is to be read as a *choice* or not. The first line, "To put this World down," is speculative, and it is "Agony" only "possibly"; there seems to be a choice involved. Later, equivocally, the variants describing the "Sacrament" of such a sacrifice vacillate between "partook" or "indorsed," so that the disciples could be either martyrs or salesmen. Death is "Patent," like a medicine, "With the Brand of the Gentile[24] Drinker / Who indorsed the Cup—." Jesus appears to be the inventor and hawker of a patent medicine—but the variants directly complicate this reading. What if the renunciation—differentiation—death—were not a choice? The "Stamp" of the "Gentile" drinker sounds less gentle than violent and possessive (and even "Brand" intimates a searing claim), and the inability to decide whether it is "indorsed" or "enforced" makes matters worse. What if the gentle drinker is, in fact, the implacable Godhead?

Then "to put this World down" is not a choice, and the "Agony" of "that old Crucifixion" is for all. What the possible equivalence of Christ with the Godhead means for the speaker is that the presence of the "Word" is not some happy human invention like a patent medicine, but the more inexorable reality of human life, and death (and Being's death), in language. *This* "Sacrament," and not "Vision," might be all that is available to humanity. And it can't be put off.

"To put this World down" then becomes the choice to write.

To put it down "like a Bundle – / And walk steady, away," is both the "Agony" of a mother abandoning her child and the acceptance of the Lockean "bundles" (of ideas) language (mis)makes of the world. The presence of the variants testifies to the "Energy" both called into being and used up by that acceptance. That the renunciation involved in putting this world down, in language and for language, might be a matter of choice is a possibility held out by the irreducibility of Christ to God, that is, his humanness. What if there is no implacable God? Then the "Scarlet way"—the Crucifixion—is precisely Sensation parsed into language at the expense of a sponsoring outside term such as Being. The "Cup" is a humane "Medicine." The paradox contained in the premise that words may both refer and not refer to an ultimate reality is played out by the tension between the variants, especially "indorsed" and "enforced," which leaves the question of reference both provisionally unanswered and ultimately unanswerable. Perhaps it is just this sort of aperture-in-closure that Cameron wishes to limn.

Dickinson explored the idea of Word as Sacrament again, possibly in 1863 after having written the poem "My Life had stood – a Loaded Gun" (Fr764). The later text (in Franklin's numbering) may be read as a variant to "My Life" (following Cameron's method) because of its marked echoes of "My Life's" final riddling formulation. The later poem, "A Word made Flesh" (Fr1715) comes from an undated transcript made by Susan Dickinson, which probably means that the original was sent to her relatively early on.[25] This poem, perhaps sent as a letter, contains no variants, as was always the case (as far as we know) when Dickinson copied her poems for others. The poem will "dwell among" its living occasion and between its sender and recipient. It makes the incarnation of relationship—as opposed to the institution of sacrifice—in words a real possibility.

> The import of that Paragraph
> "The Word made Flesh"
> Had he the faintest intimation
> Who broached it yesterday!
>
> "Made Flesh and dwelt among us"
> ───────────────
> A Word made Flesh is seldom
> And tremblingly partook
> Nor then perhaps reported
> But have I not mistook
> Each one of us has tasted
> With ecstasies of stealth
> The very food debated
> To our specific strength –
>
> A Word that breathes distinctly
> Has not the power to die
> Cohesive as the Spirit
> It may expire if He –
>
> "Made Flesh and dwelt among us"
> Could condescension be
> Like this consent of Language
> This loved Philology (Fr1715)

This poem uses imagery suggestive both of Christ's incarnation and of the sacrament of communion. In it, the thought condescends to become a word on the model of the first "Word made Flesh"—that is, thought embraces its own humanity in language. No longer tethered to an imaginary, even mythical referent such as union with the Creator, undifferentiated Being, or a time before language, language is acknowledged to be not the bringer of death, but the breath of life, our only medium. That it is spiritual, that is, imaginary, makes it capable of sustaining relation; relation in turn gives the reader the power to embrace the body as the medium of relation. With this poem the speaker embraces being in language and being a body in time. That embrace is a renunciation of the fantasy of suspension in the imagination for the vulnerability of the body; as in the "Scarlet way" of Christ, the speaker "indorses" language; we "partake" of thought which is precisely abated to word, which "fits" the human user. Though Cameron states in *Lyric Time* that "Language does not fulfill the desire it can learn how to express" (190), this poem imagines that fulfillment. Taking in the word produces an imaginative relation with a collective self "inside" the flesh—"strength."

This collective self is termed "Spirit," Spirit having the appropriate property of being, therefore, "Cohesive." "A Word that breathes distinctly" is "Cohesive as the Spirit"; each constitutes the other reciprocally. The artifact is beneficent because it "breathes" with human power. This sort of word, therefore, "Has not the power to die"—not because it is not alive in the first place, as in the word as loaded gun, but because it is coextensive with humanity. "Thought" and "word," as in Whately, are at least temporarily identified. Revising the "Loaded Gun" poem, this poem insists that the Word may expire. If language might return, alienated, to the materiality of illegible graphemes, then it is not after all wholly material. Meaning is human; it is therefore vulnerable, a collective responsibility, and personhood is as bodily and historical as it is collectively spiritual.

I have found it necessary to dismantle Cameron's argument on material, historical, and philosophical grounds in order to present an account of Dickinson which honors her skepticism and commitment to representing human consciousness as subject to death. Dickinson as often as not struggles with and even rejects a metaphysical framework which implies that language must or even can contain Being; instead, Dickinson proposes that language might contain Thought. Such competing linguistic theories focus Dickinson's composition process almost obsessively on articulation. Dickinson's variant-riddled poems, gathered in their disarray, come to us as ongoing experiment, filled as much with the consciousness of failure as with grounds for hope.

# 3

# Magical Transformations
"Necromancy Sweet," Texts, and Identity in Fascicle 8

## Eleanor Elson Heginbotham

*N*ot tucked under another poem, as are some of Emily Dickinson's shorter poems within her fascicles, but spread out boldly in the middle of a page toward the end of Fascicle 8, one of Dickinson's stranger poems grabs our attention. Written with clear large strokes (no variants) it declares its strange stridency with its exclamation points, its percussive sounds, and, primarily, the distressing prayer it offers. Indeed, it can cause the reader's hair to stand at attention:

> Ah! Necromancy Sweet!
> Ah! Wizard erudite!
> Teach me the skill,
>
> That I instill the pain
> Surgeons assuage in vain,
> Nor Herb of all the plain
> Can heal! (Fr168)[1]

Although every Dickinson reader knows that she dealt surprises with every poem, creating voices that swerve from delight and love of this life of haying and talking at fences (Fr582, F25) to despair, wishing that, like the Gnat, (s)he could "gad [her] little Being out – / And not begin – again –" (Fr444, F21), this poem seems to stand alone. Startled by its apparent cruelty, the reader wonders what happened to the dispenser of consoling letters and

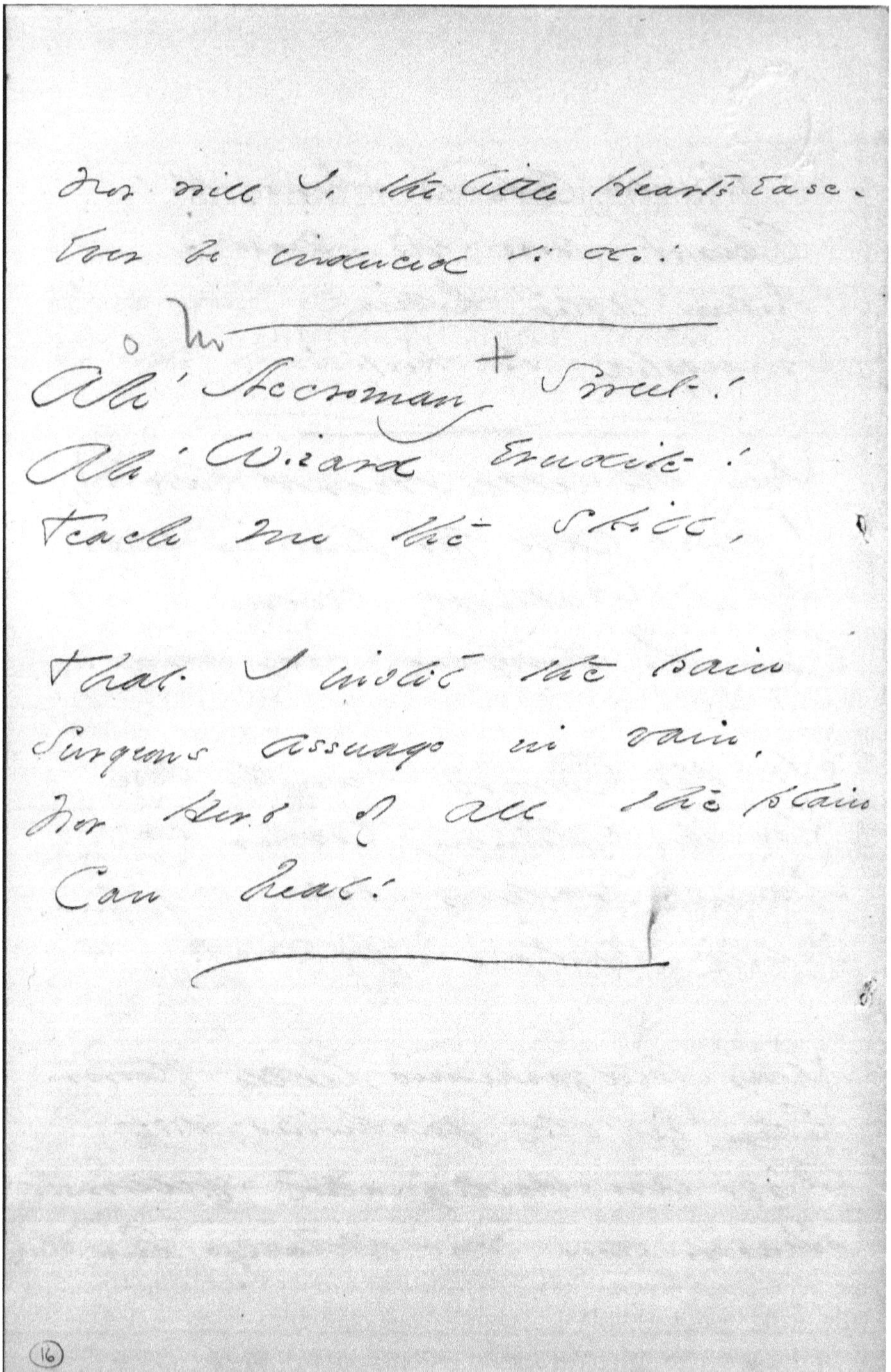

Nor will I, the Little Heart's Ease —
Ever be induced to do.

Ah! Necromancy Sweet!
Ah! Wizard Erudite!
Teach me the skill,

That I instil the pain
Surgeons assuage in vain,
Nor Herb of all the plains
Can heal!

*Figure 6.* Fascicle 8, "Ah, Necromancy Sweet!"

flowers, the poet who, in a far more famous poem, wished to "stop one Heart from breaking" (Fr982). This incantatory call for the dark side of magic or sorcery would be worth exploring whether it had been on the back of an envelope, in a letter to a friend (neither of which survives as a possibility), or as a stand-alone poem, but, in fact, it is in Fascicle 8, which has many other surprises for the attentive reader.[2]

Reading it in its fascicle setting demonstrates how context affects interpretation. There it takes its place as a penultimate climax in a grouping of poems privileging magic acts of all kinds. One business of this essay will be to show how Dickinson's placement in this twenty-poem sequence influences our understanding of it. Another—related—will be to explore how this poem and others in the fascicle reflect an interest of Dickinson's that is only recently becoming a subject of conversation and study: Dickinson's response to the rage in her own age for the occult. Finally, it will move both of those discussions—the fascicle context and the cultural context—into the realm of Dickinson's hermeneutics, her theology.

To take the first: the architecture or thematic impulses of Fascicle 8. In this remarkable gathering a gunshot transforms a deer into a high leaper and that into a suffering, struggling person; a sunset becomes a bloody battlefield that in turn morphs into a kitchen corner; flowers become poems; the pent-up force of a far-away volcano transforms itself through the poet into a reined-in, disciplined human stoic. These are not unexpected comparisons to the reader of Dickinson, or indeed of most poets. Poetry is, of course, based almost entirely on transformations. Metaphor, simile, synecdoche, metonymy, and other figures of speech transform one thing to another, often to startlingly different creatures, places, situations, ideas.[3] One of the objections to the growing community of those who encourage reading a poem in its fascicle context is that whatever one says about one text ("necromancy") in one context (Fascicle 8) could just as easily be said about Dickinson's work as a whole. In other words, say they (some of them outstanding scholars within this volume): so what that there are many transformational metaphors within Fascicle 8? Such metaphors run throughout the oeuvre, throughout, in fact, all poetry from Anglo-Saxon ballads on. One of my answers is that such a truth does not keep us from talking about other groupings in terms of their particular shape and power, even if the grouping by, say, William Wordsworth or Sylvia Plath has much in common with other groupings by that poet or with other poets from time immemorial.

Let us agree that, while we cannot know Dickinson's intention when she made her little books any more than we can know her intention when she wrote an individual lyric, we have the right—indeed, as the final poem in this sequence instructs us, the responsibility, to tease out—without insisting on our own—inferences. Unlike the groupings of most other poets, Dickinson's are unmediated by editors or printers. We are, as Suzanne Juhasz said when Ralph W. Franklin's *Manuscript Books* made doing so possible, looking "face to face with her *own* poems" (60).

That said, the magic implied and stated in the collection of poems we call Fascicle 8, the only one in which Dickinson calls on "Necromancy" for help,[4] seems a particularly compressed complex of mutually reinforcing images of the power of a text to to transform not only ideas into images and back again into ideas, but also to transform its reader and its writer. Keeping in mind the cautionary comments of Martha Nell Smith in her important essay in this volume, we might nevertheless more than provisionally accept the following: that Dickinson herself folded the five "cream, lightly ruled and embossed" stationery sheets, used the ink in her father's household to slash the marks below the slight oval design embossed on the paper, stacked the five folded sheets, and sewed them with something more like twine than like thread;[5] that early editors Mabel Loomis Todd and Thomas Wentworth Higginson respected Dickinson's work enough to keep records of how it first appeared even when they removed poems from their original settings, even (see n. 5)—keeping the thread that bound them; and that Ralph W. Franklin's heroic accomplishment in reconstituting the books offers us probable if not incontrovertible certitude about Dickinson's work in creating her little manuscript books. Beyond that, we run into those old ogres of intentional fallacies. Of course, there is no way to know whether, if Dickinson declaimed this poem as neighbors reportedly occasionally heard her do, she might have recited—or shouted—"Ah! Necromancy Sweet!" in a dramatic interpretation of Macbeth's witches or soulfully or playfully or with sophisticated wit, sharply pointed at a community that privileged flowery, inspirational, religious literature by women poets with three names.

Questions of tone become somewhat less mysterious when exploring intertextualities between poems. Why did Dickinson place this strong poem with its odd term for a specific form of transformation, "Necromancy," in the context of the nineteen poems that surround it? This essay does *not* posit that Fascicle 8—or any other of the forty—is a coded narrative about a craze for magical appearances or that, essay like, it is driven by *a* theme in the normal Carlylean/Emersonian sense. Image clusters, changing speakers, even matters of punctuation and placement of poems on pages in dialogic relationships with each other: all of these are interesting to the fascicle reader who is rewarded with more complex and open discoveries. We play with the surprises across as well as down the pages; we note refrains with variations. In short, reading Dickinson in her fascicle context—the only one she left other than the important context of poems which she slipped into letters—provides the attentive reader with the same appreciation he or she brings to the individual lyric, a term which is in itself a subject for debate as Virginia Jackson discusses it in her *Dickinson's Misery*.[6] Reading the collections—fascicles or whatever we call them (see Ellen Hart's essay in this volume)—of eleven to twenty-nine of these smaller marvels—whatever we call *them*—we may increase our respect, often our amusement, at Dickinson's wit, her care, her openness to serendipity, and, of course, her emotional and intellectual intensity and originality.

Leaving aside the question of labels for the purpose of this discussion, reading Dickinson's individual works in the context of the little thread-bound volumes that Mabel Loomis Todd called "fascicles" confirms—playfully or not—what Allen Tate—playfully or not—said: "Cotton Mather would have burned her for a witch" (quoted in Blake and Wells 167). Tate's comment is not pejorative; Dickinson's witchcraft, her power, is brewed in the words she chooses, of course, but also in the arrangement of a poem on a page. What Louise Bogan said when the Johnson variorum appeared over half a century ago—that "to read Emily Dickinson in this new text, in which every idiosyncratic habit of spelling, punctuation, diction, and localism is reproduced, is to read her in a slightly different language" (96)—is exponentially more true when one pores over the reconstituted fascicles published in 1981 by Ralph Franklin. Along with all those delights just listed, there is at least one more potential discovery in reading the fascicles, one in hot contention: reading a poem in its fascicle placement may help the reader toward (though certainly never *all the way to*) a clearer understanding of what the words so carefully chosen by that wordsmith Dickinson may have meant when she copied them into the little book, the fascicle.[7]

An earlier version of this essay posits that one way to test the thesis that placement may disclose new possibilities for interpretation—is to read the poems that appear in more than one fascicle, in light of other poems in that grouping.[8] The grouping itself becomes, as fascicle readers have noted, a long-link poem in itself, the twenty-first poem, if you will, of a twenty-poem cycle.[9] Each grouping has what I have called its own "thumbprint," its sworl of images or themes or concerns that sets it apart from others. Thus, goes my argument, a poem that is "repeated," a word used with many caveats, becomes a different poem in tone and impact through its intersection with other poems in a different sequence. It happens that Fascicle 8 contains not just one "repeated" poem ("At last, to be identified" [Fr172], a poem that Dickinson placed, in almost identical form, in a similar position, in Fascicle 21) but also the brief "Portraits are to daily faces" (Fr174), seventh in the series, which turns up again as "Pictures are to daily faces," seventeenth in this same series we call Fascicle 8. All three "repetitions"—one ("At last") expressing joy in self-identity, the other two ("Portraits/Pictures are") expressing faith in the enterprise of the artist—may somehow resonate against this call for magic—and for the power to "instill" pain.

Compiled about 1860, two years into her project of publishing her work in the form of these manuscript books,[10] this fascicle interests me for that one fulcrum—Michael Riffaterre might almost call it a "hypogram"[11]—around which, it seems to me, most of the entire little book revolves, "Necromancy." Although originally the word was reserved for the art of foretelling the future by communicating with the dead, a compelling longing in many of the poems, Dickinson here also seems to use its secondary but more general use, "magic, enchantment, sorcery." The magic she weaves through this fascicle is directly related to both "repeated" poems ("Portraits/pictures" and "At last, to be identified"), part of Dickinson's declaration of aesthetic intent.[12] Moreover, in fact, the magic is woven through most of the other poems in the sequence. Avoiding, I hope, temptations to overlay a narrative[13] or an ideology on the book, I want only to suggest that Dickinson hints throughout Fascicle 8 that she was attuned to the practices if not the possibilities of the magic, the Spiritualism, the "Necromancy" of her day and that her awareness, wary or accepting, fed her poetic vocabulary. Indeed, she could not have been unaware of it, as Paul Crumbley has ably shown in *Winds of Will: Emily Dickinson and the Sovereignty of Democratic Thought* (107–32) and as Paula Bennett's essay in this collection notes. That vocabulary, especially in Fascicle 8, surrounds Dickinson's notions of the hallowedness of an artistic project, one achieved through pain, joy, study, labor, and surprises; one that transfigures the maker of the art; and one that, she hoped and we now know, would wander down the ages for our inferences. Let those inferences begin.

## "Necromancy Sweet"?

The strange, almost sadistic seven-line single sentence, filling almost all of the left side of the open book, framed in Dickinson's characteristic horizontal lines, is fifteenth poem in a twenty-poem collection. "Ah! Necromancy – Sweet!" radiates backwards and forward through the series, informing the reading of its surrounding poems and opening up interpretive possibilities. Challenging as this poem is, to my knowledge, it has not received much scholarly attention.[14] Along with the many studies of Dickinson's religious interests, proclivities, and resistance, there are the related studies on Dickinson's poems of power, indeed of rage.[15] Most agree with Richard Sewall and Cynthia Griffin Wolff that Emily Dickinson carried on a lifelong wrestling match with the tenets of her church and the faith she had not been able to proclaim aloud as a schoolgirl. Few, however, have remarked on what some in Dickinson's circle might have regarded as a bastard offspring of traditional faiths, one that took over the imagination and even the practices of thousands in Dickinson's day: Spiritualism with its related arts and crafts. As the brief recapitulation of this almost-deviant fad of her age and place will show (later in this essay), Dickinson's metaphoric invocation of "Necromancy" was not, perhaps, as strange in Dickinson's midcentury Anglo-American world as it may seem now. Furthermore, although Dickinson's specific call for necromancy's power is unique to this poem, the call reminds us of what is more familiar: the persistent yearnings of her speakers for communion with the dead. This longing runs through Dickinson's individual poems, her fascicles, her letters, and the various scraps she left behind. Crumbley's penetrating analysis of the conduit between theology and democracy provided by the poems with a spiritualist slant illustrates the point through over fifty of Dickinson's poems, none of them from the earlier part of her oeuvre (*Winds of Will* 215–16). Thus, it would be silly to hold up Fascicle 8 as her primary revelation of this societal phenomenon. However, to look closely at this *overt* use of a term linked with spiritualism in this fascicle setting seems a worthy project. The poem's context, its placement with other poems, almost all of which involve some sort of translation of matter or spirit, provides insight into her poetic practice and her awareness of a public phenomenon.

Read in its fascicle setting, "Ah, Necromancy Sweet" is part of a network of interconnecting images. This context makes the poem simultaneously broader (more universal) and more sharply pointed (situational) than it is standing alone. This fascicle repeats (with important variations) versions of magic and transformation, that change the *poet* ("At last, to be identified," eleventh poem, halfway through the fascicle) and the *poem* (as it "wanders down the latitudes") and the *reader* who heeds the poet's call to attend to "your *inference* therefrom" ("As if some little Arctic flower," twentieth and last poem in the sequence; the "inference" underline is Dickinson's). Along the way it provides some deliciously serendipitous—or are they?—witty surprises.

The anguished pain of a wounded deer opens the fascicle with a leap. In Fascicle 8's first poem, "A *wounded* Deer—leaps highest –" (Fr181), the "extasy of death," as the hunter tells it (several poems in Fascicle 8 are secondhand stories), propels the deer to a final height before "the Brake is still!" In her own word-leap the speaker moves from that death to the death of Christ—or at least to the typography suggesting it: "The *smitten* Rock that gushes! / The *trampled* Steel that springs!" The speaker literally underlines the Christian imagery ("smitten" and "trampled"), investing the deer with a holy aura before the poem takes another turn—from the animal to the sacred to the mortal, the universal. The poem ends aphoristically, "Mirth is the mail of Anguish – / In which it cautious Arm, / Lest Anybody spy the blood / And 'you're hurt' exclaim!"[16] She will return to that image of reined-in emotion later in the fascicle, including the "Necromancy" poem, but first we turn the page to find more blood.

A "Nobody" rather than an "Anybody" (of the "Wounded Deer" poem) spies the blood in the poem that follows, "The Sun kept stooping – stooping – low! (Fr182). That poem, on the left of the opened fascicle, faces "I met a King this Afternoon" (Fr183), on the right. It takes a moment to register on that little bit of intertextuality—the "Nobody/Anybody" and the seeping blood that moves from the deer to the sunset. We are beguiled to read the poems only on their surface; when we turn the page, for example, we see two homely situations: the first (on the left), simply a (bloody) sunset over the hills, the other (on the right), a delighted glimpse of a freckled, barefoot boy and his two "ragged" friends riding in a horse-drawn wagon. However, both are just as much about a kind of magical transformation as is the wounded Deer / smitten Rock that gushes. Both actually use variants of the *word* "transformation": "On his side [the Sun's], what Transaction!" exults the speaker of the poem on the left of the opened fascicle; and the sight of the little wagon "then transported me!" says the speaker of that on the right. In the poem on the left the sunset deepens into "Armies – / So gay – So Brigadier"; on the right, the children in the wagon become "A King" and "Princes." The imagination of the poet plays with simple sights: imagination is the agent of transformation. That imagination lures the attentive reader to balance between the literal prosy setting with the suggestion of the existential dramas. Another turn of the page repeats in its own way the image cluster provided by the first three poems: on the left of the opened books are the last three quatrains of "I met a King," the top line on the page declaring, "And such a wagon!" Facing the line is the beginning of "To learn the Transport by the Pain" (Fr178). Such coincidences of language and images ("Wagon" and "Transport") may be accidental. Some critics of manuscript studies maintain that the fascicles are more scrapbook than chapbook and that Dickinson used some words so often that their pairing or intimacy in a manuscript must be accidental.[17] Nevertheless it is hard to imagine that the kind of fun such discoveries provide this reader did not also delight the writer, whatever her motivation and process for putting them there. Questions of intentionality are outside the scope of this essay—and outside the realm of our knowing,[18] but we are invited to *see* what is on the pages, make our inferences, and be moved, delighted, and entertained.

What such coincidences have to do with "Necromancy" becomes clear as we move through the fascicle, turning to more revelations, more evidence that in their fascicle context, individual poems take on new possibilities of meaning(s) and the whole becomes bigger than the sum of its parts.[19] "To learn the Transport," fourth poem in the sequence, connects in small ways to those around it as you see them on the pages: the "Barefoot Estate" at the end of the third poem is echoed, for example, in the "homesick, homesick feet" of the character in "To Learn." As the "ragged Princes" are "sovereigns" on their journey in the third poem, the pain in the fourth is "a sovereign Anguish"—and the lines are directly opposite each other. But, of course, there are much deeper interconnections. The pain and death in the first poem ("A wounded Deer") moves to a bloody sunset poem suggesting transformations in the natural and the spiritual world, and those merge to the child in a wagon morphed into a king in a coach. Where are they going? There's a provisional answer in the next ("To learn the Transport"), in which the "homesick feet" are going to a "foreign shore," where, waiting, are "'the patient Laureates' / Whose voices – trained – below – /Ascend in ceaseless Carol." From this imagined other world these voices are "inaudible, indeed, / To us, the duller scholars / Of the Mysterious Bard!" Before moving to the next poems in the grouping, it is well to remember that the business of the Spiritualist, the Necromancer, is to call on those voices so that they *will* be audible below. Of course, that is as simplistic a reading as anything else; much more is happening on these pages, so we move on to three poems that, among much else, celebrate objects that might be metaphors for poems.

## Reading the Flowers, the Letter, the Portrait: What Lives On

"If the foolish call them '*flowers*' –" (Fr179), begins the speaker of one of the most potentially rich and confusing poems in the gathering, the fifth poem of the fascicle, the first of its own little grouping, and the clever hiding place of one of the most astonishing rewards for the careful reader of the fascicle. As are most of the poems in this fascicle, this one is another spoke around that hub of "Necromancy" and the less obvious but present shadow of Spiritualism, as this cluster of poems, particularly, invokes measures against extinction: art allows the dead to visit with the living. The magic occurs on many levels; one of those is in the textured preparation for this poem ("If the foolish") with those that led up to it. To begin with, the writer of the fascicle makes the distinction in this poem between the "foolish" and the "wiser" readers, reminding "wiser" readers of the fascicle of the "patient Laureate" of the previous page/poem ("To learn the Transport"); just so, the "beclouded Eyes" of the foolish (or the wiser or the Savans) call to mind the "Blind Men [who] learn the sun" in "To Learn."

Fun as are such linguistic links, they become deeper in the context of a larger picture. To see that larger picture we remember that in the first four poems Dickinson put "To learn the Transport by the Pain" as an echo of the first, her "wounded Deer"; that the "Sovereign Anguish" of "Transport" is likewise previewed in the "Transport[ed]" children/monarch in the third poem. Clearly, so far, there have been several versions of meditations on the truth of mortality—and the sadness of death. That "Necromancy" incantation is just around the corner with all its implications of magical transformations of the dead who come to life. With "If the foolish" she begins a new group, one that includes the "flowers" of the fifth poem, the "tawny" letter, retrieved from the Ebon box of the sixth poem, and the "Portrait" of the seventh. In them the compiler of the collection offers not just solace but a triumph over death, a kind of "Necromancy Sweet." And although "If the foolish call them '*flowers* –'" may be "about" (admittedly a reductive word) other things, Dickinson's floral poems, including importantly the last in this fascicle, seem so often metaphors for the products of her industry that it seems safe to say that the self-consciously literary language of this one clarifies the "them." The "foolish" may consider them pretty and decorative and perishable; the "Savans" may try to classify them, but "those who read the 'Revelations'" understand that they (poems) may be a kind of promised land, something metaphorically as precious as that denied Moses. The poem spills over onto the right-hand side of the turned page:

> Low amid that glad Belles lettres
> Grant that we may stand –
> *Stars,* amid profound *Galaxies*
> At that grand 'Right Hand.'

Under the strong line Dickinson used to separate one lyric on a page from another is a poem as well known and oft anthologized as the previous few are not: "In Ebon Box, when years have flown" (Fr180). The "Belles lettres" of the Galaxies of some literary heaven, presided over by a God near whom the poet begs to stand, seems an introduction to this poem about what survives the dead, what speaks for the dead (a kind of "necromancy") through the dusty ages to the living. How great a miracle, how important its consequences are—the discovery of a text, a letter in this case, becomes all the more clear by *looking at* the pages on which the two poems appear, by, in the language of the first, "scanning" them, or in the language of the second, "conning" them. For there they are opposite each other,

*on the left (from Fr179):*      *and on the right (from Fr180):*

Could we stand with that Old 'Moses' –      To hold a letter to the light –
'Canaan' denied –      Grown Tawny – now, with time –
Scan like him the stately landscape      To con the faded syllables
On the other side –      That quickened us like Wine!

The written text held to the light is literally on these pages opposite the Promised Land; both are yearned for. The sight of the Promised Land, says the speaker of the poem on the left, would "deem superfluous / Many Sciences, / Not pursued by learned Angels / in scholastic skies!" It is hard to imagine a pairing that would imply more reverence about a letter. The speaker's wish to "scan" in the poem on the left, and, in the one on the right, to "con" the syllables, is the act of a reader and the wish of the writer for the reader. The poem on the right continues as the speaker brings a "flower" up from the Ebon Box with, again, the resonances of a something that outlasts death. And then the poem continues and concludes on the next page. Below the last verse of "The Ebon Box" is a puzzling little gem. It will appear, with one word changed, later in the fascicle, causing Sharon Cameron to call the doubling not so much a repetition but rather a refrain:

     Portraits are to daily faces
     As an Evening West,
     To a fine – pedantic sunshine
     In a satin Vest! (Fr174)

To my knowledge Cameron alone has explored an answer to the question of why this poem that seems a simple contrast between the actual and the virtual, the "real thing" in the Jamesian sense and the better, the representational, appears twice within nine pages.[20] It is, as she says, part of a "structural element" (*Choosing* 55). Later in her groundbreaking book Cameron says, "Thus we read connections, even equivalences, sometimes by appeal to proximity but sometimes by non-congruous associations" (116). What Cameron calls "the structural element," the connection of which this poem, "repeated" later in the book as "Pictures are to daily faces," is part of the pattern, as the speaker follows the written text held to the faded light in "The Ebon Box" with the tiny little meditation on the "Evening West." Like the "tawny letter," it is privileged to the bright light—the "pedantic sunshine"—perhaps the prosy world, the opposite of which is the lyric dark, subject of Wendy Barker's study. We see clearer in that dark, as Dickinson reminds us elsewhere. In the sequence's eighth poem, "Wait till the Majesty of Death" (Fr169), that dark, away from the "pedantic sunshine," the reader learns what is found: death has transformed the "modest Clay" to a royal state, around which "Obsequious Angels" and "the Lord of Lords" not only await but "Receive [the dead] unblushingly!"

Especially because of the quotation marks and the adjectives, the tone of this poem is ambiguous. To my ears it is playful. This reading, influenced possibly by the "Necromancy" poem coming later in the sequence, resists readings by those who focus on Dickinson's fascination with death, including such readings as John Cody's (that the poet's fascination with death propelled her inner life so much toward obsession that "she thirsted for details; it was important to learn just how the dying felt in the face of imminent dissociation" [Cody 268–69]). Cody calls this "her peculiar interest in mortality," but, of course, it was not "peculiar" to her; all around her, as we will see, Spiritualists and those who went to them for solace and connection—thousands around her—were doing something similar. The Civil War, which had barely begun in the year ascribed by Ralph Franklin to this fascicle, would exponentially increase the interest in speaking with the spirit world and gaining wisdom from it, but Drew Gilpin Faust supplies some astonishing statistics for the decade during which Dickinson *was,* presumably, compiling the fascicle. In her dense and sorrowful look at *This Republic of Suffering: Death and the American Civil War,* Faust cites the explosive nature of this trend:

> A series of spirit rappings in upstate New York in the late 1840s had intensified spreading interest in the apparent reality of communication between the living and the dead. . . . By 1853 one spiritualist estimated that thirty [spirit circles] met regularly in the city of Philadelphia alone,

and that thirty thousand mediums were operating across the country. The *Spiritualist Register* reported that just before the outbreak of war 240,000 inhabitants of New York State—6 percent of its total population—were spiritualists. (180–81)

One mission of this essay is to explore Dickinson's tone toward what amounted to a fad and to reexamine in that light the given: that, for her, immortality was indeed "the flood subject." One clue is, again, in the *look* at the poems, page against page. On the left, the leftover stanzas of "In Ebon Box" begin with "A curl, perhaps, from foreheads / Our Constancy forgot"; on the right, brow to brow, we see "Wait till the Majesty of Death / Invests so mean a brow!" And underneath the brows, the foreheads, Dickinson has copied into her book that "Portraits" poem on the left and the transformed dead on the right. Senior scholars like David Porter and Ralph Franklin may insist that such things are the coincidences of the scrapbook collector Dickinson, but to my eyes, they seem deliberate—and witty. That by no means negates the deadly seriousness of Dickinson's explorations of what happens to us when we die. We turn the page; we are now halfway through the fascicle, and there seems to be a new nuance to the tone: the reportage of the first "wounded Deer," the awe of the "Ebon Box," the witty talk of "Transport" and transfiguration becomes intense and personal.

"'Tis so much joy! 'Tis so much joy!" (Fr170), next in the series, flies across and down the page in a breathless rush to its crashing finish. "If I should fail, what poverty!" and "if indeed I fail," and then, "And if I gain!": each of the three verses sets up a subjunctive, wistful, urgent tone. Balancing joy and defeat, bliss and breath against each other, the tone is restrained until the speaker's excitement reaches a wishful crescendo:

> And if I gain! Oh Gun at sea,
> Oh Bells, that in the steeples be!
> At first, repeat it slow!
> For Heaven is a different thing,
> Conjectured, and waked sudden in –
> And might extinguish me!

So much hinges on this victory that the reader is left with the top of her head exposed, cold and hot simultaneously, in the grip of a poet whose hopes are visceral. As Jane Eberwein points out, this sense of the lure, the exhilaration of death and the Dead is as much a part of Dickinson as the mourning for the lost (*Strategies* 210). As we move toward the call on "Necromancy," the pattern emerging from the play of single lyric against lyric becomes more complex and compelling. Opposite the tentatively triumphant mood of "'Tis so much joy!" is "A fuzzy fellow, without feet –" (Fr171) with a less tentative story of transfiguration as the squat, dun caterpillar takes "*Damask Residence* – / And struts in sewing silk!" with the mission of telling "the pretty secret / Of the butterfly!"

One version of the "pretty secret" is the poem Dickinson places below that final stanza which is spilled over to the next page as a sort of preamble to the poem which will later appear, almost unchanged (readers will note that the punctuation in Fascicle 21, slightly different, is the version Franklin used for the Reader's Edition), in Fascicle 21: "At last, to be identified!" (Fr172). This tale of self-revelation brings the feet—perhaps those that appeared in the early poems—to a space "leagues" away from the old life to a new identity. The two parts of the page on the left are related: the caterpillar becomes butterfly on the top third of the page, and, below, the speaker is transformed into the inhabitant of a dark place (past midnight, past the morning star, past sunrise, past day, as she tells us). All of this is magic; all of it is transfiguration. It is the kind of sequence in which the poet's "metapoetic treatment of metaphor," as James Guthrie puts it, makes her most closely resemble "a mystic" (*Vision* 60).[21]

One of Dickinson's most famous "metapoetic metaphors" now appears on the right side of her little book, almost like an ember smoldering in that dark. As is the opening's "wounded Deer," this next long poem, "I have never seen 'Volcanoes' –" (Fr165), is a narrative. Although both narratives have been read as autobiographical reactions to one love relationship or another, and indeed they may have originated as such,[22] in this context, copied as they are in a gathering with that strange call to "Necromancy Sweet!" and anticipated with meditations on transformations, of which the largest is the passage to death, the Volcano and the Deer seem to have more to do with ways to deal with pain that transforms: through active struggle, through the quest to quiet the struggle, through containing passion with self-control. The two "as told to" narratives, "The wounded Deer" and "Volcanoes," are reversals of each other. "Mirth is the mail of Anguish," observes the hunter who reports on the wounded deer; the story he tells is of control born of the mortal wound. On the other hand, in the twelfth poem of the series, the "Travellers tell" of the surface placidity that masks the deeper explosive identity of the Volcano. "The mail of Anguish" in "The wounded Deer" becomes "the smoldering anguish" of the "appalling Ordnance" in "The still Volcano" (even in this horror Dickinson puns with "pall"). The parallel/opposing stories end the same: the deer dies in the brake; the dust in the "palpitating Vineyard" settles down over a destroyed, buried world. But in the latter, the speaker yearns for "some loving Antiquary, / On Resumption Morn" to "cry with joy, 'Pompeii'! / To the Hills return!" As in so many Dickinson poems, the mood is subjunctive: again three "ifs" frame the action as the speaker wishes for resumption, a restoration of all that has exploded, burned, died. That plea, contained in the last stanza, is on the top of the next page; under it and the usual demarcation line, is what seems a provisional answer to the cry of the Antiquarian.

The silence of the spent volcano, the smoldering ruin, leads to "Dust is the only Secret" (Fr166). The secret in the dust is "Death," pictured here as lonely ("Nobody knew 'his Father' – / Never was a Boy –" and so forth) and also as New Englandish: "Industrious! Laconic! / Punctual! Sedate," and as, oxymoronically, "Bold as a Brigand / Stiller than a Fleet!" Can this "Dust/Death" with all its sterling qualities, somehow answer the wish of the "loving Antiquary"? Taken out of its fascicle context, "Dust is the only Secret" demonstrates Cameron's thesis that "one inevitably sees an individual poem as something different from what an individual poem was before one read the fascicles. For the individual poem now is interpenetrated or saturated with the kind of connections revealed by reading Dickinson in the fascicles" (*Choosing* 174–75). Taken out of the fascicle, the poem is indeed, as Jane Eberwein calls it, "Solemn" (*Strategies* 224), but in its fascicle setting its solemnity bridges poems profoundly and wittily. It needs to be *seen*:

| On the left, the last stanza of "Volcano": | On the right, the last stanza of "Dust": |
|---|---|
| If some loving Antiquary, On Resumption Morn, Will not cry with joy, "Pompeii"! To the Hills return! | Builds, like a Bird, too! Christ robs the nest – Robin after Robin Smuggled to Rest! |

Below each of these is that solid Dickinson demarcation line; the leftover stanzas of preceding poems seem introductions to the poems below them, but they also read across the pages so that the reader imagines the compiler, Dickinson, looking up from her pile of manuscripts, smiling at the congruence she has just discovered herself. The loving Antiquary has the capacity, like the Bird, to build from bits and pieces. The Resumption Morn calls to mind the Resurrection that, according to Christian doctrine, will rob the worldly nest in order to people the next, spiritual world. And the cry for a "resumption" of Pompeii might be that of the Robins, robbed of this worldly kin, who are smuggled to rest. If that is too baroque, too much a reading in the head of the witness rather than in that of the poet, the words nevertheless exist on the page waiting for us to scan, con, study, deal with in some way. On the back side of "Birds smuggled to rest" we find—at last—the call for "Necromancy." First, though, there's another bit of the wit, witnessed only by the fascicle reader.

## What Then? Only Your Inference—and Necromancy

Under the "loving Antiquary" stanza are the first three quatrains of "Dust is the only Secret," and, on the opposite page, in exactly the same dimensions, under the last stanza of "Dust," the one about the robbed robins, are the first twelve lines of "I'm the little Heart's Ease" (Fr167). Thanks to Judith Farr's book on Dickinson's garden, we know what Dickinson must have known: that the "Hearts-Ease" is a pansy-violet that "comes up early, announcing the longed for spring." It also symbolizes bravery because it can withstand even the snow (Farr and Carter, 94). The poem thus heralds the very last poem of the sequence with its "Arctic flower." The twelve lines, of course, more than describe the flower; they echo previous poems in the group. There is a butterfly (we met it four poems back), for one thing, and the "Birds are antiquated fellows," putting together two images from those verses opposite each other ("Antiquarians" and "Robins") which appeared at the top of the opened book. Here is the entire last verse of "I'm the little 'Heart's Ease'!." It answers the question from its eighth line: "Who'll apologize for me?"

> Dear – Old fashioned, little flower!
> Eden is old fashioned, too!
> Birds are antiquated fellows!
> Heaven does not change her blue.
> [These last two lines spill onto the next page, forming almost a title to
>     "Ah! Necromancy Sweet!"]
> Nor will I, the little Heart's Ease –
> Ever be induced to do!

If the flower stands in for the poem or the poet in its loveliness and courage, it is also speaking here for a kind of steadfastness into eternity, the kind at the heart of the Spiritualists of Dickinson's day. The heated urgency of the fascicle's earlier poems—the desperation of the hurt deer, the bloodiness of the sunset, the excitement of the discoveries in the ebon box and of "at last" being "identified"—all of that which is metaphorically exploded and spent in the images of the volcano, the dust of which settles over ruins—all of that seems changed. Yes, there is sadness; the robins are robbed away from the dust and "smuggled to rest," but the "rest" to which they seem smuggled may be, in this context, the "old fashioned" Eden of the "Heart's Ease." In that case, the call on "Necromancy Sweet," centered on the page as few of Dickinson's poems are and left with a large margin of white space below, seems less strange than when read outside of this context. As the deer comes to stillness through pain and as a mountain can contain the violence of a volcano without erupting, so *human beings* come to stillness through pain; that pain can be so intense that it must erupt from the stilled volcano; that in the end, dust or death is the "only Secret": all that harsh news may be read in the poems that precede this. The Necromancer might be akin to the magician of the earlier poems, one who can transform, as it were, a little freckled boy into a king, can bring from the rubble of the inevitably shattered world, something remarkable. What cannot be assuaged is the knowledge that in the end, there is this "punctual, laconic, industrious" visitor, death.

Death would be the news—punctual, laconic, industrious—for the next five years. Paula Bennett's essay in this book raises the question of the poet's tone in Fascicle 16's famous elegy on Frazar Stearns, who "brought the horror of war home with him in his coffin." Bennett reads most of the poems in Fascicle 16 as spoken from the dead—and with an "edge" turned toward the "public, highly romanticized story." Although, according to Franklin's reckoning, the two fascicles are two years apart, those in Fascicle 16—especially seen through Bennett's sensibilities—are helpful in grappling with this fascicle's stunning invocation to necromancy: that the magician give the speaker the skill to "instill the pain / Surgeons assuage in vain." "I like a look of Agony," says one of the already dead in Fascicle 16, and "'tis so appalling – it exhilirates," says a living soldier. What happens to the dead and to those left to mourn and miss them was a subject for the poet who sought "the skill" to "instill the pain" all her writing life. One sees the skill developing through the three versions of "Safe in their Alabaster Chambers" (Fr124, F6 and F10) as Dickinson inscribed (instilled) imagery to replicate the experience that surgeons assuage in vain. Between Fascicles 6 and 10, she ups the ante of bitterness toward the enemy that takes away laughter (in Fascicle 6) and all else in Fascicle 10 ("Tribes of Eclipse").

She was not alone in her time and place. Although the expected religious systems with which Dickinson has been linked have been repeatedly studied, the rise of interest in Spiritualism which may animate "Ah! Wizard erudite" has been less so. Diary entries of the time attest to the growing fascination and scorn for the phenomenon: young Burrill Curtis, for example, wrote from Brook Farm to his father in 1843: "I hear Animal Magnatism [hypnotism] is very lively in Providence. Do you know aught new of it?" (Myerson 421). Ten years later Bronson Alcott registered in his journal for January 1, 1853: "Boston. A while at the Spiritualists' Convention which is sitting—or sleeping, rather—in the Masonic Temple [he had given a talk there] and left them to their preferred lunacies" (Shepherd 265). And three years after that—in August 1856—Alcott recorded another experience with the new movement: "Attend a conversation at Dr. B's [Henry Whitney Bellow's] on 'Spiritualism' . . . the apotheosis of idiocy and fatuity only serves to betray the latent atheism and dark superstition of multitudes in our time" (Shepherd 283). Alcott, no stranger to strangeness himself, continued to rail at the "grim goblin gods here enthroned from the vacant popular mind" and "this ghastly superstition . . . spreading fast and wide" (284). Such talk had been around since the Salem Witchcraft Trials, but the mid-nineteenth century, with its proliferation of a popular press and its plethora of Lyceum-type speaking venues, was bringing it back with a vengeance.

By the time Dickinson wrote this strange "Necromancy" poem, intellectual and popular journals, many of them read by the Dickinson circle,[23] and best-selling books[24] vividly recounted adventures in the Spiritualist trade and noted behavior like that of the famous (notorious?) adolescent daughters of a Methodist minister who were eventually hired by P. T. Barnum. People like the Fox sisters inspired so many others that there were perhaps one million believers nationwide (Kerr 9). The carnage of the Civil War would enlarge the movement even more, but that would be after Dickinson's puzzling use of "Necromancy" in Fascicle 8. The movement's "mediums" attempted to bridge the worlds of the living and the dead, sometimes in bizarre ways such as interpreting the "rapping" of deceased people. It is not surprising, then, to hear the verdict of Dickinson's fellow New England writers on "Spiritualist" practices and beliefs. Emerson called such meetings "droll bedlam"; Thoreau, "the croaking of frogs"; Oliver Wendell Holmes, "jigglery and manipulation"; and Henry James, "hocus pocus" and "insanity" (Sparks 452).[25] Some, while skeptical, were not so quick to mock the belief that the dead could correspond with the living, as Howard Kerr explains in detailed discussions of fictional characters, letters, editorials, and parodies reflecting the phenomenon.

For all the fuss over the hocus pocus elements of Spiritualism that may or may not have influenced Dickinson's "Necromancy" poem, there was something about the movement that may have resonated with her. The movement attracted strong women—women such as Sarah Grimke, Susan B. Anthony, Elizabeth Cady Stanton, and Frances Willard (Braude 70). Although Dickinson was far from a reformer, she was in her way—especially as the speakers of the poems in Fascicle 8 iterate—a proud, idiosyncratic, autonomous woman, and "Spiritualism held up a model of women's unlimited capacity for autonomous action" (Braude 201). Dickinson, then, could not *not* have been aware of and even influenced by the Spiritualist movement, its passionate followers, and its ironic or scathing detractors. The coming carnage of the war would increase interest. The "Necromancy" poem in which the poet begs for "skill" to "instill" such severe and hopeless pain is a particularly cruel phrasing of Dickinson's lifelong interest in what mystery, what "riddle," lies so "still" beyond the grave. What poets do, though, is to defy the grave. They keep the dead alive through their art, as Dickinson's Shakespeare said ("So long lives this, and this gives life to thee"). The fascicle began with instances of magic and transformation; these are synonyms for "necromancy," as is "foretelling of the future by communicating with the dead." The fascicle has another five poems, contained on the fifth folded sheet. Each, but especially the last, seems in the context of this fascicle to be about that skill of a poet—and of the reader who must herself grapple with the hard "pain" that neither "surgeons" nor nature ("herb of all the plain") can heal.

"Except to Heaven, she is nought" (Fr173), the poem which follows "Necromancy," may seem completely unrelated (and perhaps it is), but it may also be an example of what the Necromancy can do: save and reinvent the lost. Indeed, that would place the whole collection in a more orthodox tradition. Joanne Dobson, for one, reads "Except to Heaven" as one of fifty poems (two come from this fascicle) which she (Dobson) says would not have created a barrier between the poem and the reader in the nineteenth century, specifically in 1864 (132). This one (Dobson names it "Home for Heaven") appears in an imagined anthology for that year. The little poem ("Except to Heaven") posits that the little flower or the small, unnoticed person may be "nought" to all the world—but is *not* nought to Heaven or to the waiting Angels (remember the Laureates waiting above for "the duller scholars" in "To learn the Transport by the Pain," the fourth poem in the sequence?). The poem itself has made the insignificant significant, the trite fresh: quite a feat. If that seems somewhat saccharine, the next, "I cautious, scanned my little life" (Fr175), third from last, answers it with self-proclaimed cynicism but with something else as well. The speaker's first verses return to the desperation of earlier poems in the fascicle, but we also recall that many of the earlier poems valorized texts of one kind or another. The language has included scholars, letters, portraits, laureates, and acts of scanning, conning, and transforming through imagination. In this third-from-last poem, whatever the "hay" symbolizes has been harvested, winnowed, hidden, and lost. But that is not the end of the poem. After wondering whether a thief, the wind, or God himself took what was so precious, the speaker regains agency, saying, "My business is, to find!"

Lopped over to the next page—the habit throughout the little book—are the closing lines of "I cautious, scanned my little life":

> So I begin to ransack!
> How is it Hearts, with Thee?
> Art thou within the little Barn
> Love provided thee?

Under that packed quatrain/question is a poem that this reader, at least, can only read as the speaker's wistful determination to have that for which she is ransacking the barn, the "little life" that it was her business to find—the fruits of her labor and love and wit—that "business," as she repeats the word, of her life. Here is the portion of the poem below the "ransack" lines:

> If I could bribe them by a Rose
> I'd bring them every flower that grows
> From Amherst to Cashmere!
> I would not stop for night or storm –
> Or frost, or death, or anyone –
> My business were so dear!
>
> If they w'd linger for a Bird
> My Tamborin were soonest heard
> Among the April Woods!
> Unwearied all the summer long,
> Only to break in wilder song
> When Winter shook the boughs!
>
> What if they hear me!
> Who shall say

> *[And on the next page—the last]*
> That such an importunity
> May not at last avail?
> That, weary of this Beggar's face –
> They may not finally say, Yes –
> To drive her from the Hall? (Fr176)

The little life/Rose/birdsong/Beggar *will* be heard. Metaphorically like those rappers in other halls, this one will make such a ruckus that she will be driven from the Hall by those who may resist but must listen to her demands. The Necromancer not only calls forth the spirits, but he or she interprets them as well. Those thousands of Dickinson's fellow citizens, including intellectuals, who sat raptly waiting signs from the other side, are joined by the poet who wishes to know, too, what goes on beyond that swelling in the ground. In these poems, as in the séances to which the hopeful flocked, the dead are given a voice; consider the scores of proleptic poems among the almost eighteen hundred. In Dickinson's poems the dead come alive again and again as the poems are continually reinterpreted, and that is what the final poem in this twenty part sequence is all about:

> As if some little Arctic flower
> Opon the polar hem –
> Went wandering down the Latitudes
> Until it puzzled came
> To continents of summer –
> To firmaments of sun –
> To strange, bright crowds of flowers –
> And birds, of foreign tongue!
> I say, as if this little flower
> To Eden, wandered in –
> What then? Why nothing,
> Only, your *inference* therefrom! (Fr177)

The word "inference," underlined by the poet on the final line of this little book, is Dickinson's instruction, invitation, across the miles and years, to us. She speaks to us from beyond the great divide that so absorbed her, telling us—by way of metaphors for the poet and the poem, figured variously as all the contents of this poem (flowers, and birds, a letter in a box, a portrait or picture, a hay in a barn, a wounded deer, a pent-up volcano)—that we must pay attention. The language of the Spiritualists all around her, though perhaps ridiculous to many in Dickinson's day and ours, acted as objective correlatives for thoughts too complex for abstraction.

"At last, to be identified," she had exulted midway through the fascicle. Dickinson would repeat that self-identification two years later with few changes in Fascicle 21. That fascicle, too, is about "the business" of the poet, though there is no Necromancer in it. Although "At last" appears in about the same position in that later fascicle, the poem seems there to convey a less exultant, more business-like, if you will, tone. Perhaps that is because Fascicle 21 begins with a person returning home to find it absent of those she knew, to find it hostile and to flee from it. Images of darkness, burial, exhausting journeys prevail. There are no flowers or birds. Fascicle 21, in short, has a different identity, a different "thumbprint." Between the compiling of Fascicles 8 and 21 much had happened to the person exulting in her identity as one, who, through texts that are as precious as a vision of the Promised Land, can thwart death or at least burst through it. By the time, two years after 1860, when she finished copying poems (written who knows when) into the book we call Fascicle 8, a destructive war had swept through her consciousness and the whole country—something like that volcano, after which the known world seemed covered in soot. When, then, she speaks up again for the chance "to be identified," her tone has become more sober toward the urgency she feels to enact her "business" and the exigencies that stand in the way. However, she is exultant about her "business," which was, of course, to sing or to write. On the last page of *this* little book (Fascicle 8) Emily Dickinson tells us, the readers, of her work, what *our* business must be. We must have the ability and courage to *infer* what she has left in the barn, the ebon box, the air that wafts from Amherst to Cashmere. In her own way Dickinson enacts the quest of those all around her. As the journals, diaries, offhand comments, and speeches of her fellow nineteenth-century intellectuals did, she found the Spiritualist practices interesting—useful—as metaphors, and, in her most ardent wish, as realities; she must have known her little books and the poems in them would "wander down the latitudes" and speak for her from her side of the mysterious divide about which she wrote so often.

Tate's comment that linked Dickinson with Cotton Mather was no stretch. Three years before her death, Dickinson herself wrote that

> Witchcraft was hung, in History,
> But History and I
> Find all the Witchcraft that we need
> Around us, every Day (Fr1612)

For her, "Witchcraft" was in the sunset, the children, the caterpillars, the pictures and portraits, but mostly it was in the faded letters lifted from the ebon box, the texts that, like the "little Arctic flower" would wander "down the Latitudes" awaiting our "*inference* therefrom." Others of her generation might gather around tables awaiting strange rapping from the dead. Emily Dickinson found in that practice a metaphor for what readers of her fascicles do today as they stare, in perplexity and delight, at what she left on those pages.

Absent some remarkable attic discovery, we can never know Dickinson's intentions. Following her instructions, we might make educated guesses, draw *inferences* from her enormous, if mysterious, paper trail, her meta-poems about poetry and her tantalizing hints in letters. What she was *up to* when she began her project of collecting poems for her gatherings we cannot know, but we *can,* thanks to Franklin's reproductions of them, appreciate *what* she *put on* those pages. Such a study is much more entertaining and inspirational than a literal séance; it is our version of "Necromancy Sweet."

# The Precincts of Play
## Fascicle 22

### Domhnall Mitchell[1]

The twenty-three poems that comprise Emily Dickinson's Fascicle 22 were written on sheets of letter paper folded once during manufacture to create four pages or writing surfaces each: like many of their kind, six of these folded sheets were then stacked on top of, but not nested inside, each other by Dickinson before being sewn together to form a single volume.[2] The difference in construction is potentially significant: sheets folded within each other might suggest that the poems existed as linked elements in a planned and organic structure; pages placed on top of each other do not necessarily suggest any such set of relations. The distinction is similar to that between photographs in an album or computer folder and those in an exhibition or book: the former are developed and inserted, or digitally transferred, simultaneously for convenience of storage; the latter are displayed in a certain order after a lengthy process of editing and compilation. What binds poems in a fascicle, arguably, is string, and the accident of their being completed at the same time, rather than prior design.

This essay takes at its starting point the position that poems in fascicles do not have to be read as part of a cumulative and organic totality: they do not even have to be read together at all. Of the twenty-three in this fascicle, for example, only three were sent to Dickinson's friends (two, separately, to Susan Dickinson, and a third to Samuel Bowles).[3] This is a pattern that is consistent for the poems in fascicles generally: though Dickinson enclosed many poems in her letters (and sometimes *as* letters or notes), she did not distribute whole fascicles or even excerpted sequences.[4] The implication seems to have been that Dickinson herself did not find it necessary for the poems to be read in the context of their manuscript collation.[5]

An alternative view of the fascicles is to see them primarily as material archives (a form of keeping things in order), and an argument supporting this, though a more contentious one, is that they coincide with the years of Dickinson's greatest production. In the early years with few poems (1854–57), there are no fascicles, while in years with a total of 1,116 (1858–65), there are forty fascicles and approximately ten sets.[6] After 1865, when the production diminishes again, the sets become much more intermittent: there are none at all until 1871, and then nine from 1871 through 1875, at which time they cease to be made.[7] This is not conclusive evidence, but taken together in aggregate with other factors suggests that the argument for the fascicles as archives is just as compelling as, and certainly less speculative than, any other.

Nevertheless, it seems difficult to imagine that so many poems written at around the same period by a single person could not have some kind of connection: in any existence, there are concerns and interests that last a lifetime, as well as shorter phases of enthusiasm. And as Eleanor Heginbotham writes, one does not have to subscribe to a theory of the fascicles as "one large finished architectural structure" so much "as offering delight in discovering the poet/editor's play within individual books" (*Reading* ix). Heginbotham goes on, rightly in my view, to distance herself from the very few scholars who offer more fully comprehensive explanations of the fascicles—as narratives of Christian conversion or secular passion, for example—but it can be allowed nonetheless that such preoccupations do emerge, albeit more intermittently. In the fascicle under discussion there is the loss (through parting or death) of a lover, relative, or close friend in Fr461 ("We Cover Thee – Sweet Face"), for instance, *as well as* the prospect of religious election in Fr467 ("A Solemn thing within the Soul").[8] There are convergences in the imagery too: the lines "Nature – sometimes sears a Sapling – / Sometimes – scalps a Tree" from Fr457 (the second in the sequence) are very similar to the scalping of the Soul in an alternative reading for Fr477 (the twenty-second in the sequence). Such connections need not be understood as integral elements in a motivated and large-scale structure of meaning (fascicles are not chapters in a novel), but they do suggest at least the possibility of *smaller* thematic or imagistic pockets of coherence that reward closer attention. Limiting our readings to the fascicles alone, however, runs counter to our responsibilities as critics to seek the richest interpretations available—for Dickinson's use of imagery raises questions that are most adequately answered when we look inside *and* outside the fascicles. Since the word "scalp" does not appear in any of Dickinson's other poems, for example, it seems clear that its deployment may be local and immediate rather than structural or symphonic, occasioned (for example) by climatic or historical events—a lightning storm at the time of composition, for instance, or the ongoing and tumultuous Dakota conflict in the latter half of 1862. In the reading of Fascicle 22 that follows, then, the intention has been to tease out and comment on patterns of imagery within and across poems, but also to trace some of their potential trajectories in other contexts, other precincts of play—biographical, literary, and historical.

# I

Of the twenty-three poems in this fascicle, eight have four quatrains, six have two, and one has eight: of the remaining eight poems, most have at least one quatrain. In 1862, as for much of her writing life, Dickinson's standard unit of composition was the rhyming quatrain, a form she inherited and developed from ballads and, especially, from church hymns: as Martha England argues, "the hymns of Watts became involved with Emily Dickinson's vocal chords, fingers, diaphragm, and lungs very early in life" (129).[9] The meter in such poems is mostly iambic, though there is considerable variation and even some notable exceptions: Fr457, "Nature – sometimes sears a Sapling" is predominantly trochaic, for example, and Fr459 has a truncated second line that is sufficiently unusual to warrant further comment:

> "Why do I love" You, Sir?
> Because –
> The Wind does not require the Grass
> To answer – Wherefore when he pass
> She cannot keep Her place.

The abrupt switch to the third line reflects just as sudden a change of attitude to the opening question: it would seem as if the speaker begins to attempt a response, then breaks off out of reluctance, or flirtatiousness, or because the question is deemed inappropriate or unanswerable. Since the wind does not demand an explanation from the grass, she submits, the Master should not expect one from her. And indeed the rest of the poem continues to furnish examples of potentially overwhelming natural forces (wind, lightning, sun) that initiate a reaction in natural and human objects (grass, an eye, and finally the speaker) without asking for a reason. There is a logic governing the use of these images that is very like "Shall I Compare Thee to a Summer's Day": there, the speaker first rejects the opening comparison on the grounds of incompatibility ("Thou art more lovely . . . "), before cataloguing a series of anti-metaphors that always, but obliquely, contain a human referent that serves as a reminder of the beloved's presence and superiority ("too hot the eye of heaven shines," as opposed to her or his eye, for example). The speaker of Dickinson's poem declines to profess love, then, but does not deny attraction, for there are human elements to the series of natural metaphors that she deploys nonetheless: the Wind in the first stanza is male, and the stirred Grass female, for instance. The third stanza is typical of this oscillation between evasion and admission:

> The Lightning – never asked an Eye
> Wherefore it shut – when He was by –
> Because He knows it cannot speak –

The male is still identified as a force of nature, but the eye that closes (an instinctual reaction to a sudden fright; a response to something forbidden; an attempt to conceal the information that is disclosed through an eye too closely scrutinized) occupies a more neutral territory: the structural framework of the comparisons suggests that it is female, but the speaker twice invokes the third person neuter ("it") instead. There is more than one reason for this: an eye may be human, but it is not an agent, a person; or it may be that the eye belongs to a bird or an animal; or perhaps it is symbolic. In addition, the speaker is moving from the apparent recoil and displacement of the first stanza towards her own feelings in the last ("The Sunrise – Sir – compelleth Me"), from externalized nature to the personal, and "it" therefore serves as a bridge—for though there is an obvious human referent for the eye, a secondary meaning invokes flowers or plants, some of which close their petals in the kinds of weather that precede storms.[10]

The imagery of lightning in the poem links it with Fr457 ("Nature – sometimes sears a Sapling") and Fr477 ("He fumbles at your Soul"), and therefore provides an interesting test case for the thesis that Dickinson's poems reward those who read them in the context of their fascicle appearances. And yet, aside from the shared image, the poems would appear to have little in common: "Nature – sometimes sears a Sapling" commemorates a devastating but unspecified instance of hurt or loss; "'Why do I love you'" seems more like a ludic and amorous exchange (it refuses to supply a reason for love, but indicates a powerful emotional and physical response nonetheless); and the experience described in "He fumbles at your Soul" is both indeterminate and hard to read in terms of tone (is this a positive or negative experience, or one that suspends those kinds of categories?).

The eye that "cannot speak" in Fr459 is another in a series of images that appear to avoid disclosure and reveal something at the same time: while it is true that the eye cannot literally speak, it can provide very complex information through movement—closure suggests fear of some kind, or modesty, or even intense enjoyment; looking away or not looking at all suggests embarrassment or rejection; resting the eyes on someone implies interest, warmth of affection, or scrutiny. Although the primary impetus of the description may be local to the poem itself, there are several poems in this fascicle that contain references to "eye," "eyes," and to an "[eye]lid": in Fr458, Fr463, and Fr471, for example, the closure of the eye in the latter signaling death, and in Fr467, which describes the scrutiny of a Creator examining the Soul or Being. The "Windows" of Fr466 ("I dwell in Possibility") connote the ability to observe and gather information that is afforded by language and poetry, while the first and eighth lines of Fr472 ("'Tis good – the looking back on Grief") play on a discrepancy between the private and the public, between hidden pain and outwardly routine behavior or appearance. Indeed, this play with what can be seen and not seen is foregrounded in Fr474:

> You love the Lord – you cannot see –
> You write Him – every day –
> A little note – when you awake –
> And further in the Day,
>
> An Ample Letter – How you miss –
> And would delight to see –
> But then His House – is but a step –
> And mine's – in Heaven – You see –

The verb "see" is repeated incrementally here—that is, with slight variations, and three times. The first two instances are related to the organs of sight: the "you" that is addressed in the poem writes notes to a lover she cannot see (line 1) but would like to (line 6), whereas the speaker has no such possibilities, either because her lover, or the most important figure gendered as male in her life (God, Christ), is in Heaven, or because she herself is in Heaven and cannot write, visit, or hope to see. (The disappearance of "Neighbors" to "Heaven" also challenges sight in much the same way in the poem that follows, Fr476. Indeed, in Dickinson's poems generally sight is a precious but vulnerable attribute of life on earth. One of the first signs of death is the closing or "Film upon the eye" described in Fr458 but also elsewhere, perhaps most famously in "I heard a Fly buzz – when I died," a poem from F26, composed around the summer of 1863.) The "You see" that closes the poem is related to acquired knowledge, however: it means something along the lines of "it is now possible for you to understand"—and is not a reference to sight in any literal sense. In addition, the fifth and sixth lines are grammatically incomplete, for the verb "see" at the end of the sixth is missing an object or complement: it should be followed by "her" or "him," and the lack of specificity or completion has the effect of making the absence of the lover more apparent and even acute. Indeed, what is partly moving about the poem is that "you" appears six times in eight lines, whereas the personal pronoun is absent: while the identity of "you" is fairly stable, the speaker is represented only through the possessive—what belongs to her but is apart, and not who she actually is. The self is also, then, absent from the poem—or at least not fully, not avowedly present—in much the same way that the Lord is: indeed, her only partial presence is an effect of his absence.

The very first poem in the fascicle also relies on ocular imagery:

> A Prison gets to be a friend –
> Between it's Ponderous face
> And Our's – a Kinmanship express –
> And in it's narrow Eyes –
>
> We come to look with gratitude
> For the appointed Beam
> It deal us – stated as Our food –
> And hungered for – the same – (Fr456)

The verb "stated" in line 7 probably means less the past particle of "expressed verbally" than "regular, fixed or repeated," an adjectival form in a component with a missing "as" at its head ([as] stated as Our food). The literal situation is open to various forms of reconstruction, but the ponderous face might represent the thick wall of a cell, with the "narrow Eyes" and "appointed Beam" either the window or an aperture in the door through which a warden can view the prisoner: since the "eyes" are all that are visible to the inmate, the "Beam" can be understood too as an imagined smile.[11] The "narrow Eyes" might suggest windows first and foremost, partly because they are plural, and partly because of the conventional association between windows and eyes: Webster's 1828 definition of the former gives "windows of mine eyes" as one of its examples, and Mandeville was drawing on a long-established practice when he wrote that "the Eyes are the Windows of the Soul" in 1723.[12] But that the reference might be to an aperture in the door is allowable because of the element of time: the Beam is as regular as the food that is delivered during the day, and the eyes that look through the contrivance are also implied (eye-beam being common even in the poetry of Donne and others). On the other hand, the regularity could be that of the sun shining through the windows each morning at approximately the same time (and Beam is just as likely to suggest sun as eye). Dickinson does not mention *human* eyes directly, but this is not quite the 1787 Panopticon of Jeremy Bentham, the "all-seeing" prison where the inmate is under constant surveillance without the reciprocal ability to see the observer: perhaps what we can say is that in a space where she is otherwise and permanently deprived of company, Dickinson's speaker is forced to invent the illusion of eyes and a face in order to humanize her environment and preserve her sanity.[13]

Pursuing Dickinson's ocular imagery within the precinct of the fascicle itself does not lead to fully satisfactory conclusions, but it does open up links to other aspects of Dickinson's reading (Webster, Donne, Mandeville) and society (Bentham's thinking continued to have an influence in the nineteenth century, on the architecture of both prisons and asylums). Another possibility, first suggested by James Guthrie, is that the eye imagery relates to Dickinson's documented problems with her health (*Emily Dickinson's Vision* 70–71).[14] From April to November 1864, and again in 1865, Dickinson was treated for unspecified eye problems in Boston. During this first period, she wrote to Higginson: "I was ill since September, and since April, in Boston, for a Physician's care—He does not let me go, yet I work in my Prison, and make Guests for myself –" (L290, early June 1864). Of course, Fr456 was written two years earlier, in 1862, but in that year Dickinson admitted in a letter to Higginson that she had had a "terror since September" (L261)—a terror which Guthrie speculates might have been of "blindness or of near-constant confinement" (65).[15] In the most recent Dickinson biography, Alfred Habegger questions such a literal cause for the eye imagery, and writes instead that the terror was less discrete:

> The terror since September, a profound and systemic and ongoing state lasting through the winter, was the thing Dickinson had been booked to fall into. It may have begun with a moment when "the meaning goes out of things," as she put it in one of her jottings, but its essence was a recognition

of something permanent: the disconnection between her heart's absolutism and the realities of life. Painful and transforming, it brought a final sense of isolation, abandonment, rejection (436).

The prison, then, was Dickinson herself: as Guthrie says, she was "her own prison, prisoner, and imprisoner, as well as fellow-sufferer and potential liberator" (71). There is a temptation, particularly with this poet, to read lyrics as personal history in disguise, but in this case there does appear to be an overlap between the outward circumstances of Dickinson's life (the carefully managed and gradual withdrawal in her late twenties from people other than her immediate family, household staff, and a few friends) and the situation of a speaker whose prison may be little other than a room: one is reminded again of Dickinson's reported statement to her niece, locking the bedroom door, that "It's just a turn – and freedom, Matty" (Bianchi, *Face to Face* 66).

Among the more fascinating stanzas in "A Prison gets to be a friend" are the fourth and fifth:

We learn to know the Planks –
That answer to Our feet –
So miserable a sound – at first –
Not ever now – so sweet –

As plashing in the Pools –
When Memory was a Boy –
But a Demurer Circuit –
A Geometric Joy –

If one assumes that the speaker of the poem—like most of Dickinson's speakers—might be a woman, then the phrase "Memory was a Boy" seems curious: so too, though in a slightly different way, is the choice of "plashing in the Pools" as a contrast to the prison cell. The reasons for the latter may be partly formal (the alliterative echoes that are set up in the progression from "Planks" through "plashing" to "Pools": there are a number of such sounds in the poem as a whole), partly for sensory contrast (planks are hard, water is soft), and partly for opposing similarities (pools are limited spaces, too, but clearly not to the same degree as a cell or room). "Memory was a Boy" suggests a time when the speaker was not aware of all of the dimensions, sexual and social, of gender differentiation—perhaps because for much of the nineteenth century younger boys and girls both wore long skirts that were called petticoats. As a child, then, the speaker was not overly conscious of differences between boys and girls—and perhaps not even conscious that she herself was *not* a boy, or could not behave like a boy. The implication would seem to be that she is *now* painfully aware of such differences—and indeed that her present isolation has been brought about because of them. In other words, her attraction to, or for, another man or woman has led to her isolation, be it perceived or actual: the room is a prison because she is prevented from being with the lover, due to death or social disapproval or accident (the lover is already married; the lover is another woman; the lover is not aware of her interest). The innocence of the past is compared to the knowledge of the present: the pool represents a sentient experience or time less determined and fenced in by social mores. Whether we think of the child paddling or swimming in water, the contrast is clear: feet free of constrictive shoes, in sand and water, are very different from feet forced daily to walk a narrow round of planks; free too is the body of the swimmer, embraced by water, and released from the restraints of clothing. There is often a relaxation or suspension of the normal rules of behavior for children when they are around water: they can splash and dive and jump without attracting the negative attention of parents (for very often being in a pool would suggest a break from normal routines—a holiday or day out, for example). By contrast, the present is characterized by the suppression of joy, of recklessness, of indulgence—and of the capacity for sentient pleasure that emerges during physical maturity. The reward for her present captivity is supposed to be in Heaven (which presumably is like the pool in affording escape from restriction), but the speaker seems less than convinced that the reparation will be sufficient or even apt.

The idea of maturity being equated with socialization and childhood with freedom is a central tenet of Romantic poetry, and receives one of its most important expressions in Wordsworth's "Resolution and Independence."[16] But as Guthrie points out, the possibility of the poem itself as a confined space within which imaginative freedom can be exercised is also suggested by the words "feet" and "Measure" (the latter a variant for "Circuit" in the fourth stanza): he might also have mentioned the reference to "sounds" in a poem that contains a great deal of approximate alliteration (Prison, Ponderous, Planks, Pools, plashing, Posture) and the use of verbs that foreground communication as compensation for confinement (express, stated, answer).[17] Guthrie refers to Wordsworth's 1807 Sonnet beginning "Nuns fret not at their convent's narrow room; / And hermits are contented with their cells," which includes the following lines:

> In truth the prison, unto which we doom
> Ourselves, no prison is: and hence for me,
> In sundry moods, 'twas pastime to be bound
> Within the Sonnet's scanty plot of ground; (Wordsworth 199)

Wordsworth was, among other things, using this conceit to situate himself in a larger tradition of English poets including Donne ("We'll build in sonnets pretty rooms," from "The Canonization") and Keats ("If by dull rhymes our English must be chain'd," with its reference to the "fettered" sonnet and the need to find a form to "fit the naked foot of Poesy"): Dickinson is doing no less.[18] The fascicle yields evidence that by 1862 she knew that her vocation was poetry: "Without this – there is nought –" (Fr464), "I was the slightest in the House" (Fr473), and in the next fascicle, "Fame of Myself, to justify" (Fr481), suggest a preoccupation with long-term fame, and with the immortality conferred upon the writer by posterity. But perhaps the most pertinent poem in light of the present discussion is "Myself was formed – a Carpenter" (Fr475), in which the speaker describes an outsider, a judge of some kind, who comes:

> To measure our attainments –
> Had we the Art of Boards
> Sufficiently developed – He'd hire us
> At Halves –

The art of boards suggests both carpentry *and* acting or performing on the stage, and by extension creative performances in general. Dickinson's speaker rejects—as another would in "Publication is the Auction"—short-term gain or recognition for her work: "We – Temples build" she says in the end, linking her craft with that of Donne and Keats and Wordsworth, and providing further insight into "I dwell in Possibility – / A fairer House than Prose" (Fr466). The comparison of poetry with carpentry is an interesting one, not least because it enables us to read into the "Art of Boards" a form of compensation for the pain described in "Nature – sometimes sears a Sapling"; as trees are transformed into planks of wood, from which buildings are raised, suffering is changed into the no less permanent structures of art.

"A Prison gets to be a friend" has its own reference to "the Planks / That answer to our feet," of course, and the poem's perhaps most important intertextual reference is to another Romantic writer, Lord Byron: as a number of critics have pointed out before me, an important gloss on "A Prison gets to be a friend" is his "The Prisoner of Chillon" (1816), which Dickinson alludes to in several poems and mentions directly in four letters, including one in 1861 and another in 1862, the estimated date of her poem's composition.[19] Once again, "Nature – sometimes sears a Sapling" (Fr457) shows Dickinson improvising on the work of other writers—and pursuing the trail of that engagement leads us *outside* the confines of the fascicle where they first begin.

At one level, the poem can be thought of as a dramatic lyric, with Dickinson speaking in character as François Bonivard, imprisoned in the Castle of Chillon between 1530 and 1536 and kept underground for the last four years of his captivity.[20] That would provide a slightly more literal explanation for why the speaker contrasts his present confinement with a childhood past when as "a Boy" he plashed in pools (and the contrast might have been occasioned by Chillon's location at Lake Geneva in Switzerland: the great lake is the site of a prison, whereas the small pool is an arena for endless play). But there are differences as well: Byron's speaker walks on a floor of stone, Dickinson's on a floor of "Planks"; Byron's speaker is imprisoned with two of his brothers, Dickinson's is on her own; Byron's speaker is a champion of religious freedom, Dickinson's does not seem to have a cause; Byron's speaker is released at the end of the poem, Dickinson's is not (except, by implication, through death).

The disparities can be explained away to some degree. Though the floor is different in each case, for example, the detail of the walking is similar: in Byron's poem, he includes a footnote (the second) to the effect "that in the pavement the steps of Bonivard have left their traces," while in Dickinson's the Planks "answer to our feet"—which may suggest a series of sounds as much as visible imprints, but does imply reciprocity. Both brothers die in Byron's poem (the entire family appears to have been killed in actuality), and it could be argued that Dickinson chooses to concentrate on the last stage of Bonivard's captivity, when he is on his own, because of her predilection for brevity. Byron's Chillon talks about his father, his mother, and his brothers: the only suggestion of a sibling in the Dickinson poem is the younger self mentioned in stanza 4—but finding "kinship" is clearly an important element in the speaker's attempt to preserve her humanity. The two poems differ mainly in the details in this respect, because Byron's speaker moves from finding solace in the company of his two brothers to recording the horror of not being able to "move a single pace" or "see each other's face." In Dickinson's poem, the speaker is alone and able to move about with some degree of freedom (as Bonivard eventually would after the death of his two brothers), but the twin elements of "face" and affiliation are present in the first stanza, where the prison is given the attributes of a human countenance and the relationship between prisoner and cell is reconfigured as kinship. The speaker assigns human traits to inhuman objects precisely because an enforced solitude robs her of an important emotional dimension—the need for the comfort and solace that comes with other human presences.

But perhaps the crucial disparity between the poems is that Bonivard is advanced as a champion of religious freedom, whereas the motive for victimizing Dickinson's speaker—her cause, as it were—is never explicitly stated. "Liberty" is mentioned in Byron's prefatory "Sonnet on Chillon," in contrast to "the chainless Mind": the word is repeated in line 306 of the poem proper. In Dickinson's version, "Liberty" is similarly capitalized but seems to stand less for a set of political ideals or principles than more simply for the opposite of confinement. The ending is typical of the poem's revision of the original: Byron's speaker declares that the "heavy walls to me had grown / A hermitage—and all my own" (lines 377–78), but accepts his release; Dickinson's speaker appears to have no prospect of being granted freedom except through death.

Going out of the fascicles—to biography, to literary history, to other poets—in order to see different ways in which to approach a poem's possible meanings yields insights that are just as compelling as any approach based on a reading of the poem in relation to others in the fascicle or in the fascicles as a whole. For instance, the proximity of "Eyes" (line 3) and "Beams" (line 5) creates an intriguing set of associations that are anchored in the following passage from Matthew 7, where Christ speaks:

> Judge not, that ye be not judged. 2. For with what judgment ye judge, ye shall be judged: and with what measure ye mete, it shall be measured to you again. 3. And why beholdest thou the mote that is in thy brother's eye, but considerest not the beam that is in thine own eye? 4. Or how wilt thou say to thy brother, Let me pull out the mote out of thine eye; and, behold, a beam is in thine own eye? 5. Thou hypocrite, first cast out the beam out of thine own eye; and then shalt thou see clearly to cast out the mote out of thy brother's eye. (King James Version, Matt. 7,1–5)

As mentioned before, the crime for which Dickinson's speaker suffers imprisonment is never stated, and although there is pain, there is no direct expression of the speaker's innocence or guilt either. The echoes from the Bible suggest not only that the speaker's misdemeanors are relatively minor but also that those who condemn her are guilty of worse.

Where this approach to the poem differs from those who approach the fascicles as narratives is, first, that the identification of a recurrent set of images (in this case, that of eyes) does not reveal a motivated consistency (a single theme, for instance) and, second, that the imagery can be related to moments and events outside both the poem *and* the fascicle. There is a difference, in other words, between finding many lyrics that have the word "eye" and deducing from this that problems relating to seeing or being seen represent a linked element in a collective structure of meaning. The truth is that ocular images are fairly common in Dickinson's general lyric vocabulary, and that they are not used here in any clearly systematic way.[21]

## II

One of the principal arguments for studying the fascicles (though not generally the sets) in their entirety is the premise that they constitute an essentially autobiographical narrative in metrical form: to ignore this possibility is to deny perhaps the most important reason for Dickinson's writing and nonpublication.[22] The danger of such an approach is that one either reduces the grounds for interpretive engagement (one is always relating poems to a larger purpose), or that the poems become interesting primarily for people who are interested in a narrative of conversion or deferred love. Oberhaus, for example, writes that the fascicles show that Dickinson "staked all on a single goal: the hope of being among the sacred sheep at the Judgment" (157), while Shurr shows how they reveal both "her achieved sense of professional identity as a poet" and a realization that Wadsworth, whom he identifies as a secret lover and father of her child, "had removed himself so abruptly and totally—all the way across the continent—that their separation was for all practical purposes permanent, at least in this life" (84–85). If one is not interested in exploring these aspects of Dickinson's life, the narratives also become less compelling.

Other challenges remain, for there are often poems that are complex and intractable in and of themselves: they do not yield their meanings easily, if at all. Who of us can say with certainty that we know exactly what "Because I could not stop for Death" means? And if we do not know, how are we to fit it into a larger scheme of meaning? Does that intractability represent a failure on the part of the poet—an inability to rein in difficulties and subordinate them to the larger goal of the narrative? Or is the difficulty an attempt at reproducing in the reader some interpretive or theological or emotional challenge experienced by the author at a particular point in time? Does the resolution of the conversion narrative as some have formulated it undermine the seriousness of such challenges: in other words, does the sense of election mean that, like a problem in a Hollywood movie, we are briefly perturbed but reassured by the inevitability of a happy ending?

An advantage to studying the fascicles is practicality: the poems there comprise approximately half of the 1,789 that Dickinson is estimated (by Franklin) to have written, and confining oneself to these represents a considerable reduction in the amount of critical reading. For students and teachers (and increasingly for a number of researchers, beginning with Sharon Cameron), studying one or two fascicles is a manageable way of expressing general truths about Dickinson's formal practices and concerns. In class, one can certainly see an argument for limiting discussions to a fascicle or two—though to look at a list of a fascicle's contents leads one inevitably to think of what other poems the class is missing.

If the poems really *do* cohere as a single project, then it has to be admitted that more than 120 years after her death, very few people have read Emily Dickinson as she herself might have wanted. The reasons are partly related to the history of her publication by others: up until 1955, she was read in incomplete editions. Even Johnson's three-volume *Variorum* presented the poems in a sequence based on the estimated chronology of their composition: the poems as they exist in the fascicle order *today* were arranged in the following sequence by Johnson: J652, 314, 479, 480, 481, 482, 653, 654, 655, 656, 657, 483, 658, 484, 659, 485, 660, 486, 487, 488, 489, 315, and 1076. Until the publication of the fascicles in Franklin's *The Manuscript Books of Emily Dickinson* (1981), then, most nonspecialists would have read the poems out of the order of their manuscript collation. Even after that date, nonfascicle orderings have predominated, because most people are introduced to Dickinson via anthologies—at school, and especially at colleges and universities—and the selections are usually nonsequential. Of the poems in Fascicle 22, the *Norton Anthology of American Literature* (6th edition) includes three out of the total twenty-three ("Nature – sometimes sears a Sapling"; "He fumbles at your Soul"; and "Myself was formed – a Carpenter"); the *Heath Anthology of American Literature* (5th edition) has none.[23] Thomas H. Johnson's selected edition, *Final Harvest,* included seven ("Nature – sometimes sears a Sapling"; "He fumbles at your Soul"; "She dealt her pretty words like Blades"; "'Why do I love' You, Sir?"; "I was the slightest in the House"; "Myself was formed – a Carpenter"; "He fumbles at your Soul"; and "I dwell in Possibility"), but these do not appear in the order of their autograph collation.[24]

The point is not to allow the shortcomings or limitations of previous editions and anthologies to decide whether to read fascicles or not *now;* rather, the existence of the fascicles challenges us to think through our own criteria when choosing which poems we want to read, teach, and discuss. Anthologies, indeed, bring up questions of *quality* or *relevance* that many Dickinson scholars like to avoid, but the logic of selection is that some poems are more central than others—either because they are more characteristic of her imagery, her formal practices, her preoccupations as an artist, her biography, her sexuality, or her relationship to social and literary history. Comparatively few of the poems in this fascicle have been found worthy in any such regard—perhaps in part because there is a great deal of what might be deemed verbal sketching: Fr462, especially, and Fr469, for example ("Of being is a bird" and "My Garden – like the beach") appear like exercises, first attempts at coming up with and extending possible comparisons that do not go beyond the identification of similarity (a bird is like down, but down with music; if a garden is a beach, then flowers are its pearls). Fr464, "A long – long Sleep," seems like an earlier and less complex version of "Safe in their Alabaster Chambers," with its emphasis on sleep in conjunction with references to "stone" and "Noon."[25]

In terms of quality alone, a poem that is consistently selected for anthologies is the following version of Fr477, and it offers an interesting test case for determining whether a poem widely acknowledged to be of the highest quality can provide an indication or not of organic unity within a single fascicle or across the fascicles in general:

> He fumbles at your Soul
> As Players at the Keys –
> Before they drop full Music on –
> He stuns you by Degrees –
>
> Prepares your brittle substance
> For the etherial Blow
> By fainter Hammers – further heard –
> Then nearer – Then so – slow –
>
> Your Breath – has chance to straighten –
> Your Brain – to bubble cool –
> Deals One – imperial Thunderbolt –
> That peels your naked soul –
>
> When Winds hold Forests in their Paws –
> The Firmaments – are still –

Again, the drawbacks of studying the fascicles in and of themselves become clear: this poem is linked through its imagery to Fr457, "Nature – sometimes sears a Sapling," but it says very different things. The earlier poem talks of a potentially devastating wound; this one describes an experience that may be positive or negative, or that may suspend or otherwise combine those categories in new ways. Seen in the context of the fascicle alone, one might be more inclined towards reading the poem as negative in tone, and the interpretive rewards are generally limited: other contexts yield different perspectives and a greater appreciation of the poem's merits.

The peeling of the soul (the verb is "scalp" in an earlier version) and the references to shifting temperatures tally with a statement attributed to Dickinson by Thomas Wentworth Higginson: "If I read a book [and] it makes my whole body so cold no fire can ever warm me I know that is poetry. If I feel physically as if the top of my head were taken off, I know that is poetry" (L342a). Indeed, Dickinson's most positive responses to the writing and speaking of others often involve a rendering of the experience in almost physical terms—a propensity she seems to have shared with her sister-in-law Susan, who wrote of "Safe in their Alabaster Chambers" (Fr124C) that it was "remarkable as the chain lightening" and of Fr124B that "I always go to the fire and get warm after thinking of it, but I never can again" (answer to L238).[26] And as Alfred Habegger points out, Susan's image of the lightning was repeated in "I would not paint – a picture – " (Fr348), where the speaker longs for "the Art to stun myself / With Bolts – of Melody!"[27]

Though the experience being described here can be almost anything—sexual, literary, religious, even natural (the definitions of "thunder-bolt" in *Webster's* include both a shaft of lightning and an act of "fulmination; ecclesiastical denunciation")—it was certainly not unusual for sermons to be composed, and reacted to, in similar ways: the Dutchman Wilhelm Zepper compared the start of the sermon to "the opening bars of a piece of music" in his *Ars Habendi et audiendi conciones Sacras*.[28] It was Perry Miller who described a strain of preaching among early Puritans as a kind of "holy violence in the pulpit," and the speaker of "He fumbles at your Soul" (Fr477) reports an encounter that meshes with both sets of metaphor: the "Hammers" in line 7 may take up again the image of piano music established by the reference to "Keys" in the first stanza, but they are also tools capable of dealing a blow to the body (301).[29]

A preacher Dickinson is known to have admired was Charles Wadsworth, and Richard Sewall records a review from the *New York Evening Post* that compared him to Summerfield but also contended that "Wadsworth's style, it is said, is vastly bolder, his fancy more vivid, and his action more violent" (2: 450–51). Sewall notes that George Whicher (in *This Was a Poet*) assumed that "He fumbles at your soul" was about Wadsworth, but goes on to point out that Dickinson "had heard other great preachers and had been 'scalped' by them" (Sewall 2: 451). Edwards Amasa Park (1808–1900), Professor of Moral Philosophy and Metaphysics at Amherst College from 1835 to 1836, was one of them: in a letter to her brother Austin, also quoted by Alfred Habegger, she responded to a sermon on Judas delivered by Park at Amherst's First Church on November 20, 1853.

> I never heard anything like it, and don't expect to again, till we stand at the great white throne. . . . And when it was all over, and that wonderful man sat down, people stared at each other, and looked as wan and wild, as if they had seen a spirit, and wondered they had not died. (L142)

Dickinson's response is not unique: Dr. Richard Salter Storrs wrote (in a memorial) that Park's listeners often left "astonished, humiliated, with excitement in our minds, and shivers along our whole system of nerves" (Storrs 12). Park is useful for a number of reasons, not because he delivered a memorable sermon in Amherst that Dickinson attended and approved of, but because he provides insights into both the delivery and the reception of good sermons, insights that intersect with Dickinson's description of the unnamed event in Fr477 (Guest xlviii). Advising ministers on how to address their audience, Park warned that if "the words which we proclaim do not strike a responsive chord in the hearts of the choice men and women who look up to us for consolation," then they were doing something wrong (Storrs 95). And he continued: "If we leave the sensibilities torpid, it needs a larger infusion of those words which Christ defined by saying, they are spirit, they are life. If it merely charm the ear like a placid song, it is not the identical essence which is likened to the fire and the hammer" (ibid).

The experience described in "He fumbles at your Soul" echoes the kind of reception Wadsworth and Park sought to provoke: it is not defined as such, but likened to other, violent, sensations and phenomena. And note too that the response described in the third stanza is physical first ("Breath"): only in the next line is the "Brain" engaged, and then not as a means of analyzing and making sense of information, but as something that is subjected to sensory extremes and even oppositions (to "bubble" suggests boiling, for example; a "Thunderbolt" brings additional light as well as heat, but the "Winds" of the next stanza in combination with "cool" in line 10 imply colder temperatures).

The idea that successful writing somehow bypasses reason—but not the imagination or the affections—in order to strike home, aligns Dickinson's poetic method more broadly with nineteenth-century theological debates on linguistic usage that had their origins in New England Puritan discussions of how best to address an audience. The two sides of the debate are most conveniently summarized in the title of Park's "The Theology of the Intellect and That of the Feelings," a discourse given before the convention of the Congregational Ministers of New England, in Brattle Street Meeting House, on May 30, 1850.[30] Park was influenced by Friedrich Schleiermacher (1768–1834), and a connection between them was often established by his critics: David Nevins Lord (1792–1880) accused him of having been guided by "the neologists of Germany," and Charles Hodge named Schleiermacher in a widely publicized critique of Park's most celebrated sermon.[31] Though *Über die Religion* was not translated fully into English until 1893, the ideas of Schleiermacher and other German theologians circulated—not without contention—in Amherst during the first half of the nineteenth century, partly because German language and culture occupied a much more central role in American life than it does now, and partly because some of its college students and teachers had spent time in areas of Germany associated with the latest developments in theological thinking.[32] Henry Boynton Smith (1815–77), whose style of preaching impressed Dickinson like none before him, was Professor of Moral Philosophy and Metaphysics at Amherst College between October 1847 and December 1850, and "had studied in the universities of Halle and Berlin" (where Schleiermacher had taught, respectively, in 1804 and 1810).[33] Lyman Coleman (1796–1882) was married to Emily Norcross Dickinson's first cousin, Maria Flynt: a former graduate of Yale, student of theology, and minister of the Congregational Church in Belchertown, he had been a pupil of August Neander in Berlin before becoming principal of Amherst Academy (from 1844 to 1846), where Emily Dickinson took German with him.[34] The Colemans and their daughters, Olivia and Eliza, were close friends of the Dickinson sisters.[35]

The Rev. George Henry Gould (1827–99), an early family and personal friend, was another minister who "had an ear for music—the 'music of words.'"[36] Like Boynton Smith, Gould was uninterested in "the formal proclamation of abstract Christian doctrine," and believed that the language of the Bible was such that words were "far oftener used in a figurative than in a literal sense."[37]

> By the phrase "word of life," the apostle plainly refers to the Holy Scriptures, or more specifically, perhaps, to the gospel of redemption through Christ. Various terms are used by the inspired writers to designate the Bible. It is called God's law, his testimony, his commandment, statutes, oracles, and the like. The New Testament writers frequently refer to the Scriptures, under the terms, "word of truth," the "word of prophecy"; and here Paul uses the expressive phrase, "the word of life," or the life-giving word. The great fact is thus implied, as it is constantly assumed throughout the Scriptures, that God published his written truth for the simple purpose of generating spiritual life in the hearts of men. The Bible, then, is an instrument to accomplish a purpose.[38]

For Gould, the truths of the Bible lie "inert and inanimate on its written pages"—they have to be given life in human hearts through the skill of the preacher. And such sentiments are echoed in Dickinson's linguistic practice and are a theme in some of the poems—most notably Fr1577, "The Bible is an antique Volume" (Gould 156). In that poem, the line about sin being a precipice that "Others must resist" (either because sin is not difficult for the speaker to avoid, or because the speaker does not believe that the dictates of Christian morality apply to her or to him), and the general tone of the poem as a whole, are reminiscent of Mark Twain's report of a sermon given by Wadsworth, "when he gravely gave the Sunday school books a blast and spoke of 'the good little boys in them who always went to Heaven, and the bad little boys who infallibly got drowned on Sunday'" (Sewall 452). Like Wadsworth, Dickinson is not interested in terror as the mechanism by which to bring about faith. And like Wadsworth, Dickinson's speaker at the end of that poem commits to the idea of "Warbling," thus opposing poetry to overly literal interpretations of (or dependence on) the Bible: faith lies in the direction of enchantment, not fear. The *method* of the poem is parallel to its message: Dickinson seeks metaphorical, or local and contemporary, equivalents to the original stories (Eden becomes the family Homestead, from which the Dickinson family was temporarily ousted in 1840, only to return in 1855), and not dogmatic interpretations of what they mean (there is no talk of crime and its aftermath, for instance). And this emphasis on storytelling, on music, on the imaginative deployment of language and the suspension of analysis and dogma in the service of belief, links Dickinson to a number of important nineteenth-century theologians who responded to German High Criticism by accusing its proponents of failing to understand that the Bible was the vehicle not of absolutely literal but of figurative truths.[39] More importantly, it gives us a sense of Dickinson as a poet of the moment—of the lyric *now* rather than the lyric novel.

From Amherst in the 1860s to Germany in the late 1700s: from one fascicle to another; from the unnamed audience of the poems to the specific historical personalities who received some of them in letters; from lyric performance to literary history; from poetry to nineteenth-century theological debate about linguistic usage; Dickinson's poems traveled, and continue to travel, a long way beyond the hand-sewn margins of her autograph anthologies. Those anthologies will and must always be valuable and even precious—as records of her working methods and as places where her hand once moved and wrote. Nonetheless, the fact that Dickinson was willing to free individual poems from fascicles in order to send them to her correspondents allows for the possibility that they could survive on their own as autonomous aesthetic objects. Dickinson's preferred form of circulation during her lifetime was to enclose poems singly, or in small clusters of three and four, in letters or as freestanding notes, and this would appear to weaken any arguments for the fascicles as integral and deliberate selections. The poems are not satellites whose significance depends primarily on their relation to other centers of gravity—biographical, historical, or literary material: they continue to have an independent force of their own.

# 5

# "Looking at Death, is Dying"
## Fascicle 16 in a Civil War Context

### Paula Bernat Bennett

> This is pure deixis, a reality that can be projected only in the world of language. . . . It is hermetic language and the poems themselves become hermetic enclosures.
>
> —David Porter, *Dickinson: The Modern Idiom* (120, 121)

For all that "I felt a Funeral, in my Brain" (F340)—the subject of the above epigraph—is among Dickinson's most powerful poems, David Porter's frustration with it is more than understandable. Few Dickinson poems, if any, so tease the reader with emphatic statement after emphatic statement, leaving question after question in its wake. Set up as a single, clause-filled, dash-joined, non-sentence, this poem veils not just its subject but its speaker. S/he could be an observer or the corpse itself. If an observer, who? If the corpse, how could it "feel" its own burial? Then there are the other questions. Are we, for example, to take this funeral (occurring in the brain, after all) as real, or is it a trope for something else? What? Where is the speaker? What "Wrecked" him/her there? To what does the "Plank in Reason" refer, and what does its breaking signify? What sort of "plunge" does the speaker take, and what sort of "World[s]" does s/he pass on the way down? Have the worlds always been there, or are they the consequence of some (unidentified) event that is the poem's occasion? What does the speaker mean by "Finished knowing – then"? Is this an allusion to death? To insanity? To an inability to make sense of things? To unconsciousness? Is the speaker describing some sort of epistemological crisis or a spiritual one, a loss of faith perhaps? Why does the poem not end (i.e., have a period instead of a dash), especially if the speaker's consciousness ("knowing") does (i.e., is "Finished")?

As those familiar with Dickinson criticism know, scholars have answered these questions in myriad ways, each using his or her own interpretative framework—biographical, new critical, psychoanalytic, religious, feminist, and so forth to support their claim. Feminist interpreters have pointed to Dickinson's struggle with the gender issues of her day, a struggle that led her, they believe, to the brink of madness if not over it. Other scholars have forwarded other kinds of cultural or biographical contexts. Some have argued that death here is a metaphor for madness, others that both death and madness are ways of talking about consciousness or about loss of faith, or even, as Karen Ford does, about language's failure (69-70): "I, and Silence, some strange Race / Wrecked, solitary, here." Some treat the funeral as "real," if imagined, others as a placeholder for something else, experiences, for instance, that numb one out or bring one to the verge of suicidal despair. The breaking of a "Plank in Reason" has been taken as a figure for psychotic breakdown by John Cody (29) and failed faith by Cynthia Griffin Wolff, who astutely points to the literalized "plank of faith" in the religious iconography of the period (227–32). More mundanely, Judith Farr believes the poem describes "a fainting spell," with the speaker moving "from feeling to not knowing" (*Passion* 90–91). Sharon Cameron thinks "Funeral" is about ambivalence in making a thought unconscious (*Choosing* 141–44). With an unusual amount of hard evidence behind them, both Barton Levi St. Armand (*Her Culture* 108, 109) and Elizabeth Phillips (50–54) tie the poem to the death of Frazar Stearns at the battle of New Bern in March of 1862—a death that rocked not just the Dickinson family but the entire town of Amherst. I will return to Frazar Stearns shortly.

That so many specialists have read "I felt a Funeral" so diversely speaks directly to the interpretive problem lying at the heart of Dickinson's poetry, namely its indeterminacy—the absence of any sort of stabilizing framework by which her meanings can be contained. Absences, as David Porter writes, are constitutive in Dickinson's writing, "at every level: morpheme, word, phrase, poem, text, corpus, and the life as its matrix" (*Modern idiom* 5). Because they are, and because, as Porter, Cristanne Miller, and others, have argued, they require that the reader collaborate with the poet if they are to read her at all (see *Miller, Grammar,* 15–19; *Porter, Modern Idiom* 43–47; Crumbley, *Winds* 11–14), these absences make Dickinson a fabulously rich poet to explore. As she herself recognized in the slyest of puns, her verse is a "reduceless Mine" (Fr1091). But as the pile-up of interpretations for "I felt a Funeral" suggests, they also make her a very tricky read. This is not because one can go "wrong"—Dickinson being dead, how is "wrong" to be determined?—but because, given collaboration's role in the reading of her work, it is so fatally easy to think oneself "right," projecting onto the scrim of her verse one's own meaning.

Given Dickinson's indeterminacy, it is more than understandable, therefore, that scholars had hoped, with the publication of R. W. Franklin's 1981 facsimile edition of the fascicles—or "manuscript books," as he rather misleadingly calls them—that they, being self-chosen, would provide the very frameworks for interpretation her poems otherwise lack. Despite the varied and otherwise excellent work of scholars such as Dorothy Oberhaus, Eleanor Heginbotham, and Sharon Cameron, however, this has not come to pass.[1] On the contrary, although our readings of individual poems have been greatly enhanced by scholars' focus on the plays of similarity and difference among the fascicle poems themselves, the fascicles' status as free-standing interpretive units (that is, as "books") remains as contested as ever.[2] For many, the present writer included, treatments of the fascicles as independent, self-contained thematic structures only seem to multiply—this time over whole groups of poems—the temptations to projection to which, as Robert McClure Smith argues in *The Seductions of Emily Dickinson,* all Dickinson scholars are of necessity prone, the present writer—one of Smith's targets—included (1–18, 190–92).

In this chapter I will not speculate, therefore, on Dickinson's intentions when putting the poems in Fascicle 16—"I felt a Funeral's" fascicle—together. Short of finding hard evidence to the contrary, there is simply no way to know why she did what she did, be it with respect to the selection of poems, their arrangement, or her overall intentions for the fascicle as a whole. But taking St. Armand's and Phillips's reading of "I felt a Funeral" as my starting point, what I will do is show how the poems in this fascicle, all of which Franklin dates in or about the summer of 1862, can be united in relation to something else instead, namely the Civil War. In doing so, I am *not* claiming that all these poems were necessarily written with the Civil War in mind, let alone that they are consciously arranged in such a way as to say something specific about it—or about Stearns's death. Rather, I will argue that by reading them *through* the Civil War context that "I felt a Funeral" establishes, and, in particular, in relation to the horror that Stearns's death elicited in Dickinson, her family, and friends, one can find in them such unity as the fascicle possesses. This is the accidental unity of a set of poems that were written at a particular point in time when death (the single unifying thread binding the poems themselves) had overwhelming resonance for their author as for her society as a whole.[3]

In taking this approach, I hope to model an alternative way into the fascicles, one based on the assumption that if there are commonalities among fascicle poems, they are not the product of Dickinson's wish to make books, but rather the consequence of their being created by a single author, writing in a specific time, with specific concerns in mind. This approach will do nothing to solve the interpretive problems posed by Dickinson's indeterminacy in Fascicle 16 or elsewhere. To my mind, such problems are inseparable from her poetry's greatest strengths and are, therefore, a given of her verse. But as I hope to demonstrate, without making more of the fascicles than they are, insofar as these groupings bring various poems together, they can provide rich interpretive contexts for the poems they contain. And, at least where Fascicle 16 is concerned, this in itself can have a formidable impact on how we understand her in ways that reading these same poems in isolation from each other cannot have.

## Reading Fascicle 16 through "I felt a Funeral, in my Brain"

For all the centrality of "I felt a Funeral, in my Brain" to my reading of Fascicle 16, I will not discuss the poem here since I discussed both its indeterminacy and its Civil War context elsewhere, as have others as well.[4] However, I should say something at least about why I believe it is a Civil War poem and that Frazar Stearns's funeral was its occasion. The supporting evidence for both these contentions, first brought forward by St. Armand and by Phillips, can be found in the highly detailed letters, dated late March, which Dickinson wrote to her cousins, Loo and Fanny Norcross, and to Samuel Bowles. In them, Dickinson describes Stearns's death and her own family's, especially, her brother, Austin's, shocked response to it. Phillips's argument, in particular, that "I felt a Funeral," with all its dislocations and desolations, may in fact represent less Dickinson's own response than that of Austin, whose deep distress greatly perturbed the poet, seems to me to have considerable merit, and my own thinking about the poem is heavily indebted to her work. Most persuasive are the numerous verbal echoes between "I felt a Funeral" and Dickinson's letter to Bowles. "Austin is chilled," Dickinson wrote. "[H]is Brain keeps saying over 'Frazer [*sic*] is killed' – 'Frazer is killed,' just as Father told it – to Him. Two or three words of lead – that dropped so deep, they keep weighing" (L256, 399). To me, these similarities—"[H]is Brain keeps saying" / I felt a Funeral, in my Brain," "words of lead" / "Boots of Lead," "dropped so deep" / "dropped down, and down"—are simply too compelling to ignore.

At the same time, however, I would stress that this is not the only way in which "I felt a Funeral" can, or, more importantly, *should*, be read, any more than I think my readings of Fascicle 16's other poems are in any way definitive either. (Readers, for example, will see that I owe a great deal to Cameron's discussion of Fascicle 16, even though she never mentions the Civil War and our interpretations of particular poems often differ radically as a result.) But what I do want to demonstrate is what happens when, using "I felt a Funeral" as one's starting point, one reads the remaining fascicle poems with the Civil War and Stearns's death in mind. Whether or not Dickinson explicitly wrote the poems in Fascicle 16 as war poems, they were by Franklin's dating all written or, at the least, copied out by Dickinson about the same time (about summer, 1862), a time when Stearns's death would have still been relatively fresh in her mind. Intentionally or not, they all bear the impress of the war and of his death on her, whether or not we choose to read them in other ways as well, and this is how I shall approach them here.

By Franklin's account, Fascicle 16 consists of eleven poems: "Before I got my eye put out –" (Fr336B), "Of nearness to her sundered Things" (Fr337), "Tie the strings to my Life, My Lord" (Fr338), "I like a look of Agony" (Fr339), "I felt a Funeral, in my Brain" (Fr340), "'Tis so appalling – it exhilirates" (Fr341), "How noteless Men, and Pleiads, stand" (Fr342), "When we stand on the tops of Things" (Fr343), "'Twas just this time, last year, I died" (Fr344), "Afraid! Of whom am I afraid?" (Fr345), and "He showed me Hights I never saw –" (Fr346B). Of these, only one, "I like a look of Agony," is reprinted in Faith Barrett and Cristanne Miller's Civil War anthology, *"Words for the Hour."* To my knowledge, no other poem in the fascicle aside from "I felt a Funeral" has been associated with the Civil War. Yet, one way or another, all these poems engage war's defining product—death. Significantly, they do so, moreover, with a consistency not to be found in other fascicles, not even Fascicle 19, which also contains a poem closely associated with Stearns, "It dont sound so terrible – quite – as it did" (Fr384), nor Fascicle 24, which Hogue describes with such passion as a poetry of witness to the war itself (40–46).[5]

Yet tightly bound thematically as Fascicle 16's poems are, they diverge just as dramatically when it comes to the positioning of their various speakers.[6] By my count, four have posthumous speakers, two of whom are or seem to be soldiers, but all of whom, one way or another, address the relation between life and afterlife. Of the seven remaining poems, five, including "I felt a Funeral," have observer-speakers, who meditate on death from the outside, be it the experience of dying or death's impact on the living.

The positioning of the remaining two speakers is less clear, but their subject—how to deal with fear in the face of death—points to their being soldiers also. As far as I can tell, the poet's thinking about death does not evolve over the course of these poems, nor is there any narrative thread connecting them beyond the emphasis on death itself. Rather, as Leigh-Anne Marcellin observes of Dickinson's war poetry generally, the poet seems determined "to hold every position" (73), sometimes speaking for herself, sometimes having soldiers speak, sometimes voicing the thoughts of other noncombatants (see also Friedlander, "Battle of Ball's Bluff," 1582–83). Through all these works, one thing is clear, namely that in them, Dickinson is grappling one way or another with what it meant to let oneself die, to "choose" death (Cameron, *Choosing* 147), a choice to which Stearns's death at twenty-one undoubtedly gave added poignancy—and point. In volunteering, Stearns chose death over life.[7] Fascicle 16's poems seem to rethink that decision in light of its bitter conclusion, producing a poetry of what Wolosky aptly calls "endless disputation," in which nothing is really resolved ("Public and Private" 116). Since the positions Dickinson's speakers assume in these poems often contradict each other, for purposes of clarification I shall pair the poems off for analysis. Given the randomness of the fascicle's arrangement of poems, I do not think these pairings represent Dickinson's intention, nor will I address them in this way. Their presence simply reflects the workings of her mind, a mind, as Cameron, Wolosky, and so many others have demonstrated, that was given to testing and sustaining contradictory alternatives in multiple ways.[8]

## Poems with Posthumous Speakers

If scholars are now largely agreed as to the polyvocality of Dickinson's verse, that is, her use of multiple voices in her poems, they have said much less about her invention of multiple speakers, speakers, that is, who are *separate* and *distinct* from herself. This may be because while polyvocality does not of necessity rupture the lyric contract between author and reader,[9] poems spoken by imagined persons other than the author do. Or it may simply be because such poems, poems Dickinson scholars have been calling "dramatic monologues" but which are more rightly identified as "dramatic lyrics,"[10] can be, and in Dickinson certainly are, very difficult to identify, especially in the absence of unequivocal clues. Whatever the case, it was my realization that the speaker of "'Twas just this time, last year, I died" (Fr344) *was* invented and that the poem was therefore a dramatic lyric that did the most, after "I felt a Funeral" itself, to shape my thinking about Fascicle 16 as a whole. Like "Before I got my eye put out –," "Tie the strings to my Life, my Lord," and, arguably, "He showed me Hights I never saw –," "'Twas just this time" deploys a posthumous speaker. And, superficially, at any rate, the poem looks very much like those many other "posthumous" poems in which Dickinson's own dead self presumably speaks, poems such as "I often passed the Village" (Fr41) and "Because I could not stop for Death –" (Fr479). But read with an eye to the fascicle's Civil War context, the poem becomes susceptible to a very different interpretation. In this interpretation what we hear is not the voice of the poet's dead self, but that of a young soldier, one who, to judge by the poem's internal evidence, died in the first Battle of Bull Run (July 21, 1861), the year before. As it was this recognition of the poem's status as a dramatic lyric that convinced me of the importance of the fascicle's Civil War context, I begin with it and with why, for all the poem's apparent similarity to better-known posthumously spoken works,[11] it is, in fact, a very different kind of poem.

As in "'Twas just this time," so in "I often passed" and "Because I could not," Dickinson uses a travel metaphor to draw the line between the living and the dead. However, her handling of this metaphor is vastly different in the latter poems. In "I often passed," a very childlike speaker, who identifies herself through her relationship to "'Dollie'" (that is, to Susan Gilbert Dickinson), having died "Earlier, by the Dial, / Than the rest have gone," is taken past her old school to a place "stiller than the sundown" and "cooler than the dawn" (Fr41). There she lies, waiting for "Dollie" to join her. In this poem, Dickinson places herself squarely at the center of the work—this was her school, "'Dollie'" was her beloved friend, the journey that divides them was her journey. Identifying "Dickinson" as the speaker of "Because I could not stop" is trickier because both the speaker and the journey, while more detailed, are also more abstract. Of the speaker, we learn only of her clothes (and, indirectly thereby, her gender). Of her journey, we are told, that she "passed the School, where Children strove / At Recess – in the Ring – / We passed the Fields of Gazing Grain – / We passed the Setting Sun." Like one of the remote if beautiful figures of the dead on an ancient Greek stele—and distinctly unlike the speaker in "I often passed the Village"—this speaker has lost all touch with the time-bound. For her "'tis Centuries – and yet / Feels shorter than the Day / I first surmised the Horses' Heads / Were toward Eternity" (Fr479). Yet, like the speaker of "I often passed," the course of her journey is the same and its endpoint—a remote place of peace and quiet—is the same also so you could say that this is the same speaker only grown up, making both speakers surrogates for their author.

None of this holds true for the speaker of "'Twas just this time, last year" (Fr344). For one thing, although neither of the other two speakers sets out to die, having died, they both accept their fate with equanimity. Indeed, despite her youth, the speaker of "I often passed" seems to prefer death to life, looking eagerly forward to the time when "'Dollie'" joins her. In both poems, therefore, Death seems, at the least, an acceptable alternative to life, which neither speaker seems to miss all that much. Not so the speaker of "'Twas just this time," making the tone of this poem very different. Not only was this speaker unready to die, but even after death, he clings to the memories of the life that once defined him, evincing a tenderness and need neither of the other two speakers display. Carried to his resting place, he dates his death by the rustling of corn in tassel and thinks "how yellow it would look – / When Richard went to mill." He remembers "how Red – Apples wedged / The Stubble's joints between –" and how the "Carts went stooping round the fields / To take the Pumpkins in –." Harvest done, he wonders who in his family will "miss [him], least," and on Thanksgiving, would his father "multiply the plates – / To make an even sum" and whether his missing stocking will "blur the Christmas glee."

Where, that is, the female speakers of the other poems recall nothing of their human community save the schools they attended, the speaker of "'Twas just the time" remembers everything: the chores he carried out, the people with whom he worked, the holidays he and his family celebrated. Not only that, but farm boy that he is, he remembers all this with seasonal precision, continuing to follow even after death the agricultural calendar that governed his and his family's life. Beginning with the corn (which in New England ripens in late July), he counts down the "lost" months of his last (imperfect) year: corn ripening July through August, apples reddening from September through October, pumpkins harvested from late October through November, when finally Thanksgiving is held, and December comes, with Christmas rounding out the year. At this point, the pain of his loss becomes so unbearable, he turns to looking forward to that "perfect year" when his family—something neither of the other two posthumous speakers give a thought to—will join him in the afterlife and the circuit of his life will once more be complete (Fr344).

Precisely because human connections are so limited in "I often passed" and "Because I could not," there is little or no pathos in these poems. But in "'Twas just this time," pathos is everywhere—the sadness of a life unlived, symbolized by the unnatural disruption of the agricultural year and by the broken circle of family life—making hurt the poem's primary affect. But since the poem is spoken by a farm boy, this was undoubtedly

Dickinson's point. Farm boys, a goodly number as young as fifteen, made up the bulk of the armies on both sides of the war, and poets other than Dickinson also made much of this fact, using these young men's innocence and bravery and the pathos of their loss in order to underscore the terrible sacrifice asked of them and their families. That Dickinson should try her hand at such a poem at such a time is not surprising. As Benjamin Friedlander has recently argued in his highly persuasive "Dickinson and the Battle of Ball's Bluff" (1591–97), Dickinson was not only aware of the Civil War poetry published in local newspapers like the *Springfield Republican;* she wrote in response to it. Like Dickinson's, many of these poems are deeply sentimental, sometimes having the soldier tell his own story from the grave, sometimes having a fellow soldier, a family member, or the poet him- or herself telling his story for him.[12]

If the speaker of "'Twas just this time" is death's unwilling victim, the speaker of "Tie the strings to my Life, My Lord," is for no observable reason other than his own personality positively jaunty about dying. Speculating, it seems that Dickinson decided to give voice here to another soldier-type, one who, as a veteran army man rather than a young recruit, had become fatalistic about his prospects both in this life and in the afterlife.[13] Certainly, from his sly reference to riding "to the Judgment / And it's partly down Hill" (a winning line if ever there was one), this speaker, unlike the farm boy, was well-acquainted with the world. Not only is he unfazed by what now confronts him (Judgment), he seems downright eager for something new even if that "new" is life after death. Bidding a breezy goodbye "to the Life I used to live," and throwing a kiss to the Hills—a delicate allusion, perhaps, to sexual adventures—he's off to try, as he says, "by [his] own Choice and Thee [God's]" the next world, having got done with this one (Fr338). That he does see himself as having a choice strongly suggests that like Stearns, he volunteered, making not just his lack of regret, but even more, his lack of self-heroization, that much more impressive. From the way this speaker presents himself, it is clear no long funeral train or town turned upside down will attend his burial. He was a soldier and in war's lottery, death was his share. That's all.

Before leaving these two poems, I should note that in neither work does the speaker mention passing a school on his death journey. In however small a way, this puts Dickinson's notorious class prejudices in a somewhat different light. For the speakers of "I often passed" and "Because I did not," schools obviously loomed large in their minds, and their concern for schooling, which helps mark them as Dickinson surrogates, also establishes their bourgeois class status, a status neither the farm boy nor the old soldier possesses. Dickinson thus shows some sensitivity in recognizing that for them, even if they went to school, the latter was not an important part in their lives. Both men are depicted as ordinary humanity, genus Americanus, and Dickinson pays tribute to this fact by giving them poems that are most remarkable for the clarity of their diction and honesty of their thought. As such, their poems also represent what nineteenth-century sentimental verse could do at its finest. Although the thousands of men for whom these two speakers stand died unheralded, Dickinson gives them a memorial and an eloquence of their own. If one reads these poems in the usual way, identifying "Dickinson" with the speaker, all this is lost, diminishing, I would submit, the kind of poet she was.

The voice Dickinson uses in the remaining two posthumously spoken poems is far more complex, suggesting that their personae are more closely tied to Dickinson herself. Both these poems have also received far more scholarly attention than have the soldier poems. In *Choosing Not Choosing*, for example, Cameron barely gives a line or two to each of the soldier poems while devoting whole pages to "Before I got my eye put out" and "He showed me Hights." Nonetheless, although there is no clear evidence that the last two poems are spoken by soldiers, nor written with the Civil War consciously in mind, their themes fit in with the overall Civil War thematics of the fascicle itself. As Cameron argues of Fascicle 16's thematic structure generally, both these poems are about "death, vision, and choice." But where Cameron has Dickinson handling these themes in the abstract, I would suggest we look at them in relation to their historical context and, in particular, in relation to those discourses of religious consolation which in Dickinson's day took literally St. Paul's promise of new sight in the afterlife.[14] In "Before I got my Eye put out –" (Fr366), Dickinson interrogates the nature of this new sight, what in "The Tint I cannot take – is best –," she calls the "[o]ther way – to see –" acquired in the grave (Fr696). In "He showed me Hights," she focuses on the choice so many made when they voluntarily gave up their lives, exchanging one way of seeing for another. Reading the two poems this way will foreground the profound ambivalence toward the afterlife that I believe dominates each poem's conclusion, not to mention Dickinson's work as a whole, and which may well have made the rituals of sentimental consolation around the Civil War dead profoundly troubling to her, adding pain to pain.[15]

In "Before I got my eye put out," Dickinson identifies blinding with dying and dying with a new way of seeing, a way of seeing so powerful that, ironically, should one experience it while alive, the speaker says, it would strike you dead. Behind this rather bizarre logic lies the doctrine of accommodation, first elucidated by medieval theologians and later taken up by Calvin as a foundation stone of reformed biblical interpretation. In brief, the doctrine of accommodation posits that since the finite cannot contain the infinite, God made creation as a reduced version of himself that we might safely experience his magnitude through the (lesser) magnitude of the material world around us (think "All Forests – Stintless stars"). Only after death, when the soul is freed from its mortal casing, can we experience this magnitude without accommodation: an extrapolation of St. Paul's promise that after death we will see "face to face" (King James version, 1 Cor. 13:12). That this is the soul's situation in "Before I got my eye put out" seems clear. Where Dickinson diverges from theology is that for her the infinite which her speaker now apprehends in its absolute fullness is not God (God is not mentioned in the poem) but, ironically, the natural world itself, that very world God presumably created as a reduced, and hence secondary, mirroring, of himself.

What Dickinson is doing here is similar to what Sarah Piatt does in her poems on child death. The speaker's child in Piatt's elegies may well be in heaven, but what the speaker wants is her child in the flesh. Without this, no spiritual compensation can ever soothe the mother's pain.[16] For Dickinson's speaker, also, post-mortem visions of God's own majesty, no matter how awe-inspiring in themselves, can never compensate for what is lost. On the contrary, once dead, the speaker is irrevocably denied possession of what she learned to love most: the material nature defined in "the Motions of The Dipping Birds – / The Morning's Amber Road." Craving more than ever what she can now never have, the speaker is left "with just my soul / Opon the window pane – / Where other creatures put their eyes – / Incautious – of the Sun." While the poem seems to celebrate the speaker's new apprehension of God and his "creation," this image of her "soul / Opon the window pane" (Fr336) makes her sound more like a prisoner than part of that joyous community of the dead which, blinded by God's light, does not realize its loss. Read this way, the poem's concluding stanza is bitter indeed, God's revelation of his plenitude something of a twisted joke.

If there's validity to this interpretation, then this might help clarify the speaker's enormous ambivalence in "He showed me Hights, I never saw –" (Fr346B). Allegorical in nature, this poem is among Fascicle's 16's most obscure texts. Its complications are significantly multiplied, moreover, by the fact that Dickinson sent another version of the poem, with pronouns reversed, to Susan Gilbert Dickinson (Fr346), inevitably shadowing the Fascicle 16 version with the poet's frustrated passion for her sister-in-law, relevant or not. Finally, and relatively rare in a Dickinson poem, the speaker also has an interlocutor, one who, from the little she says of him, could be God or Jesus, a lover, death or even the devil—all male figures who, with the exception of the last, play important roles in Dickinson's verse. Whoever/whatever he is, he is clearly out to tempt the speaker, offering her sights she never saw—not just "Hights" but "secrets" "Morning's Nest / The Rope of Nights were put across." These are transcendent visions, as Judith Farr observes, not unlike those in the paintings of Frederick Church and Thomas Cole, artists whom her brother favored, and who depicted heavily romanticized landscapes on religious themes (Farr, *Passion* 158–59. See also St. Armand, *Her Culture* 251 and Appendix B).

In keeping with this visionary setting, the poem's controlling figure is that of mountain climbing, which the interlocutor urges the speaker to do. If she does, he says, she will witness the creation ("Morning's Nest") firsthand. This seems to suggest that she will see all things *sub specie aeternitatis* as God sees them, without accommodation, from beginning to end, morning to night, all at once. This is a heady but, as we have seen, a possibly fatal, invitation,[17] and for two stanzas, the speaker manages to resist it, unable to "find [her] 'yes.'" This speaker has no wish to rise above the world or to exchange her earthbound perspective for a sublime one. But in the final stanza, things get fuzzy. Depending on how one identifies the interlocutor, and what one assumes is the speaker's choice, the outcome is altered in different ways. "And then," the speaker explains, "He brake His Life – and lo, / A light for me, did solemn glow – / The steadier, as my face withdrew – / And could I further 'No'?" This could suggest that the interlocutor's final ploy to win the speaker's "Yes"—one her apparent withdrawal pushes him into—is to unveil himself (his light) fully to her. At this, she halts, saying— or asking rhetorically—"And could I further 'No'?" which could be read as a statement of acquiescence (F346B).[18]

But is it? Or, put another way, if it is, why does the speaker frame her "Yes" as "No"? As Cameron observes, the final line in fact leaves her choice hanging: perhaps she does, perhaps she doesn't (*Choosing* 149–51). Why? If, indeed, the fascicle "variant" of the poem is, as Farr argues, another love poem only with the pronouns reversed, then the difference between the two poems is inconsequential: the point of the poem remains "renunciation" (159). But what if, as Cameron suggests, the poem is not a variant (that is, essentially the same poem, with some words changed) but a second, stand-alone version (82), and what if in this other version the interlocutor is not the speaker's lover but God, or death or the devil, that being who thrice subjected Jesus to temptations, the last of which comes perilously close to the offer the interlocutor makes to the speaker in Dickinson's poem (Matt.

4:1–10)? Then what the speaker decides not only touches on Fascicle 16's principal themes but does so with devastating effect. For now the poem is not about giving oneself to love but about the speaker's willingness to give up her life for whatever the interlocutor is offering, which could be heaven, but which could also be hell.[19] And it is on this note of irresolution that the poem ends. Noble and naïve, Stearns rushed off to war telling his father, "If I can save my country better by dying now than living I am ready for it" (quoted in [Stearns] 73). Dickinson's speaker is more wary, and for good cause. For whatever else the light signifies, unless it is love, the speaker must die to have it, taking on faith that the promises of the promised end do not end in the grave—or worse.

## Poems Spoken by (Noncombatant) Observers

Of the remaining seven poems, five have speakers who comment on death without, presumably, being at risk of death themselves: "Of nearness to her sundered Things" (Fr337), "I felt a Funeral, in my Brain" (Fr340), "How noteless Men, and Pleiads, stand" (Fr342), "When we stand on the tops of Things –" (Fr343), and "I like a look of Agony" (Fr339). In "Of nearness to her sundered Things" (Fr337), a sentimental speaker contemplates the spiritual bonds between the living and the dead. In "How noteless Men, and Pleiads, stand," a distinctly unsentimental speaker considers the total absence of such bonds. In "When we stand on the tops of Things – ," the speaker weighs the value of positioning oneself above the fray, and watching "Things" from a treetop's (or eagle's) perspective. In "I like a look of Agony," the speaker gets down and dirty, claiming to prize the agony of death because unlike all other human emotions, death agony cannot be feigned. Insofar as these poems seem almost wilfully determined to undo each other, they reinforce Cameron's emphasis on Dickinson's strategy of "choosing not choosing" as a key element in fascicle structure. But as Marcellin observes, multipositionality is true of Dickinson's verse in any case, certainly where the war was concerned, so the fact that these noncombatants take contradictory positions is to be expected. What is surprising is the adaptability of Dickinson's style, which allowed her to negotiate her way around and about such sharp lines of difference, a phenomenon I have already touched on in my discussion of her posthumously spoken poems and will explore further here.[20]

Of the poems spoken by observers, "Of nearness to her sundered Things" is by far the most conventional, and the one that seems most likely intended to represent the thoughts of ordinary persons coping with the pain of lost loved ones. In it, Dickinson draws heavily on spiritualism, a pseudoscientific, quasi-religious discourse, whose materialist version of the afterlife gained enormous popularity during the war years.[21] For this speaker, the dead are literally always with her: "The Shapes we buried, dwell about, / Familiar, in the Rooms / Untarnished by the Sepulchre, / The Mouldering Playmate comes – / In just the Jacket that he wore – / Long buttoned in the Mold." Indeed, these spiritual "Apparitions" are so strongly present that by the poem's conclusion, it is the speaker who feels "unreal." They "Salute us, with their wings – / As we – it were – that perished – / Themself – had just remained till we rejoin them – / And 'twas they, and not ourself / That mourned" (Fr337).[22] By the summer of 1862, two of the Civil War's ten bloodiest battles, Shiloh and Fort Donelson, had occurred and given the interminable lists of the dead that, like some giant tsunami, poured off the presses after each major Civil War battle, that Dickinson's speaker would feel comforted, rather than appalled, by being surrounded by "Apparitions," makes unhappy sense.[23]

In "Of nearness to her sundered Things," the speaker has what might be called a positive relation to her dead, whose quasi-materiality, as it were, allows them to be spiritualized and sentimentalized at once. The relation between the living and the dead in "How noteless Men, and Pleiads, stand" is just the opposite. For one thing, the speaker of the latter poem is not talking specifically about her own dead, but rather about the dead in general, those who go "noteless . . . / Until a sudden sky / Reveals the fact that One is rapt / Forever from the eye."[24] For another and far more important, once dead, these people are permanently cut off from the living. They are now "Members of the Invisible, / Existing, while we stare, / In Leagueless Opportunity, / O'ertakeless, as the Air." When the speaker asks rhetorically, "Why did'nt we detain Them?" what we get by way of response is vintage Dickinson: "The Heavens, with a smile, / Sweep by our disappointed Heads, / Without a syllable –" (Fr342). In this poem, the separation between earth and heaven is as absolute as it was porous in "Of nearness," and there is no possibility of comfort coming from the latter quarter as a result. On the contrary, all that "Of nearness to her sundered Things" gives by way of comfort, "How noteless Men, and Pleiads, stand" rescinds. While the countless thousands who died in the Civil War may still "live" on another plane, from a sublunar perspective, be they noted or unnoted, we have no way of connecting to them.

Although both "Of nearness to her sundered Things" and "How noteless Men, and Pleiads, stand" deal with the same theme—the relation between the living and the dead—they do so from opposite perspectives. This pattern of opposition also holds true for the remaining pairs of poems: "When we stand on the tops of Things –" and "I like a Look of Agony" on the one hand, and "Afraid? Of whom am I Afraid?" and "'Tis so appalling, it exhilirates –," on the other. In these pairings, Dickinson uses her poems to test out conflicting positions, some of which may reflect her own thoughts, the rest of which, like "Of nearness," seem more likely to be positions she attributes to others. As a result, there is a striking amount of variation from poem to poem stylistically as well as thematically and in terms of the speaker's position. Indeed, "When we stand on the tops of Things," which I will discuss first, could even be said to double these possibilities since in itself it permits two diametrically opposed readings. In one, the poem represents Dickinson's attempt to theorize something that she herself was not—namely a person without fear. In the other, she appears to be satirizing just this latter sort of person, the person who, standing "on the tops of Things," can see all but feel nothing. Both readings focus on one of the dominant motifs of the fascicle as a whole—albeit not one Cameron identifies—fear. But where the first reading (Cameron's) assumes the poet is writing in praise of fearlessness, the second critiques fearlessness as an affect of uninvolvement. My reading will assume that the poem deals with the Civil War and should be read ironically; Cameron, as noted, reads the poem from the alternative perspective (*Choosing* 83–84n. and 147–49). Given the poem's complexity, it is certain that there are other strong readings for this (in all honesty, tortured) poem that we both have missed.

The argument of "When we stand" can be summarized as follows. "The Perfect"—those whose souls have no "flaw[s]"—are recognizable by their lack of fear. "When [they] stand on the tops of Things – / And like the Trees, look down," they do not "wink." They see things clearly ("The smoke all cleared away"). "[L]ike the Hills . . . / No lightning, scares" them, and because nothing frightens them they are "Sound," and their soundness, or what Cameron calls their "integrity" (148), helps keep the world alight: "The Stars dare shine occasionally / Opon a spotted World – / And Suns, go surer, for their Proof, / As if an axle, held –." In short, their fearlessness not only enables them to see things, as Cameron says, as a "totality," but it keeps the world going as well: the "Stars" "dare" (at least "occasionally") to shine down "Opon" our "spotted World" and the "Suns" continue in their circuit "As if an Axle, held" (Fr343). These are large claims, but are we supposed to believe them? Should we believe them, given the two qualifiers— "occasionally" and "As if"—that Dickinson slips into her final stanza? Does she really hold such an aggrandized view of the pontifications of the uninvolved as this poem seems to suggest she does?

The problem with taking the poem's argument seriously, I would suggest, lies precisely in its predication of fearlessness—and hence clarity of vision—on distance, be that distance physical, intellectual, or psychological. From the tops of trees, it is easy to look down on even a battlefield and not wink.[25] One has no dog in the fight. Blood does not spatter in one's eyes. In her essay on the eagle's perspective in Dickinson's Civil War poetry, Renée Bergland notes that "to see close at hand is to see warts and all but to see from an eagle's perspective you can imagine 'the ideal'" (148), and Oliver Wendell Holmes appears to have been of this mind, in a postbellum lecture, praising Civil War poetry that was "able to 'lift the world and the life of today into the spaceless and timeless ideal'" (quoted in Bergland 134). Similarly, Emerson, Bergland notes, advised studying things from a distance to see their ideal forms (148). But Dickinson was the author who wrote "I like a look of Agony," and what that gruesome scrutinizing of the body in pain suggests is that to study death and dying, that is, war, from a distance is to study nothing at all. To know it, one has to be there—in the lightning and the smoke,[26] in the confusion and pain. Otherwise, one's clarity, like one's "fearlessness," is no more than a function of one's safety, making a mockery of both the men who died and of war itself, which may be many things but none of them "ideal."[27]

However one chooses to read "When we stand," what is clear is that Dickinson adopts a very different relation to "Things" that make one "wink" in "I like a look of Agony," a poem which, if nothing else, confronts the reader up close and personal with those very details that seeing from the "tops of Things" makes impossible to see:

I like a look of Agony,
Because I know it's true –
Men do not sham Convulsion,
Nor simulate, a Throe –

The eyes glaze once – and that is Death –
Impossible to feign
The Beads opon the Forehead
By homely Anguish strung. (Fr339)

In sharp contrast to the convoluted argument in "When we stand on the tops of Things –," this poem's argument could not be more direct and unambiguous.[28] This is either a noncombatant speaking, possibly the poet herself, or a soldier looking down on (or remembering how it felt like to look down on) an enemy he just killed, and describing the death throes with unadorned precision, rather like a gun talking about its latest victim. So plain is the poem that there is only one metaphor in it, "the Beads opon the Forehead / By homely Anguish strung." Otherwise, it is as close to prose in its diction and syntax—and in its total lack of passion—as Dickinson ever gets. Dickinson apparently wanted to be sure that the poem's point got across. But what is the point? And why, to cite a line from another Fascicle 16 poem, did she choose to use such a "Bald – and Cold" (Fr341) voice in making it?

If, as I have argued, Dickinson produced Fascicle 16's poems not just in response to the Civil War but specifically in response to Frazar Stearns's death, she may well have wanted to puncture the idealizing aura in which the details of his death—a death that itself occurred far from Amherst— were publicly cast. Under the inspiration of one of his professors, Stearns, the beloved son of the president of Amherst College, was among the town's first volunteers, and it was at this man's feet that the twenty-one-year-old gave up his life for the Union cause. That was the public, highly romanticized story. In her letter to her cousins, Fanny and Loo Norcross, Dickinson appears to describe the funeral in the language of similarly romanticized heroism:

> 'tis least that I can do, to tell you of brave Frazer [sic] – "killed at Newbern," darlings. His big heart shot away by a "minie ball."
>
> I had read of those – I didn't think that Frazer would carry one to Eden with him. Just as he fell, in his soldier's cap, with his sword at his side, Frazer rode through Amherst. Classmates to the right of him, and classmates to the left of him, to guard his narrow face! He fell by the side of Professor Clark, his superior officer – lived ten minutes in a soldier's arms, asked twice for water – murmured just, "My God!" and passed! . . . They tell that Colonel Clark cried like a little child when he missed his pet, and could hardly resume his post. (L255, 397–98)

On the surface, at any rate, Dickinson appears to join her community in shocked grief at Stearns's death, making the letter something of an elegiac memorial.

However, as I have discussed elsewhere (see "Emily Dickinson and Her Peers" 293–94), there's an edge to Dickinson's letter that undermines its elegiac intentions if such they were. There is, for one, too much archness and too much emphasis on the pathos of a childlike Frazar, hit by a "minie ball,"[29] dying at his professor's feet. Frazar, his bereaved father declared, in a gesture of patent self-comfort, "'fell doing his duty as a Christian soldier'" (quoted in St. Armand 112). Such a sentiment might have eased a father's heart, but it's doubtful that it would have eased Dickinson's, who openly flouted duty-doing throughout her life, refusing even to participate in the war effort (L235, 377). And then there is the nod to Tennyson's "Charge of the Light Brigade" ("Classmates to the right of him, and classmates to the left of him"). Dickinson seems to be paying tribute to Tennyson's poem, but is she? Or is she parodying it, indirectly suggesting thereby that "bighearted" Frazar, like the light brigade's doomed members, blindly followed his superior's orders (and inspiration) straight into the grave. As Bergland observes, Dickinson was not a "joiner" nor given to blind patriotism (136). Stearns, her antithesis, was, and she told her Norcross cousins, he was "too brave that he could fear to die" (L256, 398). A man whom St. Armand describes as a "pragmatic Irish private" (114) put it more bluntly, commenting that for all his nobility, Stearns was "'too brave for his own good'" (quoted in [Stearns] 140).[30]

It is hard to know how deep Dickinson's outrage at the romantic trappings in which Amherst wrapped Stearns's death actually went. Certainly, her description of the memorial service has an edge, being far too neatly packaged: "Crowds came to tell him good-night, choirs sang to him, pastors told how brave he was" (L255, 398). In substituting the isolated and suffering body of "I like a look of Agony" for Stearns' heroic corpse, at least in her own mind, was she then paying her respects not to what never was but to what was—"The Beads opon the Forehead / By homely Anguish strung"? And could that help explain the chilling graphicness of the poem itself? Stearns was so mutilated, Dickinson tells Loo and Fanny, that the doctors refused to let even his father see him in his coffin. Apparently they did not trust that the distanced and removed President Stearns, who had exhorted his son to join up (St. Armand 112), would have the self-containment not to wink. Having died away from Amherst, Stearns brought the horror of war home with him in his coffin. Dickinson's poem memorializes what no one wanted to see.

## Poems Spoken by Combatants

By my reading of Fascicle 16, only two dramatic lyrics are unambiguously spoken by living soldiers: "Afraid! Of whom am I afraid?" (Fr345) and "'Tis so appalling – it exhilirates –" (Fr341). Fear is at the center of both poems. In the former, the speaker insists that his religious faith has enabled him to triumph over fear. In the latter, the speaker also claims to have triumphed over fear. However, not by asserting his faith—he mocks such professions. Rather, he has done so by stamping out hope in himself. Both poems thus touch on the single issue that seems to have troubled Dickinson the most, namely that having chosen to go to war, soldiers effectively chose death over life. This was a choice that Dickinson, with her doubts about the afterlife and her visceral wariness of publicly supported causes—a wariness blatant in her treatment of the memorial services for Stearns—had substantial difficulty understanding, let alone supporting. In the poems, both speakers have reached a point where fear of dying has finally trumped the willingness to fight and both are struggling to find some way to deal with the emotional fallout of this realization, one turning to faith, the other to a mocking form of rage. Although some readers may disagree, I think the man of faith gets the worst of it here.

The problem with the speaker of "Afraid! Of whom am I afraid?" (Fr345) is a common one: he protests too much. That is, given how firmly he states his religious convictions, one cannot help but wonder whom, exactly, he is trying to convince. True, Dickinson herself has a number of poems in which what appears to be her own voice makes similarly adamant professions of faith—"I never saw a Moor" (Fr800) for example—but these poems are dispersed through her oeuvre and do not seem to be at significant odds with what surrounds them as a result. Not so with "Afraid!" Reading the poem in the context of a fascicle containing a mere eleven poems, most of which, one way or another, raise grave doubts about the nature, and even the possibility, of an afterlife, the faith-based rebuttals that the speaker in "Afraid! Of whom am I afraid?" uses to quiet his fears cannot help but have a hollow ring. Indeed, the very emphaticness with which he renders them raises doubts in itself. If, as he claims, he has nothing to fear—not from death, or life, or from what comes after (resurrection)—why ask the question at all? The more he insists, the more fearful he sounds, the entire poem becoming what looks like a futile exercise in self-comfort as he rehearses the answer to each question like a child committing his catechism to memory:

> Afraid? Of whom am I afraid?
> Not Death – for who is He?
> The Porter of my Father's Lodge
> As much abasheth me!
>
> Of Life? 'Twere odd I fear a thing
> That comprehendeth me

In one or two existences –
Just as the case may be –

Of Resurrection? Is the East
Afraid to trust the Morn
With her fastidious forehead?
As soon impeach my Crown! (Fr345)

Whether modelled on someone Dickinson knew (Stearns, perhaps, who also agonized about religion), or created as yet another fictive "type," this soldier-speaker is very different from the posthumous speakers of "'Twas just this time" and "Tie the strings of my Life." For one thing, his diction ("abasheth," "comprehendeth," "fastidious," "impeach") marks him as well educated; for another, his family is well off. His father owns a "Lodge," which comes complete with its own "Porter."[31] This speaker can, moreover, ponder scholastic distinctions such as whether life and afterlife are one life or two, and then, with a sophisticated wave of his hand, brush the issue away. However, all these "advantages," if that is what they are, do him little good on a playing field leveled by death. On the contrary, where Dickinson's posthumous soldier-speakers exhibit the confidence of an uninterrogated faith, this speaker asks question after question. For such a man, as Dickinson knew from her own plight, the doubts that nibble at the soul were unlikely to be stilled with schoolroom logic.[32] Yet he appears to have nothing else to fall back on. He is, you could say, too educated for the gut-level situation he is in, putting all his assertions into doubt.

Doubts about the possibility of both the afterlife and resurrection have a profoundly different impact on the speaker of "'Tis so appalling – it exhilirates–" (Fr341), the poem that brings my discussion of Fascicle 16 to an end. "'Tis so appalling" is a terrifying poem, the more so because its goal is to look terror straight in the face (and not wink). In its echoes of Edgar's aside in *King Lear*—"And worse I may be yet. The worst is not / So long as we can say, 'This is the worst'" (4.1.27–28)—it reminds us that the human limits of pain are set at that point when one has nothing left to lose, and everything ceases to matter, life included. Because this poem marks the culmination of many of the issues raised by Fascicle 16's poems, I will quote it in full:

'Tis so appalling – it exhilirates –
So over Horror, it half captivates –
The Soul stares after it, secure –
To know the worst, leaves no dread more –

> To scan a Ghost, is faint –
> But grappling, conquers it –
> How easy, Torment, now –
> Suspense kept sawing so –
>
> The Truth, is Bald – and Cold –
> But that will hold –
> If any are not sure –
> We show them – prayer –
> But we, who know,
> Stop hoping, now –
>
> Looking at Death, is Dying –
> Just let go the Breath –
> And not the pillow at your cheek
> So slumbereth –
>
> Others, can wrestle –
> Your's, is done –
> And so of Wo, bleak dreaded – come,
> It sets the Fright at liberty –
> And Terror's free –
> Gay, Ghastly, Holiday! (Fr341)

As with "I felt a Funeral"—and to a lesser degree—"Before I got my eye put out," "'Tis so appalling" raises a pile of unanswered (and unanswerable) questions. Among the most basic: who is the speaker, where is he, and what occasioned the poem in the first place? These questions seem especially pointed here since, unless one believes Dickinson at least half-mad, the degree of terror the poem displays is simply way out of proportion to whatever we know she experienced in life. Not even the breakup of a deeply felt love affair, or the excruciating pain attendant on the realization of lost faith, could elicit the kind of "appalling" and "exhilirating" experience of "over Horror" that the speaker describes, at least not unless she were Sylvia Plath. And I will not deny that there are a number of Plathian moments in the poem: "To know the worst, leaves no more dread," "Suspense kept sawing so – ," "The Truth, is Bald – and Cold," "we, who know, / Stop hoping now – " "Looking at Death, is Dying," "Others can wrestle – / Your's, is done." And like Plath's last poems, these lines all seem to lead irreversibly to the quietist solution of death as the only possible remedy for the pain living in fear engenders. Standing on the tops of "Things" in such a situation will get one nowhere.

But Plath's tragedy was itself in overplus and certainly exceeded anything we know of Dickinson's situation even at its worst. The speaker of this poem is *in extremis,* has lost all hope, and urges others to do the same. Just as grappling with Ghosts is the only way to "conquer" them, so, he argues, accepting "The Truth," "Bald – and Cold," that is, without any form of consolation or hope, is the only way to wrestle Death down. "Looking at Death, [may be] Dying" but it also frees one from "Fright," albeit by setting "Fright" loose to rule as it will. This is not only a full-frontal rebuttal of all the consolations offered by the soldier-speaker in "Afraid! Of whom am I Afraid?" and the observer-speaker of "Of nearness to her sundered Things." It is a terrifying conclusion. For this speaker, however, it is also the only way to survive—if embracing death's "Bald – and Cold" "Truth" is indeed survival. "If any are not sure –," the speaker adds, with no small degree of contempt, "we show them – prayer – / But we, who know, / Stop hoping, now." This is the legend Dante placed over the gates of hell: "Abandon all hope, ye who enter here" (canto 3, line 9). And is not war a type for hell?

With these lines, the composite speaker of Fascicle 16's poems reaches bottom. It is a bottom free of God, heaven, hope. Prayer is for those who can't deal with the Truth. That is the "Terror" set loose at the poem's conclusion to enjoy its "Gay, Ghastly, Holiday"—the terror of a world in which Death is the only "Truth," and hopelessness, the only way to deal with fear. When Dickinson said in 1864 that she "sang off charnel steps" (L298, 436), it was the Civil War dead she had in mind. Whether spoken, as I believe, by a soldier or by Dickinson *in propria persona,* or by some other persona she had in mind when writing it, "'Tis so appalling – it exhilarates" is such a song. It is certainly understandable why it was not published until 1935. Reading it in a Civil War context at least helps explain how she could have written it at all, though the poem's hard-nosed position in its second stanza is not softened a whit thereby. War, I would suggest, taught Dickinson to look at the one thing she feared most—Death and tell its truth as she saw it, "Bald – and Cold."

## Conclusion

As I mentioned earlier, in choosing to discuss Fascicle 16 in terms of paired poems I am not suggesting nor do I believe that Dickinson deliberately set the fascicle up this way. There are many other ways in which these poems could be arranged for analysis, and I suspect that those reading this chapter have already found other patterns that make more sense to them. I chose this particular route because it was the most useful for me, allowing me to foreground the very kind of oppositional thinking in Dickinson of which Cameron rightly makes so much. Even if not by design, the poems in Dickinson's fascicles play off each other, and off given sets of ideas or themes, and it greatly enriches one's reading of them to view them in this way.

But I differ from Cameron in two important respects. First, in exposing the multiple contradictions and oppositions in Dickinson's work, Cameron wished to stress what she calls the heteroglossia of Dickinson's voice, a heteroglossia she contrasts to the "unitary self" (and voice) of a poet such as Walt Whitman (*Choosing* 21–24). I believe such privileging of Dickinson in opposition to Whitman does a disservice both to Whitman and to the complexity of the culture in which both poets lived and of which their verse is a part as well as a reflector. When Emerson said that "a foolish consistency" was "the hobgoblin of little minds," and Whitman said "Do I contradict myself? Very well, then I contradict myself, I am large, I contain multitudes,"[33] both men were speaking of, as well as to, a culture rife with contradiction and oppositions that one can see reflected in their works. Indeed, one need only explore the century's rich periodical and newspaper culture to know that nineteenth-century U.S. culture itself was heteroglossic, literally as well as figuratively, robustly so. And like many other poets of her period, from Henry Wadsworth Longfellow to Sarah Piatt, Dickinson, who was an avid reader of both periodicals and newspapers, brought that heteroglossia into her verse.[34]

No less important for me here, Cameron's ascription of multiplicity to Dickinson's poems still lodges diversity within the poet's own persona. The result is an implicit upholding of that "lyric contract," so fundamental to any reading of the romantic lyric, which, in the absence of any signals to the contrary, identifies the lyric speaker with the poet herself, albeit a poet who speaks (as it were) with many tongues.[35] But while Fascicle 16 contains a number of poems that may fit within this rubric (e.g., "Before I got my eye put out –," "I felt a Funeral," "How noteless Men, and Pleiads, stand," "I like a look of Agony," and "He showed me Hights I never saw –"), it also contains a substantial number in which the connection between poet and speaker seems clearly severed. If these latter poems contribute to the overall heteroglossia of Dickinson's writing, they also suggest that she adopted performative identities, stepping outside the circle of her own mentation to (re)create the thoughts of those manifestly unlike herself. As I read these personae: a New England farm boy, a battle-hardened veteran, a woman who has lost too many loved ones to death, an onlooker on war, whose distance from it allows him to idealize it, a soldier struggling to keep hold of faith in the face of fear, and a soldier who has given up all hope whatsoever and no longer fears anything.

From Lord Randal's mother and Burns's "Holy Willie" to Elizabeth Barrett Browning's "Runaway Slave," this kind of dramatic or performative poetry was, in fact, deeply embedded in the British tradition and undoubtedly traveled to the American colonies in the first boats. By the nineteenth century, it had gained enormous popularity in both literatures, and Dickinson's use of the dramatic lyric thus fits in well with nineteenth-century poetic practice. As a hybrid form between drama and lyric, the dramatic lyric was exploited not just by poets when writing what might be thought of as otherwise "traditional" lyrics (e.g., ballads and songs), but by abolitionists and other politically oriented writers who wished to create empathy for their subjects. Dickinson's handling of this genre in Fascicle 16 lacks such a political edge, but it does not lack the drive to create empathy itself. This is why the presence of these poems in Fascicle 16 gives this fascicle such stunning importance. These poems suggest a kinder, gentler Dickinson, one who was clearly engaged in the travails of others. Indeed, "'Twas just this time, last year, I died" ranks in my mind as one of the finest sentimental poems of that very sentimental century. It is a quintessential example of what sentimentality at its best could achieve. But in turning to the dramatic lyric at all, Dickinson was recognizing and acknowledging in her verse differences and possibilities among others—not just in herself. That is what I have endeavored to demonstrate here by pairing her poems, showing in the process how very different from "Dickinson" many of her speakers are and greatly extending thereby and hopefully complicating what we take to be the scope of her verse, and the nature of its concerns.[36]

# Civil War(s) and Dickinson Manuscript Book Reconstructions, Deconstructed

## Martha Nell Smith

> ... Mr. Leyda pointed to what is almost certainly a packet of poems copied in the late seventies in identical handwriting and on identical stationery that the Harvard *Poems* broke up and dispersed over a period of *six years!* The integrity of this packet is of serious biographical importance.
>
> —Rebecca Patterson, "Author's Preface," *Emily Dickinson's Imagery* xvi

> A strange scene takes place in the middle of 1891, when the biographical project [Mabel Loomis Todd's 1894 edition of Emily Dickinson's letters] has barely begun. Mabel, with Austin's collusion, begins to tamper with the overwhelming evidence of Emily's bond with Susan. A booklet containing "One Sister have I in the house / And one a hedge away" is taken apart so as to remove the poem. Emily's sewing holes are cut to disguise the poem's place in the booklet, but though the page is thus mutilated, and torn in two places, it's not destroyed for the sake of another poem on the verso. Using black ink the mutilator scores out all the lines and, most heavily, the climax "Sue – forevermore!"
>
> —Lyndall Gordon, *Lives Like Loaded Guns* 267

In the world of her writerly practice, what constituted a book of or by Emily Dickinson? Did she call or think of the binding together of texts into what we now call fascicles "bookmaking"? In our world of readerly-writerly practice, what constitutes a book of or by her? Most concur that a book of poems or letters by Emily Dickinson published by Harvard University Press is the most "authoritative." When *The Manuscript Books of Emily Dickinson* was published in 1981, the always intriguing handmade books, forty or more separate bundles of more than eight hundred poems (nearly half of what constituted her "letter" to posterity) found among her life's "detritus"—each consisting of several stationer's sheets "in folio," or folded once to make two leaves, four pages, stacked on top of one another (not interleaved), and then bound with string, threaded through two holes near the top and bottom of the left side of the versos, as one might expect for binding a notebook—gained a firmer hold on scholarly attention and on readers' imaginations. Until then, professional scholars such as Ruth Miller and Jay Leyda had certainly examined them closely, with Miller arguing for their artistic integrity. Also, scholars such as Martha Lindblom O'Keefe had privately published a lengthy study of these gatherings of Dickinson poems coterie-style, in handmade books distributed to interested readers and friends. These critics' patterns of reading were not bound by the choreographies of the Mabel Loomis Todd, Thomas Wentworth Higginson, Martha Dickinson Bianchi, Alfred Leete Hampson, Millicent Todd Bingham, and Thomas H. Johnson editions, all of which neatly separated poems from their prose contexts, and from the contexts of the handmade books, though Bianchi comes closest to retaining contexts of the orders and disorders left by Dickinson.

## Questions of Genre and Editing

Mindfulness of the handling of all of Dickinson's documents is central to the focus of this essay. My assertion that Bianchi did a better job of maintaining Dickinson's orders and disorders may seem at odds with Franklin, who in *The Editing of Emily Dickinson* claimed that the packets at Harvard, "numbered 1-40, were returned to Lavinia and thereafter were in the possession of Susan Dickinson, her daughter Martha Dickinson Bianchi, and finally Mrs. Bianchi's friend Alfred Leete Hampson. These manuscripts have been shuffled, cut up, and generally dealt with roughly. The others, numbered 80-95, along with many loose poems, remained with Mrs. Todd and passed afterwards into the possession of her daughter, Millicent Todd Bingham, who gave them to Amherst College. These packets are in good order. They have not been mutilated, and, significantly, the notebook does not indicate that any poems are missing from them" (34). Yet packet 80 was clearly mutilated when Franklin made that declaration. After more time with the documents, Franklin became increasingly aware that Todd not only mutilated manuscripts but did so with even more documents than he originally thought: "given all this, one may now reasonably identify Mrs.

Todd, rather than Lavinia or Austin Dickinson, as the person who mutilated packet 80 and, perhaps, erased the verso of 80-7" ("Emily Dickinson's Packet 27 [and 80, 14, 6]" 347).

As these anecdotes about editorial work make plain, in order to introduce Dickinson's work through the medium of print, all of her writings were resituated and reorganized from the conditions in which they were left at her death. As it did for William Blake, mass reproduction created a much wider audience for Dickinson's texts than they otherwise would have enjoyed, yet translating them into impersonal print stripped her productions of their idiosyncrasies and of the place made for each by her ordering of texts in the books she constructed and bound by thread or by a particular audience to which she sent part of her "letter to the World." All editors have tampered with her orders, including Johnson and Franklin, and, for that matter, myself. An editor of Dickinson's work cannot help but do so. This essay reflects on that fact and begins to explore the possibilities opening up to us when we recognize that all reassemblies demonstrate the *archives of our attentions* and that great reading pleasures and tremendous insights are available to those with varying methods and organizations of critical inquiry; we each in effect make our own fascicles for reading. Also crucial to keep in mind is that to see one method of organization, including precise scholarly reconstructions, as "definitive" limits readerly imaginations and interpretations unnecessarily.

Reviewing a bit of the history of the transmission and disassembly of the fascicles and the general history of the transmission of all her writings is important in order to set the stage for the critical considerations at hand. Eager to arrange her poems thematically, early editor Todd removed the strings from the fascicles and began arranging the poems according to the conventional categories invented for poetry volumes, ones which her co-editor Higginson and most readers expected—"Life," "Love," "Nature," "Time and Eternity." Producing his variorum in the heyday of New Criticism, which defined poems as closed objects, akin to a Grecian Urn, Johnson made texts for *The Poems of Emily Dickinson* that were shaped by those conditions. Consequently, he tore rhythmic lines from letters to make poems from prose, to make a lyric where Dickinson may or may not have seen one. A clear example of this editorial practice is that from an October, 17, 1851 letter to her brother Austin (L58): Johnson took the following lines and represented them as a discrete poem:

There is another sky,
Ever serene and fair,

And there is another sunshine,
Though it be darkness there;
Never mind faded forests, Austin,
Never mind silent fields –
*Here* is a little forest,
Whose leaf is ever green;
Here is a brighter garden,
Where not a frost has been;
In its unfading flowers
I hear the bright bee hum;
Prithee, my brother,
Into *my* garden come! (J2)

Working within different conditions from those of Johnson, specifically those of establishing even more "authoritative" versions of Dickinson's poems, Franklin, as a point of "correction," does not treat these lines as a separate poem, saying they are epistolary rather than poetic.

By contrast, for reasons not made clear by the editorial note, Franklin, as did William H. Shurr, accepts Johnson's (not Dickinson's, which my quotation follows) lineation in *The Letters of Emily Dickinson,* and separates as a letter "Morning / might come / by Accident, / Sister – / Night comes / by Event – / To believe the / final line of / the Card would / foreclose Faith – / Faith is *Doubt* – / Sister." Franklin says the lines immediately following—from those beginning "Show me / Eternity, and /"—conclude what he has designated as a letter to Susan Dickinson, and he calls the rest of the letter-poem a poem (Fr1658). Yet nothing in her manuscript indicates that there are two different genres on Dickinson's handwritten pages (see Smith and Vetter and #5, "Frequently Asked Questions," *Emily Dickinson Archive* for a view of the manuscript; see Hart and Smith 246 for a print translation of the letter-poem). So both Johnson and Franklin not only divorced poems from letters in which they were enclosed but also extracted poems from epistolary documents. By doing so, they establish separate genre distinctions when the differences are not so clear, in Johnson's case to make editions of *Poems* and then *Letters,* and in Franklin's case to stabilize what is recognized as a Dickinson poem. Johnson's editions assume discrete genres and showcase both letters and poems as isolated units, each numbered as if they are specimens for scientific study. Though he traced many poems to their original placement in Dickinson's handmade books, Johnson used speculative chronology as his organizing principle instead of trying to reinstate Dickinson's groupings.

What dismembering Dickinson's organizational units has cost can never be fully measured, and the fact remains that her poems, letters, and letter-poems remain torn out of their contexts. Even Franklin's meticulous reassembly of the manuscript books is a product of informed guesswork, as are his claims for the "Sets." Similarly, chronological ordering, which appears scientific, is also unreliable. Although trends in her script can be identified, from the ligated early cursive to the near-print nonligated script of her later years, in most cases Dickinson's handwriting cannot be assigned to a particular date but rather to a date range. Also, the most common fallacy found in Dickinson criticism is that when a manuscript can be dated, critics assume that is also the date of a writing's composition. All we can know is that a reliably dated manuscript conveys information about the date of copying, not of composition.

Similarly, what we can know about Franklin's two-volume *The Manuscript Books of Emily Dickinson* is that they are his conjecture of how those volumes were bound together and left at Dickinson's death. Whether his reassemblies always constitute her orders is a matter open to question. Nevertheless, when the volumes were published in 1981, her gatherings called "fascicles" or "fascicules" by Dickinson's first posthumous editors, and the implications of their organization for our interpretations, became more than an area of special interest for a few of Dickinson's readers. Among other definitions, "fascicle" connotes, as Eleanor Heginbotham points out, "a bunch, a bundle, a cluster of leaves or flowers, a tuft, a bunch of roots growing from one point" (Dickinson's own "leaves of grass," *Reading the Fascicles* 8). Sharon Cameron observes that reading the poems in the fascicles is to read them in the *contextual* sense rather than the *canonical* sense of Dickinson and that such reading "radically" reveals "a question about what constitutes the identity of the [Dickinson] poem" (*Choosing Not Choosing* 4). In *Dickinson Unbound: Paper, Process, Poetics,* Alexandra Socarides "takes up the question of how Emily Dickinson made her poems, the significance of the materials she used when doing this, and the interpretive possibilities and problems that attention to the details of poetic practice raises for this remarkable writer's work" (3). Socarides argues that Dickinson's compositional unit was the sheet folded to make these books. Visual artist Jen Bervin, who transposes Dickinson's arrangements of "+" and "x" and what we call the "dash" to produce 8' × 6' wall hangings, or quilts, notes that "By imposing conventional views of literary authorship (as expressed by book publication) and divorcing her poems from their formal integrity and its intended specificity, the implications of an unusual, complex, pervasive system are harder to understand." As do Heginbotham, Cameron, Socarides, and the contributors to his volume, and as did Leyda, Miller, and O'Keefe, Bervin examines Dickinson's fascicles to learn more about her compositional techniques.

According to Franklin, these books were not compositional, nor were they arranged and finished with a particular theme in mind (of questions of faith or secret abortive love, as has been argued): his view is that the volumes were storage units, a private record of her writings. As did Johnson for the individual poems, Franklin numbered the individual manuscript books, imparting an aura of science and so bolstering his authoritative claims. Franklin also examines pinholes, paper stains, clip impressions, and other material facts to make his case for his reassembly by attempting to recapture what was found among Dickinson's papers. All of this is laudable and created opportunities for profound advancements in the study of Dickinson and her work, as is obvious from the many provocative and generative studies of and artistic engagements with her manuscript books. What sometimes gets lost in all of these critical and creative responses is that Franklin's valuable work is the enactment of his hypotheses, not an absolute reenactment of Dickinson's orders. In Dickinson's terms, his textual world is not, then, conclusion.

## Fascicle 24 and the Civil War

Fascicle 24, the object of critical inquiry that stimulated this essay, is a wonderful witness to what might be called the "Franklin-Dickinson Books" assembled for *The Manuscript Books of Emily Dickinson:* its missing (torn away) leaves, as well as leaves with folds indicating their placement elsewhere (such as in an envelope for mailing), at least for a time, serve as poignant reminders that the manuscript books she left behind have been pawed over many times since they were last touched by Emily Dickinson. Manuscript Book 24 is also a telling example of a gathering of poems with highly suggestive resonances. Though a fair number of them clearly do belong there, it is an open question whether the documents collected as Fascicle 24 actually belong together, having been arranged and left that way for posterity by Dickinson herself. For this critical musing, occasioned by a volume of essays by scholars turning their attentions to various aspects generated by the very fact of Dickinson manuscript books left to posterity and disassembled and reassembled by various editors, I will not settle that profound question—"Are all of the books reassembled 'correctly,' with poems placed as the poet deposited them?"—but will instead use our uncertainties about their assemblies and present Franklin-choreographed order to analyze ways in which the fascicles might be taught and read as a whole.

Important to keep in mind is that whatever a writer's, reader's, or editor's intentions, all arrangements tell stories beyond those intentions. As Patterson contends in this essay's first epigraph, "The integrity of" each of the manuscript books "is of serious biographical importance." Though I am wary of Patterson's interpreting the poems biographically and literally, her observation captures a fact of our reading—the manuscript orders do tell life stories about human conditions. Also, her interpretive practice is in keeping with the other Dickinson biographers who were her near-contemporaries (Genevieve Taggard, Josephine Pollitt, George Whicher) and even with later biographers (Richard Sewall, Cynthia Griffin Wolff, Lyndall Gordon). Patterson's keen insight might be most usefully amended to say that the integrity of the manuscript books is of serious *artistic* importance.

Analyzing the resonances among the poems now identified together as Fascicle 24, readers might observe that the fascicle begins with "It sifts from Leaden Sieves –" (Fr291), a poem about winter, and then cycles backwards through the seasons (winter followed by fall followed by summer). Two poems after "It sifts" is the fall poem, "Of Brussels – it was not – " (Fr510), and then several poems later "The Trees like Tassels – hit – / and swung" effuse over the "Far Psalteries of Summer –" (Fr523). Such a reversal of the seasons presented as an order for reading is provocative, suggesting that the natural order of things, or worldly experience, has been reversed. Also arresting in this gathering of poems is that many of them are about something being overwhelmed: the first features the landscape being overwhelmed by snow, of course, and then is followed by "Like Mighty Foot Lights – burned / the Red" (Fr507), a description of a sunset so spectacular that the viewer cannot take it in but only imagines that the universe might, just might, be able to appreciate and applaud its splendors even though no pair of eyes can fully see them. After two removed poems that Franklin asserts are "A Pit – but Heaven over it –" (Fr508) and "A curious Cloud surprised the Sky" (Fr509) is "Of Brussels – it was not –" a poem about a shedding of leaves in autumn so intense that the covering of the forest floor is compared to tightly woven "Kidderminster" rugs.

Along with these images from nature that attest to its ferocity and power, Dickinson has permeated the fascicle with symbols and images that suggest the Civil War. That "curious Cloud" "'twas like a sheet with Horns; / The sheet was Blue – / The Antlers Gray – / It almost touched the Lawns." Once a reader's imagination notices that blue and gray are remarked as the colors of the overwhelming cloud, and that this poem is situated near "When I was small, a / Woman died – / Today – her Only Boy / Went up from the Potomac – / His face all Victory" (Fr518), a poem often read as a response to the horrifyingly bloody and devastating Antietam, or "Tender [Scarlet] Maryland," this collection reverberates with responses to the overpowering, devastating, and deadly national strife. Even outside of this manuscript book context, a credible interpretation of "It always felt to me – a / wrong / To that Old Moses – done –" (Fr521), a poem sympathizing with the Old Testament figure banished from the Promised Land merely for smashing his staff against a rock rather than speaking to it in order to bring forth water for the tired, hungry, thirsty Israelites, is that Dickinson's poet's eye makes visible and more palpable the plight of the disfranchised in her United States—most obviously slaves, but also women. The conditions of each were such that, like Moses, they could look at but not really possess the rich bounty of their own labors. So when Dickinson's poem cries "My justice bleeds – for thee!" the reference may be for those who in mid-nineteenth-century America could not take advantage of the liberty enjoyed by white male property owners. Surrounded by news of battles, the horrors of which defy imagination, of fellow citizens' deaths, and of escaped and recaptured slaves, any writer of Dickinson's time and circumstance inscribing "It feels a shame to be / Alive – / When Men so brave – are dead –" (Fr524) was surely thinking about the Civil War.

All of these may well point to a fascicle or manuscript book that is thematically focused on the cataclysmic national event that Dickinson and her contemporaries read about on every hand, in every journal and newspaper: the War Between the States. Though scholars such as Shira Wolosky, Eliza Richards, Reneé Bergland, Faith Barrett, Cristanne Miller, myself previously, and, in this volume, Paula Bennett, have all made credible arguments about Dickinson's attentions to the Civil War, an underappreciated fact about the Dickinson family's entanglement with the rage of domestic warfare also remains. As was true of many families, the Dickinson clan was something of a house divided against itself. When her grandfather Samuel Fowler Dickinson went bankrupt and moved to Ohio, his sons dispersed, and Samuel Fowler Dickinson, Jr., decamped to the South, eventually settling in Bibb County, Georgia, in the heart of what was known as the "plantation belt." His son Loren, Dickinson's first cousin, enlisted on April 20, 1861 (eight days after Ft. Sumter), and served in the Georgia Second Independent Infantry Battalion, Company C, locally known as the "Floyd Rifles." On January 15, 1862, he was discharged because he had been shot and "the bullet remained in his back near his spinal column," making him "a cripple unfit for duty for months to come." Loren Dickinson never renounced the Southern cause and by the end of 1862 was applying for a clerkship in the Confederacy. An unpublished family memoir called him "the sort of Southerner who thought 'Damned Yankee' was one word" (Smith, "The Civil War, Class, and the Dickinsons' Confederate Relations"). In 1909 Loren Dickinson died a disillusioned man who drank to soften the long-nursed blow of defeat.

That Fascicle 24 is as damaged a body as was Loren Dickinson's, and in a sense mirrors the rift in the extended family, having had leaves cut out, and showing obvious rearrangements, points to yet another important fact to keep in mind while contemplating the fascicles, their import, and their legacies: audience is absolutely crucial to making any text. Without an audience (including the writer herself as first reader), no text lives. The fascicles themselves, and our readings of them, are powerful reminders that readers, including editors, write their own stories on top of and for a writer's remnants. In that sense, the manuscript books are iconic and function as do figural icons such as Dickinson herself—stories of their lives and texts are perpetually being overwritten and erased, and those stories are simultaneously powerfully compelling and "powerfully contested." In "Dickinson Manuscripts in the Undergraduate Classroom," Annette Debo incisively explains the problems with Fascicle 24: how there "are no existing holographs" for two of its poems; how their placement in this fascicle is Franklin's informed supposition; and how "two other poems are split within the fascicle," are, in other words, "physically severed within" it so that "scholars have theorized that the discrete pieces make up the two separate, and complete, poems" (139). Doing so, Debo underscores how unstable are Dickinson's texts, how "fluid and alive" those instabilities are as they demand creative acts on the part of readers, and how instrumental editors and readers have been and continue to be in making "poems of Emily Dickinson," however authoritatively edited the versions encountered may be. Keeping these facts in mind is crucial for responsible interpretation.

## Questions of Editing Fascicles 2 and 19

Another mutilated grouping, Fascicle 2, underscores the importance of awareness of such problems. The marks, perhaps made by Mabel Loomis Todd and then by Jay Leyda, on the documents now gathered into that fascicle suggest that those poems were placed and left in a different order by Dickinson and that one poem now removed to a different manuscript book by Franklin was originally part of this sequence, which includes an inked-over, mutilated version of "One Sister have I in the house" (Fr5). Franklin believes that Todd labeled these manuscripts in blue pencil with the number "80" on the first poem that appears in this book, "There is a word / which bears a sword" (Fr42); Leyda had numbered all of the poems included in this gathering with a dash and a number marking the different folios; he has added "-1" to Todd's number: Yet the documents now gathered into Fascicle 2 are ordered differently from the order in which Leyda found them, and 80-7 has been moved into a different Franklin-Dickinson construction. "The Face I carry with / me – last –" (Fr395), numbered by Leyda "80-7" was apparently originally situated in the collection just before the manuscript labeled "80-8." "80-8a" was particularly offensive to Todd, as is "One Sister have I in the house" (Fr5), a loving poem about Susan Dickinson, whom Todd loathed. As Lyndall Gordon notes in one of the epigraphs to this essay, one word in the last line, "Sue – forevermore!" is notably, and much more forcefully, inked over than all the other words, and on a manuscript that features already dramatic blottings out.

Why Franklin rearranged poems that clearly were gathered side-by-side at some point and then moved one so far apart from the others ("The Face I carry" [Fr395] is now in Fascicle 19) can only partially be explained by the fact that it was copied out at a considerably (several years) later time than the other poems in what is now Fascicle 2. But even a casual reader of the fascicles knows that Dickinson herself arranged poems copied out at different times into the same gathering. In Fascicle 14, "The feet of people walking home" (Fr16, *Manuscript Books* 293–94) is in handwriting noticeably different from everything else in that book. One might argue that to include "The Face I carry with" in its place in the Leyda order leaves a blank page in the middle of the manuscript book and that surely Dickinson did not prefer, did not intend, to do that. But there are more than a few instances in which a manuscript book features a blank page in the middle of the gathering—the books numbered 11, 16, 18, 19, 21, 24, and 28 all feature such blank pages. What all of these details make clear is that for Dickinson herself, the orderings of at least some, if not all, of the manuscript books was provisional, and that readers should be mindful of that when interpreting the groupings.

Most important for this analysis, then, is not determining Franklin's specific motive in declaring that "The face I carry with" does not belong near "One Sister have I in the house"; it is, rather, in using these examples to theorize about the importance of audience in constructing meaning. The

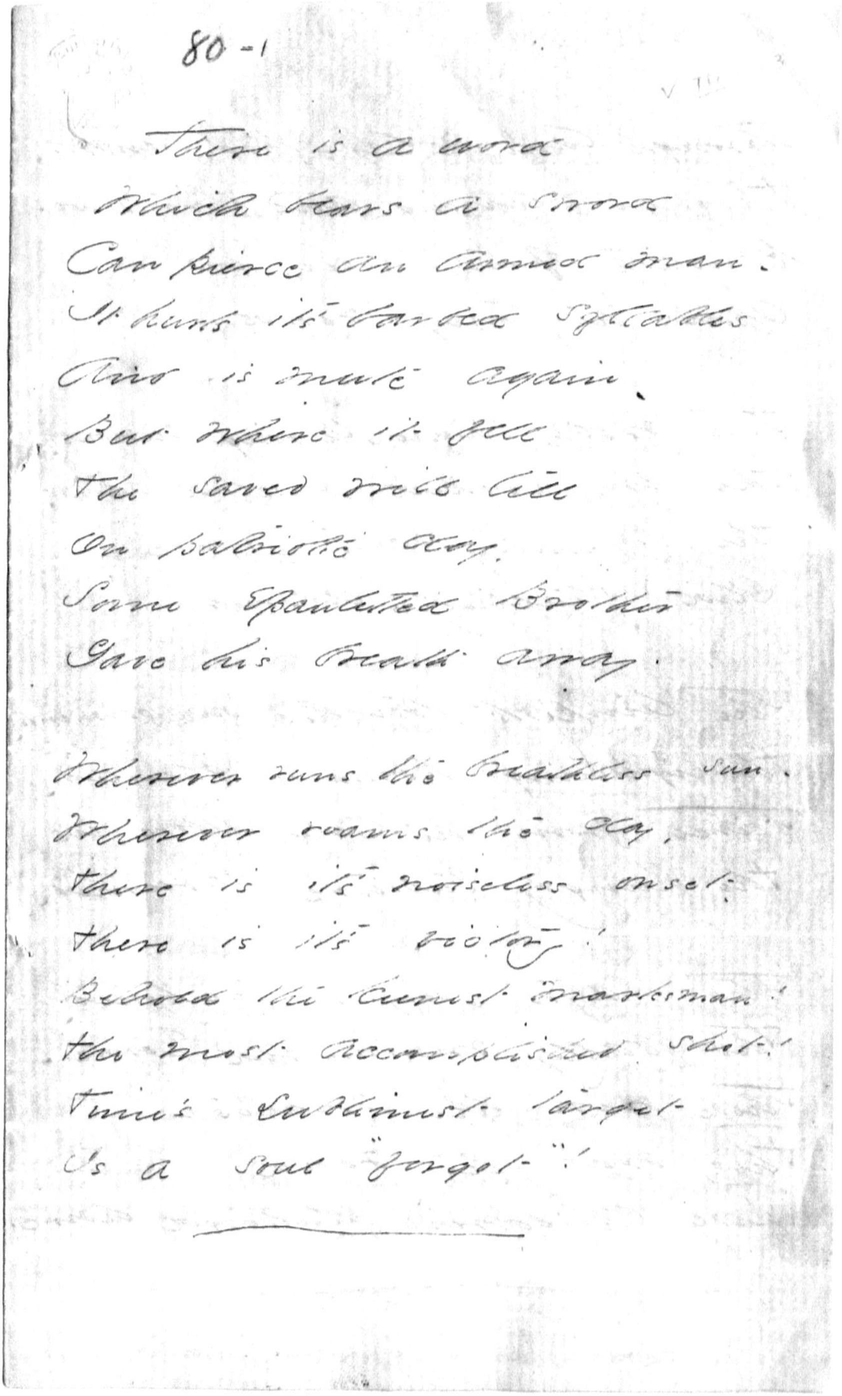

80-1

There is a word
Which bears a sword
Can pierce an armed man.
It hurls it's barbed syllables
And is mute again.
But where it fell
The saved will tell
On patriotic day.
Some epauletted Brother
Gave his breath away.

Wherever runs the breathless sun —
Wherever roams the day,
there is it's noiseless onset —
there is it's victory!
Behold the keenest marksman!
the most accomplished shot!
Time's sublimest target
Is a soul "forgot"!

*Figure 7.* Fascicle 2 (80-1), "There is a word."

*Figure 8.* Fascicle 2 (80-9), part of inked-out "One Sister have I in the house."

informed reader will recognize the provisionality of some assemblies and groupings, some of them arbitrary, some the result of informed speculation. Sometimes, in fact, groupings are as much dictated by readerly interests as are the more formal groupings made for Belknap Press. The fascicles challenge us with issues of representation, intentionalities (writerly, readerly, authorial), storytelling, and reception. We can only be nostalgic since we can never be certain that Dickinson's own orders have been restored.

As we have seen, Franklin moved from declaring that the manuscripts transmitted from Susan Dickinson to Martha Dickinson Bianchi were handled more roughly than those preserved by Mabel Loomis Todd and Millicent Todd Bingham to acknowledging that each of those handlings resulted in some damage, and that the handling of the sequence Leyda numbered 80 was assertively rough. In 1981 Franklin rearranged the sequence of the 80 group so that the poems were ordered thus:

80-1   There is a word
       Through lane it lay – thro' bramble -
80-2   The Guest is gold and crimson –
       I counted till they danced so
       Before the ice is in the pools –
       By such and such an offering

| 80-3 | It did not surprise me –
|      | When I count the seeds
| 80-8 | Bless God, he went as soldiers,
|      | If I should cease to bring a Rose
|      | One Sister have I in the house –
| 80-9 | (completion of "One Sister")
|      | "Lethe" in my flower,
|      | To venerate the simple days
|      | I've got an arrow here.
| 80-4 | I robbed the Woods –
|      | A Day! Help! Help! Another Day!
|      | Could live – *did* live –
|      | If she had been the Mistletoe
| 80-5 | My wheel is in the dark!
|      | There's something quieter than sleep
| 80-6 | I keep my pledge.
|      | Heart! We will forget him!
|      | Once more, my now bewildered Dove
|      | Baffled for just a day or two

In this sequence, 80-7 ("The face I carry with me – last –" [Fr395]) has been removed by Franklin and placed after folio H 147 at the end of the manuscript book he numbered Fascicle 19. His reasoning for doing this appears to show that at least at some point in time, "The face I carry with" was affiliated with the poems gathered into Fascicle 19. Earlier Franklin had surmised,

> It should be noted that the stationery of 80-7 does not match the other sheets in packet 80 and that the date assigned to it by the variorum is four years later than the rest of the packet. This sheet has only one poem on it ("The face I carry with me – last" [V 336]) and has been folded in thirds and addressed to someone whose name has been erased. Thus, binding the poem into packet 80 was clearly not Emily Dickinson's first intention for it. But the poem was there when Mrs. Todd indexed the manuscript in midsummer 1891, and it was there when she copied the packet in 1889. (*Editing* 72)

What Franklin suggests, then, is that Todd had moved the poem into manuscript sequence 80. What his conclusions do not take into account is the possibility that Dickinson moved the poem herself. Whether its "final" resting place as far as she was concerned was in the severely mutilated manuscript sequence in which Leyda found it or the place Franklin finally assigns can never be definitively answered. In 1967 he certainly did not think that "The face I carry with" belonged in the book he would number 19, and he in fact proposes a very different order and constitution for what would become that book in "Manuscript Order and Disorder" (*Editing* 56).

So what is important for our readerly and scholarly purposes? Does noting the provisionalities, the changing of mind by one editor, invalidate the assemblies he has made in *The Manuscript Books of Emily Dickinson*? No. But what should be taken into account and remembered is that those gatherings are the archives of Franklin's attentions and that our interpretations of those, whether we leave his orders intact or rearrange them, reflect the archives of our attentions, and all of our attentions are valid. The manuscript book that might be made of the writings we have been discussing if we restore the order in which they were found would be:

| | |
|---|---|
| 80-1 | There is a word |
| | Through lane it lay – thro' bramble – |
| 80-2 | The Guest is gold and crimson – |
| | I counted till they danced so |
| | Before the ice is in the pools – |
| | By such and such an offering |
| 80-3 | It did not surprise me – |
| | When I count the seeds |
| 80-4 | I robbed the Woods – |
| | A Day! Help! Help! Another Day! |
| | Could live – *did* live – |
| | If she had been the Mistletoe |
| 80-5 | My wheel is in the dark! |
| | There's something quieter than sleep |
| 80-6 | I keep my pledge. |
| | Heart! We will forget him! |
| | Once more, my now bewildered Dove |
| | Baffled for just a day or two – |
| 80-7 | The face I carry with |
| | (Verso of "The face I carry with" with "Sue" erased [*Open Me* 64]) |
| 80-8 | Bless God, he went as soldiers, |
| | If I should cease to bring a Rose |
| | One Sister have I in the house – |
| 80-9 | (completion of "One Sister") |
| | "Lethe" in my flower, |
| | To venerate the simple days |

144   *Chapter 6*

This arrangement emphasizes associations among the poems mutilated to remove traces of Susan's intimacies with Emily—"One Sister have I in the house" and "The Face I carry with / me – last." The first poem is about Susan and Emily's intense affections for her, and the second poem, most obviously read as one of a lover to her beloved, was addressed to Susan. Thus the book made from the sequence Leyda found and numbered 80 ends:

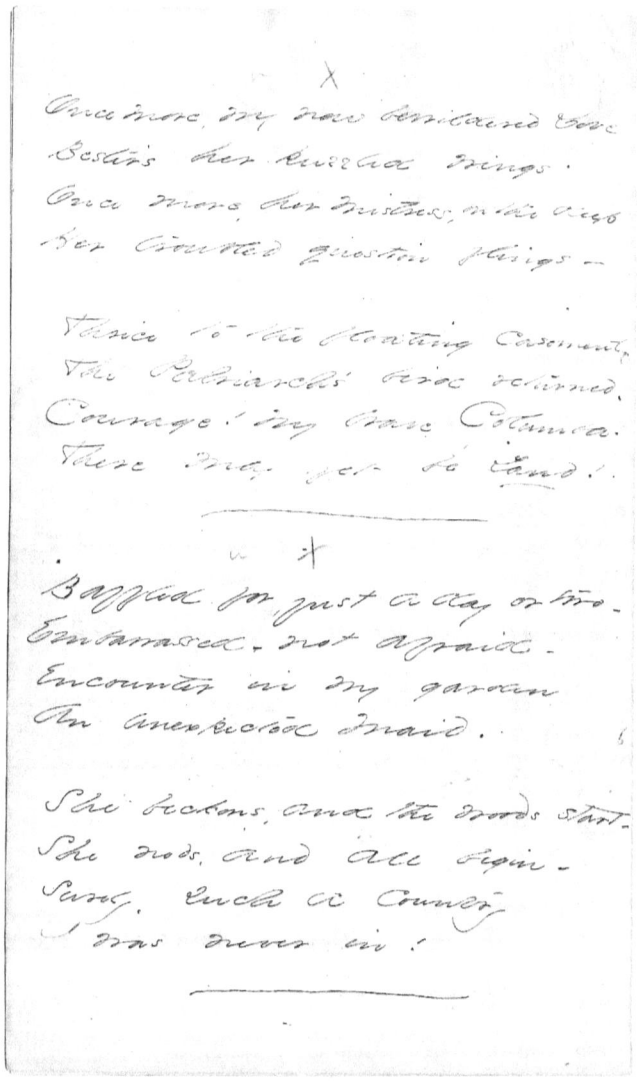

*Figure 9.* Fascicle 2 (80-6 verso, reduced; facing 80-7), "Once more my now bewildered Dove."

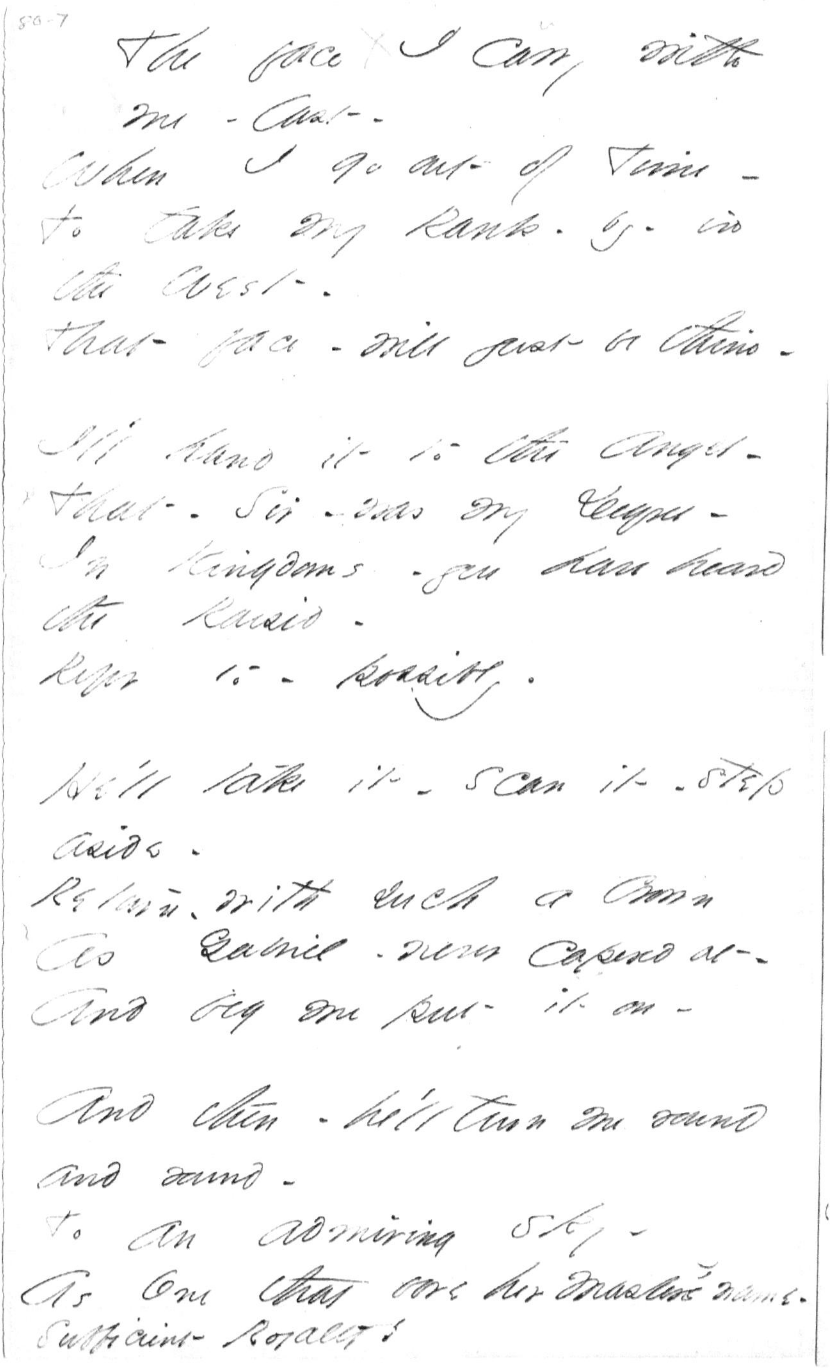

80-7

The Face I carry with
me – last –
When I go out of Time –
To take my Rank – by – in
the West –
That face – will just be thine –

I'll hand it to the Angel –
That – Sir – was my Degree –
In Kingdoms – you have heard
the Raised –
Report to – Majesty –

He'll take it – Scan it – step
aside –
Return with such a Crown
As Gabriel – never capered at –
And beg me put it on –

And then – he'll turn me round
and round –
To an admiring sky –
As One that bore her Master's name –
Sufficient Royalty!

*Figure 10.* Fascicle 19 (80-7 recto), "The Face I carry with / me – last –"

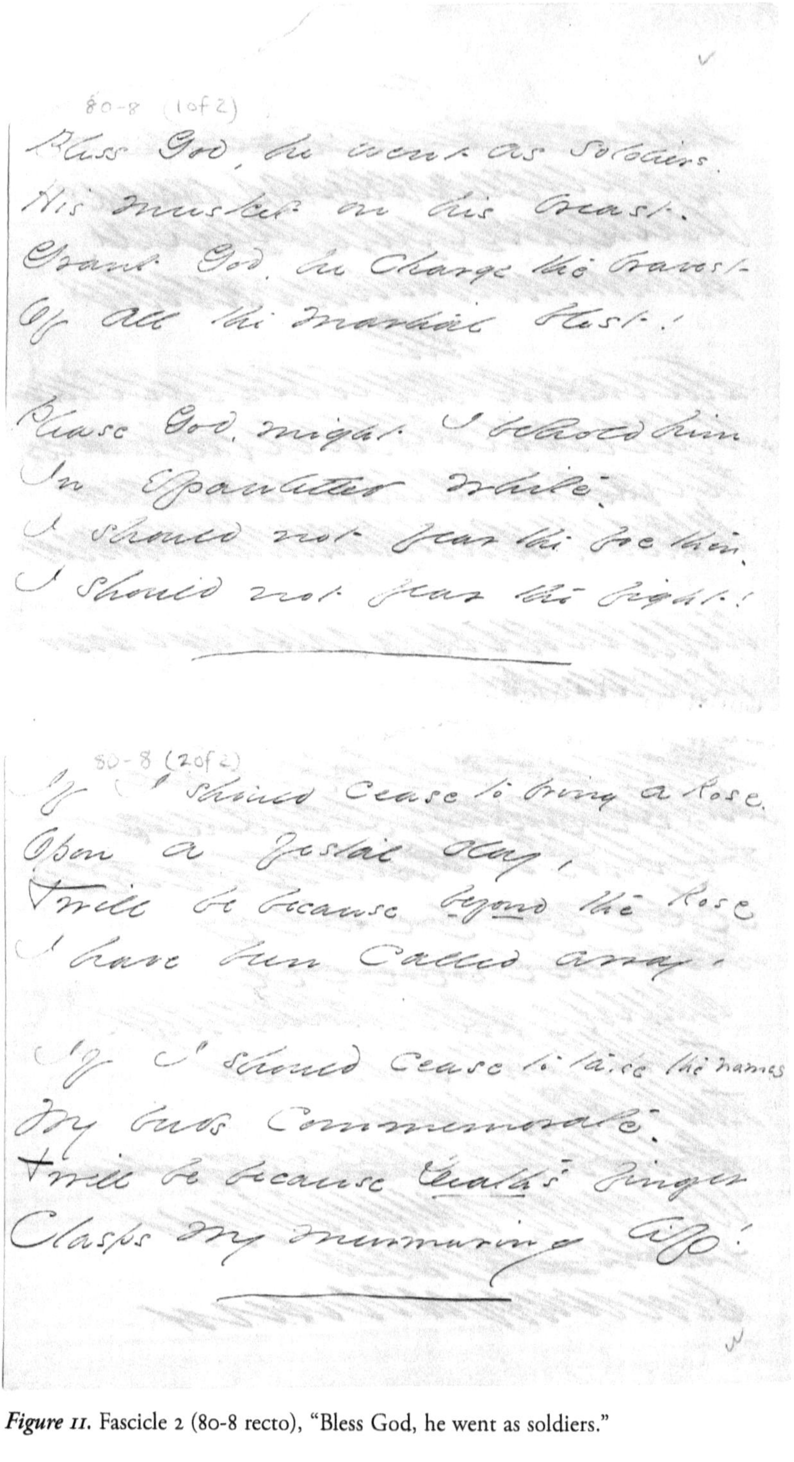

80-8 (1 of 2)

Bless God, he went as soldiers.
His musket on his breast –
Grant God, he charge the bravest
Of all the martial Host –!

Please God, might I behold him
In "Epauletted" while –
I should not fear the foe then –
I should not fear the fight –!

———

80-8 (2 of 2)

If I should cease to bring a Rose
Upon a festal day,
'Twill be because beyond the Rose
I have been called away –

If I should cease to take the names
My buds Commemorate –
'Twill be because Death's finger
Clasps my murmuring lip –!

———

*Figure 11.* Fascicle 2 (80-8 recto), "Bless God, he went as soldiers."

*Figure 12.* Fascicle 2 (80-8a), inked-over manuscripts.

This last poem of Dickinson's, finished in the 80 sequence with a transcription by Todd necessitated by her mutilations, offers the best advice for reading the sequences of writings by Emily Dickinson:

> To invest existence with a stately air
> Needs but to remember
> That the Acorn there
> Is the Elf of forests
> For the upper Air! (Fr55)

In other words, readers need not invest the orders we now have available of Dickinson's manuscripts as immutably final. While they have been created with rigor, that rigor must ever be flexible, as it is but an "Elf" compared to what might yet be realized. To "dwell in Possibility" is to own the archives of our and other readers' attentions.

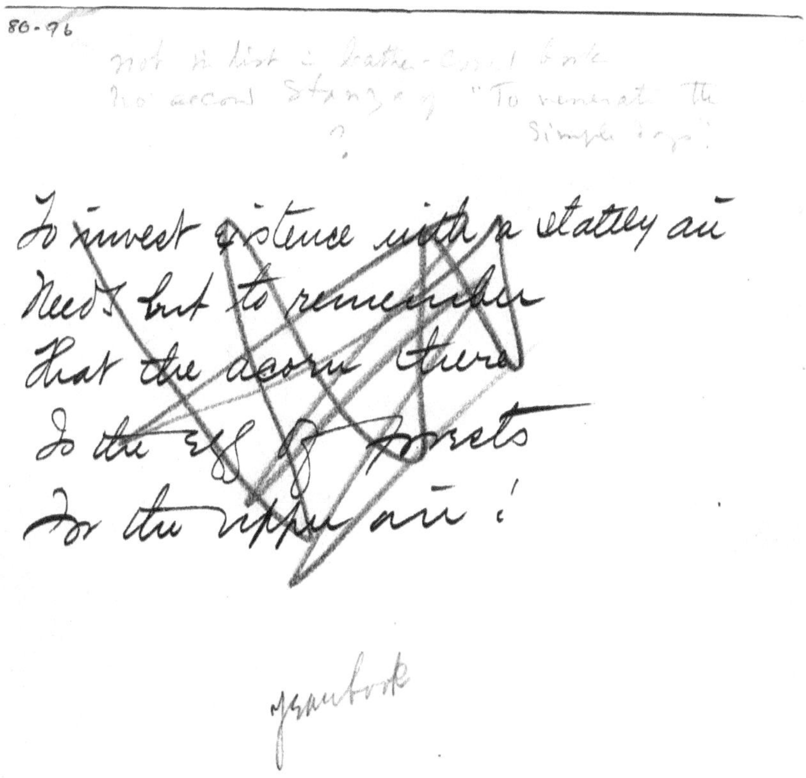

80-96

> not a list : rather-could look
> no second Stanza of "To venerate the
>                                    Simple days."

To invest existence with a stately air
Needs but to remember
That the acorn there
Is the egg of forests
For the upper air !

*Figure 13.* Fascicle 2, canceled out with pencil, transcription by Todd of second stanza of "To venerate the simple days."

# Managing Multiple Contexts
Dickinson, Genre, and the Circulation of Fascicle 1

ALEXANDRA SOCARIDES

It is impossible to write about Fascicle 1 without writing about beginnings. Even though Dickinson did not number the fascicles herself, it seems clear from the research conducted by R. W. Franklin when editing *The Manuscript Books of Emily Dickinson* and *The Poems of Emily Dickinson: Variorum Edition,* that this was, indeed, the first fascicle that she made.[1] There is the suggestion of beginnings all over the place: It includes a copy of one of Dickinson's earliest surviving poems, which she had sent to her sister-in-law, Susan Huntington Dickinson, in 1853; it contains a copy of, as far as we know, the second of Dickinson's poems to appear in print; and it employs a strategy for indicating the end of one poem and the beginning of the next that Dickinson initially used but soon discarded. Additionally, the paper that she used to make this fascicle does not appear in any other fascicle. All of this might lead us to treat Fascicle 1 as exceptional—as a first attempt or testing ground for what would later become a methodically executed practice for copying, sewing, and keeping her poems. Since we now know that Dickinson would go on to make thirty-nine more of these over the course of the next six years, it is practically impossible *not* to treat this fascicle as the extraordinary beginning of what would eventually become one of the most famous poetic projects undertaken by an American poet.[2] Yet this is precisely what this essay will aim to do.

I believe that there is a certain fascination with and emphasis placed on Dickinson's act of beginning her fascicle project because it allows the critic to designate the fascicle poems as those that demand of their readers a different kind of analysis. Because there is a moment at which Dickinson began this project and a moment at which she ended it, we are able to set this period of her writing apart and, by delimiting the scope of our analysis, take control of at least one stage of this prolific writer's oeuvre. Doing so has allowed critics to locate the controlling themes, tropes, and speakers of the fascicle poems as well as produce new readings of these poems in the context of the poems that surround them in the fascicle. This last intervention has been particularly popular, as it generates often-clarifying interpretations of poems whose meanings have previously eluded readers.[3] This occurs in relation to Fascicle 1 when, for example, Dorothy Huff Oberhaus writes that we might read the first poem as a "mock-elegy for summer" in a fascicle that indicates that "the poem's central focus is the protagonist's own vow to die" (58). In the end, not only are new readings of poems produced, but critics sometimes go on to suggest—and often quite differently—how we might characterize a whole fascicle, or the entire fascicle project, or both.[4]

While these approaches may give us new ways of thinking about the poems within the fascicles and a greater understanding of the identity of the fascicles themselves, this essay will suggest an alternative approach— one that draws us closer to the fascicles only by way of traveling away from them. Because the history of criticism on Dickinson's fascicles tells us that they are private, enclosed objects that Dickinson almost certainly did not share with her family, friends, and many correspondents, it may, at first, seem counterintuitive to think about all that existed just beyond their edges.[5] Yet I want to argue that Dickinson's actual writing practices invite such an approach, since many of the texts that she copied into the fascicles she also copied into a variety of different literal, material contexts. Instead of treating the fascicles as private sites that are divorced from the other material contexts in which Dickinson copied her poems, such an approach demands that we place a variety of diverse compositional methods in relation to each other. Doing so will allow us to see that Dickinson treated what she copied into the fascicles as mobile and flexible texts, whose ambitions, uses, and even genre could change when the opportunities presented themselves.

One of the arguments for why a consideration of the fascicles is essential to Dickinson scholarship is that, without them, we are reading individual poems that may not actually be individual poems at all. In other words, the physical context of the poems (where they were copied) matters because there may be something intertextual occurring within a fascicle that we don't have access to when we read the poems individually. But when the poems are read in their fascicle context, does our method of reading actually change? In other words, while we may be able to say more confidently what a given poem is "about," there seems to me little difference in our actual reading practice whether we are treating a poem singly or in the context of, say, twenty other poems. What we are reading are still poems; now there are simply more of them. One might say, then, that turning to the fascicle does not actually expand how we read Dickinson, but actually further entrenches the New Critical practice of divorcing poems from anything that appears or occurs outside of the poems themselves. The result, at its extreme, is that the fascicles serve as the context that actually closes down reading possibilities, precisely because they satisfy (and therefore secure) the approach that was used to read Dickinson long before we even knew there were fascicles to read.

In the face of this, I want to propose that we read the opposite of what is fixed and private. I want to read circulation. Unlike Dickinson's editors who, according to Virginia Jackson, "actively cultivated a disregard for the circumstances of Dickinson's manuscripts' circulation" (21), I want to draw attention to the texts that were copied into fascicles but that also found their way into, among other places, letters, envelopes, newspapers, and apron pockets. This is not simply about recording the fact that these texts travelled between spaces and were often read widely, although they certainly were. It is about the stakes of *not* reading this way, for, as Jackson has asserted, "by being taken out of their sociable circumstances, those manuscripts have become poems, and by becoming poems, they have been interpreted as lyrics" (21). How, then, might we read Dickinson differently when the concept of circulation is made central to our approach to the fascicles in particular?

A quick overview of the other contexts that Dickinson created for the texts of Fascicle 1 reveals that it is both impossible to regard these fascicle versions as in any way resolved or definitive and impossible to regard the fascicle itself as enclosed or private. As far as we know, at least eight of the twenty-two texts in Fascicle 1 were given some other material context besides that of the fascicle. I say "as far as we know" because any consideration of Dickinson's texts is haunted by the fact that there may have been manuscripts that were destroyed, lost, or withheld, leaving us with only part of the story.[6] At the very least, then, the poems that ended up in Fascicle 1 were also, at some point, pre-fascicle drafts written on small pieces of torn paper; texts retained in Dickinson's possession; texts copied into other fascicles; texts that ended up in print; texts that ended up in transcribed form; texts sent to Sue, Bowles, Higginson, the Norcross sisters, and several unidentified recipients; and texts that were embedded into Dickinson's letters. This is a far cry from the "enclosed textual space" with which we have come to mark the identity of fascicles (Werner 12).

Tracking Dickinson's fascicle poems through their other-than-fascicle contexts, with attention to the sometimes-minor and sometimes-major changes that she made to them, to the materials on which they were copied, and to the society of readers (sometimes intentional and sometimes not) that encountered them, makes urgent certain questions about genre that are otherwise obscured. For instance, if a piece of writing is presented as a poem in one context, then must the same words in the same order continue to be a poem once it has been placed in a different material context? How is the genre of a piece of writing affected when it is put to different uses at different historical moments? Can returning to a writer's manuscripts reveal something about the identity of a text that can't be recognized in the more accessible printed and edited versions? What difference, if any, does recontextualization (either by the writer or editor) make to the ambitions, status, and meaning of a text?

In order to address these questions, I am going to look closely at the circulation of several of the texts that Dickinson copied into Fascicle 1. I have not chosen the texts in Fascicle 1 at random, for their status as poems copied into this fascicle endows them, as we have seen above, with a sense of importance for having come first. Yet at the same time I want to make clear that these or similar questions can be asked about most of Dickinson's texts. While this is only one way to tell a story about the fascicles, my analysis aims to model a critical approach in which a focus on circulation leads to new ways of thinking about what Dickinson wrote. This is an approach that the fascicles themselves don't merely make possible, but that, as touchstones in a story of composition and circulation, they actually invite.

IN ORDER to think about the circulation of texts that we normally consider wholly uncirculated (and even uncirculatable), I want to begin with the actual poems that Dickinson sent to family and friends before she copied them into Fascicle 1. Dickinson did this with four of these poems: "On this wondrous sea" (Fr3), "Frequently the woods are pink –" (Fr24), "Nobody knows this little Rose –" (Fr11), and "Morns like these – we parted –" (Fr18). All four of these poems were sent to Sue (and the last was also sent to Louise and Frances Norcross), one as early as five years before Dickinson began making Fascicle 1. These poems were eventually copied on three of the four fascicle sheets that she would sew together, which indicates that Dickinson did not copy all precirculated poems together but instead dispersed them throughout a fascicle. Whether Dickinson was using her correspondence to test out a version of a poem before it was copied in the fascicle or was copying poems into the fascicles in order to keep a record of the poems that she was circulating, we do not know.

While knowledge of the fact that Dickinson circulated these four poems might lead us to deduce that the fascicles did not contain wholly private poems, the mass distribution of one of them really drives this point home. Dickinson may have only intended Sue to read "Nobody knows this little Rose –," but many more people than just Sue actually did. Printed on August 2, 1858, in the *Springfield Daily Republican,* this poem was titled "To Mrs.———, with a Rose. [Surreptitiously communicated to The Republican.]" and ran between a report of "Interesting Foreign Items" and the ever-eclectic column of "Special Notices," which included advertisements for everything from "Sir James Clarke's Female Pills" to the services of "Pomeroy & Ross, Undertakers." While Dickinson slightly altered the punctuation between the draft that she sent to Sue, the version that she copied onto the fascicle sheet later that summer, and the fair copy that she made two years later and retained, for the most part this poem stayed the same. Here is the fascicle version:

> Nobody knows this little Rose –
> It might a pilgrim be
> Did I not take it from the ways
> And lift it up to thee.
> Only a Bee will miss it –
> Only a Butterfly,
> Hastening from far journey –
> On it's breast to lie –
> Only a Bird will wonder –
> Only a Breeze will sigh –
> Ah Little Rose – how easy
> For such as thee to die!

If we take the title supplied by the editor as a record of fact, then we can assume that this poem was once accompanied by a dead (or dying) rose and that the poem and rose together made their journey from Dickinson's garden or desk or pathway near her house into the possession of the mysterious "Mrs.———." This poem-flower combination might have travelled in an envelope or might have been delivered by hand. Either way, the title asks the reader to assume that an actual rose was once part of the life of this poem that can only, because of the poem's appearance in a mass-produced newspaper, represent the rose through reference to it.

The first line of the poem, "Nobody knows this little Rose –," then, is more true than Dickinson may have originally meant it to be, for it is no longer that we do not "know" (as in, cannot decipher the thoughts of) this rose, but we truly cannot "know" (because we have never met) this flower. This later situation of printing that Dickinson probably did not imagine for this text can only now be read as analogous to the situation it depicts, for the poem presents an "I" who has made an otherwise overlooked rose known in the same way that "The Republican" has made the poem (and the anonymous poet) known only because of the fact that someone of hidden identity "surreptitiously communicated" the poem (and, presumably, the situation under which this someone came into possession of it) to the newspaper. In this way, the title supplied by the newspaper does more than simply tell the reader how the poem came to be printed in its pages; it also turns the rose into a metaphor for the poem itself and therefore turns these lines into the most poetic of poems. Like the rose that has been stripped of the identity that it might have had ("It might a pilgrim be"), this now widely circulated poem (the *Springfield Daily Republican* had a circulation of four thousand in 1858) is no longer an artifact of meaningful exchange between friends or lovers.[7]

In light of this, we might return to the notion with which I began and which this essay is attempting to complicate—namely the idea that the fascicles are enclosed spaces whose poems benefit from our reading them in relation to each other. If we follow that practice with "Nobody knows this little Rose –" then we lose the very component of this text's history that makes it so interesting: its status as an object of exchange between real people. Ironically, though, while the printing of this poem supplies us with this piece of its history and identity, it also urges us to suppress that knowledge, as it turns these lines into a poem about how mass circulation kills the circulated object. For, in the poem itself, the rose is missed by every element that used to surround it—"Bee," "Butterfly," "Bird," and "Breeze"— and the blame for this situation of grieving is clearly placed on the one who picked (or published) it. To read these lines this way is to treat them as constituting a poem that has a message to convey to readers of a printed poem.

The result of reading "Nobody knows this little Rose –" purely in its fascicle context or purely as a printed object is to miss the space in between, where Dickinson gave a copy to Sue, possibly (although probably not) in anticipation of her giving it to someone else. To watch, then, what Sue did with it and how the new material context of the newspaper changed it into a poem that looks as if it is addressing the very situation of its publication is to see how circulation affects the text itself. This allows us to see what we wouldn't otherwise have access to, which is that these lines address a situation of encounter and reading, albeit one that is far more intimate than the one staged by the *Springfield Daily Republican*.[8]

Since the case of "Nobody knows this little Rose –" shows us what one particularly loaded and interesting version of pre-fascicle circulation looks like, I want to turn now to two texts that Dickinson circulated *after* having copied them into the fascicle. She did this with several poems in this fascicle: "The feet of people walking home" (Fr16) (which she sent to Sue), "*Oh* if remembering were forgetting –" (Fr9) (which she sent to Bowles), and "As if I asked a common alms –" (Fr14) (which she sent to Higginson and possibly to an unidentified recipient). In these cases, Dickinson redeployed texts that she had committed to her fascicle sheets, using the situation and opportunities that circulation presented to different ends.

In the summer of 1858 Dickinson copied the lines that begin "As if I asked a common alms –" onto the final side of the second sheet of Fascicle 1 (fig. 14):

> As if I asked a common alms –
> And in my wondering hand,
> A stranger pressed a kingdom –
> And I – bewildered stand –
> As if I asked the Orient
> Had it for me a morn?
> And it sh'd lift it's purple dikes
> And flood me with the Dawn!

Many readings of this poem deal with the fascicle version I have transcribed here, forgetting (or never knowing, or not caring) that four years later Dickinson sent these same words in this same order to Higginson, and that twenty-two years after that she copied them in a draft of a letter to an unidentified recipient. Unlike what happened to "Nobody knows this little Rose –," what happened to this poem is entirely in Dickinson's hands. What isn't in her hands is how we have chosen to read (and render) that.[9]

By the time Dickinson sent Higginson the letter in which "As if I asked a common alms –" appears, they had already exchanged two letters each. Dickinson had read Higginson's article "Letter to a Young Contributor" in the April 1862 issue of the *Atlantic Monthly* and had initially written to ask: "Are you too deeply occupied to say if my Verse is alive?" She accompanied this opening letter (L260) with four poems: "Safe in their Alabaster Chambers –" (Fr124), "The nearest Dream recedes – unrealized –" (Fr304), "We play at Paste –" (Fr282), and "I'll tell you how the Sun rose –" (Fr204).[10] Three of these poems had already been copied into fascicles, and one of these had, through Dickinson's correspondence with Sue, already gone through several drafts.[11] Her second letter was accompanied by three poems—"There came a Day at Summer's full" (Fr325), "Of all the Sounds despatched abroad" (Fr334), and "South Winds jostle them –" (Fr98)—all of which had already been copied into the fascicles and one of which had already been sent to two other correspondents.[12]

Each of these seven poems had been copied out on separate sheets or leaves of stationery and enclosed, along with a letter and other poems, in an envelope. But in the case of her third letter, Dickinson did not copy "As if I asked a common alms –" onto a separate piece of paper. Instead, she included it in the body of her letter proper. Unlike the version of this letter that Johnson and Ward published in 1958 (which indents the poem and leaves white space above and below it), the manuscript of this letter reveals that Dickinson was far less interested in marking the shift from prose to poetry and back again to prose. Previously, when Dickinson had wanted Higginson to read her poems, she marked them as such by including them separately. Even when, in her correspondence with others, she copied a poem into a letter, she marked it as a poem. For instance, in three early instances in which Dickinson sent her poems to Sue, she indicated this by leaving space between her prose and the poem, by making each stanza distinct from the next, and by indicating, even when there was no room to keep a line intact, where each line begins and ends.[13] While in each of these cases there is no mistaking what a reader is reading, here it is entirely unclear.

Unlike other critics, I am not interested in marking what genre Dickinson was writing in at this moment nor am I interested in coming up with a new generic category—like the "lyrical letter" or the "letter-poem"—for this text or portion of text.[14] What I am interested in is how Dickinson uses the opportunity of a letter to take what were once lines of a poem and deploy them in a very different way. When thinking about this poem in its fascicle context, the question of the text's "purpose" or "use" seems wholly unanswerable. But in her letter to Higginson, Dickinson presents what were once lines of a poem in order to communicate something to him—something that the prose of her letter attempted to say, but didn't (or couldn't) say clearly enough. In this way, the context of epistolary

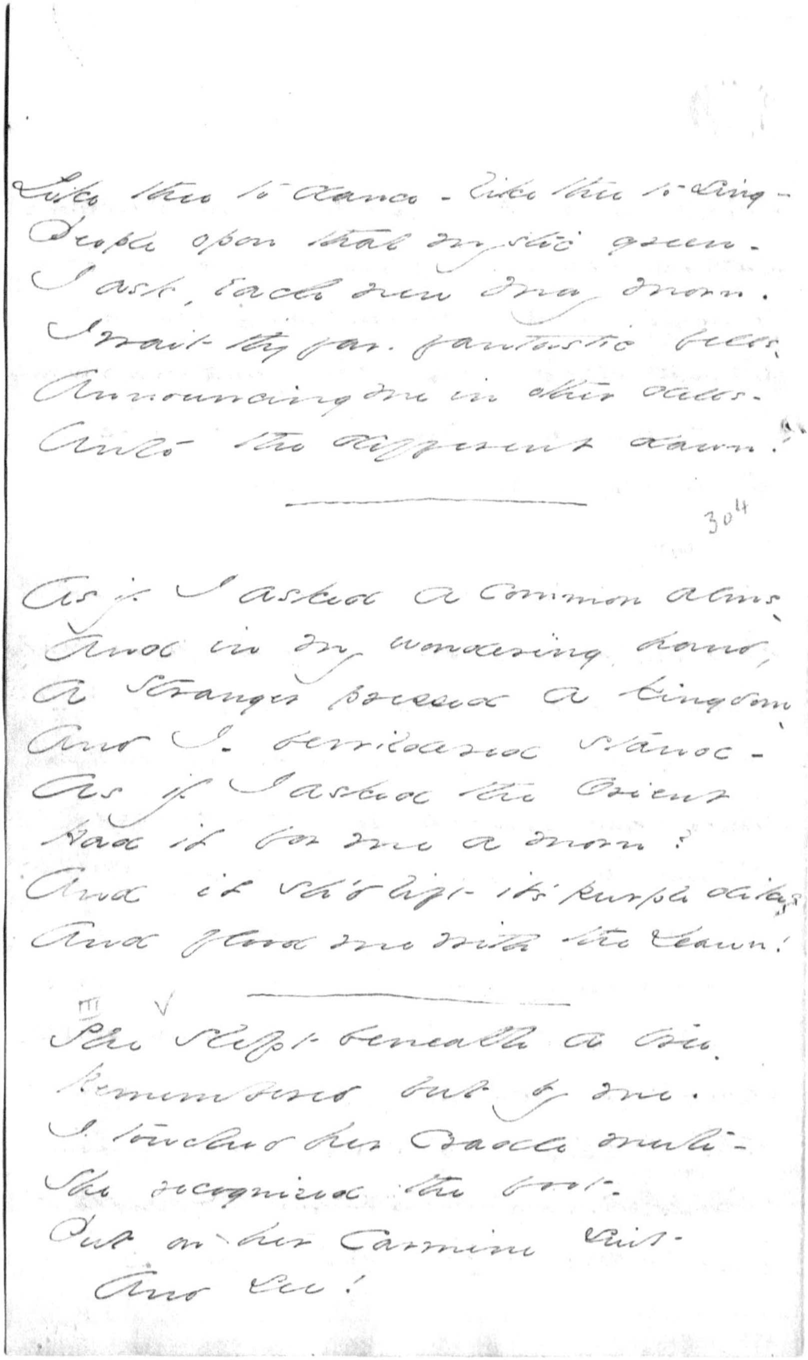

Like this to dance – like this to sing –
People upon that mystic green –
I ask, each new May morn.
I wait thy far, fantastic bells,
Announcing me in other dells,
Unto the different dawn!

---
                                        304

As if I asked a Common alms,
And in my wondering hand,
A Stranger pressed a Kingdom
And I, bewildered stand –
As if I asked the Orient
Had it for me a morn?
And it sh'd lift – it's purple dikes
And flood me with the Dawn!

---

She slept beneath a tree –
Remembered but by me.
I touched her Cradle mute –
She recognized the foot –
Put on her Carmine suit.
And see!

*Figure 14.* Fascicle 1, "As if I asked a common alms –"

82-5

The fret of people walking home
With gayer Sandals go –
The Crocus – till she rises
The Vassal of the snow –
The lips at Hallelujah
Long years of practise bore
Till bye and bye, these Bargemen
Walked singing on the shore.

Pearls are the Diver's farthings
Extorted from the Sea –
Pinions – the Seraph's wagon
Pedestrian once – as we –
Night is the morning's Canvas
Larceny – legacy –
Death, but our rapt attention
To immortality –

My figures fail to tell me
How far the Village lies –

discourse—and the imminent circulation of that discourse—provides Dickinson with the opportunity to play with the boundaries between her prose and her poetry.

In this letter Dickinson both continued to ask Higginson for guidance in the ways of writing poetry and defended herself against the criticism that he had leveled against the poems she had already sent. This must have been, to say the least, a very awkward position for her. Faced with this situation, Dickinson turned to a poem that she wrote four years earlier, long before she knew she would ever write to Higginson, and embedded these lines into the end of her letter. In doing so, she both articulated a forceful critique of him for what he had provided her with *and* softened the blow of that critique by presenting it (if he were reading the letter out loud) in regular meter and rhyme.

Given that this is a letter in which Dickinson represents herself through her use of "I" and that she has not marked the shift from prose to poetry, we can read the "I" in the phrase "As if I asked a common alms" as Dickinson herself. This is not a stretch, since the letter is all about what she has asked for in the past and what she continues to ask for from this actual reader. This "as if" is, of course, a bit of a jab at Higginson, for the "stranger" from whom these "common alms" have been requested has wholly misread the situation and instead quite inappropriately provided a "kingdom." The result is a state of bewilderment. As if, then, this situation demanded a further metaphor, Dickinson wrote that it is comparable to her having asked for "the Orient" and having instead been "shatter[ed]" with "the Dawn."[15] We can understand what Dickinson was doing here only by reading these lines as part of her letter—something that an analysis of the manuscript itself makes possible, but that a focus on its transcription or on the poem's earlier existence as a fascicle poem obscures.[16]

In short, Dickinson's manipulation of this text's format and genre can be read as her way of controlling the distance between her (as "I") and her reader (as "you"). We know that this is something she thought about over the course of her life because twenty-two years later Dickinson again revisited the lines that she had copied into Fascicle 1 and copied them as part of a letter that she addressed to an unidentified recipient (L964), this time largely ignoring her earlier punctuation and, depending on how you read it, either doing away with line breaks altogether or creating much shorter lines. In this case, the context of the exchange is different than it had been with Higginson, for here she is acknowledging the receipt of and thanking someone for a photograph of a mother and child that had been sent to her. At the same time, though, she mentions a "Book" that has been promised to her by the sender and refers to her state of "famine" without it. When she then embeds "As if I asked a common alms –" into the prose of her letter, she is clearly playing with how to balance her own sense of gratefulness and her own persistent desires.

While we might understand Dickinson using these lines in her letter to Higginson in the context of that specific friendship, I want to suggest that we think about this later case in terms of how Dickinson often returned to her fascicles later in life. She had stopped making them in 1865, but it is clear that she not only read them but rewrote parts of them over the next two decades. Whether Dickinson revised or redeployed what once had been fascicle texts, she often copied these several times, returning to them sometimes over a huge span of years, and creating a variety of different material contexts for them. In doing so, Dickinson indicated that while there is something that seems deeply personal about her texts under given circumstances, they are often widely applicable texts. Yet even when she actually circulates these texts, at the same time inviting us to question the role that circulation plays in the making and remaking of a text, their identity as fascicle poems is precisely the thing that forecloses these reading possibilities.

While we might debate whether Dickinson meant to circulate "Nobody knows this little Rose –" as widely as it was eventually circulated, there is no question that she wanted various people to read "As if I asked a common alms –," and that she wanted them to read it in various forms. In both cases a public circulation occurs because Dickinson handed or sent these texts to someone else. In the case of the next text I will discuss, Dickinson engages in a different form of circulation, one that takes place not just between people, but between fascicles themselves.

When Dickinson first copied the lines that begin "The feet of people walking home" into Fascicle 1 she also made two additional copies, both of which she retained for herself. Four years later, she sewed one of these into Fascicle 14, and the other copy remained unsewn for the rest of her life. Even though she most likely had this retained copy with her, Dickinson made a fourth copy several months after making the first three and sent it to Sue with the heading "Darling" and signed "Lovingly, Emilie." This situation raises some questions: Why would Dickinson copy this text so many times, and why would she place two quite similar versions of it in two different fascicles? Eleanor Heginbotham has offered the most extensive study of what she calls Dickinson's "duplicate poems," ultimately reading them as redeployments that affect the fascicles into which they have been copied. Of "The feet of people walking home" she writes, "Although almost identical in words and form, the poem's two differing contexts (the two fascicle groupings) offer possibilities for revision in interpretation" (116).[17]

If we treat the fascicles as "bound" objects—most critics use this language of "binding" to describe how Dickinson joined her individual, folded fascicle sheets together—then it is easy to see how we might read each fascicle as a kind of book, where each poem is essential to the ones that surround it, and where interpretation is exactly what is at stake. For instance, when writing about the context that Fascicle 14 provides for "The feet of people walking home," Heginbotham characterizes what is happening here, in contrast to the context that Fascicle 1 had provided: "this setting suggests that the poem, more innocent and almost merry in its flower-filled context of Fascicle 1, may be reflective of the frustration of a speaker (or speakers) struggling with frustration and loss" (117). Sharon Cameron employs a similar approach when she writes, "By the logic which reveals that the integrity of an entity is dictated by the fascicle binding, the same words copied in *different* fascicles must be understood to constitute two discrete poems. The difference is reflected in the disparate constructions of the meaning of the two utterances that become available. For instance, in Fascicle 1 'The feet of people walking home,' copied in 1858 and then bound, exists in a grouping that asks about the relation between nature, death, and immortality" (85).

Such readings—while enormously helpful if we are interested in understanding the identity of each fascicle—assume our critical investment in the fascicles as aesthetic objects with strict (and therefore readable) boundaries. What I want to suggest, instead, is that we read the situation as far less fixed than this, for, in reality, fascicle sheets were hardly "bound"— they were sewn together with string, often years after the actual sheets had been copied. And in the case of "The feet of people walking home," this was a far messier situation than the existence of two neatly made fascicles. There were four copies of this text that existed among Dickinson's papers around the same time, and she tried each of them out in various contexts—among the other texts copied onto a fascicle sheet, alone on a leaf of stationery, alone on a leaf of stationery that she sewed in between folded fascicle sheets, and as a note that she sent to Sue. In other words, there is something about this text that prompted Dickinson to produce different versions of it and to try out how it might work as a part of different kinds of material objects.

The version that Dickinson copied onto a sheet that she eventually sewed into Fascicle 1 reads:

The feet of people walking home
With gayer sandals go –
The crocus – till she rises –
The vassal of the snow –
The lips at Hallelujah
Long years of practise bore –
Till bye and bye, these Bargemen
Walked – singing – on the shore.

Pearls are the Diver's farthings,
Extorted from the sea –
Pinions – the Seraph's wagon –
Pedestrian once – as we –
Night is the morning's canvas –
Larceny – legacy –
Death – but our rapt attention
To immortality.

My figures fail to tell me
How far the village lies –
Whose peasants are the angels –
Whose cantons dot the skies –
My Classics vail their faces –
My faith that Dark adores –
Which from it's solemn abbeys –
Such resurrection pours!

Dickinson altered some of the punctuation in the other drafts and, in the case of the version that she sent to Sue, she put it in quatrains. But other than that, this text remained relatively the same throughout its many drafts, indicating that Dickinson was not engaging in a revision process. Instead, I would like to suggest, she was multiplying its fairly similar versions precisely to see which of the possible material contexts might fit (or answer, or complement) it best.

Given the content of this text, it should not surprise us that Dickinson tested it out in various places. Combining a performance of waiting for death with a series of metaphors about distance and ignorance, this is a strange text that has neither a clear message nor an emotional center. Instead, it is composed of various attempts to see, hear, name, measure, and know—all of which end in a form of failure. That is not to say that it is itself a failure, but instead that because of this, it is ripe for the multiple kinds of circulation to which Dickinson subjects it. By circulating the text, even within contexts that are for her eyes only, she tests it out—in isolation, as part of different groups, and as a message.

On the one hand, my point is that to study just the fascicles, or to study an individual fascicle, is to miss all of this. But on the other hand, I am not rejecting the fascicles as units of study, for I only achieved my prior point by reading deeply into the fascicle itself. Along those lines, and in conclusion, I want to turn to one last text from Fascicle 1, one that, as far as we know, Dickinson did not circulate. That being said, it is related to the three texts that I have considered in this essay precisely because it is part of the same fascicle. In other words, if I was not thinking about Fascicle 1 as a unit worthy of attention, I might never have connected them, and yet I want to suggest how such connections can be surprisingly fruitful, albeit not in the way we might expect.

"If those I loved were lost" (Fr20) is the "one exception," according to Franklin, to Dickinson's practice of destroying her pre-fascicle "worksheets" (11). Eventually copied into Fascicle 1, this text was originally written on a scrap of stationery that had been folded vertically at its center such that it had four panels on which Dickinson could write (fig. 15). Despite having this room, Dickinson contained this draft on the first side only, where she wrote:

> If those I loved    's
> were lost The Crier
>     note
> ~~would~~ voice
> would tell me –
> If those I loved
> were found, the
> bells of Ghent
> would sing,
> Did those I loved
> repose, The Daisy
> Would impel
> me – Philip
> ~~questioned eager~~
> ~~I, my riddle~~

*Figure 15.* Pre-fascicle draft of "If those I loved were lost."

~~bring~~ when bewil
dered – bore his riddle
in –

One of the things that this draft makes visible is that Dickinson grappled with certain moments in these lines more than others. She was unclear whether she wanted the "Crier" to sound a "note" or use his "voice," and she seems entirely unsure whether Philip actively "questioned" or whether he was passively "bewildered." What is also interesting about Dickinson's revision to the final move is that in the crossed-out version the "I" owns a riddle that he or she bears and in the not-crossed-out version the "I" does nothing and the riddle belongs solely to Philip.

While it is, indeed, fascinating to see Dickinson struggling with her word choice (I find myself absorbed by thinking about the difference between "note" and "voice," given that one marks the Crier as particularly birdlike while the other suggests he is human), I want to shift our attention to the material on which Dickinson copied these words. As I noted earlier, Dickinson had three other panels on which she could have written these words, yet she crams them all in here. Right from the start she is preserving space, for, on the second line, she places what we now think of as the beginning of a next line, "The Crier," right after "were lost." This is our first indication that in an initial draft Dickinson didn't seem to care about indicating what she had in mind as later line breaks, that she had not yet conceived of where her lines would break, or that these were not yet "lines" when she wrote them here. Now that we know the poem that she copied into Fascicle 1—the one that exists both in manuscript and transcription with clearly marked line breaks—it is almost impossible not to read the space between "lost" and "The" as a silent beat that would later become an actual line break. But if we can rid ourselves of that habit and read the words that appear on this panel of a scrap, then what we can see (and hear) is that as the thought proceeds, it catches a rhythm, one that will later manifest visually as line breaks. In other words, the poem that begins "If those I loved were lost," as it would be copied onto the third sheet of Dickinson's first fascicle, had a pre-life not as a poem, per se, but as words set down as prose.

Dickinson's choice of material to set these words on tells us that something contradictory is happening here. On the one hand, had she wanted to indicate line breaks, she had ample room to do so, as the other three panels remain blank. But on the other hand, by folding this scrap of paper, Dickinson limited herself to a small column of space, making it difficult for her to indicate line breaks had she wanted to. What's important, though, is that Dickinson chose this very particular kind of material, one that provided this tension between thoughts set down as prose or verse.

While "If those I loved were lost" seeks to name the very kind of communication that will bear utterly necessary information, these lines were never sent to anyone (either in draft form or fascicle form), as far as we know. Yet from this early draft, before it had the chance to be solidified as a fascicle poem, we can see that Dickinson's compositional practice was highly attuned to the role of circulation in the making of a text. The summer that she wrote this pre-fascicle draft, "Nobody knows this little Rose –" was published in the *Springfield Daily Republican,* an event that would show Dickinson that what one intends as intimate is actually often utterly public. She would also write "As if I asked a common alms –," a poem that would later be incorporated into her prose, reversing the process by which "If those I loved were lost" came to have distinct lines. And while we do not have access to any kind of pre-fascicle draft of "The feet of people walking home," the number of copies that she made is itself a bearing of her message, even if, as in the case of "If those I loved were lost," she doesn't know exactly what that message is.

If a study of the fascicles limits itself to what is actually contained within them, then the eclectic kind of work that Dickinson was doing as she made and remade these texts is obscured, for most of this work gets done in pre-fascicle and post-fascicle drafts, not in the fascicles themselves. That being said, if we never look at the fascicles as units of composition that are ripe for analysis, then we miss seeing how Dickinson's sometimes disparate-seeming preoccupations (in process as well as content) are often clustered together. While I am advocating for a reading of the fascicles that takes these issues into account, it is important to acknowledge that the kinds of readings I have argued for here are meant to be suggestive. My impulse to read Dickinson's move across material contexts, while largely informed by my work with her manuscripts, comes out of a desire to present an alternative way of thinking about Dickinson's fascicles and her experimentation with the poetic conventions and generic boundaries they make visible.

In an essay that has spent very little time looking at the fascicles themselves, I hope that my emphasis on circulation has illuminated several things about them. First, even though Dickinson made the fascicles for only six years at the beginning of her writing career, they were present in her writing processes until the very end of her life. Second, by treating her fascicle texts as definitive, we overlook the fact that a certain degree of flexibility was built into the fascicles themselves, a flexibility that allowed Dickinson to deploy these texts in a variety of ways. If they had been fixed in the fascicles, Dickinson would not only have been unable to place them in new material contexts, but she would not have been free to alter their properties and purposes. Third, by turning to the non-fascicle texts that are related to the fascicle-texts, we are confronted with Dickinson's actual correspondence in a way that we normally treat separately. Thinking about the relationship of Dickinson's letters and poems is crucial, precisely because it allows us to break free of having to choose between Dickinson the private poet and Dickinson the social correspondent. And finally, while Dickinson's fascicles have been characterized as enclosed spaces, I hope to have shown that the various modes of puncture and circulation that Dickinson employed renders the fascicles far more porous than we have previously thought. One of the most fruitful things about looking closely at Fascicle 1 is that we can see that all of this was present from the very beginning.

# Manuscript Study, Fascicle Study
## Appreciating Dickinson's Prosody

ELLEN LOUISE HART

*This* essay is for readers who want to think in new ways about Dickinson's verse theory, the technical aspects of her versification. I argue here that manuscript features in her handwritten work are expressive visual strategies creating and highlighting aspects of her prosody; that her poems in manuscript offer readers more information about the prosody than standard print editions can provide; and that the fascicles and sets present a body of work in which prosodic developments, experiments, and innovations can be traced.[1]

Although manuscripts are now available on Harvard's Dickinson Archive, I refer to images accessible to readers, teachers, students, and critics in Franklin's 1981 *Manuscript Books of Emily Dickinson,* a photofacsimile edition that is relatively affordable, and available in many libraries. The chronology of fascicles and sets established by Franklin is essential to tracing developments in the poems, and yet I do not believe that the work can be dated as precisely as Franklin sometimes claims. In the introduction to his 1998 variorum edition, the editor explains that his evidence for dating the documents, the poems in manuscript and not their composition, includes handwriting; writing papers; embossment and watermarks; occasional stains. Expert observation of these characteristics leads to educated speculation. Franklin acknowledges: "It should be clear that dating is a judgment, albeit an informed one, subject to imprecision that increases across time" (variorum edition, 39). He notes particular difficulties determining endings and beginnings of certain years, including 1861 and 1862,

1864 and 1865, and he explains that with fascicles and sets after 1865, "dating becomes more difficult" (38). In *The Manuscript Books* he qualifies dating with "about" in relation to each year, whereas in the variorum he regularly places manuscripts in a particular season of the assigned year.[2] In this essay I use the more approximate dating of the *Manuscript Books,* according to which the earliest poems in the series can be dated "about 1858" and the latest "early 1876" and "about 1877." Franklin's meticulous work establishes an invaluable chronology that allows readers to follow Dickinson's prosodic shifts and changes over a period of nearly twenty years.

A one-stanza poem in Fascicle 3, "about 1859," looks like this:

I hide myself within my flower
That wearing on your breast –
You – unsuspecting, wear me too –
And angels know the rest! (Fr80)

A later version, in Fascicle 40, "about 1864," looks like this:

I hide myself – within
my flower,
That fading from your
Vase –
You – unsuspecting – feel for
me –
Almost – a loneliness –

The earlier poem is a Common Measure quatrain, which traditionally consists of four beats in lines 1 and 3, three beats in lines 2 and 4; the pattern abbreviates as 4.3.4.3. This form is also described as "hymn meter" and "ballad meter." In the language of conventional scansion these are tetrameter and trimeter lines. The later poem is a variation of the form. The conventional Common Measure rhyme scheme is "full" rhyme for lines 2 and 4; here, "breast" and "rest." The later poem varies the meter in the final line where there are two beats, not three, and organizes sound in alliterative patterns, consonantal threads: of "s" in "-self," "unsuspecting," "almost"; of "f" in "-self," "flower," "fading," "from," "feel," "for"; "l" in "feel," "almost," "loneliness"; "m" in "myself," "my," "from," "me," "almost." There are the assonances of "hide myself," "almost" and "loneliness," and the "near," or "slant," rhyme of "Vase" and "loneliness." Division of metrical lines 1, 2, and 3, and midline dashes, slow the pace, encourage articulation of each syllable, and emphasize words by centering them, or positioning them before or after a pause set out by a break. The varied rhythm and intricately interwoven sound patterns of the poem's second version are characteristic of poems after the early 1860s, which increasingly employ strategies of spatial prosody.

Through focused, observant reading of manuscripts, new poems appear, and are heard with intensified clarity. Readers can learn to recognize signifying characteristics of the handwriting during various periods of the work, including multiple forms of letters with different shapes, sizes, and degrees of flourish for the upper and lower cases, "A/a," "C/c," "S/s," for example. Often whether a letter is capitalized or not is a matter of studied interpretation. Differentiating dashes and commas can be challenging. Dashes have various appearances: long and short, horizontal and angled, some pointing up, others down, some toward the left or the right. Dividing metrical, or measured, lines results in visual lines that enhance the sound of individual syllables, protect against slurring and promote what nineteenth-century elocutionists refer to as "distinct utterance," add extrametrical stress, establish rhythmic phrasing, prevent metrical patterns from becoming monotonous or "sing song," and multiply ambiguities while suggesting interpretive emphasis. Combining manuscript study with fascicle study here, I hope to model a process and encourage readers to be confident, precise, and exacting; to probe for subtle nuances of meaning; and to take deepening delight in the rich array of visual strategies contributing to Dickinson's complex aural art.[3]

The practice of dividing measured lines may have begun in the earliest fascicle poems as a way to avoid excessive "crowding," that is, fitting words into a line by running up against the edge of the sheet, in smaller handwriting, often in print lettering, which takes less space. Concern for neat, legible handwriting would be compatible with Dickinson's reputation at Amherst Academy, where she wrote a column for *Forest Leaves,* a student publication remembered by a friend as "all in script" and "passed around the school": "Emily's" script was "very beautiful—small, clear, and finished" (Buckingham, *Reception* 350). "Small" describes the handwriting of the first three fascicles in relation to Fascicle 4, "about 1859," when space between words is increasing; and by Fascicle 8, "about 1860," lettering is larger.

Crowding to keep metrical lines physically intact is a strategy Dickinson sometimes uses, which raises the questions: What does it mean when she does not crowd? What choices is she making? What are her priorities for each metrical line? In my view the most important effects of visual lines are to preserve sound integrity, create rhythm, and suggest interpretive emphasis. One exception, where fitting poems to space does dictate line arrangements, is summed up by Franklin's comment that Dickinson's "unit" "in one sense had always been the sheet" (*MB* xii). In certain cases throughout the fascicles and sets, as writing approaches the bottom of a sheet, Dickinson crowds one or two lines toward the end of a poem so all lines appear on a single page. For example, in the opening line of a poem in Fascicle 9, "He was weak, and I was strong – / then –," she divides the metrical line, keeping the visual parallel with the third line of the stanza: "I was weak, and He was strong / then –." But in the final stanza, lines 1 and 3 use smaller handwriting to keep lines together and fit the whole stanza into the sheet's remaining space. About five years later a single-stanza poem in set 6a, "about 1865," shows a similar concern:

> The Definition of
> Beauty is
> That Definition is none –
> Of Heaven, easing Analysis –
> Since Heaven and He are One. (Fr797)

The first measured line is shorter than the last by one character (counting as "characters" are letters, one space between words, and punctuation marks), yet the shorter line is divided and the longer line is squeezed into the space to keep the poem visually intact. Priorities for dividing the first line seem to be to slow the pace, to center and emphasize "Definition," and to emphasize "Beauty."

In Fascicles 9, "about 1860," and 10, "about 1860 and 1861," Dickinson begins to divide metrical lines more often than in the previous eight fascicles. In Fascicles 1 and 2, both dated "about 1858," and Fascicle 3, "about 1858 and 1859," there are no poems in which metrical lines are divided. In Fascicle 4, "about 1859," four of the sixteen poems have stanzas in which some lines are divided. Poems in Fascicles 5 and 6, dated "about 1859," are without line division; Fascicle 7, "about 1859," has one poem with one divided line; Fascicle 8, "about 1860," has no divided lines. Then in Fascicle 9, "about 1860," nineteen of the twenty-nine poems have divided lines, and in Fascicle 10, "about 1860 and 1861," sixteen of twenty-two poems have divided lines. Here is the full text, in my print translation, of a poem in Fascicle 10: the two-stanza draft version of "Safe in their Alabaster / chambers." Franklin dates the fascicle "about 1860 and 1861," and this manuscript "about 1861."

> Safe in their Alabaster
> chambers –

Untouched by Morning –
And untouched by Noon –
Lie the meek members of
the Resurrection –
Rafter of Satin – and Roof
of Stone!

Grand go the Years – in the
Crescent – above them –
Worlds scoop their Arcs –
And Firmaments – row –
Diadems – drop – and Doges –
surrender –
Soundless as dots – on a
Disc of snow – (Fr124)

In editing terms, a "print translation" is a limited "diplomatic transcription." "Diplomatic" derives from "diploma," meaning a document folded in half. A diplomatic transcription represents a manuscript as accurately as type or print will allow, and may include a description of features that are difficult or impossible to represent typographically. A complete diplomatic transcription of this poem would describe certain letters that stand out in the manuscript, elaborately formed capitals, in particular, and would make note of the length and angle of dashes. It would also provide a measurement of a line drawn beneath the second stanza, separating the pair of stanzas from two that follow. (These may be versions of an alternative second stanza, or versions of a third stanza.) Commentary of this kind is unnecessary here, however, since Franklin's edition makes the manuscript image available.[4]

There are five existing manuscript versions of the poem, including a version in Fascicle 6.[5] Dickinson's line divisions create rhythm, sometimes varying, sometimes supporting the metrical pattern. The text of the poem's first stanza, below, shows metrical lines with stressed syllables underlined.

    x       x  x    x
S<u>a</u>fe in their <u>A</u>lab<u>a</u>ster ch<u>a</u>mbers –
x  x      x
<u>Un</u>t<u>ou</u>ched by M<u>o</u>rning –
    x  x      x
And <u>un</u>t<u>ou</u>ched by N<u>oo</u>n –

```
    x      x   x                    x
```
Lie the meek members of the Resurrection –
```
X       x            x     x
```
Rafter of Satin – and Roof of Stone!

Lines 1, 4, and 5 have four beats; lines 2 and 3 have three beats. "Beats" are also known as "strong stresses."

Linguist Sandra Chung offers useful alternative terms for metrical analysis: "Emily Dickinson wrote almost all of her poetry in a metrical form clearly connected to the meter of English-language folk verse and hymns. Hence, the terms used by literary scholars to describe her verse (e.g. ballad stanza, hymn meters, common meter; see England and Sparrow 1966, Johnson 1955, Lindberg-Seyersted 1968, Porter 1966). Adopting the perspective of Burling (1966), Attridge (1982), Hayes and MacEachern (1998), Kiparsky (2006), and others, we [Chung and Hart] say that Dickinson wrote in four beat verse, a *family* of rhythmic forms that are arguably simple, accessible, and universal compared to, say, iambic pentameter. Four-beat verse is ubiquitous in English folk songs, nursery rhymes, greeting cards, and political chants." Chung notes that Dickinson "experimented with this form. As Thomas Johnson put it, her 'great contribution to English prosody was that she perceived how to gain new effects by exploring the possibilities within traditional metric patterns' (1955:86)."[6] "The meter is phonologically well-defined, clearly recognizable, and related to a very familiar meter; readers have no trouble perceiving (hearing) it," Chung writes. She explains that "the pauses, intonation, etc. of performance are superimposed on the poem's underlying (metrical) organization," that "the visual lines are superimposed on the meter; to the extent that they fail to coincide with the meter, they suggest new ways of perceiving (reading / delivering) the poems."[7]

By omitting line divisions editors restrict lines. When an edited line does not correspond with the visual lines, the two do not sound the same and do not have the same meaning. Division of metrical lines distributes the centers of the verse, helping to avoid "mid line slackening," the term Robert Shaw uses in his study *Blank Verse,* and promoting what Seamus Heaney refers to as a "mid-line dynamic."[8] Short visual lines direct focus to words in the center of a metrical line rather than at the line's end. In "Safe in their Alabaster / chambers," "Alabaster" receives more emphasis than it would if the eye moved more quickly across the page to "chambers." Separating "Alabaster" from "chambers" weakens the syntactical bond, and the adjective resonates, creating a lingering impression of hard, white stone, before the noun dominates and the focus moves to "chambers." In this way images and scenes unfold piece by piece, and our perception changes. Textures, dimensions, layers of meaning come into view gradually. Like her "Players at the Keys – / Before they drop full Music / on – /," Dickinson "stuns you by Degrees" (Fr477, F22).

Why does the division of a metrical line occur in one place and not another? In "Rafter of Satin – and Roof / of Stone" the break avoids the muffled echo "Roof of," which decreased space between words in the first part of the line might have allowed. But the awkward sound could detract from the acoustic impact of "Stone." Instead, every syllable in the line stands out, with the integrity of its sound protected. In "Lie the meek members of / the Resurrection –" if "of" after "members" were not so widely spaced, the article would follow on the same line, but article and noun together carry more weight. Compare the visual lines with the metrical line: "Lie the meek members of the Resurrection –" In the former, "Meek members" are at the center of the scene. The ultimately powerful "Resurrection" does not dominate the line until a reader has the opportunity to wonder: "'members' of what?" The word evokes images of body parts, and of incomplete human beings who must unite with some other power to become whole. "Lie" receives more stress in the shorter, slower line: Is belief in life after death a "lie" the "meek" tell themselves? Is it possible to be "safe" without lying meekly in a state of unconsciousness? In another version of the poem, the "meek" "sleep" rather than "lie." Sleep is re-creational and less passive (as Hamlet notes, to sleep is to dream).

In a version of "Safe in their alabaster chambers" in Fascicle 6, where the first stanza is similar to the first stanza of the version in Fascicle 10, and the second stanza is different, there are no divisions. The longest line, "Sleep the meek members of the Resurrection," is squeezed into one row, with "Resurrection" finishing in tiny print. A year or so later when Dickinson revises the line, she divides it.

In the second stanza midline dashes create pauses that work in some ways similar to line division. As the poet Mary Jo Salter points out, "dashes are like line breaks within a line—and they can double or triple meaning" (from a talk on "The Music of Emily Dickinson," April 12, 2007). Dashes hold back "row": "And Firmaments – row –." Line division slows the advance of "snow": "Soundless as dots – on a / Disc of snow –." As a result of the break, more emphasis is placed on "Disc," the final figure of circles, partial circles, and circular movements in a sequence: "Crescent," "scoop," "Arcs," "row," "Diadems," "dots," "Disc." In the lines "Grand go the Years – in the / Crescent – above them –" a dash prevents the slurring of "Years in," avoiding "yearzin." Breaks allow us to see and hear each word and syllable individually. They assure visual and acoustic clarity, which is crucial for a poetry where sound is organized through alliteration.

The first stanza features a kind of rhyme often associated with Dickinson's poetry, "slant rhyme": "Noon" and "Stone." However, the term is imprecise, and in studies of Dickinson's prosody this form of rhyme is removed from a larger context. Concentration on "slant rhyme" isolates consonance and assonance from other kinds of alliteration and sound repetition, and limits readers' awareness of Dickinson's "range of rhyme."[9] "Alliteration" has various definitions, depending on the prosodist. It may refer specifically to initial letter repetition, sometimes known as "head rhyme"; in other cases, it encompasses consonance—the repetition of initial, medial, and final consonants—and assonance, the repetition of vowel sounds. I use the broadest definition. Alliteration is often demoted in prosody studies, considered a feature of "light" verse, too simple for sustained analysis, more of an ornament or device than a structure. In Dickinson's writing, both poetry and prose, alliteration serves many purposes, including rhythmic variety and rhetorical persuasion, and the full achievement of her rich and diverse use of the sound structure depends on her innovative visual strategies of manuscript.[10]

Alliteration in "Safe in their Alabaster / chambers" often supports beats: "*meek mem*bers," "*Raf*ter of *Sat*in – and *Roof* / of *Stone*," "*Sound*less as *dots* – on a / *Disc* of *snow*." In a number of places a beat falls on an alliterated syllable in a capitalized word, and the word receives triple emphasis: "Noon," "Rafter," "Disc." In other cases alliteration adds emphasis to an unstressed word, "go" in "Grand go," or it adds to the articulation, accentuation, and emphasis of syllables less likely to receive full sound even when carrying a beat, as in "Un—" of "Untouched."

Poet and prosodist Wendy Bishop points out that alliteration is partly a visual device (406). The strategies increasing acoustic and semantic possibilities include Dickinson's capitalizations. Since handwriting allows gradations, sizing letters becomes another way of assigning degrees of emphasis. Capitalizing significant words is common in nineteenth-century writing. In his 1824 *English Grammar*, Lindley Murray explains that although it was once "the custom to begin every noun with a capital," eventually capitalization came to designate certain words as "remarkably emphatic" (248). Dickinson exploits and extends this practice, capitalizing many nouns and also adjectives.[11] Letters take various forms and sizes. Metrical lines often begin with a large, ornate capital. There are midsize letters formed as small capitals. Some letters with similar forms appear in four or five sizes, blurring upper- and lower-case distinctions. In "Safe in their Alabaster /

chambers" there are at least six different forms and sizes of "S/s," with the "S" in "Safe" the largest. This kind of lettering enhances the emphatic effect of alliteration.

In *Middle English Alliterative Poetry and Its Literary Background,* David Lawton explains that alliteration provides "systematic linking" (28). Alliterative threads in "Safe in their Alabaster / chambers" link parts of measured lines and connect one line to the next to form tightly woven stanzas. From the poem's first word to the last, "s" repeats in initial, medial, and final positions. This pattern is set in the opening line with "Safe," "Alabaster," "chambers." In another series, "-r," "-er," "-ers" repeat ("their," "Alabaster," "chambers") with a sound somewhat grinding and awkward to pronounce, setting up a slightly discordant, and, following "Safe," possibly ironic, note. Repetition of "n"—"Untouched," "Morning," "Untouched," "Noon"—in a sequence of two-syllable words, then one syllable, moves the lines in a lilting, hypnotic rhythm. Alliterative series in the stanza develop, extend, intertwine: "meek members"; "Resurrection," "Rafter," "Roof." Alliterative, parallel phrasing, "Rafter of Satin – and Roof / of Stone!," with the midline dash and line division, sets out rhythmic repetition while avoiding predictability. The effect of the consonantal rhyme of "Noon" and "Stone" is intensified by the series "untouched," "untouched," "Morning," "Resurrection," "Satin."

In the last lines of the second stanza, until the final word, every noun, verb, and adjective alliterates in an emphatic series of initial and medial "d's":

> Diadems – drop – and Doges –
> surrender –
> Soundless as dots – on a
> Disc of snow –

Centering "dots" highlights the strange, ambiguous image—blood? earth? ink? Dashes and divisions enhance sound repetition in the alliterative progression that represents sequential events, movement in time. "Surrender" and "Soundless"; the plurals, "Diadems," "Doges," "dots"; and "Disc" conclude the central consonantal chain of "S/s" beginning with "Safe," ending with "snow," the first word connecting with the last in a cycle of sounds. "Exact" rhyme (also called "true," "pure," "full" rhyme) in end-rhyme position pulls readers to the line's last word. The one exact rhyme in "Safe in their Alabaster / chambers," "row" and "snow," creates closure. Harmonizing connections suggest a peacefulness that can coexist with mystery, change, and uncertainty. Arguably, the closing lines of this poem, with their intricate, intermingled alliterative threads, are among the most memorable (alliteration adds to memorability) and haunting in Dickinson's poetry.

A thorough analysis of how alliteration works in Dickinson's writing can build on the critical commentary on her rhyme. Discussion of her unconventional forms begins in 1862 with her own comment to Thomas Higginson. Early in their correspondence, in a letter postmarked "Amherst Ms Jun 7 1862," Dickinson appears to defend her rhymes, explaining that she "could not drop the Bells whose jingling cooled my Tramp" (L265). In several instances Dickinson uses "syllable" as a homonymic pun, rhyming as if it were pronounced "sylla-bell": in "I could suffice for Him, / I knew," in "My Syllable rebelled"; and in "For this – accepted Breath," "Get Gabriel – to tell – the royal Syllable –." Writing to Higginson she seems to be saying that her rhyming syllables slow, or "cool," the verses, varying her meter, or her "tramp," one of her frequent puns on the movement of "feet." Robert Shaw, in *Blank Verse*, speculates that "jingle" and "Bells" are references to Edgar Allan Poe, whose poem "The Bells" stands out as a masterpiece of rhythm: "To the tintinnabulation that so musically wells / From the bells, bells, bells, bells / Bells, bells, bells – / From the jingling and the tinkling of the bells." Shaw notes that Emerson refers to Poe as the "jingle man" and describes him as an "indefatigable rhymer" (81).

A twentieth-century contributor to the discussion of Dickinson's rhyme, George Frisbie Whicher, in his 1938 critical biography, *This Was a Poet*, states that "no poet before her had made such constant use of approximate rhymes as she did" (244). Whicher's definition of "approximate rhyme" includes "imperfect rhyme," "vowel rhyme," and "suspended rhyme." Thomas Johnson, in the introduction to his 1961 selected poems, *Final Harvest*, describes Dickinson as "a prosodist experimenting in rhyme" (xi). In his 1955 *Interpretive Biography* he writes that for sound repetition in American poetry, Dickinson's "unorthodox," "supple," "varied" (86) rhymes "enormously extended . . . the range of variation within controlled limits" (87), and he points out that her additions to rhymed pairings previously "allowable in English verse" are bold and innovative. Brita Lindberg-Seyersted, in *The Voice of the Poet: Aspects of Style in the Poetry of Emily Dickinson* (1968), concentrates on rhyme while identifying Dickinson's "fondness for alliteration" (208n). She traces "alliterating constructions" in individual poems, and finds Dickinson "conscious of the value of this device to highlight structurally and semantically important words" (207).

Percy G. Adams's *Graces of Harmony: Alliteration, Assonance, and Consonance in Eighteenth-Century British Poetry* (1977) is the rare study of alliteration with a substantial section on Dickinson. Adams shows that along with that of Keats, Coleridge, Shelley, and Robert Browning, Dickinson's poetry "employs [phonal] repetitions," "deliberately, artistically, sometimes heavily" (170). He writes that she "is not only unique with her invigorating images and quick twists of wit; she is intriguing in her use of phonic recurrences" (172) and concludes: Dickinson "replaces end rhyme with consonance far more than any poet before her, often preferring it" (173). Making a similar case, James Guthrie finds that no other poet "of her generation" uses "near rhymes" so frequently ("Near Rhymes" 70). Explaining that "taken as a whole, rhyme can be regarded as a scale ranging from no rhyme at all to exact rhyme, with dozens of gradations in between that poets can employ to modulate their sound," Guthrie describes Dickinson using "a network of related sounds to hold her poems together, combining assonance, consonance, and near and exact rhyme" (71).

In fact, among the 4,840 rhymes Timothy Morris has counted in poems from 1858 to 1865, "exact rhyme is the most common type"; however, Morris continues, "nearly as common is consonantal rhyme, where the final consonants, but not the preceding vowels, are identical" (161). "It has become a given of Dickinson criticism that the poet's style never changed," writes Morris, taking issue with Charles Anderson's 1960 study of Dickinson's rhyme, in *Emily Dickinson's Poetry: Stairway of Surprise,* and its conclusion that "there are no marked periods in her career, no significant curve of development in her artistic powers" (157). Morris argues that "by measuring Dickinson's patterns of rhyme and enjambment, we can see that these formal contours of her verse changed over time, especially from 1858 to 1865" (158) and that the fascicles "can be used to show how Dickinson's use of rhyme and enjambment developed over time" (160). In this important essay, Morris maintains that "the development of Dickinson's style deserves more critical attention" (158).[12]

In the only book-length study of Dickinson focused entirely on rhyme, *Positive as Sound: Emily Dickinson's Rhyme* (1990), Judy Jo Small treats her "uncommon handling" of it (214). Like Morris, whose work she cites, Small finds that "consonantal rhymes" "make up most of Dickinson's unconventional rhymes" (219). Creating "progressions and dynamic modulations of rhyme that help shape and support the structure and movement of whole poems," Small writes, Dickinson was "exploring and exploiting rhyme differences" (217) and, through experimentation, "devising a poetry with a radically new *sound*" (28). Small, too, concludes that Dickinson's "acoustic texture merits far more attention" (206). Dickinson was not alone in her time. As Cristanne Miller notes in "The Sound of Shifting Paradigms, or Hearing Dickinson in the Twenty-First Century" (2004), "the formal experiments of nineteenth-century American poetry are overwhelmingly centered on sound play, especially rhythmic (generally metrical) variation, rhyme, and alliteration and assonance" (207). Miller continues: "Patterns of nineteenth-century poetry itself indicate that poetry was primarily an aural . . . art: poetic innovation was based on alliteration, assonance, multiple and elaborate rhyme schemes, varying meters, and other rhythmic structures" (207–8). My position aligns with Miller's on hearing Dickinson, and then diverges with my argument that in order to hear acutely, readers must see the visual lines.

As Adams explains in *Graces of Harmony,* assonance and consonance provide a poet with "a means of stressing the rhythmic peaks in a line" (29). In building rhythmic structures, Dickinson draws on her instruction in rhetoric and prosody provided by eighteenth- and nineteenth-century grammar and elocution textbooks.[13] After 1795 Lindley Murray's *English Grammar* replaced Noah Webster's grammar to become the most widely used grammar textbook in American schools. Murray identifies the field as a "science," composed of four elements. The first, orthography—from the Greek "orthos," meaning "correct," and "grapho," "to write"—he defines as the "power and proper use" of letters of the alphabet. Etymology, syntax, and prosody are the elements that follow (13).[14] Murray explains that the study of prosody "teaches the true PRONUNCIATION of words, comprising ACCENT, QUANTITY, EMPHASIS, PAUSE, and TONE," and "the laws of VERSIFICATION" (204; capitalization his). He concludes: "As there are few persons who do not sometimes read poetical composition, it seems necessary to give the student some idea of that part of grammar, which explains the principles of versification; that, in reading poetry, he may be the better able to judge of its correctness, and relish its beauties" (220).

"Distinct utterance" is the term commonly used by nineteenth-century grammarians and elocutionists to refer to precise articulation. In his 1810 *Elements of Elocution,* John Walker claims that "wherever there is contradistinction in the sense of the words, there ought to be emphasis in the pronunciation of them," and "wherever we place emphasis, we suggest the idea of contradistinction" (199). Allen Weld's 1856 revised edition of *English Grammar,* illustrated by exercises in composition, analyzing, and parsing, instructs: "Let the class practice simultaneously, on the different sounds of these letters, with a full and distinct utterance" (5). Thomas Sheridan in his 1803 *Course of Lectures on Elocution* expresses the urgent need for clear, correct pronunciation in oral reading: "The first, and most essential point in articulation, is distinctness," and "the chief force of indistinctness is too great precipitancy of speech" (34). "Precipitancy," another shared term (also used by the well-known elocutionist Isaac Watts), refers to the critical fault in oral performance of rushing headlong, and, as if falling from a "precipice," slurring words.

Ebenezer Porter's *Rhetorical Reader,* consisting of instructions for "regulating the voice, with a rhetorical notation, illustrating inflection, emphasis, and modulation" (title page), was the elocution manual used at Amherst Academy when Dickinson studied there. (At the time, her father served as a trustee, and, presumably, helped select the textbooks.) Porter defines emphasis as "a distinctive utterance of words which are especially significant, with such a degree and kind of stress, as conveys their meaning in the best manner." His manual provides practice exercises, including the following sentences, to be read out loud:

"The magistrates ought to prove the declaration."
"'Magistrates ought?' or 'Magistrate sought?'"

"Who ever imagined such an ocean to exist?"
"Who ever imagined such a notion to exist?"[15]

Lindley Murray explains that "for the purpose of marking the different pauses which the sense, and an accurate pronunciation, require," writers use "points," commas and dashes, or "stops," periods (234). He notes that "feet and pauses are the constituent parts of verse" (220), and that a dash is "properly" placed "where a significant pause is required" (243). A long history of commentary on Dickinson's dash explains its use for rhetorical emphasis and metrical variety. In "Emily Dickinson: Poetry and Punctuation," a 1963 article in the *Saturday Review,* Edith Wylder, a pioneer of the first wave of manuscript studies, identifies the mark as an adaptation of a "unique notational system" devised by Porter in his *Rhetorical Reader.* Wylder argues that the angled dashes are based on symbols indicating voice inflection—rising and falling tones, and the monotone. In 1971, in *The Last Face: Emily Dickinson's Manuscripts,* Wylder elaborates on this theory, arguing that the markings assist Dickinson in "creating in written form the precision of meaning inherent in the tone of the human voice" (4). Whereas Dickinson probably did not design the dash to approximate Porter's elocutionary notations, Wylder illuminates Dickinson's use of the dash when she makes the connection between the poet's innovative punctuation and Porter's instruction, and when she explains that "the variety of emphasis that Dickinson's punctuation affords successfully counterbalances . . . the potential rigidity of her hymnal meters" (40). Christina Pugh, in "Ghosts of Meter: Dickinson, After Long Silence," reiterates Wylder's argument: "Dickinson's syntactical elisions and ubiquitous dash work to resist an already-established and very familiar metrical norm" (6).[16]

Following Lindberg-Seyersted, Cristanne Miller explains that "although nineteenth-century writers frequently used dashes, especially in informal writing, Dickinson generally used them more disruptively, more often, and in more various ways than her contemporaries did. Most often, Dickinson's dashes imitate the starts and stops of speech" ("Dickinson's Language: Interpreting Truth Told Slant" 78). Like Wylder and Lindberg-Seyersted, Miller points out that "in the middle of a sentence, for example, dashes may isolate words for emphasis" (78). Miller goes on to say that dashes also "mark off sentence fragments, giving the effect of impulsiveness or strong emotion ('Of Course – I prayed – / And did God care?'); at other times the dash creates an effect of breathlessness or hesitation ('When – suddenly – my Riches shrank – / A Goblin – drank my Dew –'). A dash may usher in abrupt changes of subject or metaphor, as though Dickinson feels greater freedom to articulate the associative leaps of her thinking when she is not bound by conventional punctuation" (78–79).[17]

Whereas dashes at the ends of measured lines are prominent beginning with the first fascicles, in Fascicles 9 and 10 dashes occur frequently within lines: "What is – 'paradise,'" she writes in Fascicle 9; in 10, "And Firmaments – row –." As dashes diversify, one function is to encourage "distinct utterance" of alliterative patterns. For example, here is the last stanza of "Musicians wrestle everywhere," in Fascicle 9:

> Some – say – it is "the Spheres" – at play !
> Some say – that bright Majority
> Of vanished Dames – and Men !
> Some – think it Service in the place
> When we – with late – celestial face –
> Please God – shall ascertain ! (Fr229)

Notice: "Some," "say," "Spheres," "Some," "say," "Dames," "Some," "Service," "place," "celestial," "face," "please," "ascertain." Dashes setting out pauses with repetitions vary timing and rhythm: "Some – say –," "Some say –," "Some – think."

One type of dash that most print editions erase is exclamatory. Fascicle 4 includes two poems with the earliest usage of the "exclamatory dash," my term for a mark that throughout the fascicles and sets often follows an interjection, such as "Ah" and "Oh," and occasionally an address. In the last stanza of "Heart not so heavy as mine": "Oh Bugle – by the window" (Fr88, F4), and in the opening line, "Soul – Wilt thou toss again?" (Fr89,

F4), dashes are elevated above the base of the writing line, unlike commas, which Dickinson draws at or beneath the base. And yet the Franklin and the Johnson editions represent these marks consistently as commas, though Franklin makes one notable exception.

In Fascicle 9 there are several poems that use the exclamatory dash. See, for example, in "For this – accepted Breath" (Fr230): "Ah – what a royal sake"; in "We don't cry – Tim and I" (Fr231): "But – Oh – so high !"; and in "Dying ! Dying in the night !" (Fr222): "This way – Jesus – Let him pass !" In the latter example even though a comma would not precede the start of a new sentence, Franklin, and Johnson, print the line as "This way, Jesus, Let him pass!" Misrepresenting this inventive mark removes an indicator of emotional tone. The erasure of the exclamatory dash represents the many editorial decisions in Dickinson's publication history that muffle her rhythms and tones, and interfere with meaning.

The exception Franklin makes (not Johnson) is in Fascicle 11, "about 1861," in the last stanza of "Wild nights – Wild nights!" (Fr269): "Rowing in Eden – / Ah – the Sea!" Franklin prints the mark after "Ah" not as a comma but as a dash. In this one instance only, as far as I can tell, Franklin allows that an exclamatory dash is a dash—even though his level mark misconfigures it (as most of us do because of publishers' limitations). Perhaps he was moved by two influential works of textual studies that have helped make the manuscript image of this well-known poem especially prominent: Wylder's *The Last Face* (1971), and Martha Nell Smith's *Rowing in Eden: Rereading Emily Dickinson* (1992). Referring to "marks resembling a dash" as "'irregular' notations," Wylder specifies that a notation she calls an "angular slant" is often placed "after an interjection above the writing line" (8). When she coordinates notations with Ebenezer Porter's "inflectional symbols," she identifies the exclamatory dash as one of "the rising slides" (69).[18] In her print translation of "Wild nights – Wild nights !" Wylder places an elevated, short, angled dash after "Ah" (77).[19] An image of this manuscript serves as the cover for *Rowing in Eden: Rereading Emily Dickinson*, and Smith describes the mark as an "ecstatic exclamation mark without a point" (65). She reprints Higginson and Todd's rendition from *Poems by Emily Dickinson: Second Series* (1891), where the dash is replaced by an exclamation point: "Ah! the sea!" (Smith 65).[20]

Dickinson's punctuation puzzles and fascinates her wide readership. In her young adult novel, *A Voice of Her Own: Becoming Emily Dickinson* (2009), Barbara Dana quotes Lindley Murray's *English Grammar*: "The dash, though often used improperly by hasty writers, may be used with propriety, where the sentence breaks off abruptly; where a significant pause is required; or when there is an unexpected turn in the sentiment" (168).

Dana pictures Dickinson as a young writer declaring, "When I think of my love for the dash I fear I join the ranks of the improper, hasty and incoherent writers. . . . But I love it so—its liveliness, its thrust, its enviable ability to include a thought, yet separate that same just far enough from its preceding colleagues to keep the meaning straight. Its boldness, its daring, its sense of abandon! And the freedom, the effortless flow" (168). Literature students are introduced to the mark through textbooks such as *The Norton Anthology of American Literature,* which states that the dash "may have been used systematically for rhetorical emphasis or musical pointing" (Gottesman et al. 2351). Even those who know little about Dickinson do know that she used unusual punctuation: the mark commands attention in the popular imagination, as well as among Dickinson scholars. Critical commentary on the dash will advance when the marks are represented accurately in print and digital editions, and when the dash is no longer singled out and instead is studied in the context of other expressive manuscript features.

Dickinson explores another graphic form of emphasis, and then limits it after the early 1860s. In this poem in Fascicle 10,

> Faith is a fine invention
> For Gentlemen who see –
> But Microscopes are prudent
> In an Emergency ! (Fr202)

notice the underlining. Fascicle 10 has an unusually high number of poems with dense underlining; this opening stanza, for example:

> The Sun – just touched the
> Morning –
> The Morning – Happy thing –
> Supposed that He had come
> to dwell –
> And Life would all be Spring ! (Fr246)

The following poem has four stanzas. Every line has at least one word underlined, most have two; three lines have three or four underlined words.

> If He dissolve – then – there
> is nothing – more –
> Eclipse – at Midnight –
> It was dark – before – (Fr251)

In *English Grammar* Lindley Murray warns:

> There is one error, against which it is particularly proper to caution the learner; namely, that of multiplying emphatical words too much. It is only by a prudent reserve in the use of them, that we can give them any weight. If they recur too often; if a speaker or reader attempts to render everything which he expresses of high importance, by a multitude of strong emphases, we soon learn to pay little regard to them. To crowd every sentence with emphatical words, is like crowding all the pages of a book with italic characters, which, as to the effect, is just the same as to use no such distinctions at all. (215)

It may be that Dickinson came to the same conclusion. After Fascicle 10 there are far fewer underlinings. (In the fascicles and sets Dickinson uses underlining as she revises poems to indicate a selection from the list of possible alternatives to replace a word or phrase.) In Franklin's chronology, the first three hundred poems have the greatest number of underlined words. But after the early 1860s this was no longer one of Dickinson's primary ways to show emphasis. Pauses set out by midline dashes and divisions of metrical lines were serving that purpose.

And then in the mid-1860s, when a greater number of poems divide lines, when there are more divided lines per poem, and division is likely to come earlier in a metrical line, there is a decreased use of punctuation, especially the midline dash. (Franklin makes a related point: "In the mid-1860s [Dickinson] reduced the amount and force of punctuation in the poems" [*Reading Edition* 10].) In Set 7, "about 1865," "Knows how to forget!" (Fr391) uses standard punctuation, including commas in conventional places. The only mid-line dash is exclamatory: "Ah – to be erudite/Enough to know!" In Fascicle 19, "about 1862," an earlier version of the poem has mid-line dashes in one or two of the lines in each of the four stanzas.

A poem from Set 10, in my print translation below, has five stanzas, each with four measured lines. Of these twenty lines, all but two, the last line of the first stanza and the last line of the last stanza, are divided.

> To disappear
> enhances –
> The Man who
> runs away
> Is gilded for
> an instant
> With Immortality

But yesterday
a Vagrant
Today in Memory
lain
With superstitious
value –
We tamper with
Again

But Never – far
as Honor
Removes the paltry
Thing
And impotent
to cherish
We hasten to
adorn –

Of Death the
sternest feature
That just as
we discern
The Quality
defies us –
Securest gathered
then

The Fruit
perverse to plucking
But leaning to
the Sight
With the extatic
limit
Of unobtained Delight. (Fr1239)[21]

"Safe in their Alabaster / chambers" has fifteen dashes in ten measured lines: four of the five in the first stanza come at the ends of measured lines, and one is within the line; in the second stanza each measured line has an end dash, and there are seven dashes within lines. Compare this with the total of five dashes in the twenty measured lines of "To disappear /

enhances" (Fr1239). Print editions and print translations using conventional type, including mine, fail to represent differences among dashes, though the distinctions are significant for interpretation. The argument set out in "To disappear / enhances" moves through four rhetorical sections, and Dickinson uses three long dashes to indicate shifts. The longest dash, drawn with a slight wave as a flourish, closes the aphoristic opening. With "To" appearing slightly indented, the visual lines might serve as a title—a text with an explication to follow. The second section plays on the trope of "the Man who / runs away," a beloved who is recreated and perfected in the minds of those who miss him. The "vagrant" is "in Memory lain," possibly a pun on "Memory Lane." But memory is unreliable; we cannot see the person the way he, or she, was, and we cannot see them where they are now. But we hold out the "gilded" hope that they have achieved immortality, which is what we desire for ourselves. Angry at the abandonment, we, the bereaved, devalue the beloved, who becomes "the paltry Thing," "the worthless One" in Dickinson's alliterative variant. The mortal is "paltry"—the word derives from dialectical German for "rag"; and so we "adorn" them, making their image more beautiful than reality, dressing them in better clothing. ("Adorn" sounds like "adore.")

The second long dash, at the end of stanza 3, closes the second section and marks the move in stanza 4 to a reflection on death's lesson—that in observing the dying we lose sight at the moment we attain clarity, recognizing a human being's flawed magnificence just as we lose track of who they really are. The third long dash concludes this thought and leads to the final revelation: we can never know whether our desires for love or knowledge will be fulfilled, thus ensuring that the pleasures of desiring will never end.

This complex wisdom poem depends on line division and enjambment to convey its twists and turns. Here Dickinson varies Common Measure:

To disapp*ear* / enh*a*nces –
The M*a*n who / r*u*ns aw*ay*
Is g*i*lded for / an *i*nstant
With *I*mmort*a*lity

This stanza has a 3+.3.2+.2+ pattern. (To show that an unstressed syllable, or syllables, follow the last beat in a line, I use the plus sign. In traditional scansion these would be called "3f" and "2f" lines, with "feminine," that is, "weak and unstressed," line endings. Of course, I want to avoid this problematic "f" designation.) Dickinson uses the 2+ and 3+ lines in this poem with enjambment to represent the movement of thought. (Several times in letters and poems Dickinson refers to her writing as "thought.") Timothy Morris, in "The Development of Dickinson's Style," writes that "Dickinson began by using conventional hymn-like end-stopping. Her earliest poems are heavily end stopped, and the first fascicle poems, in 1858–59, show only infrequent enjambment. But from 1860 to 1865, the amount of enjambment in her poetry grows steadily." Morris calculates that "by 1864, more than one-third of her quatrains are enjambed" (164). He concludes that "even more than her rhyme, Dickinson's characteristic enjambment is probably the one formal element that makes her quatrains sound so distinctive" (163). Manuscript study invites further analysis of Dickinson's use of enjambment in relation to alliteration, range of rhyme, and divided metrical lines.

The variation on Common Measure in "To disappear / enhances" carries the authority of the form, while allowing for lines closer to emphatic speech. Line division frequently supports the stress pattern by adding pauses before or after the beats, as in the first stanza where there is greater stress on "disappear" than there would be without the pause introduced by division. Small words are stressed in similar ways, such as "for," in "Is gilded for / an instant," where division also draws attention to the consonance of "for" and "Im*mor*tality." In the final stanza, "to" in "But leaning to / the Sight"—note the alliterative "*t*'s"—is articulated, and "Sight" has greater impact.

Line division supports alliteration, adding to the emphasis it provides and the accentuation it requires. A break between "disappear" and "enhances" makes it less likely that "pear" and "en" will be run together, and more likely that the parallel structure, each word has three syllables, and the consonance, "s," will be heard. "Enhances" positioned alone on a line, "Man" centered in the line, "an instant" after a line break: the arrangements strengthen the assonance. "But yesterday / a Vagrant" minimizes the echo of "day" with "a," and "day" alliterates more gracefully with "Vagrant." Note the pattern of "er," "or," "ar": "Never," "far," "Honor," "yesterday," "Memory," "superstitious," "tamper." In the fourth and fifth stanzas, in the lines "Securest gathered / then [stanza break] The Fruit," enjambment adds to the effect of "Securest" consonating with "Fruit," and with "Sight," "Extatic," "limit," "unobtained," and "Delight."

Dickinson often chooses for possible substitution alternate words that continue alliterative threads. In the first stanza, "The Man who" would become "The Man that," and "tinctured" would replace "gilded" to alliterate with "instant" and "Immortality." "T" continues in the next stanza with "But," "yesterday," "Vagrant," "Today," "tamper," and the alternate for "value" which might be "merit" or, more likely, "moment," which is underlined. In the fourth stanza, "Excellence," where all three syllables fit the pattern, could substitute for "Quality," adding to the stanza's thread of "*s*'s": "sternest," or its alternate, "sharpest," and "just as," "discern," "defies us," and "Securest." The practice of listing alliterative substitutions begins in the early 1860s. Two alternate stanzas for "Safe in their Alabaster / chambers" continue the thread of "*s*'s." One stanza begins "Springs – shake the sills – / But – the Echoes – stiffen," and ends "Staples – of Ages – have / buckled – there"; the other, "Springs – shake the seals – / But the silence – stiffens," concluding, "Midnight in Marble – / Refutes – the Suns." This selection principle is further evidence of alliteration's central role in the way Dickinson organizes sound.

The first four stanzas of "To disappear / enhances" use assonance and consonance, or "slant" rhyme, in the Common Measure end-rhyme positions, lines 2 and 4: "away" and "Immortality"; "lain" and "Again"; "Thing" (or its alternate, "one") and "adorn"; "discern," and "then." In a departure from the assonantal and consonantal pattern, in the final stanza the rhyme is "near exact" ("near" because a one-syllable word is considered to rhyme inexactly with a two-syllable word), announcing closure: "Sight" and "Delight."

In the later poems of the sets, Dickinson's spatial prosody includes varying the amount of space, the distance, between two words in a line, which creates pauses, without dashes. Here is my print translation of the first three metrical lines of the fourth stanza with words spaced to represent the relative spacing of the manuscript lines:

Of   Death the
sternest   feature
That just   as
we   discern
The   Quality
defies us –

Nineteenth-century handwriting instruction does not condone irregular spacing between words. Penmanship manuals make clear that this was not the norm, that it was a flaw. The 1873 edition of *The Payson, Dunton, and Scribner Manual of Penmanship* remarks that "It is a very common fault to place the words too far apart" (37). *Gaskell's Compendium of Forms, Educational, Social, Legal, and Commercial; Embracing a Complete Self-Teaching Course in Penmanship and Bookkeeping, and Aid to English Composition; Including Orthography, Capital Letters, Punctuation, Compo-*

*sition, Elocution, Oratory, Rhetoric, Letter Writing, etc,* in 1881, explains in a section on "Spacing": "The spaces between letters and between words should be as uniform in manuscript as in print. The rule is to leave just space enough between the words to write the small m; between letters just enough to avoid crowding" (32).[22] In "To disappear / enhances" a greater amount of space after "Of" creates a dramatic pause before "Death." "That just," together, reads quickly; then a pause before "as," followed by a line division, slows the pace, giving us time to wonder: "'just as' what?" This prosodic device for regulating space invites readers into a deeper dialogue with the poem.

Involving readers—getting us to read closely, listen carefully, and think—is central to Dickinson's poetics. In my contribution to *Wider than the Sky: Essays and Meditations on the Healing Power of Emily Dickinson,* "May the Circle Be Unbroken: Reading Emily Dickinson After 9/11," I tell the following story about a spring 2004 marathon reading of Dickinson's poetry at the Emily Dickinson Museum:

> Participants at the community reading were seriously engaged as they read; one organization after another took its place in the circle of chairs and became absorbed in the poetry as if settling into a study group. One of my favorite moments was when a young woman's turn came to read and she sat studying the page. "Oh," she said, when she looked up and saw us waiting for her, "I was still thinking about the last poem." (MacKenzie and Dana 81).

The novelist Jeanette Winterson writes: "When people say that poetry is a luxury, or an option, or for the educated middle classes, or that it shouldn't be read at school because it is irrelevant, I suspect the people doing the saying have had things pretty easy. A tough life needs a tough language—and that is what poetry is" (40). Dickinson created tough prosodic forms: durable, flexible, capacious. Her readers need new editions and new ways of reading that bring these forms to life.

# "This – was my finallest / Occasion –"

## Fascicle 40 and Dickinson's Aesthetic of Intrinsic Renown

PAUL CRUMBLEY

After completing Fascicle 40 in early 1864, Dickinson ceased binding her manuscript books and two years later entered a four-year period of infrequent writing that Ralph W. Franklin has characterized as "without fascicles or sets or even many poems" (*Poems* 26). This is the same period during which the volume of Dickinson's correspondence declined to a level Thomas H. Johnson has described as "the smallest by far that Emily Dickinson is known to have written during her mature years" (*Letters* 448). My approach to Fascicle 40 anticipates this future lull in production by reading the poems it contains as consistent with a transitional phase in Dickinson's development as a poet. To clarify this dimension of the fascicle, I position it within an ongoing meditation on the public life of poems that was part of Dickinson's thinking as early as 1863 when she transcribed "Publication – is the Auction" (Fr788) and appears to have concluded by 1877 when she responds to Thomas Wentworth Higginson's poem "Decoration" with a poem of her own in which she states that true poetic achievement may be "Too intrinsic for Renown –" (L583).[1]

That Dickinson should contemplate the nature of publication and authorial fame during the months she assembled Fascicle 40 makes sense for the simple reason that she had created a substantial body of work capable of standing on its own, but her language also reflects sensitivity to widely publicized copyright debates that repeatedly raised questions about the political, legal, and philosophical foundations of literary ownership. These public debates provide a broad cultural context that is helpful in interpreting Dickinson's concern with authorship at the moment she was completing her fortieth manuscript book and thinking back over the approximately 251 poems or letter-poems that she is estimated to have sent by the end of 1864 as part of her correspondence (Franklin, *Poems* 1547–57).[2] The circulation and limited print publication of these poems, which achieved a kind of high point in 1864, might also have led Dickinson to realize that her poems had lives of their own. A number of the fascicle's poems support this possibility by indicating Dickinson's wish to observe her poems and determine how they were being absorbed by the world around her. For this reason, these poems and indeed the whole of Fascicle 40 can be read as Dickinson's dawning recognition that she wanted her work to enter the life of language itself, invisibly fusing with the thoughts of others.

Despite the presence of this thematic consistency, though, I do not read the six bifolia and twenty-one poems that make up Fascicle 40 as forming a coherent narrative.[3] Instead, I build on Sharon Cameron's argument that "if there is a story in the fascicles, it is told discontinuously" (*Choosing* 56). Cameron identifies "'returned to' moments" that "function as variants of something, though what is being returned to and departed from is never, within the limits of one lyric entity, fully in view" (56). Following Cameron's lead, I do not attempt to resolve meaning definitively but rather tease out one of many potential variants, this one gaining support from public debate surrounding the disposition of literary property and Dickinson's relationship to her poems as revealed in her life and letters. As Eleanor Heginbotham has stated in her book on the fascicles, "context shapes interpretation" and it is not "illogical to see what proximate poems can tell us about each other" and what they "suggest about the concerns of the author at the moment she bound them together" (xi).

The fascicle binding is of course significant, as it is that which sets the fascicle apart as a distinct literary gathering and allows for the sense of proximity that Heginbotham mentions. In my reading of the fascicle, however, I take direction from Franklin's early observation that the bifolium sheet was Dickinson's primary "unit" of composition (*MB* xii) and treat each sheet as representing a greater coherence than the fascicle as a whole.[4] Fascicle 40 thus emerges as a gathering of six sheets constituting twenty-one bifolia poems that cluster around central issues related to reading and writing, circulation and reception, and departures from conventional modes of conduct, all of which are appropriate for a poet formulating an aesthetic directed to intrinsic rather than public renown. The first bifolium is primarily concerned with reading, reception, and distribution. These poems present a speaker who *reads* "Bulletins all Day / From Immortality" (Fr820), one who imagines how best to reach an audience in "Wert Thou but ill – that / I might show thee" (Fr821), and a speaker who envisions the management of her poems as the harvest of a crop she describes as "In Consummated Bloom – " (Fr822). The second bifolium identifies "A nearness to Tremendousness –" that one poet/speaker attains by refusing the "Laws" of literary convention described as "Contentment's quiet Suburb" (Fr824). Speakers in the third sheet pursue a new obsession that replaces the security of "Wealth" and "Station" (Fr827) with the risky circulation of flowers that symbolize poems. The next bifolium, the fourth, vastly expands the temporal context for assessing personal achievement, looking beyond "The Admirations – and / Contempts – of time –" (Fr830; *MB* 987). The fifth sheet concentrates on the problem of reader reception, imagining how "I shall be perfect – in / His sight –" (Fr834; *MB* 991). The fascicle's sixth and final bifolium positions fame beyond acceptance or rejection in the present moment and anticipates a "Hint of Glory" (Fr838). The speaker of this concluding poem enters the darkness of night with "Faith" in "a Revolution" to come that will reveal "New Horizons" (Fr839).

Major events shaping Dickinson's life in 1864 would have sharpened her sensitivity to the brevity of life and the impossibility of controlling the public response to her poems. Edward Hitchcock died in February and Thomas Wentworth Higginson entered the second year of his military deployment to South Carolina. Letters provide evidence of personal anxiety provoked by the continuation of the Civil War and the eye treatments that took Dickinson to Boston in February and again from April through November. As Karen Dandurand has noted, 1864 also marked the "the unparalleled publication of five of [Dickinson's] poems within two months" (257). More important than the number of poems may be the fact that "Flowers – Well – if anybody" (Fr95) appeared in four different settings and "Blazing in Gold and quenching in Purple" (Fr321) in three, making for a total of ten print publications, by far the most of any year.[5] Dandurand identifies the likely significance this reprinting of poems would have held for Dickinson: "she probably would have seen that two of her poems were reprinted and would have understood what this implied—that the poems might reappear again, in other newspapers: they had become 'public property'" (257). The most reprinted of her poems, "Flowers – Well – if anybody," considers the impossibility of explaining what poems are, stating instead that they operate according to a "system of aesthetics" the speaker describes as "Far superior to mine." The appearance of this and other anonymously published poems in settings Dickinson had not selected and could not control would have heightened her awareness that poetry acquires new life through readers. There is "Too much pathos in their faces," the speaker of "Flowers – Well – if anybody" admits, "For a simple breast like mine –."

Dickinson's recognition that she had so little direct influence over the success or failure of her poems gave rise to letters in which she blends artistic concerns with expressions of anxiety over the outcome of the Civil War. Her fluctuating and intertwined emotions are vividly conveyed in a letter to her nieces Louise and Francis Norcross in which she conflates public grief brought on by the war with the appearance of a new poem by Robert Browning. Dickinson begins this letter that was probably written in 1864 by acknowledging, "Sorrow seems more general than it did, and not the estate of a few persons, since the war began" (L436). She then mentions that the new poem by Browning reminded her of her own poetry: "I remembered that I, myself, in my smaller way, sang off charnel steps. Every day life feels mightier, and what we have the power to be, more stupendous." This conjunction of loss and future promise characterizes the general mood of Fascicle 40 where multiple poems contemplate the poet's release of poetry that passes into the larger world and the uncertainty of artistic reward that comes from the world's reception.

Dickinson incorporated the first stanza from the poem that opens the fascicle—"The only news I know" (Fr820)—in a June 1864 letter to Higginson that similarly juxtaposes anxiety and promise:

> I wish to see you more than before I failed – Will you tell me your health?
> I am surprised and anxious, since receiving your note –
> The only News I know
> Is Bulletins all day
> From Immortality. (*Poems* 776–77)

In this instance, Dickinson's anxiety appears most directly related to Higginson's health. Her own eye problems appear to have intensified her desire to "see" Higginson; the phrase "before I failed" reflecting her current diminished vision. The sense of promise implied by "Bulletins . . . / From Immortality" is notably dampened by the likelihood that Dickinson intertwines newspaper reports from the front announcing the heroic sacrifices of soldiers with information she receives about the public life of poems like "Flowers – Well – if anybody" (Fr95).

Many scholars have remarked on Dickinson's reflective state of mind during the time that she was working on Fascicle 40. Alfred Habegger describes Dickinson's stylistic development as moving away from "present, extreme, and exclamatory feeling" toward "a story line in which the speaker gives a respectful account of what she has achieved" (472). Writing specifically of 1864, Habegger delineates a time of transition that might easily apply to artistic self-awareness: "In 1864 we begin to see poems registering a sense that the struggles of youth and early maturity are over" (482). To substantiate this point, Habegger cites "The Admirations – and Contempts – of time –" (Fr830), the twelfth of the twenty-one poems in Fascicle 40.

James R. Guthrie's extensive study of Dickinson's visual impairment details the single most significant physiological development contributing to the reflective and anticipatory mood so pronounced in the fascicle. Indeed, it is difficult not to agree with Guthrie's argument that "illness itself [was] a governing factor in Dickinson's development as a poet" (*Vision* 4). The part of Guthrie's careful analysis that most directly applies to the position I am developing here has less to do with the direct influence of her illness, however, than with his acknowledgment that during this period of her life Dickinson was actively thinking through her relationship to her poems, especially in terms of ownership. In an illuminating discussion of "It sifts from Leaden Sieves –" (Fr291), Guthrie explains that through a revision of the poem that took place between 1862 and 1865,[6] Dickinson significantly altered the poem's logic in order to emphasize "the mechanism of poetic language rather than the poet's controlling vision" (151). Guthrie's conclusion that Dickinson removed "the presence of her own body from [the poem] so that it could assume a life of its own" parallels my own sense that Fascicle 40 investigates the lives poems achieve independent of the poets who compose them.

Páraic Finnerty agrees with Guthrie that Dickinson's visual impairment and the treatment she underwent informed her view of the public life of poems, only for him Dickinson's understanding of language is directly linked to a shift in her relationship to Shakespeare that also took place at this time. Noting that Dickinson's "public engagement with Shakespeare, and much of her praise of him, comes after her eye trouble in the mid-1860s," Finnerty argues that Dickinson openly praises Shakespeare only after the era of her own greatest production was over (132). The preceding years of intense creativity mark a period when Dickinson does not mention Shakespeare precisely because for her Shakespeare was a living presence with whom she collaborated as she would "a literary friend" (137); her dearth of references reflects Dickinson's intimate engagement with his work. Finnerty points out that Dickinson shared this approach to collaboration with other nineteenth-century American women who similarly "transformed Shakespeare, developing his plots and characters to address issues important to them as women" (116). According to this logic, Dickinson "demonstrates the expected knowledge of Shakespeare's works by imaginatively transforming them." Such reasoning equates fame with intrinsic renown by linking literary influence to the absorption of authorial language rather than the naming of authors and discrete literary texts. Accordingly, the appearance of references to Shakespeare that surface in Dickinson's writing after her eye treatments suggests that in the years following the completion of Fascicle 40 her attitude toward Shakespeare altered and she became more willing to acknowledge his influence. Fascicle 40 might in this context coincide with the end of a phase when Dickinson viewed herself as establishing a body of work capable of influence equal to Shakespeare's and the beginning of active reflection on the world's reception of that work.

The third bifolium provides what may be the clearest examination of the poet's relationship to her poems that I consider a primary preoccupation of the entire fascicle. It contains "I hide myself – within my flower" (Fr80C),[7] the one poem that also appears in another fascicle, and concludes with "Between My Country – / and the Others –" (Fr829), another poem in which flowers play a prominent role as metaphors for poetry. These poems communicate the poet's concealment in her poems and the way poems connect the poet to other people. The second flower poem's closing lines state that "Flowers – negotiate / between us – / As Ministry." Read in the company of these two poems, the first poem in the bifolium, "All forgot for recollecting" (Fr827), describes the sudden alteration of consciousness that takes place with the discovery of new love or when a poet chooses a new relationship with readers.

All forgot +for recollecting     +through
Just a paltry One – All forsook, for just
A Stranger's
New Accompanying –

+Grace of Wealth, and     + Grace of Rank – and – Grace of Fortune
Grace of Station
Less accounted than
An unknown +Esteem     +content
possessing –
Estimate – Who can –

Home effaced – Her
faces dwindled –
Nature – altered small –

Sun – if shown – or
Storm – if shattered –
Overlooked I all –

Dropped – my fate – a
timid Pebble –
In thy bolder Sea –
+Prove – me – Sweet – if        +Ask
I regret it –
Prove Myself – of Thee –

We are told that all is forgotten for "just a Stranger's / New Accompanying"; even "Home" is "effaced" for "An unknown Esteem." The passage of poetry into another's world is most directly established in the fourth and final stanza where the speaker describes having "Dropped – my fate – a / timid Pebble – / In thy bolder Sea –," after which she waits for the lover or reader to "Prove – me – Sweet – if / I regret it – / Prove Myself – of Thee." One function of these lines would be to declare that the speaker now awaits her reader/lover's response in order to assess the ultimate value of her efforts. Of particular interest is the metaphorical proposition that even the most passionate of embraces might yet render success or failure difficult to determine; after all, how noticeable could even the most profound impact be when it involves a pebble entering the sea? As Dorothy Huff Oberhaus has pointed out, the modifier of "Sea" is "bolder," "a verbal play on "boulder" that further accentuates the insignificance of the pebble (110). Such imagery might also evoke the perplexity of a poet who wonders how to measure success when the desired outcome is immersion in language.

Dickinson once again uses the pebble metaphor in an April 1882 letter she sent Thomas Niles of Roberts Brothers after he requested poems for publication. In that letter, she asks Niles to "accept a Pebble" (L725), referring to "How happy is the little Stone" (Fr1570E), the poem she enclosed. The poem presents the stone as "rambl[ing] in the Road alone" where "A passing Universe put on" her "Coat of elemental Brown," an inauspicious-seeming act that Dickinson casts as fulfilling the poem's "absolute Decree / In casual simplicity –." Her language tells Niles that her poem is already in the world—though in a manner entirely unlike the commercial publication he has in mind. More to the point, even, she informs him that her poem has already achieved success, even though its fame is casual and simple, not attached to public renown. The reference to a pebble in Fascicle 40 may indeed express a like belief in intrinsic renown, only at this earlier stage of her life the fame she contemplates is presented as a future possibility rather than an accomplished fact.

The release of poems into the world that is taken up in the two flower poems and alluded to through the pebble reference is further explored in the remaining bifolium poem where the speaker appears to be addressing her poems, expressing anxiety about letting them go. She opens by acknowledging the comfort her creations have given her:

> Had I not This, or
> This, I said,
> Appealing to Myself,
> In a moment of prosperity –
> Inadequate – were Life – (Fr828)

A speaker similar to Dickinson casts her eyes over the poetic output of many years and declares that the poems that fill her manuscript books have given her life meaning. Extending the metaphor of a poet-to-poem conversation to the next stanza, Dickinson uses quotation marks to present the poems she has just addressed as responding with voices of their own:

> "Thou has not Me,
> nor Me" – it said
> In moment of Reverse –
> "And yet Thou art
> industrious –
> No need – had'st Thou – of us –"?

One of the first things to notice here is Dickinson's careful use of pronouns. Initially, the language framed in quotation marks is associated with a singular "it" (as in "it said") that may refer to the speaker's "Life" mentioned at the very end of the preceding stanza. At the same time, though, the speaking entity identifies itself as composed of two "me's," presupposing more than one speaker. The final two lines then present this speaking entity as addressing the speaker as "Thou" and defining itself as "us," thereby thoroughly frustrating any efforts either to separate or conjoin singular and plural speakers. The simplest solution to this conundrum is to treat the lines as a riddle that asks what it is that can be both singular and plural, part and not part of the self. Given the poet-to-poem trope of the first stanza, we might conclude that the poems alluded to as "This" and "This" in the first line of the poem correspond here to "Me" and "Me," urging the conclusion that poems are simultaneously part of and not part of the poet who creates them. If indeed the poems are speaking to the poet, they are informing her that they have in some crucial sense always been part of the larger world. More importantly, even, they ask what possible need she might have for them given that she is "industrious" and in theory capable of producing more. The point being that the proper function of the writer is to write, not cling to the products of past writing.

This emphasis on the *act* of writing, rather than its material outcomes, provides the focus for the final two stanzas of the poem. Here the poet declares that future growth depends on not letting completed poems get in the way of her desire to write:

> My need – was all I had –
> I said –
> The need did not
> reduce
> Because the food – exterminate –
> The hunger – does not cease –
>
> But diligence – is sharper –
> Proportioned to the chance –
> To feed upon the
> Retrograde –
> Enfeebles – the Advance –

The logic that so aggressively binds these two stanzas turns on the perception that writing, like hunger and diligence, is a need that is never absolutely satisfied. Just as food can "exterminate" appetite temporarily but fails to eradicate hunger, so too do poems meet the immediate need of the poet but not eliminate the desire that fired that need in the first place. More to the point, the poem seems to be saying that past poems constitute a form of "Retrograde" accomplishment that diminishes poetic power ("Enfeebles") if mistakenly viewed as a continued source of artistic nourishment. It would be far better to sharpen one's diligence through responsiveness to "chance." If we take the speaker of the poem to be a poet, then the function of the poem is to convey the poet's discovery that her poems have lives of their own and that her particular development as a poet is best achieved by dedicating herself to new writing rather than asserting ownership over her past creations. The poem's closest approximation to perfect end rhyme links "chance" to "Advance," accentuating recognition that attentiveness to the unpredictable and unprecedented is crucial to future artistic growth.

To explain what Dickinson might have had in mind when referring to poems that are not the possession of the poet and that succeed through lives of their own, it helps to look briefly at the copyright debates that significantly shaped nineteenth-century American culture's definition of authorial ownership. Dickinson would have known that throughout the course of her life American authors sought to extend proprietary rights over literary productions by claiming that notions of property based on the writings of John Locke justified their doing so as an extension of natural rights. One of the most active proponents of authorial copyright was Noah Webster, who, as an Amherst resident of considerable fame, author of the dictionary owned by Dickinson's family, and grandfather of Dickinson's friend Emily Fowler, would have brought this debate close to home. Siva Vaidhyanathan states in *Copyrights and Copywrongs* that Webster was instrumental in establishing the Copyright Law of 1831 that extended copyright protection from fourteen "to twenty-eight years (renewable for fourteen more)" and that he was a tireless advocate for "perpetual copyright protection" (45). Driving efforts like Webster's was the conviction that authors ought to enjoy the same natural rights to property ownership that the legal system associated with the ownership of landed estates or other forms of material property.

Through a series of copyright acts that began with the 1790 Copyright Act and—as far as Dickinson is concerned, included the 1831, the 1851, and the 1870 Copyright Acts—the American judicial system increasingly sided with authors, extending protection for literary property based on the Lockean understanding of natural law, according to which ownership is founded on the principle that individuals own their bodies and can acquire additional property by investing the labor of their bodies in the natural world.[8] Melissa J. Homestead succinctly describes the legal status of authorship based on Locke:

> Thus, according to Locke, man acquired property rights by mixing his labor with common materials, and civil government had a fundamental duty to protect those property rights acquired through labor. Advocates of copyright transformed Locke's laboring body and hands into the author's laboring mind. Similarly, they transformed Locke's material objects removed from the state of nature and made a man's own through physical labor (such as trees transformed into lumber to build a house)

into words and ideas from the common store transformed by the author's intellectual labors of invention, arrangement, and selection into works of literature. (26)

The writer's mind derives its power to acquire property from the precedent provided by the labor of an isolated and thereby original body. Critically, the focus on originality made possible through isolated acts implies that authority for the ownership of literary property depends on the privacy of individuals whose labor generates products that bear the imprint of a unique, natural, and unmediated self. As a consequence of this reasoning, the productions of authors were viewed as the unencumbered expressions of the private self.[9]

Virtually all scholarly accounts of the nineteenth-century copyright debate acknowledge that the core issue was how to balance public access to knowledge with the need to provide authorial incentives. Much of the nineteenth century was absorbed in very public debates surrounding revisions of the copyright law that sought a legal distinction separating a collective intellectual commons from the particular expressions of ideas achieved by individual authors.[10] Legal scholars Monroe E. Price and Malla Pollack describe "the complexity of copyright in a free society" as posing a particularly vexing legal challenge: "how does one calibrate a legal structure so as to provide adequate incentives for creativity without, at the same time, discouraging the inventive scholarship that comes from the exploitation of existing ideas?" (452). What may well have concerned Dickinson most was the manner in which copyright legislation that was proposed as a means to liberate authors from slavery within a highly exploitative commercial marketplace inadvertently restricted authorial freedom by narrowing the scope of literary expression.

This is precisely what took place by means of a circular logic that applied all too often to nineteenth-century female authors who were entering the literary marketplace in unprecedented numbers. In her discussion of the Copyright Act of 1909, Homestead identifies a broad-based restriction of authorial expression that had perhaps inadvertently accompanied the publication industry's advocacy of copyright from the time it was first enacted. She explains that the expansion of authorial protection initially arose from the mistaken expectation that legal protection would lead to "increased freedom and power for authors," when in fact "publishers instead increasingly 'managed' authorial production" (259). Based on their assessments of market demand, "publishers increasingly intervened in the artistic process" so that what seemed at first an "expansion of author's rights was thus ultimately a triumph of corporate interests" (259). In other words, authorial representations of the private self came under increasing pressure to conform to publicly accepted views of private experience.

Stacy Margolis addresses this specific topic in *The Public Life of Privacy in Nineteenth-Century American Literature* where she argues that during this period writers—in this case, novelists—consciously explored the way public assumptions about the private self, or what she terms "publicness," acted "as a condition of intelligibility" (14). As I hope my preceding description of Fascicle 40 indicates, Dickinson drew attention to this very issue by concentrating attention on the distinct experiences of individual readers, rather than conformity to publicly determined values and actions. In an important sense, the concept of intrinsic renown requires the perception that language acquires power as it is informed by the distinct circumstances of individual readers. Thus, in "All forgot for recollecting" the speaker forsakes "All" that is familiar "for just / A Stranger's / New Accompanying –." There is no sense of language imposing or confirming conformity; rather, language is distinguished by ceaseless mutability. As the speaker of "Had I not this – or / This, I said" concludes: "To feed upon the / Retrograde – / Enfeebles the Advance –."

In her efforts to extricate her own writing from public constructions of privacy, Dickinson reveals her sympathy for the utilitarian side of the copyright wars that questioned the founding of literary ownership on originality. Fundamental to the utilitarian position was the view that authorship was an activity understood as "communicative and participatory" (Rice 92). Utilitarians viewed authors as pursuing their craft by drawing on the circulation of ideas already present in the public domain, adding to that store of ideas through participation that was fundamentally public in nature. In the eyes of utilitarians, copyright was a legal device designed purely for the purpose of providing authors incentives that would then increase the public circulation of ideas. Thomas Jefferson presented a classic utilitarian summary of authorship in an 1813 letter to Isaac MacPherson:

> "If nature has made any one thing less susceptible than all others of exclusive property, it is the action of the thinking power called an idea, which an individual may exclusively possess as long as he keeps it to himself; but the moment it is divulged, it forces itself into the possession of everyone, and the receiver cannot dispose himself of it." (quoted in Vaidhyanathan 23)

In opposition to this view, copyright advocates magnified the material dimension of authorship, giving particular weight to the literary product of the writer's labor. As the speaker of "Had I not This, or / This, I said" makes plain, however, an important reason for Dickinson's resistance to copyright was her recognition that the language authors use to construct their art has a public life that cannot be separated from the private experience of the author.

The clearest example of Dickinson's calculus for breaking the grip of publicly defined versions of privacy and shaping an aesthetic that privileges the unpredicted but actual experiences of readers appears in "Publication – is the Auction" (Fr788), a poem probably composed around 1863—the year before her creation of Fascicle 40. More than any other poem in the Dickinson corpus, "Publication – is the Auction" provides insight into the mind of the woman writer who imagines how best to elude entrapment in the authorial body demanded by copyright. The poem's concern with ownership and the body may also be understood as Dickinson's effort to think through the implications of property rights in general and the extent that ownership and economic slavery are intertwined. In this poem, what begins as a dismissive rejection of the commercial motive for publication quickly becomes a much more thoughtful assessment of democratic poetics, the literary marketplace, and the limits of authorial property rights:

> Publication – is the Auction
> Of the Mind of Man –
> Poverty – be justifying
> For so foul a thing
>
> Possibly – but We – would rather
> From Our Garrett go
> White – unto the White Creator –
> Than invest – Our Snow –
>
> Thought belong to Him who gave it
> Then – to Him Who bear
> It's Corporeal illustration – sell
> The Royal Air –
>
> In the Parcel – Be the Merchant
> Of the Heavenly Grace –
> But reduce no Human Spirit
> To Disgrace of Price –

The analysis of publication conducted through this poem passes through three phases, each of which constitutes a specific authorial option. Taken together, these alternative postures, or voices, focus the poem's discussion of publication on the issue of originality, or what Mark Rose describes as the "doctrine of originality" that arose "as a central value in cultural production . . . in precisely the same period as the notion of the author's property right" (6). Rose's observation that "the representation of the author as a creator who is entitled to profit from his intellectual labor came into being through a blending of literary and legal discourses" (6) affirms the primary role attributed to privacy as a necessary adjunct to original creation. It is in response to this assertion of privacy that Dickinson speaks most powerfully in this poem.[11]

All three of the perspectives sketched in the poem treat as a given the role that economics plays in imagining approaches to publication. The opening stanza presents a speaker who appears to disdain the economics of publication while paradoxically retaining confidence in the larger system of exchange; the problem she cites is one of taste that carries with it implications of class and gender. A genteel woman would never permit her private writing to enter the marketplace, but perhaps the demands of poverty would justify such degradation. In this case, the speaker grants that donning the commercial female body may be justified for those whose need is great, but that the process of accepting the public determination of that body is a form of commodification and hence slavery that the speaker will not accept for herself. In a curious inversion of the "author-slave analogy" that Homestead associates with the arguments in favor of copyright (9, 49–51), Dickinson presents copyright as enabling authors to profit by their labor, but in doing so entering economic slavery by assuming a commercialized female body.[12] Beginning the poem in this way may obliquely signal Dickinson's own contemplation of commercial publication during the early years of fascicle composition, an option that she distances herself from through the speaker of this poem.

The voice that opens the second stanza is more contemplative; this speaker appears to weigh her initial judgment, then reject it as unsuited to her particular preferences. She chooses not to be enslaved within the body of the conventional female author, but signals her refusal by an act of denial that reifies the economic and legal system that negatively defines her. The language of the stanza holds open the possibility that the speaker is rethinking her position even as she declares it. When she uses the plural pronouns "We" and "Our," she conflates the royal "we" with the idea that she is acting for others. This speaker anticipates her fate at the hands of publishers and openly admits her distaste for such an outcome. She understands all too clearly that to "invest – Our Snow" would be to "invest" in both the monetary sense and in terms of dress—it would require tainting the pure snow of the insufficiently "public" and hence unintelligible female subject by assuming the guise of conventional female authorship. The problem is that her disdainful refusal to pursue publication here results in a form of inaction that potentially perpetuates the protocols of property and ownership she finds so distasteful: she remains secluded within property she perceives as safe ("Our Garret") and takes into that retreat property that she believes she can protect in the interest of herself and others ("Our Snow"). At this point in the poem, the repetition of the word "White" in line 7 significantly magnifies the racial implications of such a choice, suggesting that the speaker subscribes to a racist ideology that understands creation as supporting the race-based privilege of whites. Such a position is ultimately unacceptable not only because it fails to make the actual experiences of women publicly intelligible but because it also reveals the speaker's complicity in the cultural definition of nonwhites as "Other." This the speaker cannot do because she is altogether too aware that her interest in publication is motivated by a desire to escape the category of "Other" imposed on women writers who stand outside the protocols of print culture. The logic of the first two stanzas demonstrates that the speaker's inaction perpetuates the auction of the female writer by placing unintelligible women in the same category of "Other" that denies the humanity of nonwhites. Karen Sanchez-Eppler makes this point in a different but related context when she writes that Dickinson "does not project her fears onto the bodies of some poor 'Other,' safely cordoned off by class or race. Rather, she recognizes this dangerous body as her own" (130).

The third and fourth stanzas introduce yet another voice that builds on the first two by continuing in the idiom of capitalist discourse but with the added twist of suggesting that items of greatest value can never be the property of distinct individuals. Instead, the body is presented as the vehicle for "Thought"—a commodity that receives value prior to embodiment through the agency of "Him who gave it"—that originates in an invisible source that exceeds the apprehension of "Him Who bear[s] / It's Corporeal illustration." Read in the context of copyright debate, this source of thought acts as a divinely inspired intellectual commons out of which the "Royal Air" emerges as the utilitarian circulation of "Heavenly Grace." The body is not the creator of literary property after all; instead, the body is the vehicle for already created "Thought" and therefore incapable of becoming the locus for private and hence original creation.[13]

The injunction delivered in the final seven lines instructs those authors who must seek commercial publication in the honest and democratic fulfillment of their duties. If sell they must, they are to "sell / The Royal Air"; that is, the contents of the "Parcel" and not the parcel. This is a direct reversal of the basis for copyright that presents authors as justified in marketing the particular expression they give to ideas extracted from the intellectual commons. Such a finely drawn distinction between the corporeal poem and the message conveyed through linguistic embodiment demands that the article of value is not human creation but "Heavenly Grace"; not the body but that which is never more than partially embodied or always emerging out of invisibility. The alternative would be to market the body and thereby "reduce . . . Human Spirit / To Disgrace of Price," to engage in a form of misrepresentation that erases knowledge of the true source of value.[14] Elevating the body of the poem above its message and then reifying the body *as* message consolidates a publicly intelligible female body that retroactively casts as "Other" all deviations from that body. The marketplace requirement that value be placed in the textual body affirms a form of ownership that confuses the true origin of thought with the human artifice that served as its momentary habitation. To market the artifice, the poem tells us, is to presume the power to make static the circulation of thought that is the primary utilitarian aim of publication in a democratic culture.[15]

Dickinson's insistence that the textual body function as a vehicle for the circulation of thought and not the foundation for authorial control is very much at the heart of her June 1877 letter to Higginson that contains her poetic rejoinder to his poem "Decoration." To appreciate her response, it is necessary to understand that Higginson's poem is about the memorializing of the dead on what we now call Memorial Day. Significantly, his speaker chooses to place flowers on the untended grave of a nameless woman rather than add yet another bouquet to the tombs of men who perished in battle during the Civil War. Dickinson's words, "Lay this Laurel on the One / Too intrinsic for Renown –" (Fr1428C), similarly affirm the honor due those whose contributions are great but largely undetected. In her careful analysis of this letter and the poem it contains, Mary Loeffelholz concludes that Dickinson "demonstrated to Higginson both the care with which she read him and the ingenuity with which she rewrote him" ("'Decoration'" 677). In other words, Dickinson's poem accomplishes what the speaker of "Publication – is the Auction" says good poetry ought to do: transmit meaning from one reader to another so that no particular reader misapprehends it as personal property. With this gesture, Dickinson simultaneously honors Higginson by giving new form to the thought his poem illustrates and shows her acceptance of fame as absorption in the language of others.

The poem I take my title from addresses the difficulty the poet faces when seeking to confirm this version of fame. "The first Day that / I was a Life" (Fr823) opens the second bifolium with the sudden discovery that the end to life may not be an end after all. When viewed in the context of a "tenderer Experiment," life may in fact persist:

The first Day that
I was a Life
I recollect it – How
still –
The last Day that
I was a Life
I recollect it – as well –

'Twas stiller – though
the first
Was still –
'Twas empty – but
the first
Was full –

This – was my finallest
Occasion –
But then
My tenderer Experiment
Toward Men –

"Which choose I"?
That – I cannot say –
"Which choose They"?
Question Memory!

The speaker's immediate qualification of the statement "This – was my finallest / Occasion –" that appears in the third stanza is unavoidably perplexing. Having declared in the first two stanzas that her life has reached its end ("The last Day that / I was a Life"), why does the speaker suddenly arrest her train of thought as if she has just remembered something she had overlooked? "But then / My tenderer Experiment / Toward Men –," she muses, recalling an ongoing experiment, not a life that has ended. Hints as to what this "tenderer Experiment" might be appear in the final stanza, where the speaker enters a conversation with herself that directly associates the experiment with choices made by the speaker and an unspecified "They." First she asks a question in quotation marks, "'Which choose I'?" as if asking herself whether she chooses the view that her life has in some sense ended, or the alternative view that her life continues as part of the experiment. Her response is that she "cannot say –," an admission that she quickly follows with yet another question in quotation marks: "'Which choose They'?" This question is then succeeded by a final command not in quotation marks: "Question Memory!" These words indicate that whether her life has ended or not depends on choices made by others and that the success of the experiment will depend on information held in memory.

Read within the context of other poems in the fascicle, together with Dickinson's understanding of the role readers play in the circulation of thought, the poem states that the speaker's decision about the continuation of her life now rests with readers. As Oberhaus has explained, the speaker "longs for readers for her 'Experiment Toward Men' and cannot be certain if she will ever have them" (20). What makes her experiment an experiment is its innovative and risky departure from publicly determined versions of the private self; what makes it "tenderer" is its dependence on readers and its embrace of the unconventional or illegible features of their experience.

A surprising number of poems in this fascicle cluster around the idea that the poet must rely on the choices of others to determine whether the tenderer experiment has succeeded; many also propose that because success can be hard or impossible to detect, some degree of uncertainty may be inescapable. As previously noted, "All forgot for recollecting" (Fr827), the first poem in the third bifolium, explores the question of which actions and what forms of recognition endure. The closing stanza suggests that the speaker has risked all on entering the memory of another, admitting that she "Dropped – my fate – a / timid Pebble – / In thy bolder Sea –." That personal actions can be justified through their power to inform the lives of others is reiterated in the second poem of the fifth bifolium, where the speaker describes actions that are absorbed by others but bent to purposes different from those that originally motivated them. This speaker begins by stating, "He who in Himself believes – / Fraud cannot presume" (Fr835)—a rejection of the publicly legible or fraudulent private self—and concludes that such a belief "Cannot perish, though / it fail / Every second time – / But defaced Vicariously – / For Some Other Shame." This is to say that the reader who experiences the poem's power to evoke shame may indeed displace the poet's shame with her own, but entry into the life of the reader is what matters, not retention of the poet's identity. "Wert Thou but ill – that / I might show thee" (Fr821), the second poem of the first bifolium, concentrates on ways to capture the attention of a lover or a reader.[16] This speaker repeatedly addresses a specific "Thou" with the aim of identifying a need she might meet and by that means win admission into the other's life. "Wert Thou but stranger / in ungracious country – / And Mine – the Door / Thou paused at," she states in the second stanza; in the third she imagines yet another need she could meet: "Accused – wert Thou / and Myself – Tribunal –." The poem concludes with the speaker stating, "No Service hast Thou, / I would not +achieve it –" ("+attempt"). We could say that the speaker in this poem emphasizes the importance of identifying the reader's need, where the speaker of "Had I not This, or / This, I said" places greatest emphasis on the poet's need.

As if to round out her reflections on the relationships poems maintain with poets and readers, Dickinson's speaker in "Fitter to see Him, I / may be" (Fr834), the first poem of the fifth bifolium, worries that she might lose a reader or lover who once admired her because she has changed so much in his absence. "I only must not grow / so new / That +He'll mistake – and ask for me / Of me" ("+He"), she cautions herself in the fifth stanza, only to repeat her concern in the next: "I only must not change / so fair / He'll sigh – +'the Other – She is Where'?" ("+Real One"). In the end, though, the speaker reconciles herself to the possibility that the "He" she seeks to please may "perceive the other / Truth / Opon an Excellenter Youth." Without denying the pain such a loss would provoke, the speaker affirms the growth that has ultimately led her away from the lover or reader when she states that what she has become is "The Beauty that reward / Him +most –" ("+best"). What matters in the end is that the inspiration the other provided has led to the further development of the poet's art; the reader's failure to keep pace with the poet's growth is secondary to heightened artistic accomplishment. Here again, the poet's or lover's need is given emphasis, suggesting that through the poems in this fascicle Dickinson is exploring ways to assess the lives poems enter once they are part of a larger world that includes both the poet and readers of the poems.

Perhaps it should come as no surprise, then, that a number of the poems in the same fascicle deal specifically with the question of new birth and how best to embrace it. In the fourth bifolium, Dickinson assembles what might well be her most dazzling effort to track the poet's initial motivation and the personal experience that attends poetic creation. Taken together, the four poems transcribed onto this sheet represent movement from intellectual contemplation of death and new life to immediate, subjective entry into the process of change itself. The first poem, "The Admirations – and / Contempts – of time –" (Fr830), alludes directly to Christian resurrection through reference to the "Open Tomb" that simultaneously signals Jesus's death and his return to life. The poem does not, however, treat this event as the original precedent for experiences to come. Instead, Jesus is presented as embodying a broad pre-existing principle that the speaker draws on to justify an artistic transformation that will cast present experience in a wholly new light. "Dying," she observes in the first stanza, provides "as it were / a Hight" that "Reorganizes Estimate" so that "what We saw / not / We distinguish clear –." Death, we are told, yields an elevated perspective that enables an expanded view of experience. This is different from recumbence in the bosom of the Lord and the peace of the Heavenly Kingdom.

Here it is tempting to say that this speaker's determination to face new life directly, without the mediation of Christ, echoes the position of the speaker in "'Unto Me'? I do not / know you –" (Fr825), the third poem of sheet 2, who denies knowledge of "'Jesus – late / of Judea –.'" Rather than accepting Jesus's offer to convey her to heaven where he tells her she can "'Occupy my +House'" ("+Breast"), she chooses not to respond.[17] Like that earlier speaker, this speaker is more concerned with the journey new life offers than arrival at a point of rest. By means of "Compound Vision," that she defines as "The Finite – furnished / With the Infinite," the speaker imagines casting her vision "Back – toward Time – / And forward – / Toward the God of Him –." At this point it becomes possible to interpret death as not a passage from time to timelessness but another kind of death altogether, one that retains the experience of time by placing the perceiver both in and out of it. If we view what is being described not as literal death but as the poet's release of poems that enter the stream of time, we can also imagine that the speaker is describing what happens to the poet who contemplates intrinsic renown and who writes poems that expand the linguistic commons. Her personal compound vision would in this case include reflection on the entry of her poems into history plus her belief that in doing so her words contribute to the inspiration of future poets.

The next poem in the bifolium, "Till Death – is narrow / Loving –" (Fr831), further develops the concept of compound vision by exploring the proper role of poetic imitation and the way a writer integrates in her own writing the influence of those who preceded her. The poem explains that each new work retroactively affirms a history of poetic influence that binds the poet to the past at the same time that it directs that influence forward toward artistic expression appropriate to the future poet's historical moment. Framed in this manner, the poem presents the poet's compound vision as looking both ways—toward time and toward eternity. This is achieved when life is modeled on the conduct of another whose death so diminishes mortal experience that art becomes a means of expressing the beauty now absent. The first line of the poem, "Till death – is narrow / Loving –," establishes the poem's focus on an expansive love not bound by the span of a particular life. Unlike Christian marriage vows where the words "until death do us part" focus attention on the duration of mortal life only, Dickinson's language pointedly affirms that the poet's reach cannot be so neatly confined. The speaker instructs us that escape from such constraints may be accomplished by imitating "He whose loss / procures you / Such Destitution that / Your Life too abject for / itself / Thenceforward imitate –."

According to Páraic Finnerty's line of argumentation, these words of Dickinson's could be applied to her own relationship with Shakespeare, as Shakespeare remained forever alive for Dickinson because his genius continually inspired fresh creation: "Despite acknowledgements of Shakespeare's 'firm' and fixed genius, he remained 'just published' because readers redeployed him, his plays becoming displaced by that which had more contemporary or personal relevance" (Finnerty 116). Dickinson's deep respect for Shakespeare's ability to meet the artistic needs of his own historical moment provokes her effort to fill the gap she senses in her day. She goes about this through imitation of the thought that flowed through his language, not his style. Therefore, as Finnerty puts it, "while [Dickinson] shows deference to Shakespeare's thoughts, the poet modifies, fragments, and adds to his lines, converting his iambic pentameter into her own preferred hymnal meter" (121).

In the final stanza of "Till Death – is narrow / Loving," Dickinson's speaker describes the process of imitation as advancing until the poet assumes "Resemblance perfect." At this point mortal imitation fuses with spiritual reach so that the poet imitator becomes an extension of the thought the poet precursor gave voice to in the past. Addressing the aspiring poet directly, Dickinson's speaker observes that when such resemblance is attained, "Yourself, for His pursuit / Delight of Nature – abdicate." When the poet of the present imbibes the creative spirit of past creative genius, she turns her attention to the infinite. Nature, or the world of the living moment, becomes a lens through which eternity is freshly framed. The solid rhyme that links "imitate" of stanza 2 with "abdicate" of stanza 3 further establishes the message that proper imitation includes a shared dedication to the future. One might even say that such imitation does indeed "Exhibit Love – somewhat" (the final line of the poem) because the momentary illustration of that love always meets the needs of the present even as it extends to the works of poets to come. Thus, the poet's compound vision brings the past into the present as a means of achieving what the speaker of "The Admirations – and / Contempts – of time –" described as looking "forward – / Toward the God of Him –."

The final two poems of the fourth bifolium continue the third-person investigation of compound vision taken up in the first two poems but do so by exploring the ways poetic creation alters the outward and inward life of the poet. In the first of these, "'Tis Sunrise – little Maid – / Hast Thou" (Fr832), Dickinson treats the subject of the poem, the little maid, as if she were a poet who has abdicated nature, as advocated by the speaker of the previous poem. Central to the poem is what appears to be the maid's sudden departure from established patterns of daily behavior that have been regulated by the stations of the sun. Whether it be morning, noon, or night, the maid is described by the speaker as behaving contrary to convention. In the first stanza, "'Tis Sunrise" and the maid has not assumed her "Station in the Day"; in the second, the speaker wonders that even at "Noon" the maid is "sleeping / yet"; and in the third stanza the speaker discovers that for the little maid night has somehow displaced morning: "That Night should be to thee / Instead of Morning. . . ." Over the course of the poem's three stanzas, the speaker gradually realizes that the little maid has died, but the speaker's response to this death, and hence the nature of the death itself, is highly unusual. At first the speaker appears caught by surprise, but by the end she expresses regret at not having been included in the maid's "Plan to Die": "Had'st / thou broached / Thy little Plan to Die – / Dissuade thee, if I c'd not, Sweet, / I might have aided – thee –." Given the previous two poems' focus on the relationship between dying and the acquisition of vision, and this poem's presentation of death as part of a plan, we might conclude that a newly acquired vision has led the maid to abandon mortal life, but this may not be entirely what Dickinson has in mind.

The appearance of the word "industry" at the very end of the first stanza resonates with the word "industrious" that appeared in "Had I not This or / This, I said" where it referred to the poet/speaker's writing of poems. Treating that poem as a point of reference for this one, we might conclude that when the speaker here urges the little maid to "Retrieve thine industry –," she means that the maid should continue writing poems. In this case, the poem can be read as an outside observer's reflections on a poet's decision to stop writing poems, or as a poet's contemplation of how an outside observer might respond to her own decision to stop writing poems. What might finally be most significant about this poem is that the speaker overcomes her opposition to such a plan and ultimately expresses support. It may be acceptable, the poem tells us, for the poet to end her life as a writer.

The fourth and final poem of this fourth bifolium provides an explanation of why the poet is attracted to the possibility of bringing her writing to an end. "Pain – expands the Time –" (Fr833) explains that the interior experience of the poet is fraught with pain produced by the departure of precursor poets and the present poet's uncertainty that her efforts to fill the gap created by that absence will succeed. The expansion of time that is the subject of the first stanza presents pain as the poet's experience of her role as the outer edge of history that advances through the narrow seeming confines of her own mind:

Pain – expands the Time –
Ages +coil within                    +lurk
The minute Circumference
Of a single Brain –

The pain the speaker describes here acts as a corollary of the "Life too abject for / itself" mentioned in the second poem in this bifolium, "Till Death is narrow / Loving –." Pain as described here is the poet's subjective encounter with history, the looking "Back – toward Time" that the speaker of the first poem in this bifolium presents as one half of compound vision. Sensing the accomplishments of poets from past ages, the poet acknowledges her role as one of their company but in doing so feels the weight of those "Ages +coil within" ("+lurk"). Recognition of one's greatness, this speaker tells us, registers as pain, pain that comes from feeling the gap in the present age that no other poet can fill.

A different but related pain is described in the second stanza when the poet of the present age recognizes that the lives of the poems she made to meet the needs of her moment may be impossible to evaluate. Time contracts because evidence of the sent poems' passage into the linguistic commons does not arrive, and yet the poet remains impatient:

Pain contracts – the Time –
Occupied with Shot
+ Gammuts of Eternities              +Triplets
+Are as they were not –              +flit – show

The poems bearing the coiled ages of the past that the poet has released ("Shot") into the world—have so far yielded only silence. Dickinson's variant of "Triplets" for "Gammuts" draws additional attention to the musical and prosodic character of the encapsulated eternities that poems are, while the variants of "flit – show" for "Are" magnify the hard truth that time's fleet passage has so far shown an absence of detectable renown. This, then, is the pain of the poet who circulates poems with the knowledge that word of her success may never be forthcoming.

That such an understanding of poetic circulation and, ultimately, fame equates success with absorption and results in invisibility is a matter taken up in the final poem of the fascicle, "Unfulfilled to Observation –" (Fr839).

> Unfulfilled to Observation –
> Incomplete – to Eye –
> But to Faith – a Revolution
> In Locality –
>
> Unto Us – the Suns
> extinguish –
> To our Opposite –
> New Horizons – they
> +embellish –                           +Replenish
> +Fronting Us – with Night.    +Turning Us – their Night.

If the poem can be read as the statement of a poet reflecting on the fate of her "tenderer Experiment," then it describes the poet's recognition that poetry is given new form and meaning in the experience of her readers. Such poetry may well be "Unfulfilled to Observation" and "Incomplete – to Eye" while achieving fulfillment through a revolution in locality that situates meaning in the mind of the reader. That is what the first stanza tells us; the second implies that such an outcome is natural. Just as suns pass from one hemisphere to another, illuminating "New Horizons" for others whose lives we may never witness, so poetry defines new horizons, enabling others to discover new worlds while the poet confronts the night that precedes her next creation. By insisting on the motion of the sun, Dickinson magnifies the continuum of light and dark, day and night, so that even the poet's darkness is linked to the illumination of others and the ultimate return of light that will show the poet new horizons. Unlike the little maid who refused to "Retrieve [her] industry" in "'Tis Sunrise – Little Maid," this speaker remains industrious, writing on as a poet whose faith in the power of her words sustains her in the face of undetectable renown. The variant of "Replenish" for the word "embellish" in the seventh line here reinforces this first-person speaker's confidence in the promise of a new day.

I will leave the fascicle here, not because I have exhausted it, or even fairly scratched the surface, but because the final poem of the fascicle so clearly articulates the concern with endings and beginnings that is central to my reading of the fascicle. This concluding speaker captures the general attitude Dickinson may well have adopted as the era of her greatest poetic productivity was drawing to a close and she wondered what the ultimate outcome would be. Through the speakers of Fascicle 40, Dickinson unflinchingly declares that when poetry contributes most directly to the deepest spiritual and artistic aspirations of the poet's historical moment, it does so by entering the linguistic lives of readers and becoming intrinsic to their cultural self-understanding. Perhaps she saw then that the preservation and control of her poems ran contrary to her aim of releasing them into the world and allowing them to enter the lives of others. This realization may have led Dickinson to stop binding her poems after completing her fortieth fascicle, to write on unbound sheets in 1865, and to scale down her writing to the extent that she probably produced no more than ten and twelve poems per year from 1866 through 1869 (Franklin, *Poems* 1533). These new poems, and those to come after 1869, would pursue new directions, as might be expected, but that is another story.

# Coda from *My Emily Dickinson*[1]

## Susan Howe

*Among the tantalizing fragments Emily Dickinson left for our inference is this one: "Have you ever read one of her Poems backward, because the plunge from the front overturned you? I sometimes (often have, many times) have—A something overtakes the Mind—" (PF30, Letters III, 916). Almost 30 years ago, Susan Howe's meditation on reading Dickinson in her own manuscript form noted of this passage that it is "a hint as to Emily Dickinson's working process" in that the poet "found sense in the chance meeting of words" (My Emily Dickinson 23–24). We began this volume with the foundational discussion by Sharon Cameron. We end it by turning "backward" from the contemporary scholarly studies of this book, each of which probes the possible "what" of the fascicles, to Howe's reminder of why she, distinguished scholar and recipient of Yale's Bollingen Prize, among many other awards—and so many of us—approach the mysteries of the forty books Dickinson left, as she left each individual poem within them, for our own discoveries.—Eds.*

When Thoreau wrote his introduction to *A Week on the Concord and Merrimack Rivers*, he ended by remembering how he had often stood on the banks of the Musketaquid, or Grass-ground, River, which English settlers had renamed Concord. The Concord's current followed the same law in a system of time and all that is known. He liked to watch this current that was for him an emblem of all progress. Weeds under the surface bent gently downstream shaken by watery wind. Chips, sticks, logs, and even tree stems drifted past. There came a day at the end of the summer or the beginning of autumn, when he resolved to launch a boat from shore and let the river carry him.

    Emily Dickinson is my emblematical Concord River.
    I am heading toward certain discoveries . . . .

# NOTES

## Chapter 1

1. Certainly the history of Dickinson criticism from the 1890s to the present, as the quotations above indicate, has preserved a consistent account of the poet. It has stressed the separations in the poems (among grammatical and syntactical units), as well as the separation of any given utterance from a decipherable situation that it could be said to represent; and it has stressed vexed connections among them. Specifically, as the chronology of the poems is not seen to signal development, critics are deprived of one conventional way of discussing the poetry, and this deprivation is often countered by certain primitive groupings of the poems, according to thematic similarities, formal properties, evaluative assessments which discriminate poems that are successful from those that are not—with the constant implication that there is no inherent way of understanding relations among the poems. The taxonomies advanced for Dickinson's poems are different from those advanced for other poets, because when the poems are sorted it is precisely to emphasize idiosyncrasies and repetitions (of traits, themes, syntactic features), as if what Dickinson had to teach us were that there is no way to comprehend the alien except by the most critically reductive strategies of categorizing and comparison.

2. In this essay I primarily exemplify the ways in which poems are associated, rather than only the ways in which variants to words in lines are associated. However, as variants to words in the line and variant poems are central features of the fascicle text, both are discussed. For an amplified discussion of the two subjects, see Cameron, *Choosing*.

3. The vast majority of my references to Dickinson's poems reproduce them as they appear in Franklin's three-volume variorum edition. Throughout, whenever a poem is initially cited, Fr and the number assigned by Franklin follow in parentheses. When in my discussion I consider a single line that includes variants, I enclose the variants in brackets with slash marks separating the alternative words. When I discuss variants without quoting a whole line, brackets are omitted, and a slash mark alone indicates the presence of alternatives. In a few cases, where Franklin's variorum text seems not to fully capture the ambiguities of the fascicles to which my argument draws attention—

the specific order of variants within the same fascicle, for example, or the interlineation and/or deletion of words within the same poem—I direct the reader to the two-volume facsimile, *Manuscript Books,* abbreviated *MB* and cited by page number.

4. The sets have many of the characteristics of the fascicles except that they were not stab-bound and tied. According to Franklin, Dickinson stopped *binding* fascicle sheets around 1864, though there are a few unbound sheets as early as 1862 (set 1 is dated 1862 by Franklin; sets 2–4, 1864). In the late 1860s Dickinson stopped *copying* fascicle sheets. In the 1870s she began copying fascicle sheets again (sets 5–7 are dated between 1864 and 1866, though, as noted, the majority of the poems in the remaining sets [8–15] are from the 1870s), but she never again bound them (see *MB* xii–xiii). For a concise discussion of the differences among the bound fascicles, the unbound fascicle sheets, the worksheets, and the miscellaneous fair copies, as well as for Franklin's speculations about the ways Dickinson variously used the bound fascicles, and for a detailed description of how Franklin reassembled them, see the introduction to *Manuscript Books.*

5. It is important to reiterate that this and the following assertions about Dickinson's intentions with respect to the fascicles are speculative. While the following pages produce an empirical argument about how the fascicles work, and about what the fascicles are, the basis of that argument is, and could only be, speculative.

6. The earliest fascicles have no variants; the first occurrence of a variant is in Fascicle 5, and there are only five other variants for poems through Fascicle 10. These variants, often multiple and not uniformly positioned at the end of the poem, as in the Johnson edition, are sometimes signaled in the facsimile text by the little "+" signs that Dickinson used near a word to indicate variants to that word. In the facsimile text the variants appear in the following diverse positions: at the end of the poem, to the side of the poem, and underneath or above a particular stanza, word, or line. Sometimes the variants to words are virtually inseparable from the text, as in the second stanza of "I think the Hemlock" (*MB* 439; Fr400). Frequently a variant appears above the word: "The [maddest/nearest] dream – recedes – unrealized –" (*MB* 285; Fr304). Or to the side of the line: "The Cordiality of Death – / Who [drills/nails] his Welcome in –" (*MB* 212; Fr243). Or to the side of and at right angles to the poem, as in "There is a pain – so utter –" (*MB* 544; Fr515) and "Like Some Old fashioned Miracle –" (*MB* 449; Fr408). Or underneath the word, as in "Of Bronze – and Blaze –": "An Island in dishonored Grass – / Whom none but [Daisies/Beetles –] know" (*MB* 269; Fr319). In the same poem another variant ("manners") is also noted below the word ("attitudes") that is on the line. But a third variant appears at the end of the poem, "An/Some – Island," making it seem that different ways of noting variants indicate different ways of understanding alternatives in relation to each other. Only in the later years of the copying are the variants positioned characteristically at the poem's end, Dickinson having apparently standardized her placement of them.

Infrequently Dickinson drew a line through words to signal their replacement by alternatives. See, e.g., *MB* 340 (Fr339), "I like a look of Agony," in which in the first line of the second stanza, "Death comes," is decisively crossed out and replaced by "The Eyes glaze once – and that is Death –," and *MB* 275–77 (Fr325), "There came a Day – at Summer's full –," where substantive decisions against word choices are marked by lines through those words, with the preferred alternatives unambiguously chosen. I say "unambiguously chosen," but even here the choice unambiguously made may subsequently have been *un*made. A second fair copy, for which no manuscript is extant, presumably written after the fascicle copying, is reproduced in facsimile on four pages preceding the title page of *Poems by Emily Dickinson,* Second Series, ed. T. W. Higginson and Mabel Loomis Todd (1891). That fair copy adopts some of the canceled fascicle readings which had appeared (erroneously) to have been definitively deleted. There Dickinson restores words in the second, third, and penultimate stanzas.

However exceptional, these excisions insist, by distinction, that Dickinson's typical way of *noting* variants is not random but indicates her way of *understanding* variants. I elaborate in the body of the text.

7. In the fascicles Dickinson often, though not always, drew a line after the variants that concluded a poem, thereby indicating an end to the unit of sense. But because the poems are ordered and bound and because there are sometimes several poems to the bifolium, the collocation oppositely implies a potential relation among poems. (In Fascicle 14, where poems from 1861, 1858, 1862 are bound in that sequence, the implications of "order" are differently unmistakable.)

Moreover, within the bifolium, the method of copying is varied. It is varied because, as indicated, a line is frequently but not always drawn after a poem, and because, although the bifolia are customarily filled, there are instances of blank half-rectos and -versos. This is particularly the case in Fascicle 11, where whole sheets and half sheets are left blank. But there is also a three-quarters blank first verso in Fascicle 15; nine blank lines and a blank verso conclude Fascicle 18, while in Fascicle 13 the first bifolium contains a three-quarters blank second recto. Such variations indicate that Dickinson may be regulating *which,* as well as *how many,* poems belong in a particular bifolium. The method of copying is also varied because, while the fascicles are ordinarily composed of single, folded sheets—with a disjunct leaf or slip added rarely, where necessary, to continue a poem—Fascicle 11 contains as many as four disjunct leaves (see Franklin's tables for Dickinson's manner of accommodating overflow of poems and for the locations of disjunct leaves within particular fascicles, in *Manuscript Books* 1413 and 1414, respectively).

Further, while Dickinson characteristically tries to complete a poem on a single page, and if it runs over, it characteristically does so by as many as four lines, in Fascicle 11 there are only two lines on the verso of the fourth sheet. Finally, although Franklin is right to say that the sheet or bifolium is the unit of *manuscript* integrity (an assumption borne out by Dickinson's manner of accommodating overflow from the sheet), the sheet or bifolium is not the unit of *thematic* integrity.

8. The relation "among" the fascicles is itself problematic because, in Franklin's words, Dickinson "did not number or otherwise label" or index them (*MB* x). Thus, though in the facsimile they are now arranged according to a presumed chronology, it is only arbitrarily that Fascicle 13 precedes Fascicle 14. This is the case because, while one can determine that certain fascicles were copied in the same year, it is now impossible to determine the particular order in which they were copied within that year. Fascicle 13 would seem to precede Fascicle 14 in that the former dates from 1861 while the latter has poems which Franklin dates from 1862, as well as from 1858 and 1861. But Fascicle 11, too, has poems from 1861, and Fascicle 12 has poems from 1861 as well as 1860. Moreover, by virtue of these different dates, it would appear that in binding the sheets Dickinson worked from a pool of manuscripts, and therefore the exact relation

of Fascicle 13 to Fascicle 14, if Dickinson intended one, cannot be surmised. Fascicles 11 through 14 are the most problematic of the fascicles, since in them the binding practices are inconsistent. Specifically, Dickinson there deviates from her practice of binding poems presumably copied in the same year.

9. Herbert was anthologized in Chambers's *Cyclopaedia of English Literature*, as he also was in Griswold's *Sacred Poets of England and America* (New York: Appleton; dated 1849 on the title page and 1848 on the copyright page). Susan Gilbert Dickinson owned the 1844 edition of the *Cyclopaedia* published in Edinburgh by William and Robert Chambers; Edward Dickinson's copy was printed in Boston in 1847 by Gould, Kendall, and Lincoln. A separate edition of *The Temple* was owned by Susan Gilbert Dickinson. Finally, although there is no proof that Dickinson read Shakespeare's sonnets, since her letters do not allude to them in particular, Edward Dickinson had a copy of the sonnets in his eight-volume 1853 edition of Shakespeare's *Comedies, Histories, Tragedies, and Poems*, which we know Dickinson had read, and which Richard Sewall tells us Edward Dickinson purchased in 1857; see *Life* 2:467, as well as Capps, 12, 68–69. See, too, Sewall's list of books in the Dickinson Collection at Houghton Library, some of them, as indicated by the library's register, containing markings "probably" or "perhaps" by Dickinson (*Life* 2:678–79). Dickinson mentions Tennyson and Barrett Browning in her letters, and the collections of their poems owned by the Dickinson family are in the Houghton Library.

10. See, e.g., the discussion of Fr304, "The [maddest/nearest] dream – recedes – unrealized –," in which I argue that the variants must be considered in relation to each other rather than as alternative possibilities: "maddest" and "nearest"; "maddest" because "nearest"—the intoxication being caused by the proximity, not simply conjunctive but, perhaps more strongly, consequent (in *Choosing* 63–66). With respect to variants like these Dickinson sets up a situation that seems exclusionary, and, in letting both alternatives stand she refuses choices she presents as inevitable.

11. Other poems in Fascicle 23 about the apprehension of death ("The Whole of it came not at once – / 'Twas Murder by degrees –" [Fr485], "Presentiment – is that long Shadow – on the Lawn –" [Fr487], "He fought like those Who've nought to lose –" [Fr480]) and about apprehension of another's death ("You constituted Time – / I deemed Eternity / A Revelation of Yourself –" [Fr488]) substantiate that possible reading.

## Chapter 2

1. Cameron notes, "It is important to reiterate that this and the following assertions about Dickinson's intentions with respect to the fascicles are speculative. While the following pages produce an empirical argument about how the fascicles work, and about what the fascicles are, the basis of that argument is, and could only be, speculative" (7, n. 6).

2. "The position of the speakers [ . . . ] is beyond, inhuman, indifferent, sublime" (182).

3. David Porter, in *Dickinson: The Modern Idiom*, complained memorably that Dickinson had no "project." The poems were seemingly written one after another, each a new start wholly unrelated to its predecessors, and as often as not unable to get past that start. There was no "development," and thus Dickinson's potential greatness went

unrealized. A genius ought to comprehend a world, if not the world; Dickinson was plainly no match for her subject matter, taking stab after stab at articulation. Ultimately for Porter this is what makes Dickinson "modern," but he is also clearly disappointed in what he takes to be her failure.

Perhaps this brooding analysis has been what's prompted any number of attempts to demonstrate that Dickinson does have a project, does develop, and does comprehend a world. Much of that work has focused on the fascicles; it has seemed important to show that either the little booklets present thematic sequences (Rosenthal and Gall), or that the fascicles in their entirety present a narrative (Shurr). The most sophisticated of these, Cameron's, marshals a magisterial deconstructionist machinery to demonstrate that Dickinson is engaged in an ultimately metaphysical project.

But Porter's disappointment in Dickinson's evident incoherence, and Cameron's beautiful account of that incoherence as coherence with Being, has resulted in the dueling deconstructionists obscuring the actual field of play. Neither has paid attention to the philosophical and rhetorical problems, terms, and commitments available to Dickinson in her time. Thus they (and we) miss the sources of her thought and practice in Locke and Hume's philosophical skepticism. Why should her philosophical commitments matter, especially to these physical objects, the manuscripts? Because the way she wrote, from the propositional starts of her poems down to her generation of variants, was an engagement with what she was taught to think about language.

4. McGann says, regarding manuscript works such as Blake's and Dickinson's, "At this point we should be able to see the theoretical importance of these texts for criticism. They are peculiarly significant because they reveal the paradox implicit in the concept of authorial intention. In their earliest 'completed' forms these texts remain more or less wholly under the author's control, yet as a class they are texts for which the editorial concept of intention has no meaning. These texts show, in other words, that the concept of authorial intention only comes into force for criticism when (paradoxically) the artist's work begins to engage with social structures and functions. The fully authoritative text is therefore always one which has been socially produced; as a result, the critical standard for what constitutes authoritativeness cannot rest with the author and his intentions alone" (75). Earlier he remarks that only a Romantic conception of authorship and editing privileges the author alone, and regards any interventions beyond the manuscript as contaminations (51). It could be argued, of course, that Dickinson is therefore thoroughgoingly Romantic. But her release of poems into letters to her friends suggests that she accepts the interventions of a copying culture in manuscript.

5. In the Introduction. See Bruce Clary's discussion of Franklin's several assertions about the fascicles in his dissertation, "Emily Dickinson's Menagerie."

6. Alexandra Socarides's argument in "Rethinking the Fascicles" concurs with Franklin that the unit of composition is the sheet, and proposes that we adjust our reading methods to reflect that (84).

7. Clary objects to certain scholars' tendency to use anomalous features—such as the presence of mixed-dated poems in Fascicle 14—to justify Dickinson's sequencing intention—when such anomalous features are not statistically significant enough to warrant the assumption (100).

8. In this respect I must differ from Socarides, who similarly consults the archives, but finds that fascicle-making is not prevalent (*Dickinson Unbound* 79). This is probably

because, as she observes, there is no ready way to find examples, as they are not archived as a category.

9. See Suzanne Spring's dissertation, "Forming Letters," for this and other information concerning composition practices at Mt. Holyoke. Richard Green Parker's *Aids to English Composition,* in a section entitled "Suggestions to Teachers" (304–7), is probably the source of these practices. See Alexandra Socarides for complementary work on nineteenth-century manuscript practices.

10. In Mabel Loomis Todd's edition of the *Letters of Emily Dickinson,* Todd records the reflections of Emily Fowler Ford. They did the paper, called *Forest Leaves,* for two years at the Amherst Academy, and Dickinson, the wit, did the "comic's column" (128). "This paper was all in script, and was passed around the school, where the contributions were easily recognized from the handwriting, which is Emily Dickinson's case was very beautiful—small, clear, finished. [Dickinson's bits were irresistible:] One bit was stolen by a roguish editor for the College paper, where her touch was instantly recognized; and there were two paragraphs in the *Springfield Republican*" (129).

11. Lucy Schulz notes, in her essay "Constructing Composition Books," in *Archives of Instruction,* "Beginning students copied alphabet letters and numbers and short words onto their slates; they responded to assignments in school readers (important to remember that school readers have a longer history than composition textbooks) and practiced what they learned by 'filling in the blanks' of a passage, a practice often known as 'ellipticals'" (151).

12. For at least circumstantial evidence that Dickinson experienced this popular mode of training, see Fr116, "Our share of night to bear –" which contains the line "Our blank in bliss to fill." See Scheurer on Dickinson's schooling.

13. More sophisticated are exercises provided by Richard Green Parker, in his *Aids to English Composition,* in which one is to find substitutes for given words or paraphrases; these hone one's ability to distinguish fine shades of meaning among synonyms, which, he contends, are never truly synonymous. "The nice distinctions which exist among some words commonly reputed synonymous having now been pointed out" (43), he recommends that the tutor exercise his pupils in substituting phrases and not simply words while composing their sentences (44).

> In the sentences which follow, it is required to change the words as in the following examples. The student will notice that every change of words will, in most cases, produce some corresponding change in the idea; but, as the object of the exercise is to give him a command of language, it is not deemed important in these Exercises to exact a strict verbal accuracy.
>
> Example 1st.  He continued the work without *stopping.*
> He continued the work without *resting.*
> He continued the work without *cessation.*
> He continued the work without *intermission.*
> He continued the work without *delay.*
> He continued the work without *leaving off.*
> He continued the work without *interruption.*
> He continued the work without *obstacle.*
> He continued the work without *impediment,* &C. [44–45]

Students were similarly made to practice generating synonyms in verse, referred to Crabb's *English Synonymes,* and exercised in translation in order to achieve flexibility and control in English. Dickinson especially would have been aware that, as Parker puts it, "[T]o the poet especially a familiar acquaintance with expressions of similar meaning is absolutely indispensable. Confined as he is to certain rules, it is often the case, that a long word must be substitute for a short one, or a short one for a long, in order to produce the necessary succession of syllables to constitute the measure, or the harmony, of his verses" (40–41). As Parker's pronouncement perhaps suggests, composition exercises were not limited to prose. Quoting *Murray's Grammar* on the practice of poetic composition, Parker affirms that requiring it

> will copiously enlarge the writer's stock of expressions [ . . . ] It will at the same time, produce a more important and beautiful effect,—it will enrich the intellectual store of thought; for, while in search for an epithet, for an example, or a periphrase, he is obliged to view the subject in all of its possible bearings and relations, that he may choose such particular word or phrase, as shall exhibit it in the most advantageous light. And what study more effectual to call into action the powers of the mind, to exercise the judgment, to whet the sagacity, and give birth to a variety of ideas, which might otherwise have lain for ever [*sic*] dormant? For these weighty considerations, the practice of verse-making has been recommended by Locke, Chesterfield, Franklin, &c, &c. [242]

14. American Antiquarian Society Online catalog: Notes. Kittredge listing.

15. Note that Campbell's nominalist identification of thought and word always gives way to the more skeptical account of Hume's associationism; a word and a thought are still theoretically distinct, as also in Locke.

16. Whether Dickinson read Campbell directly is a question of some interest. Undoubtedly she was familiar with the basic claims as they were filtered down to her through Newman (who enthusiastically quotes Campbell) and Whately. See Nan Johnson's *Nineteenth-Century Rhetoric in North America* for a comprehensive discussion of the promulgation and diffusion of Campbell's rhetorical ideas in the works of Newman, Blair, and Whately. Mt. Holyoke's library may have held a copy as early as Dickinson's tenure, and it is likely that Amherst College's library kept a few copies for the industrious, since Campbell was a required text for seniors during her brother Austin's tenure and her young adulthood. Amherst College's clubs, such as the Alexandrian, kept Campbell among the several thousand volumes available to members—and perhaps to their extremely well-connected sisters. (Special Collections at Amherst has an undated catalogue of the society's library holdings. Anneliese Ostendarp's "The Athenian Society Library" is also helpful, as is George Cutting's *Student Life at Amherst College.*) One has only to remember that Edward Dickinson wrote the checks (as treasurer)—and that George Gould published Emily's valentine in the college's literary magazine, *The Indicator* (in 1850), to realize that her ties to that environment must have been quite intimate. For a survey of Emily's friendships with young men at the College, see Sewall's "Early Friendships II" (ch. 18), esp. pp. 418–20. At least one letter (L191) suggests that Dickinson had free access to the Amherst College library.

17. Berlin notes the intellectual lineage: "The qualities of good style—correctness,

perspicuity, vivacity, euphony—are adapted from Campbell. The kinds of style—e.g., concise and diffuse, forcible and vehement—are lifted directly from Blair" (38). And, as Nan Johnson notes, Whately also synthesizes Campbell and Blair (50).

18. H#2559, w/ signature "E. Dickinson 1839." See Lowenberg, *Emily Dickinson's Textbooks* and Bryan Short on Dickinson's "New Rhetoric."

19. Dickinson's "expedient" of varying her metaphors around what has been called an absent center may very well have to do with this caution.

20. For McIntosh, see the introduction, pp. 14-15; for Hagenbüchle, see the whole of "Sign and Process."

21. See Dickinson's poem beginning "Publication is the Auction" for an example of these two rhetorics at work. The speaker is both loath to "invest" her snow—to dress or undress in public—and to appear at all, while the Thought is clearly able to be incarnated.

22. My representations of the poems are derived from the manuscripts and the Franklin editions. I therefore adopt the practice of representing a stanza's lines whole rather than broken (at a page edge), but I also seek to represent the variants as they appear, with crosses, interlineations, or crowding the bottom, rather than imposing an editorial apparatus not Dickinson's own.

23. In this case, the variants do not simply reflect a struggle but actively represent it, as in "Shall I take thee."

24. "Gentile" has to be read as "genteel" or "gentle"—see Lucy Goodale's letter of 6/8/1838: "so you think I have improved in penmanship. E. says I do not write as I did when I came here. I do not know how it happens. Our teachers tell us that although it used to be considered very gentile to write fine, it is not now. But I hope you will not criticise on this for I have written it, as few lines at a time with the first pen I could find and besides all this with a book for my writing table [ . . . . ]" (Mt. Holyoke, Special Collections).

25. Sue made the transcripts some time after Dickinson's death, though it is clear she was transcribing poems the "family" had received for years. Dickinson sent twenty-one poems in autograph which still survive to Sue in 1863, on the very high end of her average throughout the years. Poem 1651 may have been written and sent to Sue in 1863 as well. While it's not necessary to demonstrate temporal proximity in order to justify considering these poems together, Dickinson had a habit of reiterating or reformulating pieces of language she liked—from poems to letters, from letters to poems. While some "scraps" reappear as many as eight years after their introduction, Johnson used repeated phrasing to correlate the composition dates of poems and letters.

# Chapter 3

1. As much as possible, when I quote a poem from the *Manuscript Books of Emily Dickinson*, I will endeavor to recreate her punctuation and spelling. To my eye, the marks after the two "ah's" are closer to exclamation points than to commas, which is the way they appear in Franklin's three-volume variorum as well as in the Reader's Edition. It is true that elsewhere the distinction is more obvious. The two exclamation points at the end of the first two and last lines are not ambiguous; each shows a decided period

under the slash mark, but the mark is perched above the line unlike the clear comma after line 5. From the beginning of this essay, then, we are up against questions that can never be fully decided—but the importance of which, as Ellen Louise Hart in this volume shows, are important.

2. The Poems of Fascicle 8

| First lines | Franklin Franklin's Number | Notes* | First Publication |
|---|---|---|---|
| A *Wounded* Deer – leaps highest – | 181 | copy to Susan lost | 1890 |
| The Sun kept stooping – stooping – low! | 182 | copy to Sue in pencil | 1910 |
| I met a King this Afternoon! | 183 | no known copies | 1893 |
| | | | |
| To learn the Transport by the Pain – | 178 | another version to Sue | 1891 |
| If the foolish call them "*flowers*" – | 179 | no known copies | 1896 |
| In Ebon Box, when years have flown | 180 | no known copies | 1935 |
| Portraits are to daily faces | 174 | two versions in F8 | 1891 |
| | | | |
| Wait till the Majesty of Death | 169 | no known copies | 1891 |
| 'Tis so much joy! 'Tis so much joy! | 170 | no known copies | 1895 |
| A fuzzy fellow, without feet, | 171 | no known copies | 1929 |
| At last, to be identified! | 172 | duplicate in F21 | 1890 |
| | | | |
| I have never seen 'Volcanoes' – | 165 | no known copies | 1945 |
| Dust is the only Secret. – | 166 | copy to Sue | 1914 |
| I'm the little "Heart's Ease"! | 167 | no known copies | 1893 |
| **Ah, Necromancy Sweet!** | **168** | **no known copies** | **1929** |
| | | | |
| Except to Heaven, she is nought, | 173 | copy to Sue | 1890 |
| Pictures are to daily faces | 174 | two (variants) in F8 | 1891 |
| I cautious, scanned my little life – | 175 | no known copies | 1929 |
| If I could bribe them by a Rose | 176 | no known copies | 1935 |
| As if some little Arctic flower | 177 | no known copies | 1890 |

*Obviously any of the poems for which Franklin records no other recipient may have gone to the many people in Dickinson's epistolary range. As Jane Eberwein and Cindy MacKenzie note in their *Reading Emily Dickinson's Letters,* the over one thousand letters available, published in the three-volume Thomas Johnson collection, "represent only about one-tenth of the letters Dickinson actually wrote" (1). Within those missing letters may be copies of any of these poems.

3. Updating the theory, we might say—grossly oversimplifying the discussion—that semiosis takes up where mimesis leaves off. Books on semiotics update such words by explaining why semiosis (the study of signs—of the language and figures in the work) is more relevant to conversations about poetry than is mimesis (the starting point in reading a poem for its literal coherence). This is offered with apologies to such texts as Michael Riffaterre's *Semiotics of Poetry* and Robert Scholes's *Semiotics and Interpretation.* The process (its pleasures and problems) of reading poetry, say such theoreticians, lies

in the ability to recognize and respond to implied and stated comparisons/contrasts, to move from the literal to the figurative and vice versa. They say a great deal more, but let this be enough for this essay's focus on magical transformations, something highly relevant to a discussion of semiotics.

4. Admittedly, Dickinson also calls on a "Necromancer! Landlord!" in "What inn is this" (Fr100, F5), in which, apparently, a newly dead person explores the new home; she also refers to the art in two of the four versions of "A Dew sufficed itself" (Fr1372), all playful uses. In "Nature affects to be sedate" (Fr1176), written in pencil on a fragment of stationery, she seems to begin a more serious experimentation with the practice: "But let our observation shut / Her practices extend / To Necromancy and the Trades / Remote to understand / Behold our spacious Citizen [Nature] Unto a Juggler turned –."

5. Some twenty years ago while I worked on another project at Harvard's Houghton Library, a kind keeper of its treasures showed me a fascicle page. It was, then, within a vault-like closet that was within a room holding Dickinson furniture that was within the Amy Lowell collection. She pulled out a manila folder from a green box (such as is used for magazines). Within that folder was one sheet—I wish I could remember *which*, for such an opportunity never came again. The miracle to me was that the three holes were intact—not torn—and that the string was included in the folder. To my eyes it was twine, something thicker than sewing thread and thinner than cooking twine. Having heard for years that Dickinson's early editors virtually tore the delicately constructed books apart, I changed my view to respect the care with which that thread had been pulled through those holes—and kept for such eyes as mine.

6. Jackson calls into question the very term "lyric," particularly with its association of first-person, primary private emotion. See her questions on "a series of lyrics" or "one big lyric" (58) and "public and private" materials (60ff). As for the term "fascicle": see Heginbotham, *Reading the Fascicles* 8 for a review of possible other terms and the history of Mabel Loomis Todd's use of the term, one which continues as an alternate to "Manuscript Books."

7. See Heginbotham, *Reading the Fascicles of Emily Dickinson* 9–13 and "Dwelling in Possibilities" 20–28 for a review of cautionary comments, some by the most distinguished names of the founding scholars of Emily Dickinson, including Ralph W. Franklin. To put their argument too simply, the fascicles are more like scrapbooks, made for filing purposes, than consciously created little books that today might be called chapbooks, each with a carefully chosen beginning and end and careful arrangements of poems next to other poems.

8. See (again) Heginbotham, *Reading the Fascicles of Emily Dickinson*. Much of it is predicated on reading poems within fascicles in which Dickinson "repeated" a poem. Influenced by Neil Fraistat's 1986 study of poets from Horace to Whitman (Dickinson was not included), *Poems in Their Places*, on contextual reading, I compared the same poem in a new context in four pairs: Fascicles 1 and 14, both of which include "The feet of people walking home" (Fr16); Fascicles 3 and 40, which include "I hide myself – within my flower" (Fr80); Fascicles 6 and 10, which contain radically different versions of "Safe in their Alabaster Chambers –" (Fr124); and Fascicles 8 (without this essay's focus on the "Necromancy" poem) and 21 in which the poet/speaker revels: "At last – to be identified" (Fr172). See *Reading* 155 and Franklin, *MB* 1415 for the more complete list of "duplicated" poems. Ellen Hart's essay in this volume discusses the different versions of "Safe in their Alabaster Chambers –" (Fr126).

9. See, among many others: Ruth Miller, who, working with a previous and now discredited ordering, was nevertheless prescient in observing that, while readers should not seek to find a single event or subject reflected in any fascicle, single fascicles "have polar feelings" (248) and that we must "let Emily's choice guide them" (8); Rosenthal and Gall, who connect the cycles with the sequences of Whitman and with modernist long-link poems, compare a fascicle to "a magnetic or electrical field . . . created by its component parts and transformed by those same parts" (101); Willis Buckingham, who, reviewing the *Manuscript Books,* says that "Each fascicle . . . may well constitute an intended sequence of interrelated poems" (614); and not last but certainly among the most compelling to try to describe the fascicles, Sharon Cameron, whose entire complex book I oversimplify with this excerpt, says, "to read the poems in the fascicles is to see that the contextual sense of Dickinson is not the canonical sense of Dickinson" (*Choosing* 19) and that "To see a poem contextualized by a fascicle is sometimes to see that it has an altogether different, rather than only a relationally more complex meaning when it is read in sequence rather than as an isolated lyric" (32). In fairness, some major Dickinsonian pioneers have offered cautionary comments about the value of reading the poems in their fascicle comments. For a sample of such critics, see Heginbotham, *Reading* 13–14 and 157 n. 10. Just so, this volume includes vigorous disagreements on the subject. See Hubbard's essay, for example.

10. We do not know what Dickinson herself called the "Fascicles," the name given the books by Mabel Loomis Todd from the word for "a bundle" (and related to the word for "symbol of power"). Tantalizing possible references are to "My books—so good to turn" (Fr512, F24) and similar poems; "a little manuscript volume of yours," and "what portfolios of verses you must have," as Helen Hunt Jackson spoke of something from Dickinson (L937a); and "a pamphlet," as a letter from Dickinson to Bowles suggests (L193). Emerson had much to say about the "portfolio" poets, but that term connotes the work of an amateur, a term few Dickinsonians would accept for these poems.

11. Michael Riffaterre's *Semiotics of Poetry* describes the "hypogram," the unseen hub in a poem about which its stated language and images revolve. He does not mention Dickinson in his work, but her habit of the elided subject or pronoun referent and the games she frequently plays via circuitous or incomplete syntax and sometimes wild metaphors make her a great test case. The text of a poem, says Riffaterre, is something that "results from the transformation of a word or sentence into a text, or the transformation of texts into a larger whole." Hence," he continues, "a constant component of poetic significance is that the poem's language looks as much like a ritual or a game (in many cases the poem is akin to a generalized pun) . . . as it does like a means of conveying sense." The reader's job, he says, is to perceive rather than to rationalize "what the detour turns about" (164). In other words, Michael Riffaterre is talking about what Dickinson calls "inference" in the last line of this fascicle.

12. See *Reading the Fascicles,* chapter 1 for a discussion of the way Dickinson centers the collection of Fascicle 21 with "They shut me up in Prose" (Fr445) opposite "This was a Poet" (Fr446). The two poems contrast the effects and purposes of prose (daily life, dullness) with those of poetry (freedom, readiness to bloom, ability to unsettle the reader) privileging the writer's task: to surprise her readers.

13. It now seems redundant to criticize the thesis of William H. Shurr in one of the earliest of the fascicle studies. Shurr posits that Dickinson's "There came a Day . . ." (Fr325, F13) marks a high point in a relationship with "the Master," whom he too-

confidently names as Charles Wadsworth. Further, in his book, he claims that the entire fascicle project is an account of the affair between the two. In order to make eight-hundred-plus poems fit this storyline, he leaps and lingers through all forty little books.

14. Barbara Mossberg alone, I think, takes on the poem, linking it (interesting in the fascicle context—which she does not mention) with the volcano poems. In discussing "Ah, Necromancy Sweet!" Mossberg speaks of the "sinister satisfaction of the 'Ah'": "Only evil takes pleasure in evil," she says. "The witch is the poet wanting the pain she inflicts to be immortal, incurable, irremediable—as permanent as the word" (192). David Porter mentions it in his first book on Dickinson, but only to discuss Dickinson's idiosyncratic use of the subjunctive mood (137). The poem does not make it onto the interesting list of "Poems with Spiritualist Implications," appendix to Paul Crumbley's important article on "Dickinson's Use of Spiritualism" (251).

15. See, for example, Christopher Benfey, who says that "My Life had stood" (Fr764, F34) "is about possession by the daemon . . . about the knowledge that power in a woman can seem destructive, and that you cannot live without the daemon once it has possessed you" (87). Paula Bennett's reading of the same poem is much the same: "My Life had stood," she says, "perfectly captures the nature, the difficulties, the risks involved in [the] task of self-definition and self-empowerment" (*My Life A Loaded Gun* [5]). In the poem, continues Bennett, "she is murderous. She is a gun. Her rage is part of her being" (7). More generally, Wendy Barker says that "at the heart of her own darkness lurked a monster at times as terrifying as the sun itself: her own energy, of necessity, often suppressed, loomed like a powerful force that seemed more akin to Satan than to God" (28). And E. Miller Budick's study of the "symbolic vitality of Dickinson's language" speaks of the "turbulence" and "cosmic disruption" of Dickinson's diction and rhyme (13), saying that "her poems parade before us words veritably gone mad, words that . . . masquerade as the absoluteness of cosmic law" (43). An important overview of Dickinson's spirituality is that by Joseph Raab (1998).

16. The "Mirth of Mail," along with the images in the second stanza, calls to mind "The Rock of Ages." Barton Levi St. Armand compares the poem to Thoreau's comment that "Your ticket to the boxes admits you to the pit also" ("Heavenly Rewards" 232); Joanne Feit Diehl offers a reading through the "Romantic Imagination," and says that Dickinson fuses "the threat of the Edwardsean pit with the Emersonian faith in the self," and in so doing, subverts Emersonian power" (182); Judith Farr, in a similar vein, says that Dickinson's art "is founded on thrilling loss" (*Passion* 182); most recently, Alfred Habegger has weighed in, considering the poem part of Dickinson's relationship to Bowles. "A wounded Deer" with its Old Testament typography ("smitten rock") is, says Habegger, Dickinson's response to their disagreement about women in the public sphere, "a portent of what lay ahead for the tortured writer" (392).

17. Such debates are the focus of Margaret Dickie's "Dickinson in Context" (1995); Mary Loeffelholz's "What Is a Fascicle?" (1999); Cristanne Miller's "Whose Dickinson?" (2000); and Heginbotham's "Reading Dickinson" (2008, 90–91). The latter is one of several essays, including those by Tim Morris and Alexandra Socarides, that touch on the subject in *A Companion to Emily Dickinson*, edited by Martha Nell Smith and Mary Loeffelholz. Of course, the debate really began with the earliest reviews of the Manuscript Books, particularly those of Rosenthal and Gall (1983) and William Buckingham (1984), and the denigration of such studies by David Porter ("Dickinson's

Readers" 1984 and Ralph Franklin himself (1983). See Heginbotham, "Dwelling in Possibilities" 19–26.

18. For discussions of the "intentional fallacy" in such criticism, see Heginbotham, "Dwelling" 39–41.

19. As with the first poem in the fascicle, the next two have attracted critical commentaries in other contexts. For example, Joanne Feit Diehl has noted the Keatsian quality of the "terrifying" figures in "To learn the Transport." In her reading the "patient 'Laureates'" suggest God, "the mysterious Bard" (102). I would add to Diehl's reading the element of play (even admitting the "anguish") brought to the gravity of Bardolotry. Readings like those of Diehl and mine in this section seem to complicate at least one poem that Dickinson's earliest readers thought simple: an "Anonymous" reviewer in 1892 says that "To learn the Transport" "has a sweet, sympathetic note"; Martha Hale Shackford, however, notes "the subtlest harmonies" wrought out of "apparent contradictions and discords" (Blake and Wells 49 and 86).

20. Cameron notes that the version with "Portraits," which appears in the second bifolium, and the second, which varies only in the word "Pictures," appears in the fifth and last bifolium. "Because something is being narrated," says Cameron, "the double instances *cannot* be seen as variants . . . but rather in terms of refrains" (*Choosing* 87). Cameron calls such serendipity "so idiosyncratic that it appears almost unprecedented in nineteenth-century American Poetry" (56). Bernard Frank, who does not note the near duplication nor the fascicle setting, concludes that there is no preference by Dickinson for either the "Portrait" or the "Pedantic Sunshine" in what he nicely calls "a mixed elegy" (202).

21. Guthrie speaks of Dickinson's willingness to risk all through her poetry, of her "Promethean spirit" as she "makes forays into a place where it is always 'north'" (*Vision* 61).

22. For example, Judith Farr speaks of it as part of the conversation with Master (*Passion* 213); coming just short of specifying him, Farr notes that Dickinson "herself was a volcano that concealed fiery depths beneath her quiet demeanor" and that Samuel Bowles called her "half angel, half demon" (214–15).

23. *Harper's* (April 1852), in a learned and level tone; *Putnam's* (January 1853), presented in Horace Greeley's "Modern 'Spiritualism'"; and *Knickerbocker,* not so likely part of the Dickinson household but one that may have made its way into conversations by their learned friends (April 1851, June 1852, August 1854—a satire). The so-called Rochester Rappings were of particular interest and were especially the butt of satire (Kucich 36–54). Journals that featured the movement included *American Whig Review* 14 (December 1851); *Atlantic Monthly* (1859); *Gleason's Pictorial Magazine* 4 (June 1853); *Brownson's Quarterly Review* (1854 and 1860); five different "Editor's Drawer" columns in *Harper's* in 1852–53; *Graham's Magazine* (1855); *New York Tribune* (1850); and an article by John Greenleaf Whittier in *United States Magazine and Democratic Review* 13 (1843). On this subject, too, see Russell M. Goldfarb and Clare Goldfarb's *Spiritualism and Nineteenth Century Letters*, 422–32.

24. For example, Orestes Brownson's *Spirit Rapper,* published in 1854 (Kerr 65) was a popular book circulated in Boston in 1854, as was C.W. Roback's *The Mysteries of Astrology and Wonders of Magic, including a History of the Rise and Progress of Astrology and the Various Branches of Necromancy.*

25. James Russell Lowell in 1851 turned his contempt into the humorous "The Unhappy Lot of Mr. Knott" (Kerr 22); in 1852 Artemus Ward, did so in "Among the Spirits"; and in 1856 Herman Melville did the same in "The Apple Tree." Among those whose irony on the subject verged on glee were Mark Twain (Samuel Clemens), William Dean Howells, and Henry James. On the other hand, just about every member of the famous Beecher clan, including Harriet, reflected a serious concern in the subject, free from irony (Kerr 22–33). Braude notes that "the power of Emerson's ideas helped fuel the movement he despised" (45). Even though Emerson and Thoreau spurned the movement, their lectures were enthusiastically attended by Spiritualists. The point of all this is that it would have been difficult for Dickinson not to have experienced the wave of spiritualism (and its interest in necromancy).

## Chapter 4

1. My thanks to Anja Angelsen, Paul Goring, Jeremy Hawthorn, and Eli Løfaldli for contributions made during the writing of this essay, and to Paul Crumbley and Eleanor Heginbotham for comments and advice.

2. For an earlier and fuller treatment of the larger implications of this method of binding, see Alexandra Socarides, "Rethinking the Fascicles: Dickinson's Writing, Copying, and Binding Practices." Ralph Franklin describes the paper as folio (folded during manufacture, at which stage an embossment is added, G. & T. within a decorated vertical oval measuring 1.5 cm × 1.5 cm). The paper, he reports, is laid, cream, and blue-ruled (*MB* 482). The manuscript fascicle is MS Am 1118.3 (104–8) at Houghton Reading Room, Harvard College Library.

3. The notes to Susan were Fr457A, MS Am 1118.3 (292); and Fr477A MS Am 1118.3 (262). Susan received only two poems out of twenty-three: in 1862 as a whole, she received (in Franklin's estimate) about eighteen of the 227 poems composed in the course of that year. Had the significance of those poems relied in any important way on their immediate or overall placement in a fascicle sequence, one would have thought that Dickinson would want to reflect that in some way. Of course, their placement in an overall and ongoing sequence could not have been reflected: Dickinson did not cease compiling poems in this way until much later, in the 1870s. There is also the possibility that withholding other poems from a fascicle helped her to disguise their larger meaning: sending only two was a form of camouflage. But this would suggest that Dickinson did not want to reveal significant aspects of her life to Susan, something most readers no longer accept, or that her audience, if she had one, was not local and known to her. However we choose to read this, it seems clear that Dickinson believed that the poems were quite capable of standing on their own.

4. Franklin records several exchanges between Dickinson and Henry Vaughan Emmons in 1853 and 1854 suggesting that she might have lent him "individual sheets, containing a few poems on each, unbound" (*MB* 8–9, 20).

5. This is not quite the same as saying that Dickinson did not *want* the poems to be read in the order of the fascicles. The motive then would be a desire to *hide* their contents and carefully to leak poems that had would not betray the story they contain. The two best-known interpretations of the fascicles are Dorothy Huff Oberhaus, *Emily*

*Dickinson's Fascicles: Method and Meaning*, and William Shurr, *The Marriage of Emily Dickinson: A Study of the Fascicles*. But I should not be understood as saying that poems chosen for inclusion in correspondence are necessarily the best, either: Dickinson did not always retain copies of the poems sent in letters, and the choice of poem was often tailored to the correspondent—which is why Susan Dickinson, a devout Christian, often received more orthodox poems.

6. The distribution of poems by year was: 1858–43 poems; 1859–82; 1860–54; 1861–88; 1862–227; 1863–295; 1864–98; and 1865–229. These figures do not include working drafts. Of course, not all of the poems were included in the fascicles and sets. And many critics would argue the opposite: that the volume of poems in years with fascicles compared to years without suggests that the poems in years with are part of a massive poetic project united by an overall purpose or design.

7. And as R. W. Franklin writes in an appendix to his 1981 edition, seventeen poems were twice entered in the fascicles and sets: four are the same; two have a single variant, and the others "show substantial variation in their appearances, with the repetition recording further work on the poem" (*MB* 1415).

8. It was William Shurr who argued that the fascicles tell the tale of an impossible love affair between Dickinson and a married man, by whom she had a child: this man predeceases her. He claimed that there were "many poems which refer to a loved person as already dead," and that one of these ("We cover thee–sweet face –," Fr461, F22), "describes such a mysterious death, of someone deeply loved by Dickinson" (177). Dorothy Huff Oberhaus emphasizes the fascicles as a narrative of Christian doubt and faith, in which Dickinson "staked all on a single goal: the hope of being among the sacred sheep at the Judgment." She reads "A solemn thing within the Soul" as deriving from a recurrent Christian and devotional tradition where the cultivation of souls is compared to harvesting (63).

9. Three of the poems in F22 were sent to friends: two to Susan Dickinson, and one to Samuel Bowles. The ones to Susan (Fr457 "Nature – sometimes sears a Sapling" and Fr477 "He fumbles at your Soul") were thought to have been sent before they were recorded in the fascicle: in both instances, the latter version was altered from consecutive lines of verse in letters to lines divided by quatrains (eight lines to two quatrains in the first; twelve lines and a couplet to three quatrains and a couplet in the second). The one to Bowles (Fr478 "Just Once! Oh Least Request!") was sent after it had been recorded in the fascicle, and in both versions there are two quatrains.

10. The gentiana nivalis, for example.

11. Beam can also suggest any large piece of timber, either in a building or a ship—and Dickinson plays on the convergence of eye-beam and structural support in very deliberate ways: the repeated event in the prison is what keeps her speaker from falling apart. It sustains her.

12. The literal situation might also include the following: the speaker recalls standing outside the prison before being admitted and confined there; the speaker is outside the prison at a regular time to visit someone inside. Bernard Mandeville, *THE FABLE OF THE BEES: OR, Private Vices, Publick Benefits. The SECOND EDITION, Enlarged with many ADDITIONS. AS ALSO An ESSAY on CHARITY and CHARITY-SCHOOLS. And a Search into The NATURE of SOCIETY* (LONDON: Printed for *Edmund Parker* at the *Bible* and *Crown* in *Lombard-Street*, 1723), 62. Not mentioning human eyes may

mean that the contrivance in question is a precursor to the Judas Hole—the earliest usage of that term is 1865, according to the *OED*, but there were apertures that performed a similar function (Burchfield 1:1517).

13. In *Discipline and Punish,* Michel Foucault writes: "In view of this, Bentham laid down the principle that power should be visible and unverifiable. Visible: the inmate will constantly have before his eyes the tall outline of the central tower from which he is spied upon. Unverifiable: the inmate must never know whether he is being looked at any one moment; but he must be sure that he may always be so. In order to make the presence or absence of the inspector unverifiable, so that the prisoners, in their cells, cannot even see a shadow, Bentham envisaged not only venetian blinds on the windows of the central observation hall, but, on the inside, partitions that intersected the hall at right angles and, in order to pass from one quarter to the other, not doors but zig-zag openings; for the slightest noise, a gleam of light, a brightness in a half-opened door would betray the presence of the guardian. The Panopticon is a machine for dissociating the see/being seen dyad: in the peripheric ring, one is totally seen, without ever seeing; in the central tower, one sees everything without ever being seen" (196–97).

14. Nor can the error be blamed on erroneous dating: in Johnson's edition of the poems, which Guthrie used, J65 is attributed to 1862, however (*Poems of Emily Dickinson* 2:503–4).

15. For a more detailed look at Dickinson's illness, see Norbert Hirschhorn and Polly Longsworth 316.

16. William Wordsworth, *Poetical Works,* 155–57. The word "plashy" is associated in the poem with the young hare "who is running races in her mirth": much of its action from the eighth stanza onwards takes place beside "a pool bare to the eye of heaven" (156).

17. James R. Guthrie, *Emily Dickinson's Vision:* 186, n. 8. Guthrie's reading of the self-conscious element in the poem is in a footnote: What is slightly unappealing about the self-conscious argument is that it suggests that poetry is a substitute for real life, and a rather poor one at that.

18. John Donne, "The Canonization." John Keats, "If by dull rhymes our English must be chained," in *The Complete Poems,* 521.

19. L233 was to the unknown recipient addressed as "Master," in 1861; L249 to Samuel Bowles in early 1862; L293 to Lavinia in 1864; L1042, one of the last, to Higginson in the spring of 1886. This connection between the poem and "The Prisoner of Chillon" is most comprehensively advanced by Jane Donahue Eberwein in *Dickinson: Strategies of Limitation,* 87–88. For a psychological discussion, see Vivian Pollak, *Dickinson: The Anxiety of Gender,* 129–31. There the phrase "When Memory was a Boy" is associated with the recovery of a "prelapsarian past" (134).

20. Bonivard in *Encyclopædia Britannica Online,*

21. For example, "see" is used 146 times (and is the 32nd most common of her words); "eye" 92 times (58th most common), and "eyes" 88 (61st).

22. In *Emily Dickinson's Fascicles,* Oberhaus attends mainly to the fascicles, not the sets. Martha Lindblom O'Keefe's privately printed *This Edifice: Studies in the Structure of the Fascicles of the Poetry of Emily Dickinson* also stops at the fortieth fascicle.

23. Nina Baym, gen. ed., *The Norton Anthology of American Literature,* 6th ed.. Paul Lauter, *The Heath Anthology of American Literature,* 5th ed.

24. Thomas H. Johnson, *Final Harvest: Emily Dickinson's Poems*. Using Johnson's numbering, the poems appear as 314, 315, 479, 480, 486, 488, and 657; in Franklin's ordering of Johnson's numbers, these should have appeared as 314, 479, 480, 657, 486, 488, and 315.

25. The poem's use of "s" and "l" combinations in particular is characteristic of this fascicle's attention to language as a system of sounds as well as sense: here it is "long sleep"; "Stretch of limb"; "stir of Lid"; in Fr457, it is "Fainter leaves" and "further Seasons."

26. *Letters*, 2.379–80.

27. Habegger 440. Habegger also makes the same connection between Susan's letter and Higginson's report of Dickinson's comment.

28. Perry Miller 336. Zepper's book, a manual on preaching organized according to traditional rhetorical categories (exordium, narration, proposition, conformation, confutation and epilogue) was published in 1598: the comparison was a traditional one, then.

29. Dickinson's own fondness for playing and listening to the piano is recorded by several of her friends: her pianoforte is currently housed at Harvard, where it is described thus: "Pianoforte; Renaissance revival square piano; floral and scroll carved legs and apron. Hallet, Davis & Co., Boston, Massachusetts; circa 1845. Brazilian rosewood, Brazilian rosewood veneer, spruce, ivory, iron; height 93.9 cm., width 207.0 cm., depth 99.0 cm. Emily Dickinson received this piano from her father in 1845, when she was fourteen." Dickinson Family Artifacts (Dickinson Room), Houghton Library, Harvard University.

30. After leaving Amherst College, Park went on to become the Bartlett professor of sacred rhetoric at Andover Theological Seminary (1836–47), and then Professor of systematic theology at Andover, "arguably the most important position in nineteenth-century divinity" (Bruce Kulick, introduction to Park *Memorial Collection* n.p.). Park was described as "the greatest theologian of his time, the greatest American theologian since Jonathan Edwards" (Albert H. Plumb, "The Relation of Professor Park's Theology to His Sermons," in Park, *Memorial Collection*, 6), albeit a more liberal version whose Common Place Book criticized Edwards for too much emphasis on everlasting punishment and God's wrath (see Vanderpool 291).

31. Lord, *Review of Professor Park's Theologies*, 37. The review comes to fifty-eight pages, testimony to the significance of Park's sermon. For a major critique of the Theology of the Feelings, directed particularly at Horace Bushnell, see Charles Hodge, *Essays and Reviews* (New York: Robert Carter & Brothers, 1857), 539–633.

32. Schleiermacher, *On Religion: Speeches to Its Cultured Despisers*. There were earlier publications: *A Critical Essay on the Gospel of Saint Luke*, trans. Connop Thirlwall (London: John Taylor, 1825); *Brief Outline of the Study of Theology, Drawn Up to Serve as the Basis of Introductory Lectures*, trans. William Farrer (Edinburgh: T. & T. Clark, 1850); and *The Life of Schleiermacher as Unfolded in His Autobiography and Letters*, trans. Frederica Rowan (London: Smith, Elder and co., 1860), and reviewed by the Rev. W. L. Gage in "Schleiermacher as a Man," *New Englander and Yale Review* 21, no. 80 (July 1862): 427–42. These are in English: Amherst College has copies of the works in German dating from 1828. Dickinson, of course, studied German at the Amherst Academy.

33. Sewall 359. Johnson and Ward *Letters* 1:64. Smith had moved to Europe for health reasons, first to Paris, France, in 1837, and then to Germany, where he embarked on a course of study that took him to Halle and Berlin between 1838 and 1840, when he returned to America. J. Alfred Guest, *Amherst College Biographical Record, 1963: Biographical Record of the Graduates and Non-Graduates of the Classes of 1822–1962 Inclusive* (Amherst, MA: Trustees of Amherst College, 1963), xlv. A review of *Henry Boynton Smith: His Life and Work* (New York: A. C. Armstrong & Son, 1881) mentions August Neander in Berlin and F. A. G. Tholuck at Halle as the most prominent of the lecturers he heard (*New Englander and Yale Review* 40, no. 163 [November 1881]: 796). Dickinson wrote (in 1848, to Austin, while she was at South Hadley), that "Professor. Smith. preached here last Sabbath & such sermons I never heard in my life. We were all charmed with him & dreaded to have him close." Pomeroy Belden, a hellfire preacher, she was less impressed by: in the same letter she notes that he had been invited to South Hadley but hoped that "it *will*, WILL not be until my year is out" (L22).

34. He is alluded to in L9, to Abiah Root (12 January 1846): "I don't go to school this winter except to a recitation in German. Mr. C[oleman] has a very large class, and father thought that I might never have another opportunity to study it" (L9). Coleman's friendship with Neander resulted in the former's *A Church without a Bishop: The Apostolical and Primitive Church, Popular in Its Government, and Simple in Its Worship* (Boston: Gould, Kendall and Lincoln, 1844), including an introductory essay, by Dr. Augustus Neander.

35. See the entry on Coleman in Johnson and Ward *Letters* 3, p.936. The connections between Amherst College and German institutions of higher learning did not end in the 1840s: Richard Henry Mather (class of 1857) studied at the University of Berlin (1858–59) and later became Instructor of Greek at Amherst College (1859–61: he was an assistant professor there between 1861 and 1864). See Guest, *Amherst College Biographical Record, 1973* p. 84.

36. The phrase is from Gould's daughter, Nellie Gould-Smith, in her introduction to *In What Life Consists, and Other Sermons*. The phrase "music of words" is quoted in Habegger 311: he also discusses the possibility of a romantic attachment between Gould and Dickinson (238–39). As Habegger also points out, Gould was one of the five editors of the Amherst College *Indicator*, published in June 1849 and April 1850. In the Amherst College library edition, his name is written in pencil beside a pen-portrait, and the reader is informed that he takes "a *high stand*" wherever he goes (*The Indicator* 2 [1849–50]: 30: Gould was over six feet tall). Dickinson had a valentine letter published in *The Indicator* (*Letters* 1:92). For a discussion of its contents, see Erkkila 144–45.

37. Gould 166–67. The second phrase is a formulation by Nellie Gould-Smith, in her introduction.

38. "The Word of Life," *In What Life Consists* 155.

39. For an early and comprehensive discussion of the connections between Dickinson and German Higher Criticism, see Maria Stuart, "Contesting the Word: Emily Dickinson and the Higher Critics" (Unpublished PhD thesis: Darwin College, Cambridge, 1994). For a discussion of the German philosophical influence on American theology and Amherst's educational culture, see Jed Deppman, *Trying to Think with Emily Dickinson* (Amherst: University of Massachusetts Press, 2008).

## Chapter 5

1. In grouping Oberhaus, Heginbotham, and Cameron together, I am not suggesting these three works should be conflated with each other, but merely pointing out that none has achieved one of their principal goals: namely persuading readers that the fascicles provide stable contexts for the reading of the poems themselves. Taken individually, all these scholars, including those with whom I disagree the most, have, as I say, greatly enriched our understanding of individual poems and of the synergy that passes between them in the fascicle context (to my mind, fascicle scholarship's greatest contribution to date). But the problem of fascicle unity itself, at least in this writer's opinion, is irresolvable given the way Dickinson writes. For a more nuanced treatment of some of these scholars, see Crumbley's essay on Fascicle 40 in this book. (See 192, 247 n.1, 248 n.3)

2. In *Choosing not Choosing,* Cameron sought a way out of the problem of fascicle unity by shifting the burden of analysis away from the thematic and toward structural issues instead. Taking as her model the poet's habit of leaving variants in place, Cameron argues that the individual fascicles are structured along analogous lines. Just as Dickinson left multiple word choices as, effectively, *parts* of her poems, refusing to choose between them, so with the fascicle groupings. By offering readers multiple viewpoints on one or more ideas, they allow Dickinson to mediate through her poems' arrangements a prismatic, even disjunctive, "self," that chooses and "not chooses" at the same time. This is a powerful thesis that avoids or at least puts the brakes on what has been the most arguable aspect of fascicle readings: the desire to make individual fascicles tell unified narratives. However, while I agree that Dickinson's poems, in the fascicles as well as outside them, offer multiple (and often contradictory) viewpoints, I see no need to tie this multi-perspectivalness to fascicle structure itself. (See Socarides for a similar critique.)

3. In email correspondence, Vivian Pollak pointed out, rightly, that I am substituting chronological "unity" for thematic or structural unity. This is unquestionably true, and it puts my entire argument on a speculative basis since there is no way to be sure Dickinson did not copy into Fascicle 16 poems written at a much earlier date. However, I believe there are enough poems in the fascicle that "work" better if one assumes they were written in response to the war to justify my approach. Among the most important of these poems are "'Twas just this time, last year, I died" (Fr344), "Tie the strings of my Life, My Lord" (Fr338), and "'Tis so appalling – it exhilirates –" (Fr341). On the other hand, there are at least two poems, "Before I got my eye put out –" (F336B) and "He showed me Hights I never saw –" (Fr346B), which could well have been written without the war in mind. For a Gothic reading of F16, see Wardrop in Martin (142–64).

4. See "Emily Dickinson and Her Peers" 290–95. Also see St. Armand 108–9 and Phillips 46–51. My treatment of "I felt a Funeral" in this essay represents a condensed version of my comments on the poem in the earlier essay.

5. The evidence for "It dont sound so terrible – quite – as it did –" (Fr384) is quite strong—consisting, again, of verbal echoes in Dickinson's letter to Bowles. However, the poem's title line makes clear that the impact of Stearns's "murder," as Dickinson calls it in this poem (and in the Bowles letter), was fading by late summer when, according to Franklin, Fascicle 19 was put together. That this poem coexists with poems such as "The

Grass so little has to do" (Fr379B), and "I cannot dance opon my Toes –" (F381B), also in Fascicle 19, thus urges strongly *against* taking the unusual degree of thematic unity in Fascicle 16 as a model for other fascicles. In this respect, Fascicle 16, which at eleven poems is the smallest of the fascicles, may well be unique.

6. The multi-perspectivalness of Dickinson's Civil War poetry has been pointed out by many different scholars. Barrett, for example, notes that "[w]hile some of [Dickinson's Civil War poems] are marked by Dickinson's characteristic oblique and indirect stances, still others read like conventional elegies and sentimental depictions of soldiers' Christian martyrdom on the battlefield" ("Introduction," 18). Similarly, Friedlander describes Dickinson's "wartime writing" as "encompass[ing] multiple, contradictory forms of response, a diversity of representational strategies and of the attitudes expressed that strongly suggest a project of coming to terms with war" ("Battle of Ball's Bluff" 1583). To my knowledge, only Phillips and Marcellin suggest that Dickinson actually used the voices of others (i.e., dramatic monologues, or as I shall call them, dramatic lyrics) in diversifying her approach, a position rebutted by Richards ("'How News'" 163–64). Although I agree with Richards that Dickinson was keenly aware of her fragmentary knowledge of war itself, like Phillips, Barrett, Marcellin, and Friedlander, I do not think this stopped her from trying to imagine how others (both soldiers and noncombatants) responded to it. Indeed, the very line I have taken for my title, "Looking at Death, is Dying," suggests that Dickinson's intense scrutinizing of others was based on a strong belief in empathic connection. The main point, however, is that all these scholars agree on the substantial diversity of Dickinson's Civil War verse, a point also made at book length by Wolosky as well as in her essay on Dickinson's Civil War poetry in Pollak.

7. "I am quite ready to die an *ignominious* death, as a private or officer, or do anything for our beloved country," Stearns said to his father (quoted in [Stearns] 78). See also St. Armand 114). St. Armand believes that Stearns was in fact hoping for a martyr's death, in which case, he achieved at least half his goal. The other half I leave to God.

8. Along with Cameron, one could list Wolosky ("Emily Dickinson," in Bercovitch 427–80, Crumbley 11-4), Marcellin, and Messmer, whose monograph, *A Vice for Voices,* addresses Dickinson's multiple voices in her letters.

9. For more on lyric contract see notes 35 and 36, and pages 111, 128–29 of this essay.

10. Although "dramatic monologue" has been the term of choice today for any poem employing an imagined speaker, Browning, the putative inventor of the genre, did not use it. According to Páraic Finnerty in "'It does not mean me, but a supposed person': Browning, Dickinson and the Dramatic Lyric," the term "was first used in the mid-nineteenth century . . . [but it] was not fully defined until 1908, when the American critic Samuel Silas Curry classified it as one end of a conversation." Browning's own terminology stressed the hybrid nature of his verse, variously identifying his poems as "dramatic pieces," "dramatic lyrics," "dramatic idylls," or "dramatic romances." In *The Poetical Works Complete 1833–1868,* he says of his poems that "the majority" might come "under the head of 'Dramatic Pieces'; being, though often *Lyric in expression,* always *Dramatic in principle,* and so many utterances of so many imaginary persons, not mine" (Italics mine. Quoted in Browning, *The Poems and Plays* 3). "Dramatic lyrics" best describes Dickinson's practice as well as that of other Anglo-American poets of the period. In such poems, which in themselves, I would argue, constitute a lyric subgenre, the poet explicitly blurs the line between the lyric and the dramatic by (effectively) fulfilling all

the criteria for the lyric (meter, rhyme, stanzaic pattern, etc.), save one, the speaker's imaginary status, or, put another way, his or her objectification. These poems thus introduced the possibility of "objectivity" (that is, a realist stance) into the heart of that most subjective and personal of poetic genres, the poem of the poet's "I," precisely the kind of poem that until recently most scholars assumed Dickinson wrote to the exclusion of everything else.

11. Along with Finnerty, Cristanne Miller has also recently adopted the term "dramatic lyrics" for this subset of poems in Dickinson's opus. (See *Reading in Time: Emily Dickinson and the Nineteenth Century,* 12, 148, 207n.27, 241n. 43) It is possible that Dickinson's use of personae will become the next big issue on Dickinson criticism, as it goes directly to the heart of how we read her, even as Virginia Jackson argues (*Misery* 6–7).

By definition, posthumously spoken poems involve invented speakers; however, some of Dickinson's posthumous poems make a clear identification with the poet, while others, just as clearly, do not. The real problem lies with those many poems, be they posthumously spoken or not, which can be read fruitfully both ways at once, for example, in Fascicle 16: "Before I got my eye put out," "He showed me Hights," and "I like a Look of Anguish."

12. See, for example, the following poems in Browne: Anonymous, "Enlisted To-Day" (45–47); Margaret Junkin Preston, "Only a Private" (69–70); Forceythe Willson, "Boy Brittan" (74–77); Francis O. Ticknor, "Little Giffen of Tennessee" (78–79); Walt Whitman, "Come up from the fields, father" (133–35); Maria La Coste, "Somebody's Darling" (174–75); and Kate Putnam Osgood, "Driving Home the Cows" (213–14). For an extremely helpful site listing online resources for Civil War poetry, see http://www.loc.gov/rr/program/bib/lcpoetry/cwanth.html (accessed December 23, 2009).

13. For some poems featuring veteran soldiers see in Browne: Bayard Taylor, "Scott and the Veteran" (43–45); Elizabeth Stuart Phelps, "Malvern Hill" (110), and Forceythe Willson, "The Old Sergeant" (151). I should add that although Dickinson was clearly drawing on stereotypes for both "'Twas just this time" and "Tie the strings," in each case, the poem bears her own stamp.

14. "For now we see through a glass, darkly; but then face to face; now I know in part; but then shall I know even as also I am known" (King James version 1 Cor. 13:12). Spiritualist forms of consolation were especially instrumental in popularizing the literalization of sight in the afterlife both during and after the war and heavily influenced nominally Christian writers such as Elizabeth Stuart Phelps, concerned with salvaging what they could of an embittered faith. See Phelps and McGarry. Discussing both the Civil War and the nineteenth century's cult of a "love religion," St. Armand touches on Dickinson's links to spiritualism in *Emily Dickinson and Her Culture* (99–101, 147).

15. For a perceptive comparison of Dickinson's attitude towards volunteerism and that of Julia Ward Howe, see Bergland 134–45.

16. See in Piatt, for example, "Her Blindness in Grief" (49–51), "That New World" (61), "Comfort by a Coffin" (64 and 65). Nowhere do these two strong women poets come closer than in their shared skepticism regarding the efficacy and, indeed, good faith of conventional forms of consolation.

17. In Exod. 33:20, God says: "Thou canst not see my face: for there shall no man see me, and live." In "To pile like Thunder to it's close," Dickinson puts it more succinctly: "For none see God and live –" (Fr1353).

18. Both Farr (*Passion* 158–60) and Cameron (81–83, 149–51) read "I showed her Hights" (F346A), and "He showed me Hights" (F346B) as concluding in rejection. I also lean toward that view. However, the conclusion of "He showed me Hights" is sufficiently ambiguous that it can fairly be listed as a posthumously spoken poem for purposes of discussion here. Certainly it deals with what one can reasonably hope to "see"/"know" after death.

19. As Wolosky observes, Dickinson was profoundly ambivalent over the question of self-sacrifice for the greater good, which, of course, is the soldier's first duty ( "Public and Private" 118–25). At points, as in "The Martyr Poets – did not tell –" (Fr665), which I follow St. Armand in interpreting as about soldiers (112), she appears to pay homage to their self-sacrifice, but in other poems, like "It feels a shame to be Alive –," she appears to question whether the sacrifice was worth it or not (Fr524).

20. Basing his thinking on "When I was small, a Woman died –" (F518), Friedlander argues that Dickinson was intrigued with the idea of publishing and that, in its patriotic fervor, this poem shows signs of her intention to fit her verse to the marketplace (1584–85). Although, as I have demonstrated, I too think Dickinson drew on popular Civil War poetry, I do not think Friedlander's further assumption—that Dickinson was "testing" alternatives with the marketplace in mind—is necessary to explain her derivativeness, nor the contradictions to which it gave rise.

21. Spiritualism's rise and progress in the nineteenth century and its impact on women writers in particular has been canvassed with some thoroughness from different angles by Braude; Buescher; Bennett, in *Poets;* and Goldsmith.

22. For a similar emptying out of the speaker's immediate reality in another spiritualist poem, see my discussion of "Sister Josie" by Clara Longdon in Bennett, *Poets* 118–19.

23. In total, Shiloh cost 110,053 lives and Fort Donelson, 32,167.

24. One suspects that "rapt"'s derivation from *rapere*—to seize, carry off, plunder, or rape—is operative in this poem, albeit subliminally.

25. According to the 1859 *Webster's,* to wink, which shares the same root as "to wince," is to shut one's eyes briefly. Meanings for the phrase "To wink at" include "to seem not to see" and "to overlook, as something not perfectly agreeable." In the context of Dickinson's poem, not winking would then mean being able to look steadfastly at something that is disagreeable, as, for example, the speaker does in "I like a look of Agony" (Fr339), the poem I treat next, and, as I discuss below, as Stearns's father was spared having to do by the doctors who handled the young man's body on its return to Amherst.

26. Dickinson's emphasis on smoke and lightning strongly urges a reading of "When we stand" as a Civil War poem. See, for example, Piatt's "My Dead Fairies." Here the mother-speaker tries to protect her son from the ugly realities of war, by substituting his "rain" over the "blood" she cannot say, and using "lightning" for gunfire, saying of the "fairies" (i.e., the confederate soldiers) that they were "drowned in drops of – 'Rain?' / They were burned to death with lightning" (19). "Smoke," of course, was conventionally associated with battle, as, for example, in President Stearns's remarkable last sketch of his son, published in the memorial volume *Adjutant Stearns* (1862): "as soon as the smoke had cleared away, and the roar of cannon ceased, a beautiful bird rose and hovered over the camp, and sang. . . . Thus calmly rise the spirits of Christian soldiers" (158).

Stearns's point—that once the smoke has cleared one can see clearly (and praise God with a calm mind)—is so eerily close to that in Dickinson's poem, that it is hard not to wonder if he was the butt of the poem's sarcasm. The book itself was in the Dickinsons' library.

27. Commenting on "My Triumph lasted till the Drums" (F1212), Wolosky contrasts Dickinson with Julia Ward Howe, noting that Dickinson "eschews such a visionary grasp of the whole, remaining caught instead in a fragmentary present. And her ultimate image of repudiation is a 'Bayonet,' whose contrition offers 'nothing' to the dead it neither redeems nor restores" ("Public and Private" 113).

28. Interestingly "I like a look" is a rewrite of a much earlier and much less successful poem, "A throe opon the features –" (F105B, Fascicle 5), suggesting that the war sharpened Dickinson's pen as well as her thoughts on death.

29. "Minie balls" were a kind of muzzle-loading rifle bullet, named after their inventor, Claude Etienne Minié. However, given Dickinson's emphasis on the contrast between Frazar's "big" heart and the comparatively tiny size of the ball that killed him, a submerged graphic pun on either "minim," which according to *Webster's* (1859) literally meant "something exceeding small," or on "miniature," seems possible here.

30. See also pp. 104–14, for St. Armand's full discussion of Stearns's importance to Dickinson, her family, and the town of Amherst.

31. According to the 1859 *Webster's,* a lodge was "a small house, or habitation, in a park or forest," and a porter was "a man that has the charge of a door or gate; a doorkeeper." Their presence in this poem is odd enough to suggest that Dickinson is making a specific point with them. As a noun, "lodge" appears only once in her poetry, and "porter" is used only twice. Neither word is used in her letters in the sense used in this poem.

32. See "This World is not conclusion" (F373; Fascicle 18): "It beckons, and it baffles – / Philosophy, dont know – / . . . / Narcotics cannot still the Tooth / That nibbles at the soul –." Also written, according to Franklin, in the summer of 1862, this poem strongly suggests that Dickinson's dark night of the soul was precipitated, as Wolosky argues, by the war.

33. In "Self-Reliance," Emerson, *Essays First series,* http://www.emersoncentral.com/selfreliance.htm (accessed December 23, 2009), and Whitman, "Song of Myself," section 52, lines 1324–26).

The content of this and the next paragraph is deeply indebted to Vivian Pollak, who in an extended phone conversation walked me through the distinctions I wished to make between poems generally expressive of Dickinson's polyvocality (or heteroglossia) and dramatic lyrics.

34. Beginning with Reynolds, *Beneath the American Renaissance,* literary studies of the heteroglossic nature of nineteenth-century culture are legion. Some of the more important for me are Danky, Fahs, Haralson, Lehuu, Levine, Lott, Okker, Price and Smith, Sizer, Wald, and the essays in Bennett, Kilcup, and Schweighauser. For single-author studies and for anthologies, see the "Works Cited and Recommended" section by Schweighauser in Bennett, Kilcup, and Schweighauser. Bluntly, there is almost nothing in Schweighauser's capacious bibliography that does not support or provide evidence for the heterogeneity of nineteenth-century culture and the poetry to which it gave rise.

35. As Virginia Jackson argues, the romantic lyric (putatively, the poem of the poet's "I") was not an all-dominating form in the nineteenth century. It only became so under the aegis of the New Criticism in the 1930s, when what she and Yopie Prins call "lyrical reading" received its academic imprimatur. Browning's importance lies in the fact that he was the first to create a theoretical space between dramatic lyrics and the romantic lyric, against which he was revolting. Browning's defense of his own, as he saw it, realist, poetic is encapsulated in the poetic prologue to his last volume, *Asolando*. It hardly needs saying, however, that such a theorization of the breaking of the "lyric contract" was only possible once the contract itself had been established—as it was in the *Lyrical Ballads*. That is, the seeds for lyrical reading and hence for the romantic lyric's ultimate triumph were laid in 1798, flying in the face of centuries of verse (e.g., sonnet sequences, satires, epics, Provencal love poetry, and so on) wherein the role of convention in the construction of speakers and the situations they described was taken for granted. In this sense Dickinson's inordinate use of "I" did make her a pivotal figure of great importance. The question now is, how far can her "I" be trusted, or, put another way, when she uses "I," how do we know it is Dickinson speaking or a "supposed person"? Can we? Or has that aspect of her work become permanently destabilized as well?

36. On this point Phillips writes, "The critics who assume that the origins of ["I felt a Funeral"]'s images and events are only in the poet's preoccupation with the self deny the efficacy of imaginative intelligence in transfiguring perceptions of the experiences of others as well as oneself into evocative language. But those critics also deny Emily Dickinson a measure of her humanity" (52), a point I view as well taken.

## Chapter 7

1. See *Manuscript Books of Emily Dickinson* 1–18; and *Poems of Emily Dickinson: Variorum Edition* 57–58, 63–85.

2. For some readers this is far more than simply the beginning of a practice; it is the beginning of a structure, sequence, or narrative that will come to fruition in the thirty-nine fascicles that follow. See Oberhaus, *Emily Dickinson's Fascicles*, in which she argues that Fascicle 40 is "a carefully constructed poetic sequence and the triumphant conclusion of a long single work, the account of a spiritual and poetic pilgrimage that begins with the first fascicle's first poem" (3). See also Shurr, *The Marriage of Emily Dickinson*, in which, starting with Fascicle 1, he maps the "phases or stages of the events" that he argues unfold chronologically over the course of the fascicles (5). See Heginbotham, *Dwelling in Possibilities*, in which she reads each fascicle as its own sequence. Heginbotham does not directly link the first to the last, but instead analyzes the connections among and between various fascicles, calling the first fascicle the "impressionistic introduction to the fascicle project" (120).

3. For one explanation of how this works, see Cameron, *Choosing Not Choosing* 3–29.

4. For characterizations of Fascicle 1, see Cameron, *Choosing Not Choosing*, where she refers to it as "a grouping that asks about the relation between nature, death and immortality" and suggests the questions that it poses: "Is death part of nature or does

it mark the end of nature? Can death be redeemed in nature or can it only be rectified by immortality?" (85). See also Paul Crumbley's article, "Fascicle One: The Gambler's Recollection," in which he argues that "The twenty poems that make up the first fascicle trace three cycles, each of which shows speakers moving into or away from the memory of consensual selfhood epitomized by the gambler." Last, see Heginbotham, *Dwelling in Possibilities*, for a study of the relation between Fascicle 1 and Fascicle 14, in which she describes the setting of Fascicle 1 as "a woodsy garden" and argues that the poems move through time, "beginning with the autumn of the gentian and moving to the summer of the rose" (120).

5. See Werner, *Emily Dickinson's Open Folios: Scenes of Reading, Surfaces of Writing*, where she argues that each "volume" of the fascicles "constitutes a 'room of her own,' an enclosed textual space in which Dickinson explored the contents of privacy and power" (12). See also Dickie, "Dickinson in Context," where she suggests the insular nature of the fascicles by arguing that they create a problem for feminist critics because they give us a picture of "the poet in her workshop at a point when feminist critics have been working to bring her out into the world" (321).

6. For instance, we know that there were often pre-fascicle drafts that Dickinson usually destroyed once she copied a poem onto fascicle paper and that Dickinson also often made drafts of her letters, which she destroyed once she made a copy suitable for sending. More problematically, we know that certain correspondents—for instance, her cousins Louise and Frances Norcross—were selective about which of Dickinson's letters and poems they chose to share with Dickinson's editors. The Norcross sisters also edited and transcribed many of Dickinson's writings themselves instead of handing over the originals. For this reason, it is hard to know the extent of what Dickinson sent them and what these documents looked like. (See White, "Letter to the Light: Discoveries in Dickinson's Correspondence," 2–4, where she reproduces a recently discovered full letter to the Norcross sisters, therefore giving readers some insight into what they cut from Dickinson's letters.) For many critics, the most problematic situation is that many of Dickinson's manuscripts were mutilated, erased, and destroyed by one or more persons. Most fingers point at Austin Dickinson and Mabel Loomis Todd, both of whom had something at stake in tempering Dickinson's expressions of affection for her sister-in-law, Sue. For a thorough discussion of the role that Austin Dickinson and Mabel Loomis Todd have played in the reception of Dickinson's poems and letters, see Smith, *Rowing in Eden: Rereading Emily Dickinson*, 10–49.

7. Many thanks to Maggie Humberston at the Lyman and Merrie Wood Museum of Springfield History, who was able to find these circulation numbers for me.

8. For other readings of this poem, see Dandurand, "Another Dickinson Poem," 434–37; and Petrino 153.

9. See chapter 2 of Socarides, *Dickinson Unbound*, where I undertake a more thorough investigation of this text and, in particular, the issues about genre that it raises.

10. While Johnson and Ward suggest that Dickinson may have enclosed a poem in her letter of January 11, 1862, to Samuel Bowles, this poem has never been identified and therefore the enclosures to Higginson have, for a long time, been considered her first. See *Letters of Emily Dickinson*, 390–91.

11. "Safe in their Alabaster Chambers –" (Fr124) had been sent to Sue in three different states of revision, had been published in the *Springfield Daily Republican* on March

1, 1862, and had been copied into both Fascicle 6 and Fascicle 10. For the rich history of the writing, revision, and publication of "Safe in their Alabaster Chambers – ," see *Poems of Emily Dickinson* (1998), 159–64, and Hart and Smith, *Open Me Carefully: Emily Dickinson's Intimate Letters to Susan Huntington Dickinson,* 97–100. "I'll tell you how the Sun rose –" (Fr204) and "The nearest Dream recedes – unrealized –" (Fr304) had been copied into Fascicles 10 and 14 respectively, the first in early 1861 and the second in early 1862. "We play at Paste –" (Fr282) is the only poem that had not already been copied into a fascicle and may not have been sent to anyone prior to its inclusion in this letter. According to Franklin, three years later Dickinson made a fair copy of this poem on embossed notepaper with the heading "Emily" and signature "Emily," although it was not folded or sent. See *Poems of Emily Dickinson* (1998), 300.

12. Although Higginson said the enclosures were "Your Riches, taught me, poverty –" (Fr418) and "A bird came down the walk" (Fr359)—see *Letters of Emily Dickinson* (1958), 405—Johnson decided otherwise, and Franklin concurs with Johnson's assessment. "There came a Day at Summer's full" (Fr325) had been copied into Fascicle 13, "Of all the Sounds despatched abroad" (Fr334) into Fascicle 12, and "South Winds jostle them –" (Fr98), in addition to having been sent to Louise and Frances Norcross as well as Thomas Gilbert, had been copied into Fascicle 5.

13. See L74a and L74c, L173, and L198. Many thanks to Leslie Morris and the staff of the Houghton Library at Harvard University, who gave me access to these unpublished manuscripts.

14. For a strict marking of what genre Dickinson is writing in when, see Mitchell, *Measures of Possibility: Emily Dickinson's Manuscripts.* For a discussion of the "lyrical letter," see Hewitt, *Correspondence and American Literature, 1770–1865,* 142–72. For a discussion of Dickinson's "letter-poems," see Hart and Smith xxv–xxvi.

15. Note that the word "flood" in the fascicle version has been changed to "shatter." This was not indicated as a variant in the fascicle and is the only word that has been changed.

16. Many thanks to Eric Fraser at the Boston Public Library for giving me access to this manuscript, which is reproduced in full in Socarides, *Dickinson Unbound,* 61–63.

17. See Heginbotham, *Dwelling in Possibilities,* 116. See 125–32 for an extensive study of this poem in both the Fascicle 1 and Fascicle 14 contexts.

# Chapter 8

1. For consistency with the essays here, I use "fascicles," the name used by some of Dickinson's most influential editors. Mabel Loomis Todd refers to "fascicules." R. W. Franklin uses "fascicles," departing from his predecessor, Thomas H. Johnson, who calls them "packets." I prefer "manuscript volumes," a common nineteenth-century term. Helen Hunt Jackson wrote to Dickinson: "I have a little manuscript volume with a few of your verses in it—and I read them very often" (L444a). Lavinia Dickinson used the term while working with the poems she discovered after her sister's death. "Sets" is the name Franklin gives to his organized groups of unbound sheets where stationeries match, and poems are arranged on the page as they are in the fascicles: "sets" are "grouped here by similarity of paper and date" (*MB* xi).

2. In *Open Me Carefully: Emily Dickinson's Intimate Letters to Susan Huntington Dickinson*, Martha Nell Smith and I assign documents to the early, middle, and late periods of each decade, unless there is reliable evidence for specification.

3. Debate in Dickinson studies over whether line breaks are intentional, or a matter of line length and paper size, began soon after the publication of Franklin's facsimile edition. Poet, painter, and literary theorist Susan Howe was among the first to challenge the editor's claim that the divisions are accidents. See the section of Franklin's introduction to the variorum, pages 34–36, beginning: "Available space ordinarily determined the physical line breaks in Dickinson's poems." Franklin writes that his edition, "unconstrained by incidental characteristics of the artifact," "restores the lines, though also recording the turnovers" (35–36). A section called "Division" lists the last word of each physical line that differs from the measured line, without rationale for or explanation of how this information might be used.

See Susan Howe's "'These Flames and Generosities of the Heart': Emily Dickinson and the Illogic of Sumptuary Values," in *Sulfur: A Literary Bi-Annual of the Whole Art* (1991); a later version of this groundbreaking essay appears in her collection *The Birth-mark: Unsettling the Wilderness in American Literary History* (1993). A version from 1986, "Women and Their Effect in the Distance," is included in *Ironwood* 28.

A number of Dickinson scholars disagree with Howe and support Franklin's position. See work by Jay Ladin, Cristanne Miller, Domhnall Mitchell, Christina Pugh, and John Shoptaw. My own views were originally influenced by Howe and by manuscript scholar and textual editor Martha Nell Smith. I am also indebted to the work of Marta Werner and Jerome McGann.

4. Franklin's text and my own differ from Johnson's in two instances: Johnson capitalizes the "c" in "chambers" and the "s" in "snow," whereas I do not, and Franklin does not.

5. See Smith, Hart, Vetter, and Werner, *The Dickinson Electronic Archives*, "Emily Dickinson Writing a Poem," for images of versions in the fascicle and those sent to Susan Dickinson and Thomas Wentworth Higginson.

6. Chung and Hart, "Meter and Lineation in Emily Dickinson's Verse," an unpublished paper presented at Poetics Fest, University of California at Santa Cruz, April 21, 2007.

7. Email correspondence, July 2008.

8. I am grateful to Tilly Shaw, my dissertation adviser at the University of California, Santa Cruz, for providing me with the phrase "distributes the centers of the verse." In the introduction to his verse translation of *Beowulf*, Heaney discusses the midline dynamic of alliterative poetry, explaining that "where end-rhyme puts the most prominent aural feature at the end of the verse, alliteration creates a dynamic across the middle of the line" (xix).

9. I first encountered the term "range of rhyme" in James Guthrie's 1989 essay, "Near Rhymes and Reason: Style and Personality in Dickinson's Poetry," where Guthrie's analysis of style is useful, yet marred by his problematic claim that her choice of near rhyme serves as evidence that her style is "self-referential" and her personality "eccentric" (75).

10. I make similar points in two other essays. See "Hearing the Visual Lines: How Manuscript Study Can Contribute to an Understanding of Dickinson's Prosody," with

Sandra Chung; and "Alliteration, Emphasis, and Spatial Prosody in Dickinson's Manuscript Letters."

11. In editing Dickinson's writings, identifying capitalizations can be difficult. Johnson's penciled notes, as he edited poems at Harvard University's Houghton Library, show that he occasionally crossed out a letter and changed his reading of a capitalization, especially with "O/o" and "C/c." Franklin's capitalizations sometimes differ from Johnson's, as noted above. Martha Nell Smith and I did not always agree on capitalizations for our transcripts of manuscript poems in "Emily Dickinson's Correspondences: A Born-Digital Textual Inquiry." In "Editorial Notes" to the electronic edition we record our differences.

12. "The Development of Dickinson's Style" deserves more attention. Morris calculates that "eighty-eight percent of Dickinson's rhymes are of three phonetic types: exact, consonantal, and vowel rhymes," that the early poems mainly employ exact rhyme, "80.4 % in 1850–1854, down to 68.1% in 1858, then in 1864, 28.3% and in 1865, 29.9%" (162). I disagree with Morris when he maintains that "after 1865, Dickinson wrote so little poetry that analysis of trends is not reliable" and that she "stopped her great outpouring of poetry in 1866, and the technique she had developed through so many hundreds of poems shows no strong growth in any direction thereafter" (163). However, his conclusion that "rhyme and enjambment developed over time" will lead to new directions in fascicle scholarship and prosody studies.

13. In two previously published essays on Dickinson's prosody, I discuss at greater length the role of studies in elocution and handwriting on her visual strategies of manuscript. See "Hearing the Visual Lines," with Sandra Chung; and "Alliteration, Emphasis, and Spatial Prosody in Dickinson's Manuscript Letters."

14. It is striking that prosody, an area of knowledge that today most people know little about—few even know the word, or they assume it involves prose—was once routinely studied in grammar classes in American schools. In two previously published essays on Dickinson's prosody, I discuss at greater length the role of her studies in elocution and handwriting on her visual strategies of manuscript. See "Hearing the Visual Lines," with Sandra Chung; and "Alliteration, Emphasis, and Spatial Prosody in Dickinson's Manuscript Letters."

15. I use the same examples from Ebenezer Porter in "Hearing the Visual Lines," and I also discuss Porter's work in "Alliteration, Emphasis, and Spatial Prosody in Dickinson's Manuscript Letters." The instruction of this particular elocutionist, so well known to Dickinson, is the most effective way to show the meticulous care readers were urged to take in articulating each consonant and vowel.

16. Another critic to explain the importance of the dash as a "tool" that "graphically suggests sound and meaning" is Brita Lindberg-Seyersted, who writes in her 1968 study, *The Voice of the Poet:* "Whereas punctuation in general was becoming more syntactical and more fixed as the nineteenth century advanced, Emily Dickinson never abandoned the rhetorical basis" (196). Lindberg-Seyersted sees the dashes as "pointings" and describes them as "indicators of 'the pause of anticipation or suspense'" and "'as giving the stress of italics' to certain words" (196). Lindberg-Seyersted explains in a footnote that her quotations are from "'Stops' or How to Punctuate," by George Paul Macdonnell, writing as Paul Allardyce, published in London in 1884. For an overview of critical theories on Dickinson's dash before 1968, see Lindberg-

Seyersted's complete section on "Punctuation and Other Graphic Representations of Sound and Meaning," 180–96.

17. See also Paul Crumbley's *Inflections of the Pen.*

18. Wylder agrees with Porter that "various attitudes or tones [are] conveyed through the different vocal inflections," and concludes that a "rising slide" "indicates that the word it follows is heard with an upward slide," and that "such an intonation conveys attitudes of question, incomplete thought, tender emotion, or something implied or insinuated." She notes that the mark may appear "high above" the word, and that "the higher the slide, the more intensive the inflection heard with the word, or the more emphatic the attitude conveyed" (68–69).

19. "Wild nights – Wild nights !" is the first of four manuscript images included in *The Last Face;* see Wylder's print translation of the poem on page 77.

20. In *Open Me Carefully,* Smith and I did not have the option of using alternative typography to represent the multifaceted dashes; we use the symbol of an apostrophe to denote the mark. See, for example, "Ah – Teneriffe !" (121) where exclamatory dashes appear in three places, including after the signature at the end of the poem, "Emily –." (In the correspondence to Susan Dickinson, the exclamatory dash often follows Dickinson's signature.) Fascicle 35's "Ah – Teneriffe – receding / Mountain," "about 1863," also uses the exclamatory dash, after "Ah" in the opening line, above, and in the last lines: "Ah – Teneriffe – We're / pleading still –."

21. In the second stanza Franklin does not capitalize "Again"; Johnson does.

22. I also make this point in "Hearing the Visual Lines," and in "Alliteration, Emphasis, and Spatial Prosody in Dickinson's Manuscript Letters."

## Chapter 9

1. In referring to the fascicle as a meditation, I draw on a key term in Dorothy Huff Oberhaus's important study of Fascicle 40. In *Emily Dickinson's Fascicles: Method and Meaning,* Oberhaus situates the poems in "The Christian meditative tradition," arguing that "the fortieth fascicle is a carefully constructed poetic sequence and the triumphant conclusion of a long single work, the account of a spiritual and poetic pilgrimage that begins with the first fascicle's first poem" (3). My aim in this essay is not to refute Oberhaus but rather to draw on her careful readings as they contribute to my own interest in a different kind of meditation: Dickinson's artistic meditation on the life of poems and her role as a poet. Mine is an alternative analysis in which Jesus does not play the central role that Oberhaus attributes to him. In keeping with my more secular orientation, I identify lovers and readers where Oberhaus identifies Jesus and readers as primary addressees. Readers interested in a meticulous reading of the poems as part of a Christian conversion narrative should read the Oberhaus book. For additional scholarship on the religious significance of the fascicles, readers might also consult Martha O'Keefe's 1986 work, *This Edifice: Studies in the Structure of the Fascicles of the Poetry of Emily Dickinson.* The reading I present here does not propose a coherent narrative that unites either the poems of Fascicle 40 or the poems that make up all forty fascicles. I am more interested in the way poems in Fascicle 40 provide a thematic rather than a narrative meditation.

2. We do not of course possess a complete record of Dickinson's correspondence, so it is impossible to know for certain how many of her poems she would have distributed through letters at this point in her life. It is safe to say that by this time she had sent out *at least* 251 poems.

3. Though my reading is not connected to narrative, important scholarly work has proposed narrative structures for the forty fascicles. I have mentioned in note 1 that Dorothy Huff Oberhaus presents the fascicles as contributing to a Christian conversion narrative. Ruth Miller, the first scholar to publish a study of the complete fascicles, also identified clear narrative features, only for her each individual fascicle contained a narrative the main features of which were repeated in all forty: "Each is a narrative structure designed to recreate the experience of the woman as she strives for acceptance or knowledge, is rebuffed or fails because of her limitations, but then by an act of will, forces herself to be patient in order to survive, fixes her hopes on another world where Jesus and God await her, and remains content meanwhile with herself alone" (249). The most controversial scholarly effort to identify a narrative that unites all the fascicles was provided by William Shurr in *The Marriage of Emily Dickinson: A Study of the Fascicles*. Drawing on what he refers to as "snatches of narrative . . . that connect to establish a 'program' which is carried on throughout the fascicles and beyond" (4), Shurr argues that the "narrative core of Dickinson's fascicle poetry is the classic love triangle involving the married couple and the outsider" (30). For Shurr, the married couple was the clergyman Charles Wadsworth and his wife, and Dickinson was the outsider. Readers interested in the narrative dimensions of Dickinson's fascicles would benefit by consulting these works.

4. I should point out that in constructing Fascicle 40 Dickinson used a "greenish white, and blue-ruled" paper (Franklin, *MB* 974) that Franklin designates as "SUPER (blue rule)" (1408). This paper does not appear in any other bound fascicle and shows up on only one other occasion as one of the two sheets that make up Set 4 (1022). Dickinson's choice of paper does distinguish this fascicle from other bound fascicles, though it is difficult to say how significant this might be. Her tendency was to use the same paper for a series of fascicles, but this pattern changed with the last three fascicles, where she uses a different kind of paper for each one. It is tempting to speculate that her inconsistent use of paper is one indication that consistency itself was becoming less important and that she was already questioning the value of material consistency that here applies to common paper choice and will later extend to the stacking and binding of individual sheets. Whether this was part of an emerging wish to free poems from material forms of containment represented by common paper choice and stab binding is impossible to say with any certainty.

5. According to R. W. Franklin's record of "Poems Published in Dickinson's Lifetime," there were a total of seven years when Dickinson poems appeared in print: 1852, 1858, 1861, 1862, 1864, 1866, and 1878 (*Poems*, 1531–21). Of these, 1864 is the only year when more than one of her poems was printed. The most appearances of any poem in any other year was two: "I taste a liquor never brewed" (Fr207, F12) appeared twice in 1862 and "A narrow Fellow in the Grass" (Fr1096) twice in 1866.

6. R. W. Franklin identifies five variants of the poem, for which he estimates the dates of composition to be "about 1862, 1863, 1865, 1871, and 1883" (*Poems*, 311). Guthrie concentrates his discussion on the version of the poem that Franklin identifies as

written in around 1865 (312). Guthrie cites the date of composition as 1864, the date assigned by Thomas H. Johnson (233).

7. I have presented the first lines of "I hide myself – within / my flower," as they appear in Fascicle 40. The first line of Fr80A does not include a dash or a comma.

8. Concern with the political outcomes of copyright legislation reflects sensitivity to tensions widely viewed as inherent within the legal establishment of literary property. This is a point stressed by L. Ray Patterson and Stanley W. Lindberg in the early pages of *The Nature of Copyright: A Law of Users' Rights*. They state first that "the primary purpose of copyright . . . is to promote the public welfare by the advancement of knowledge" and second that from "its statutory beginnings in early-eighteenth-century England, copyright has been the product of a precarious attempt to balance the rights of the creators—and those of their publishers—with the rights of users, present and future" (2) In what follows, I outline the way Dickinson illuminates the tendency among authors and within the reading public to forget the precariousness of the balance struck between private and public interests. I present Dickinson as concerned about the ease with which private and authorial legal rights take precedence over public and communal interests to the detriment of American democracy. By drawing attention to this concern within Dickinson's writing, I hope to show that while her *approach* to copyright and literary ownership may be distinctive, her *conclusions* place her in the company of other writers, politicians, and citizens.

9. What I am describing here is the importance of Locke in establishing the legal status of the author as perceived in terms of possessive individualism. In *The Political Theory of Possessive Individualism: Hobbes to Locke,* C. B. MacPherson describes the essential makeup of the possessive individual: "As with Hobbes, Locke's deduction starts with the individual and moves out to society and the state, but, again as with Hobbes, the individual with which he starts has already been created in the image of the market man. Individuals are by nature equally free from the jurisdiction of others" (269). Gillian Brown affirms the crucial role of Locke in *Domestic Individualism: Imagining Self in Nineteenth-Century America* where she writes that "by the mid-eighteenth century the notion of individual rights promulgated in the political philosophies of Hobbes and Locke comprised an article of cultural faith" (2).

10. For an overview of public awareness of and interest in copyright debates, see Melissa Homestead's *American Women Authors and Literary Property, 1822–1869,* especially 4–11.

11. Here it is worth noting that in making what may appear to be a bold statement about the duties of democratic authorship Dickinson is in actuality entering a prominent cultural debate while also affirming a meaning inherent within the etymological history of "property." Alan Hyde's etymological analysis in *Bodies of Law* makes plain the way Dickinson's concern with the public character of property reflects a dimension of the word's history that has been overshadowed by the term's specialized function in legal discourse. "The central pun involved in every invocation of 'property,'" he observes, "is inherent in its name: *property,* however defined, always mimetically represents both a supposed private, individual, isolated self (*propre,* one's own), and, at the same time, the proper, as defined publicly or socially through the social conventions that give us *propriety, propre* (clean)" (54).

12. Benjamin Friedlander's essay on "Publication – is the Auction," "Auctions of the

Mind: Emily Dickinson and Abolition," provides a careful exploration of the poem's treatment of publication as a form of slavery. Though his conclusions differ from mine, he effectively outlines the social and economic dimensions of the poem.

13. Mitchell presents a much different interpretation of Dickinson's approach to authorial ownership in *Measures of Possibility*. There he writes, " . . . in the same way that the Divine Author gives life (and perhaps even imaginative ideas) to humans, the human author—the genius or originator—passes these meanings on to the reader, who 'bears' but does not own or originate them . . . " (286). Mitchell presents Dickinson as standing in opposition to the utilitarian position I have been describing and concludes that in "Publication – is the Auction" Dickinson argues that authorial ownership should extend to the ideas themselves and not the particular embodiment or expression of those ideas. Central to his interpretation of the poem is his belief that originating power somehow passes from the divine to the poet but stops there and does not pass from poet to reader. I read the poem as claiming that originating power is never transferred from the divine source to the poet or to the reader; instead, it circulates through them equally. For a fascinating presentation of a completely different way to read this poem in light of copyright legislation see 267–70. See also 78–83 in *Monarch of Perception* where Mitchell acknowledges a broader range of interpretive possibilities for this poem though he arrives at the same ultimate conclusion.

14. Marlon B. Ross establishes the precedent for displacement of the message by the medium as far back as the medieval scribal practice of textual embellishment. Because embellishment "brings attention to the prideful self with its intrinsically fallible apprehension of divine authority and its constant yearning to claim God's authority as its own," "the scribe's unpaid labor for the profit of salvation contains within itself the tendency to degenerate into paid labor for mere profit, whether it be worldly fame or monetary gain" (234).

15. There are a great many Dickinson poems that stress the importance of the poet as vehicle for a message that lives on in readers and is not to be confused with the person of the legal author. "The poets light but Lamps" (Fr930), "A word is dead, when it is said" (Fr278), "A word made Flesh is seldom" (Fr1715), "To pile like Thunder to it's close" (Fr1353), and "I would not paint – a picture" (Fr348, F17) are but a few prominent examples.

16. Oberhaus concludes of this poem that the speaker wonders "will she ever have readers for her 'Experiment'?" and "will her poems serve them as she intends?" (53). Oberhaus also equates positive answers to these questions with spiritual salvation. I do not rule out this possibility, but rather choose to concentrate more narrowly on the poem's commentary on the poet's relationship to readers.

17. The poem that follows "'Unto Me'? I do not / know you –" in the second bifolium is "Denial – is the only / fact" (Fr826), a poem in which the speaker teases out the implications of denial. I read this poem as lending credibility to the possibility that the speaker of the previous poem has indeed denied Jesus's offer of a heavenly home. The fact that in the final line of the first stanza the speaker of this poem links denial to "The Day the Heaven died –" would further reinforce this reading.

## Chapter 10

1. "Introduction" by Susan Howe, from *My Emily Dickinson*, copyright 1985 by Susan Howe. Reprinted by permission of New Directions Publishing Corp. Berkeley, CA: North Atlantic Books, 1985. Republished by New Directions, 2007.

# WORKS CITED

## Primary Sources

Dickinson, Emily. *Emily Dickinson Archive: An Open-Access Website for the Manuscripts of Emily Dickinson.* Cambridge: Houghton Library and Harvard University Press. http://edickinson.org.

———. *Emily Dickinson's Correspondences: A Born-Digital Textual Inquiry.* Ed. Martha Nell Smith and Lara Vetter, with Ellen Louise Hart, consulting editor. Charlottesville: University of Virginia Press, Rotunda New Digital Scholarship, 2008 to the present. http://rotunda.upress.virginia.edu/edc.

———. *Final Harvest: Emily Dickinson's Poems.* Ed. Thomas H. Johnson. Boston: Little Brown, 1961.

———. *The Letters of Emily Dickinson.* Ed. Thomas H. Johnson and Theodora Ward. 3 vols. Cambridge, MA: Belknap Press of Harvard University Press, 1958.

———. *The Manuscript Books of Emily Dickinson.* Ed. R. W. Franklin. 2 vols. Cambridge, MA: Belknap Press of Harvard University Press, 1981.

———. *The Poems of Emily Dickinson, Including variant readings critically compared with all known manuscripts.* Ed. Thomas H. Johnson. Cambridge, MA: Belknap Press of Harvard University Press, 1955.

———. *The Poems of Emily Dickinson: Reading Edition.* Ed. R. W. Franklin. Cambridge, MA: Belknap Press of Harvard University Press, 1999.

———. *Poems by Emily Dickinson: Second Series.* Ed. T. W. Higginson and Mabel Loomis Todd. Boston: Roberts Brothers, 1891.

———. *The Poems of Emily Dickinson: Variorum Edition.* Ed. R. W. Franklin. 3 vols. Cambridge, MA: Belknap Press of Harvard University Press, 1998.

## Secondary Sources

Adams, Percy G. *Graces of Harmony: Alliteration, Assonance, and Consonance in Eighteenth-Century British Poetry.* Athens, GA: University of Georgia Press, 1977.

Alcott, Bronson. In Shepherd 280–85.

Anderson, Charles R. *Emily Dickinson's Poetry: Stairway of Surprise*. New York: Holt, Reinhart, and Winston, 1960.
Attridge, Derek. *The Rhythms of English Poetry*. New York and London: Longman, 1982.
Barker, Wendy. *Lunacy of Light: Emily Dickinson and the Experience of Metaphor*. Carbondale: Southern Illinois University Press, 1987.
Barrett, Faith. "Introduction." In Barrett and Miller 1–22.
Barrett, Faith and Cristanne Miller, eds. *"Words for the Hour": A New Anthology of American Civil War Poetry*. Amherst and Boston: University of Massachusetts Press, 2005.
Baym, Nina, gen ed. *The Norton Anthology of American Literature*. 6th ed. New York: Norton, 2002.
Benfey, Christopher. *Emily Dickinson: Lives of a Poet*. New York: George Braziller, 1986.
Bennett, Paula. "Emily Dickinson and Her Peers." In Lauter, *Companion*, 284–315.
———. *My Life a Loaded Gun: Female Creativity and Feminist Poetics*. Boston: Beacon Press, 1986.
———. *Poets in the Public Sphere: The Emancipatory Project of American Women's Poetry, 1800–1900*. Princeton, NJ: Princeton University Press, 2003.
Bennett, Paula Bernat, Karen L. Kilcup, and Philipp Schweighauser, eds. *Teaching Nineteenth-Century American Poetry*. New York: Modern Language Association, 2007.
Bentham, Jeremy. *The Panopticon Writings*. Ed. Miran Bozovic. London: Verso, 1995.
Bercovitch, Sacvan, gen. ed. *The Cambridge History of American Literature*. Vol. 4, *Nineteenth-Century Poetry, 1800–1910*. Cambridge: Cambridge University Press, 2004.
Bergland, Renée. "The Eagle's Eye: Dickinson's View of Battle." In Smith and Loeffelholz 132–56.
Berlin, James A. *Writing Instruction in Nineteenth-Century American Colleges*. Carbondale: Southern Illinois University Press, 1984
Bervin, Jen. *The Dickinson Fascicles Online*. http://www.jenbervin.com/html/dickinson.html.
Bianchi, Martha Dickinson. *Emily Dickinson Face to Face*. Boston: Houghton Mifflin, 1932.
———, ed. *The Life and Letters of Emily Dickinson*. Boston and New York: Houghton Mifflin, 1924.
Bishop, Wendy. *Thirteen Ways of Looking for a Poem: A Guide to Writing Poetry*. New York: Longman, 2000.
Blake, Caesar R. and Carlton F. Wells. *The Recognition of Emily Dickinson*. Ann Arbor: University of Michigan Press, 1964.
Bogan, Louise. "Emily Dickinson." In *A Poet's Alphabet: Reflections on the Literary Art and Vocation,* ed. Robert Phelps and Ruth Limmer. New York: McGraw-Hill, 1970. 88–103.
Bonivard, François. *Encyclopædia Britannica Online*, accessed September 22, 2006. http://search.eb.com/eb/article-9080619.
Brantley, Richard E. *Experience and Faith: The Late-Romantic Imagination of Emily Dickinson*. New York: Palgrave Macmillan, 2004.
Braude, Ann. *Radical Spirits: Spiritualism and Women's Rights in Nineteenth-Century America*. Boston: Beacon, 1989.
Brodhead, Richard H. "Veiled Ladies: Toward a History of Antebellum Entertainment." *American Literary History* 1, no. 2 (1989): 273–94.

Brown, Gillian. *Domestic Individualism: Imagining Self in Nineteenth-Century America*. Berkeley: University of California Press, 1990.
Browne, Francis. *Bugle-Echoes: A Collection of Poems of the Civil War, Northern and Southern*. Ed. Francis F. Browne. New York: White, Stokes, & Allen, 1886.
Browning, Elizabeth Barrett. "The Runaway Slave at Pilgrim's Point." In *Poems of Elizabeth Barrett Browning*. Vol. 3. New York: James Miller, 1867. 14–24.
Browning, Robert. *The Poems and Plays of Robert Browning*. New York: Modern Library, 1934.
Buckingham, Willis J., ed. *Emily Dickinson's Reception in the 1890s: A Documentary History*. Pittsburgh, PA: University of Pittsburgh Press, 1989.
———. Review of *Manuscript Books*. *American Literature* 54 (1984): 613–14.
Budick, E. Miller. *Emily Dickinson and the Life of Language: A Study in Symbolic Poetics*. Baton Rouge: Louisiana State University Press, 1985.
Buescher, John B. *The Other Side of Salvation: Spiritualism and the Nineteenth-Century Religious Experience*. Boston: Skinner House Books, 2004.
Burchfield, Robert, ed. *The Compact Edition of the Oxford English Dictionary*. 3 vols. Oxford: Oxford University Press, 1987.
Burns, Robert. "Holy Willie." *RobertBurns.org*. http://www.robertburns.org/works/58.shtml (accessed August 21, 2010).
Cameron, Sharon. *Choosing Not Choosing: Dickinson's Fascicles*. Chicago and London: University of Chicago Press, 1992.
———. *Lyric Time: Dickinson and the Limits of Genre*. Baltimore: Johns Hopkins University Press, 1979.
Campbell, George. *Philosophy of Rhetoric*. Ed. Lloyd F. Bitzer. Carbondale: Southern Illinois University Press, 1963.
Capps, Jack L. *Emily Dickinson's Reading, 1836–1886*. Cambridge, MA: Harvard University Press, 1966.
Carr, Jean Ferguson, Stephen L. Carr, and Lucille M. Schultz. *Archives of Instruction: Nineteenth-Century Rhetorics, Readers, and Composition Books in the United States*. Carbondale: Southern Illinois University Press, 2005.
Chambers, William and Robert Chambers. *Cyclopaedia of English Literature: A Selection of the Choicest Productions of English Authors*. 2 vols. Boston: Gould, Kendall & Lincoln, 1847 [and in Edinburg: Robert Chambers, 1844].
Chung, Sandra and Ellen Louise Hart. "Meter and Lineation in Emily Dickinson's Verse." Unpublished paper, presented at Poetics Fest, April 21, 2007, University of California at Santa Cruz.
"Civil War Poetry: Selected Bibliography of Online Anthologies and Collections, Library of Congress Resources." http://www.loc.gov/rr/program/bib/lcpoetry/cwanth.html (accessed August 21, 2010).
Clary, Bruce W. *Emily Dickinson's Menagerie: The Fascicles as Poetic Scrapbooks*. PhD diss., Kansas State University, 1998. Ann Arbor, MI: UMI, 1998.
Cody, John. *After Great Pain: The Inner Life of Emily Dickinson*. Cambridge, MA: Belknap Press of Harvard University Press, 1971.
Crumbley, Paul. "Dickinson's Dialogic Voice." In Grabher, Hagenbüchle, and Miller. 93–109.
———. "Dickinson's Uses of Spiritualism: The 'Nature' of Democratic Belief." In Smith and Loeffelholz 235–257.

———. "Fascicle 1: The Gambler's Recollection." *Dickinson Electronic Archives.* http://archive.emilydickinson.org/fascicle/crumbley.html

———. *Inflections of the Pen: Dash and Voice in Emily Dickinson.* Lexington: University Press of Kentucky, 1997.

———. *Winds of Will: Emily Dickinson and the Sovereignty of Democratic Thought.* Tuscaloosa: University of Alabama Press, 2010.

Cutting, George R. *Student Life at Amherst College: Its Organizations, Their Membership and History.* Amherst, MA: Hatch and Williams, 1871.

Dana, Barbara. *A Voice of Her Own: Becoming Emily Dickinson.* New York: HarperCollins, 2009.

Dandurand, Karen. "Another Dickinson Poem Published in Her Lifetime." *American Literature* 53, no.3 (1982): 434–37.

———. "Dickinson and the Public." In *Dickinson and Audience,* ed. Martin Orzeck and Robert Weisbuch. Ann Arbor: University of Michigan Press, 1996. 255–77.

Danky, James P. and Wayne A. Wiegand, eds. *Print Culture in a Diverse America.* Urbana: University of Illinois Press, 1998.

Davis, Robert Henry. Scrapbook collection. Class of 1868. Amherst College Archives and Special Collections.

Debo, Annette. "Dickinson Manuscripts in the Undergraduate Classroom." *College Literature* 27, no. 3 (2000): 130–43.

Decker, William Merrill. *Epistolary Practices: Letter Writing in America Before Telecommunications.* Chapel Hill: University of North Carolina Press, 1998.

Deppman, Jed. *Trying to Think With Emily Dickinson.* Amherst: University of Massachusetts Press, 2008.

Dickie, Margaret. "Dickinson in Context." *American Literary History* 7, no. 2 (Summer 1995): 320–33.

Diehl, Joanne Feit. *Dickinson and the Romantic Imagination.* Princeton, NJ: Princeton University Press, 1981.

Dobson, Joanne. *Dickinson and the Strategies of Reticence: The Woman Writer in Nineteenth-Century America.* Bloomington: Indiana University Press, 1989.

Donne, John. "The Canonization." In *The Metaphysical Poets,* intro. and ed. Helen Gardner. Harmondsworth: Penguin, 1980. 61–62.

Eberwein, Jane Donahue. *Dickinson: Strategies of Limitation.* Amherst: University of Massachusetts Press, 1985.

———. "Dickinson's Local, Global, and Cosmic Perspectives." In Grabher, Hagenbüchle, and Miller 27–43.

———. "Is Immortality True?: Salvaging Faith in an Age of Upheavals." In Pollak, *A Historical Guide to Emily Dickinson,* 67–102.

Eberwein, Jane Donahue and Cindy MacKenzie. *Reading Emily Dickinson's Letters: Critical Essays.* Amherst: University of Massachusetts Press, 2009.

Emerson, Benjamin Kendall. Papers. Box 5, Folder 13. Compositions. Amherst: Amherst College Archives and Special Collections.

Emerson, Ralph Waldo. "New Poetry." In *Ralph Waldo Emerson: Essays and Lectures,* ed. Joel Porte. New York: Library of America, 1983. 1169–1173.

———. "Self-Reliance." In *Essays, First Series. Ralph Waldo Emerson Texts.* http://www.emersoncentral.com/selfreliance.htm (accessed December 23, 2009).

England, Martha Winburn. *Hymns Unbidden: Donne, Herbert, Blake, Emily Dickinson and the Hymnographers.* Astor: New York Public Library, 1966.

Erkkila, Betsy. "Dickinson and the Art of Politics." In Pollak, *A Historical Guide to Emily Dickinson,* 113–74.

Ezell, Margaret J. M. *Social Authorship and the Advent of Print.* Baltimore: Johns Hopkins University Press, 1999.

Fahs, Alice. *The Imagined Civil War: Popular Literature of the North and South, 1861–1865.* Chapel Hill: University of North Carolina Press, 2003.

Farr, Judith, ed. *Emily Dickinson: A Collection of Critical Essays.* New Jersey: Prentice Hall, 1996.

———. *The Passion of Emily Dickinson.* Cambridge, MA: Harvard University Press, 1992.

Farr, Judith and Louise Carter. *The Gardens of Emily Dickinson.* Cambridge, MA: Harvard University Press, 2004.

Fast, Robin Riley and Christine Mack Gordon, eds. *Approaches to Teaching Dickinson's Poetry.* New York: Modern Language Association, 1989.

Faust, Drew Gilpin. *This Republic of Suffering: Death and the American Civil War.* New York: Vintage Civil War Library, 2008.

Finnerty, Páraic. *Emily Dickinson's Shakespeare.* Amherst: University of Massachusetts Press, 2006.

———. "'It does not mean me, but a supposed person': Browning, Dickinson and the Dramatic Lyric." Unpublished manuscript, November 2011.

Ford, Karen. *Gender and the Poetics of Excess: Moments of Brocade.* Jackson: University Press of Mississippi, 1997.

Foucault, Michel. *Discipline and Punish: The Birth of the Prison.* Trans. Alan Sheridan. New York: Vintage Books, 1995.

Fraistat, Neil. *The Poem and the Book: Interpreting Collections of Romantic Poetry.* Chapel Hill: University of North Carolina Press, 1986.

Frank, Bernard. "Dickinson's 'Portraits are to Daily Faces.'" *Explicator* 60, no. 4 (2002): 200–202.

Frank, Lucy. "'Bought with a Price': Elizabeth Stuart Phelps and the Commodification of Heaven in Postbellum America." *ESQ: A Journal of the American Renaissance* 55, no. 2 (2009): 165–92.

Franklin, R. W. *The Editing of Emily Dickinson: A Reconsideration.* Madison: University of Wisconsin Press, 1967.

———. "The Emily Dickinson Fascicles." *Studies in Bibliography* 36 (1983): 1–20.

———. "Emily Dickinson's Packet 27 (and 80, 14, and 6)." *Harvard Library Bulletin* 27, no. 3 (1979): 342–48.

Friedlander, Benjamin. "Auctions of the Mind: Emily Dickinson and Abolition." *Arizona Quarterly* 54 (Spring 1998): 1–25.

———. "Emily Dickinson and the Battle of Ball's Bluff." *PMLA* 124, no. 5 (October 2009): 1582–99.

Gardner, Thomas. *A Door Ajar: Contemporary Writers and Emily Dickinson.* Oxford: Oxford University Press, 2006.

Garner, Dwight. "Books of the Times: On a Path to Salvation: Jane Austen as a Guide." Review of *Why Be Happy When You Could Be Normal?,* by Jeanette Winterson. *New York Times,* March 9, 2011.

Gaskell, George Arthur. *Gaskell's Compendium of Forms, Educational, Social, Legal, and Commercial; Embracing a Complete Self-Teaching Course in Penmanship and Bookkeeping, and Aid to English Composition; Including Orthography, Capital Letters, Punctuation, Composition, Elocution, Oratory, Rhetoric, Letter Writing, etc.* Chicago: W. M. Farrar, 1881.

Goldfarb, Russell M. and Clare R. Goldfarb. *Spiritualism and Nineteenth-Century Letters.* Cranbury, NJ: Associated University Press, 1978.

Goldsmith, Barbara. *Other Powers: The Age of Suffrage, Spiritualism, and the Scandalous Victoria Woodhull.* New York: HarperCollins, 1998.

Goodale, Lucy Thurston. Papers, 1832–41. Class of '41. Mount Holyoke Archives and Special Collections.

Gordon, Lyndall. *Lives Like Loaded Guns: Emily Dickinson and Her Family's Feuds.* London and New York: Viking, 2010.

Gottesman, Ronald, Francis Murphy, B. Laurence Holland, Hershel Parker, David Kalstone, and William H. Pritchard, eds. *The Norton Anthology of American Literature.* Vol. 1. New York: Norton, 1979.

Gould, George H. *In What Life Consists, and Other Sermons.* Boston & Chicago: Pilgrim Press, 1903.

Grabher, Gudrun, Roland Hagenbüchle, and Cristanne Miller, eds. *The Emily Dickinson Handbook.* Amherst: University of Massachusetts Press, 1998.

Griswold, Rufus. *Sacred Poets of England and America.* New York: Appleton, 1849.

Grossman, Allen R. *The Sighted Singer: Two Works on Poetry for Readers and Writers.* Contains *Summa Lyrica: A Primer of the Commonplaces in Speculative Poetics.* Baltimore: Johns Hopkins University Press, 1992.

Guest, J. Alfred, ed. *Biographical Record of the Graduates and non-Graduates of the classes of 1822–1971 Inclusive.* Amherst, MA: The Trustees of Amherst College, 1973.

Guthrie, James R. *Emily Dickinson's Vision: Illness and Identity in Her Poetry.* Gainesville: University Press of Florida, 1998.

———. "Near Rhymes and Reason: Style and Personality in Dickinson's Poetry." In Fast and Gordon 70–77.

Habegger, Alfred. *My Wars Are Laid Away in Books: The Life of Emily Dickinson.* New York: Random House, 2001.

Hagenbüchle, Roland. "Sign and Process: The Concept of Language in Emerson and Dickinson." *ESQ: A Journal of the American Renaissance* 25, no. 3 (1979): 137–55.

Haralson, Eric, ed. *Encyclopedia of American Poetry: The Nineteenth Century.* Chicago: Fitzroy Dearborn, 1998.

Hardy, Josephine Kingsley. MS 0778 Josephine Kingsley Hardy Papers. Series 2, "Casket of Gems," essay 7; series 2, "What Employment Brings the Most Happiness" composition. Mount Holyoke College Archives and Special Collections.

Hart, Ellen Louise. "Alliteration, Emphasis, and Spatial Prosody in Dickinson's Manuscript Letters." In Eberwein and MacKenzie 213–39.

———. "May the Circle Be Unbroken: Reading Emily Dickinson after 9/11." In MacKenzie and Dana 69–82.

Hart, Ellen Louise with Sandra Chung. "Hearing the Visual Lines: How Manuscript Study Can Contribute to an Understanding of Dickinson's Prosody." In Smith and Loeffelholz 348–67.

Hart, Ellen Louise and Martha Nell Smith, eds. *Open Me Carefully: Emily Dickinson's Intimate Letters to Susan Huntington Dickinson.* Ashfield, MA: Paris Press, 1998.

Hartman, Geoffrey. *Criticism in the Wilderness: The Study of Literature.* New Haven, CT: Yale University Press, 1980.

Heaney, Seamus. "Old English Language and Poetics: Introduction." *Beowulf, A New Verse Translation,* ed. Daniel Donoghue. New York: Norton Critical Edition, 2000.

Heginbotham, Eleanor Elson. "Dwelling in Possibilities: The Fascicles of Emily Dickinson." PhD diss., University of Maryland, 1992.

———. "Reading Dickinson in Her Context: The Fascicles." In Smith and Loeffelholz 288–308.

———. *Reading the Fascicles of Emily Dickinson: Dwelling in Possibilities.* Columbus: The Ohio State University Press, 2003.

Hewitt, Elizabeth. *Correspondence and American Literature, 1770–1865.* Cambridge and New York: Cambridge University Press, 2004.

Higginson, Thomas Wentworth. "Emily Dickinson's Letters." *Atlantic Monthly* 68 (October 1891): 444–56.

———. "Letter to a Young Contributor." *Atlantic Monthly* 9 (April 1862): 401–11.

Hirschhorn, Norbert and Polly Longsworth. "'Medicine Posthumous': A New Look at Emily Dickinson's Medical Conditions." *The New England Quarterly* 69, no. 2 (June 1996): 299–316.

Hodge, Charles. *Essays and Reviews.* New York: Robert Carter and Brothers, 1857.

Hogue, Cynthia. "'lives – like Dollars': Dickinson and the Poetics of Witness." *Emily Dickinson Journal* 15, no. 2 (2006): 40–46.

Holmes, Janet. *The Ms of M Y Kin.* Exeter, UK: Shearsman Books, 2009.

Homestead, Melissa J. *American Women Authors and Literary Property, 1822–1869.* New York: Cambridge University Press, 2005.

Howe, Susan. *The Birth-Mark: Unsettling the Wilderness in American Literary History.* Hanover, NH: Wesleyan University Press, 1993.

———. *My Emily Dickinson.* Berkeley, CA: North Atlantic Books, 1985. Republished by New Directions, 2007.

———. "'These Flames and Generosities of the Heart: Emily Dickinson and the Illogic of Sumptuary Values." *Sulfur: A Literary Bi-Annual of the Whole Art* 28 (Spring 1991): 134–55.

———. "Women and Their Effect in the Distance." *Ironwood* 28 (1986): 58–91.

Hyde, Alan. *Bodies of Law.* Princeton, NJ: Princeton University Press, 1997.

Jackson, Virginia. *Dickinson's Misery: A Theory of Lyric Reading.* Princeton, NJ: Princeton University Press, 2005.

Jackson, Virginia and Yopie Prins. "Lyrical Studies." *Victorian Literature and Culture* 7, no. 3 (1999): 521–30.

Johnson, Nan. *Nineteenth-Century Rhetoric in North America.* Carbondale: Southern Illinois University Press, 1991.

Johnson, Thomas. *Emily Dickinson: An Interpretive Biography.* Cambridge, MA: Harvard University Press, 1955.

Juhasz, Suzanne. Review of Manuscript Books. English Language Notes, December 1983, 57.

Keats, John. *The Complete Poems.* Ed. Miriam Allott. Harlow: Longman, 1970.

Kerr, Howard. *Mediums, and Spirit-Rappers, and Roaring Radicals: Spiritualism in American Literature, 1850–1900*. Urbana: University of Illinois Press, 1972.
Kittredge, Charles Baker. Sermons. Folder 1. American Antiquarian Society.
Kucich, John. *Ghostly Communion: Cross-Cultural Spiritualism in Nineteenth-Century American Literature*. Hanover, NH: Dartmouth College Press, 2004.
Lambert, Robert Graham, Jr. *A Critical Study of Emily Dickinson's Letters: The Prose of a Poet*. Lewiston, NY: Mellen University Press, 1996.
Lauter, Paul, ed. *A Companion to American Literature and Culture*. Oxford: Wiley-Blackwell, 2010.
Lawton, David. "Middle English Alliterative Poetry: An Introduction." *Middle English Alliterative Poetry and Its Literary Background: Seven Essays*. Suffolk: Boydell & Brewer, 1982.
Lease, Benjamin. *Emily Dickinson's Readings of Men and Books*. New York: St. Martin's Press, 1990.
Lehuu, Isabelle. *Carnival on the Page: Popular Print Media in Antebellum America*. Chapel Hill: University of North Carolina Press, 2000.
Leyda, Jay. *The Years and Hours of Emily Dickinson*. 2 vols. New Haven, CT: Yale University Press, 1960.
Lindberg-Seyersted, Brita. *The Voice of the Poet: Aspects of Style in the Poetry of Emily Dickinson*. Cambridge, MA: Harvard University Press, 1968.
Loeffelholz, Mary. "Dickinson's 'Decoration.'" *ELH* 72 (2005): 663–89.
———. "What Is a Fascicle?" *Harvard Library Bulletin* 10, no. 1 (1999): 23–42.
Lord, David Nevins. *Review of Professor Park's Theologies of the Intellect and of the Feelings*. New York: F. Knight, 1850.
Lott, Eric. *Love and Theft: Blackface Minstrelsy and the American Working Class*. New York: Oxford University Press, 1993.
Lowenberg, Carlton. *Emily Dickinson's Textbooks*. Lafayette, CA: Carlton Lowenberg, 1986.
Lundin, Roger. *Emily Dickinson and the Art of Belief*. Grand Rapids, MI: Eerdmans, 1998.
MacKenzie, Cindy and Barbara Dana, eds. *Wider Than the Sky: Essays and Meditations on the Healing Power of Emily Dickinson*. Kent, OH: Kent State University Press, 2007.
MacPherson, C. B. *The Political Theory of Possessive Individualism: Hobbes to Locke*. Oxford: Clarendon Press, 1962.
Mann, John. "Dickinson's Letters to Higginson." In Fast and Gordon 39–46.
Marcellin, Leigh-Anne Urbanowicz. "'Singing off the Charnel Steps': Soldiers and Mourners in Emily Dickinson's War Poetry." *Emily Dickinson Journal* 11, no. 2 (2000): 64–74.
Margolis, Stacey. *The Public Life of Privacy in Nineteenth-Century American Literature*. Durham, NC: Duke University Press, 2005.
Martin, Wendy. *The Cambridge Companion to Emily Dickinson*. Cambridge: Cambridge University Press, 2002.
McCormack, Jerusha Hull. "Domesticating Delphi: Emily Dickinson and the Electromagnetic Telegraph." *American Quarterly* 55, no. 4 (2003): 569–601.
McGann, Jerome. *A Critique of Modern Textual Criticism*. Charlottesville: University Press of Virginia, 1992.

McGarry, Molly. *Ghosts of Futures Past: Spiritualism and the Cultural Politics of Nineteenth-Century America.* Berkeley: University of California Press, 2008.

McIntosh, James. *Nimble Believing: Dickinson and the Unknown.* Ann Arbor: University of Michigan Press, 2000.

Messmer, Marietta. *A Vice for Voices: Reading Emily Dickinson's Correspondence.* Amherst: University of Massachusetts Press, 2001.

Michael, Ian. *The Teaching of English: From the Sixteenth Century to 1870.* Cambridge: Cambridge University Press, 1987.

Miller, Cristanne. "Dickinson's Language: Interpreting Truth Told Slant." In Fast and Gordon 78–84.

———. *Emily Dickinson: A Poet's Grammar.* Cambridge, MA, and London: Harvard University Press, 1987.

———. *Reading in Time: Emily Dickinson and the Nineteenth Century.* Amherst: University of Massachusetts Press, 2012.

———. "The Sound of Shifting Paradigms, or Hearing Dickinson in the Twenty-First Century." In Pollak, *A Historical Guide to Emily Dickinson,* 201–34.

———. "Whose Dickinson?" *American Literary History* 12, no. 2 (2000): 230–53.

Miller, Perry. *The New England Mind: The Seventeenth Century.* Cambridge, MA: Belknap Press of Harvard University Press, 1939; rpt. 1963.

Miller, Ruth. *The Poetry of Emily Dickinson.* Middletown, CT: Wesleyan University Press, 1968.

Mitchell, Domhnall. *Emily Dickinson: Monarch of Perception.* Amherst: University of Massachusetts Press, 2000.

———. *Measures of Possibility: Emily Dickinson's Manuscripts.* Amherst: University of Massachusetts Press, 2005.

Morris, Timothy. "The Development of Dickinson's Style." In *On Dickinson: The Best from American Literature,* ed. Edwin H. Cady and Louis J. Budd. Durham, NC: Duke University Press, 1990. 157–172.

Mossberg, Barbara. *Emily Dickinson: When a Writer Is a Daughter.* Bloomington: Indiana University Press, 1982.

Murray, Lindley. *English Grammar.* Bridgeport, CT: Josiah B. Baldwin. 1824 (facsmile reproduction with an introduction by Charlotte Downey. Delmar, NY: Scholars' Facsimiles and Reprints, 1981).

Myerson, Joel. "James Burrill Curtis and Brook Farm." *New England Quarterly* 51 (1978): 396–423.

Newman, Samuel P. *A practical system of rhetoric, or, The principles and rules of style inferred from examples of writing, to which is added a historical dissertation on English style.* 5th ed. Andover: Gould and Newman. New York: H. Griffin and Co. 1835. Charlotte Downey, intro. Delmar, NY: Scholars' Facsimiles & Reprints, 1995.

Oberhaus, Dorothy Huff. *Emily Dickinson's Fascicles: Method and Meaning.* University Park: Pennsylvania State University Press, 1995.

O'Keefe, Martha Lindblom. *This Edifice: Studies in the Structure of the Fascicles of the Poetry of Emily Dickinson.* Chevy Chase, MD: Mrs. John A. O'Keefe, 1986.

Okker, Patricia. *Our Sister Editors: Sarah J. Hale and the Tradition of Nineteenth-Century Women Editors.* Athens: University of Georgia Press, 1995.

Ostendarp, Anneliese M. "The Athenian Society Library, 1821–1846: The Student Literary Society Library and the Academic Library." SUNY Albany, School of Library and Information Science, August 2, 1985.
Park, Edwards A. *Memorial Collection of Sermons by Edwards A. Park, compiled by his daughter.* Boston: Pilgrim Press, 1902.
Park, Edwards Amasa and Bruce Kuklick. Introduction to *Edwards Amasa Park: Selected Essays,* ed. Bruce Kuklick. New York: Garland, 1987.
Parker, Richard Green. *Aids to English Composition, Prepared for Students of All Grades; Embracing Specimens and Examples of School and College Exercises and Most of the Higher Departments of English Composition, Both in Prose and Verse.* 20th ed. New York: Harper and Bros, 1852. (1845.)
Patterson, L. Ray and Stanley W. Lindberg. *The Nature of Copyright: A Law of Users' Rights.* Athens: University of Georgia Press, 1991.
Patterson, Rebecca. *Emily Dickinson's Imagery.* Ed. Margaret Freeman. Amherst: University of Massachusetts Press, 1979.
Payson, J. W., S. Dunton, and W. M. Scribner. *Payson, Dunton, and Scribner Manual of Penmanship.* New York: Potter, Ainsworth, 1873.
Peiss, Kathy. "Going Public: Women in Nineteenth-Century Cultural History." *American Literary History* 3, no. 4 (1991): 817–28.
Petrino, Elizabeth A. *Emily Dickinson and Her Contemporaries: Women's Verse in America: 1820–1885.* Hanover, NH: University of New England, 1998.
Phelps, Elizabeth Stuart. *Three Spiritualist Novels.* Ed. Nina Baym. University of Illinois Press, 2000.
Phillips, Elizabeth. *Emily Dickinson: Personae and Performance.* University Park: Pennsylvania State University Press, 1996.
Piatt, Sarah. *Palace-Burner: The Selected Poetry of Sarah Piatt.* Ed. Paula Bernat Bennett. Urbana: University of Illinois Press, 2000.
Pollak, Vivian, ed. *A Historical Guide to Emily Dickinson.* Oxford: Oxford University Press, 2004.
———. *Dickinson: The Anxiety of Gender.* Ithaca, NY: Cornell University Press, 1984.
Porter, David. *The Art of Emily Dickinson's Early Poetry.* Cambridge, MA: Harvard University Press, 1966.
———. *Dickinson: The Modern Idiom.* Cambridge, MA: Harvard University Press, 1981.
Porter, Ebenezer. *The Rhetorical Reader, Consisting of Instructions for Regulating the Voice.* New York: Mark H. Newman, 1835.
Price, Kenneth M. and Susan Belasco Smith, eds. *Periodical Literature in Nineteenth-Century America.* Charlottesville: University of Virginia Press, 1995.
Price, Monroe E. and Malla Pollack. "The Author in Copyright: Notes for the Literary Critic." In Woodmansee and Jaszi 439–56.
Pugh, Christina. "Ghosts of Meter: Dickinson, After Long Silence." *Emily Dickinson Journal* 16, no. 2 (2007): 1–24.
Quinn, Carol. "Dickinson, Telegraphy, and the Aurora Borealis." *Emily Dickinson Journal* 13, no. 2 (2004): 58–78.
Raab, Joseph. "The Metapoetic Element in Dickinson." In Grabher, Hagenbüchle, and Miller 273–95.

Rice, Grantland S. *The Transformation of Authorship in America.* Chicago: University of Chicago Press, 1997.
Richards, Eliza. *Gender and the Poetics of Reception in Poe's Circle.* New York: Cambridge University Press, 2004.
———. "'How News Must Feel When Traveling': Dickinson and Civil War Media." In Smith and Loeffelholz 160–79.
Ricks, Christopher. *The Force of Poetry.* Oxford: Oxford University Press / Clarendon Press, 1984.
Riffaterre, Michael. *Semiotics of Poetry.* Bloomington: Indiana University Press, 1984.
Rose, Mark. *Authors and Owners: The Invention of Copyright.* Cambridge, MA: Harvard University Press, 1993.
Rosenthal, Macha L. and Sally M. Gall. *The Modern Poetic Sequence: The Genius of Modern Poetry.* Oxford: Oxford University Press, 1983.
Ross, Marlon B. "Authority and Authenticity: Scribbling Authors and the Genius of Print in Eighteenth-Century England." In Woodmansee and Jaszi 231–57.
St. Armand, Barton Levi. *Emily Dickinson and Her Culture: The Soul's Society.* New York: Cambridge University Press, 1984.
———. "Heavenly Rewards of Merit: Recontextualizing Emily Dickinson's 'Checks.'" In Yamakawa 219–38.
Sanchez-Eppler, Karen. *Touching Liberty: Abolition, Feminism, and the Politics of the Body.* Berkeley: University of California Press, 1993.
Salska, Agnieszka. "Dickinson's Letters." In Grabher, Hagenbüchle, and Miller 163–80.
Salter, Mary Jo. "The Music of Emily Dickinson." Public address, April 12, 2007. Dallas: Southern Methodist University.
Scheurer, Erika. "'[S]o of course there was Speaking and Composition—': Dickinson's Early Schooling as a Writer." *Emily Dickinson Journal* 18, no. 1 (2009): 1–21.
Schleiermacher, Friedrich. *On Religion: Speeches to Its Cultured Despisers.* Trans. and ed. Richard Crouter. Cambridge: Cambridge University Press, 1996.
Scholes, Robert. *Semiotics and Interpretation.* New Haven, CT: Yale University Press, 1982.
Schultz, Lucille M. *The Young Composers: Composition's Beginnings in Nineteenth-Century Schools.* Southern Illinois University Press, 1999.
Schweighauser, Philipp. "Works Cited and Recommended." In Bennett, Kilcup, and Schweighauser 357–92.
Sewall, Richard. *The Life of Emily Dickinson.* 2 vols. New York: Farrar, Straus and Giroux, 1974.
Shaw, Robert B. *Blank Verse: A Guide to Its History and Use.* Athens: Ohio University Press, 2007.
Shepherd, Odell, ed. *The Journals of Bronson Alcott.* Boston: Little, Brown, 1938.
Sheridan, Thomas. *Course of Lectures on Elocution.* New York: O. Penniman, 1803.
Shoptaw, John. "Listening to Dickinson." *Representations* 86 (Spring 2004): 20–52.
Short, Bryan C. "Emily Dickinson and the Scottish New Rhetoric." *Emily Dickinson Journal* 5, no. 2 (Fall 1996): 261–66.
Shurr, William B. *The Marriage of Emily Dickinson: A Study of the Fascicles.* Lexington: University Press of Kentucky, 1983.
Small, Judy Jo. *Positive as Sound: Emily Dickinson's Rhyme.* Athens: University of Georgia Press, 1990.

Smith, Martha Nell. "The Civil War, Class, and the Dickinsons' Confederate Relations." In *The Classroom Electric,* ed. Kenneth Price and Martha Nell Smith. Charlottesville: Institute for Advanced Technology in the Humanities, 2000. http://www.classroomelectric.org/volume2/smith.

———. "Suppressing the Books of Susan in Emily Dickinson." In *Epistolary Histories: Letters, Fiction, Culture,* ed. Amanda Gilroy and W. M. Verhoeven. Charlottesville: University Press of Virginia, 2000. 101–24.

———. *Rowing in Eden: Rereading Emily Dickinson.* Austin: University of Texas Press, 1992.

Smith, Martha Nell and Mary Loeffelholz. *A Companion to Emily Dickinson.* Oxford: Blackwell, 2008.

Smith, Martha Nell, Marta Werner, Jessica Beard, and Julie Enszer, eds., Ellen Louise Hart, consulting editor. *Dickinson Electronic Archives* http://emilydickinson.org Available: 2012 to the present. Smith, Martha Nell, Ellen Louise Hart, Lara Vetter, and Marta Werner, eds. 1994–2012.

Smith, Robert McClure. *The Seductions of Emily Dickinson.* Tuscaloosa and London: University of Alabama Press, 1996.

Socarides, Alexandra. *Dickinson Unbound: Paper, Process, Poetics.* Oxford and New York: Oxford University Press, 2012.

———"The Poetics of Interruption: Dickinson, Death, and the Fascicles." In Smith and Loeffelholz 309–33.

———. "Rethinking the Fascicles: Dickinson's Writing, Copying, and Binding Practices." *Emily Dickinson Journal* 15, no. 2 (2006): 69–94.

Sparks, Robert. "Review: *Spiritualism and Nineteenth Century Letters,* by Russell M. and Clare R. Goldfarb." *New England Quarterly* 51 (1978): 452–54.

Spring, Suzanne B. "Forming Letters: Mount Holyoke, Emily Dickinson, and Nineteenth-Century Epistolary Compositions." PhD diss., University of Michigan, 2005.

[Stearns, William Augustus]. *Adjutant Stearns.* Boston: Massachusetts Sabbath School Society, 1872.

Stonum, Gary. *The Dickinson Sublime.* Madison: University of Wisconsin Press, 1990.

Storrs, Richard Salter. "Tribute." In Park, *Memorial Collection of Sermon.*

Stuart, Marie. "Contesting the Word: Emily Dickinson and the Higher Critics." PhD diss., Darwin College, Cambridge, 1994.

Tate, Allen. Article in *Symposium,* April 1932. Rpt: *The Recognition of Emily Dickinson,* ed. Caesar Blake and Carlton Wells. Ann Arbor: University of Michigan Press, 1964. 153–67.

Todd, Mabel Loomis, ed. *The Letters of Emily Dickinson.* 2 vols. Boston: Roberts Brothers, 1894.

———, ed. *The Letters of Emily Dickinson.* New York and London: Harper & Brothers, 1931.

Vaidhyanathan, Siva. *Copyrights and Copywrongs: The Rise of Intellectual Property and How It Threatens Creativity.* New York: New York University Press, 2001.

Vanderpool, Harold Young. "The Andover Conservatives: Apologetics, Biblical Criticism and Theological Change at the Andover Theological Seminary, 1808–1880." PhD diss., Harvard University, 1971.

Wadsworth, Charles. *Sermons by Charles Wadsworth, D. D.* New York: Eagle Book & Job Printing Department, 1905.

Wald, Priscilla. *Constituting Americans: Cultural Anxiety and Narrative Form.* Durham, NC: Duke University Press, 1995.
Walker, John. *Elements of Elocution.* Boston: D. Mallory & Co., 1810.
Ward, Theodora. *The Capsule of the Mind: Chapters in the Life of Emily Dickinson.* Cambridge, MA: Belknap Press of Harvard University Press, 1961.
Wardrop, Daneen. "Emily Dickinson and the Gothic in Fascicle 16." In Martin 142–64.
Washburn, Eliza. School compositions, c.1840? box 1 folder 22. Washburn Family papers. American Antiquarian Society.
Weisbuch, Robert. *Emily Dickinson's Poetry.* Chicago: University of Chicago Press, 1975.
———. "Whitman and Dickinson." *American Literary Scholarship: An Annual,* 1983: 87–94.
Weld, Allen H. *English Grammar, illustrated by exercises in composition, analyzing, and parsing.* Rev. ed. Boston: Sanborn, Carter, and Bazin; Portland, ME: Sanborn and Carter; Detroit, MI: John A. Kerr, 1856.
Werner, Marta L., ed. *Emily Dickinson's Open Folios: Scenes of Reading, Surfaces of Writing.* Ann Arbor: University of Michigan Press, 1995.
Whately, Richard. *Elements of Rhetoric, Comprising the Substance of the Article . . .* Boston: James Munroe and Co, 1839.
Whicher, George Frisbie. *This Was a Poet: A Critical Biography of Emily Dickinson.* New York: Scribner's, 1938.
White, Melissa. "Letter to the Light: Discoveries in Dickinson's Correspondence." *Emily Dickinson Journal* 16, no. 1 (Spring 2007): 1–26.
Whitman, Walt. *Leaves of Grass and Other Poems.* New York: Norton, 2002.
Winterson, Jeanette. *Why Be Happy When You Could Be Normal?* Toronto: Knopf Canada, 2011.
Wohlpart, James A. "A New Redemption: Emily Dickinson's Poetic in Fascicle 22 and 'I Dwell in Possibility.'" *South Atlantic Review* 66, no. 1 (Winter 2001): 50–83.
Wolff, Cynthia Griffin. *Emily Dickinson.* New York: Knopf, 1986.
Wolosky, Shira. *Emily Dickinson: A Voice of War.* New Haven, CT: Yale University Press, 1984.
———. "Public and Private in Dickinson's War Poetry." In Pollak 103–31.
Woodmansee, Martha. "On the Author Effect: Recovering Collectivity." In Woodmansee and Jaszi 14–28.
Woodmansee, Martha and Peter Jaszi, eds. *The Construction of Authorship: Textual Appropriation in Law and Literature.* Durham, NC: Duke University Press, 1994.
Wordsworth, William. *The Poetical Works of Wordsworth.* Ed. Thomas Hutchinson. London: Oxford University Press, 1964.
Wylder, Edith. "Emily Dickinson: Poetry and Punctuation." *Saturday Review,* March 30, 1963, 26–27, 74.
———. *The Last Face: Emily Dickinson's Manuscripts.* Albuquerque: University of New Mexico Press, 1971.
Yamakawa, Tomoaki, ed. *After a Hundred Years: Essays on Emily Dickinson.* Kyoto, Japan: Emily Dickinson Society of Japan, 1988.
Yeats, W. B. *Selected Poems and Four Plays.* Ed. M. L. Rosenthal. New York: Scribner, 1996.

# CONTRIBUTORS

**Paula Bernat Bennett,** professor emerita from Southern Illinois University Carbondale, is the author of a number of books and articles, including *Poets in the Public Sphere: The Emancipatory Project of American Women's Poetry, 1800–1900; Emily Dickinson: Woman Poet;* and *My Life a Loaded Gun: Female Creativity and Feminist Poetics.* With Karen Kilcup and Philipp Schweighauser, she co-edited *Teaching Nineteenth-Century American Poetry* for the MLA Options for Teaching series.

**Sharon Cameron** is William R. Kenan, Jr., Professor of English at Johns Hopkins University. She is the author of seven books: *Lyric Time: Dickinson and the Limits of Genre; The Corporeal Self: Allegories of the Body in Melville and Hawthorne; Writing Nature: Henry Thoreau's Journal; Thinking in Henry James; Choosing Not Choosing: Dickinson's Fascicles; Beautiful Work: A Meditation on Pain;* and *Impersonality: Seven Essays.*

**Paul Crumbley** is a professor of English at Utah State University and author of *Inflections of the Pen: Dash and Voice in Emily Dickinson* and *Winds of Will: Emily Dickinson and the Sovereignty of Democratic Thought.* Other books include *The Search for a Common Language: Environmental Writing and Education; Body My House: The Work and Life of May Swenson,* and *The Student's Encyclopedia of Great American Writers,* Volume 2, 1830–1900. He is a past president of the Emily Dickinson International Society and currently serves on the Board of Directors.

**Ellen Louise Hart,** editor and textual critic, writes about the history of Dickinson's manuscripts and about prosody and the visual line in the correspondences and verse. Her work has appeared in at least ten major collections and journals. In 1998, with Martha Nell Smith, she co-edited *Open Me Carefully: Emily Dickinson's Intimate Letters to Susan Huntington Dickinson.* She serves as an associate editor for the Dickinson Electronic Archives, and on electronic editions of Susan Dickinson. Hart served on the Board of the Emily Dickinson International Society and has taught in the Writing Program at UC Santa Cruz. Currently she teaches at Portland Community College and at Portland State University in Portland, Oregon.

**Eleanor Elson Heginbotham,** professor emerita, Concordia University, is the author of *Reading the Fascicles of Emily Dickinson: Dwelling in Possibilities* (Columbus: The Ohio State University Press, 2003) and some dozen essays on Dickinson (and others) in collections and journals, including essays on Dickinson's Milton and Dickinson's George Eliot in the *Emily Dickinson Journal*. She continues to teach in the Washington, DC area and serves on the Board of the Emily Dickinson International Society as Member-at-Large.

**Susan Howe's** *My Emily Dickinson* (1985) and *Unsettling the Wilderness in American Literary History* (1993), named "International Book of the Year" by the *Times Literary Supplement* (among her numerous volumes of ground-breaking poetry and criticism), have pointed the way in Dickinson studies. Elected as Chancellor of the Academy of American Poets in 2000, she has been the recipient of many awards, including Yale University's 2011 Bollingen Prize in American Poetry.

**Melanie Hubbard,** an independent scholar, is writing a book on Emily Dickinson's rhetoric and poetics, for which she won an NEH award; she has published articles in *The Emily Dickinson Journal* and *MOSAIC*. She has also contributed essays to *Dickinson and Philosophy* (2013) and *Emily Dickinson in Context* (2013). Her book of poems, *We Have With Us Your Sky,* was published in 2012 by Subito Press.

**Domhnall Mitchell** teaches nineteenth-century American Literature at the Norwegian University of Science and Technology. He has written two books on Emily Dickinson for the University of Massachusetts Press and edited another on her international reception for Continuum. With Paul Goring and Jeremy Hawthorn he has authored *Studying Literature: The Essential Companion for Bloomsbury Academic*. His essays have appeared in *American Literature, The Emily Dickinson Journal, Legacy,* and *Nineteenth-Century Literature*.

Professor of English and Distinguished Scholar-Teacher at the University of Maryland, **Martha Nell Smith** is the author/editor of five books on Emily Dickinson, as well as a digital scholarly edition, *Emily Dickinson's Correspondences: A Born-Digital Textual Inquiry* (2008) and the *Dickinson Electronic Archives* (1994 to the present). She is on the Advisory Board of Harvard University Press's Emily Dickinson Archive (2013) and is working on a biography of Susan. She has received the Livingston College Distinguished Alumni Award from Rutgers University, has been named an ADVANCE Fellow at the University of Maryland, and is President of the Emily Dickinson International Society.

**Alexandra Socarides** is associate professor of English at the University of Missouri. Her book, *Dickinson Unbound: Paper, Process, Poetics,* was published by Oxford University Press in 2012. She has published articles on Dickinson in *the Emily Dickinson Journal, A Companion to Emily Dickinson,* and *Emily Dickinson in Context*. She serves on the board of the Emily Dickinson International Society.

# INDEX OF FIRST LINES

A bird came down the walk (Fr359), 244n12
A Charm invests a face (Fr430, F15), 27
A curious Cloud surprised the Sky (Fr509, F24), 136
A Day! Help! Help! (Fr58, F2), 142
A Dew sufficed itself (Fr1372), 228n4
A fuzzy fellow, without feet – (Fr171, F8), 76, 227
A long – long Sleep – (Fr463, F22), 90, 100
A narrow Fellow in the Grass (Fr1096), 248n5
A nearness to Tremendousness – (Fr824, F40), 22, 193
A Pit – but Heaven over it – (Fr508, F24), 25, 136
A Prison gets to be a friend – (Fr456, F22), 6, 91, 93, 96
A Solemn thing within the Soul (Fr467, F22), 87, 90, 233n8
A throe opon the features (Fr105B, F5), 241n28
A Word dropped careless on a Page (Fr1268), 50
A word is dead, when it is said (Fr278), 250n15
A Word made Flesh is seldom (Fr1715), 5, 61, 250n15
A *wounded* Deer – leaps highest – (Fr181, F8), 70–71, 227n2, 230n16

Afraid! Of whom am I afraid? (Fr345, F16), 110, 123–25, 127
After great pain, a formal feeling comes – (Fr1372, F18), 23, 228n4
Ah! Necromancy Sweet! (Fr168, F8), 63, 66, 68–69, 78
Ah – Teneriffe – Receding / Mountain (Fr752, F36)
All forgot for recollecting (Fr827, F40), 193, 196, 202, 208
As if I asked a common alms – (Fr14, F1), 156–61, 167, 244n15
As if some little Arctic flower (Fr177, F8), 69, 83, 227n2
At last – to be identified – (Fr172, F8 and F21), 68–69, 76, 228n8
At least – to pray – is left – is left (Fr377, F18), 21, 23
Baffled for just a day or two – (Fr66, F2), 142, 143
Because I could not stop for Death – (Fr479, F23), 25, 32, 98, 112,
Before I got my eye put out (F336B, F16), 110, 112, 115–16, 126, 128, 237n3, 239n11
Before the ice is in the pools – (Fr46, F2), 142, 143
Behind Me – dips Eternity – (Fr743, F36), 22
Bereaved of all, I went abroad – (Fr886, F39), 22

267

Bereavement in their death to feel (Fr756, F34), 26
Between My Country – and the Others – (Fr829, F40), 196
Blazing in Gold and quenching in Purple (Fr321, F13), 193
Bless God [Please God], he went as soldiers (Fr52, F2), 142, 143, 146
Bound – a trouble – (Fr240A, F9 and 36), 16
By such and such an offering (Fr47, F2), 141, 143
Could live – *did* live – (Fr59, F2), 142, 143
Denial – is the only fact (Fr826, F40), 250n17
Dust is the only Secret (Fr166, F8), 77, 78, 227n2
Dying! Dying in the night! (Fr222, F9), 183
Essential Oils – are wrung – (Fr772, F34), 26
Except to Heaven, she is naught (Fr173, F8), 81, 227n2
"Faith" is a fine invention (Fr202, F10), 184
Fame of Myself, to justify (Fr481, F23), 95
Fitter to see Him, I may be (Fr834, F40), 209
Flowers – Well – if anybody (Fr95, F4), 193–94
For this – accepted Breath (Fr230, F9), 178, 183
Frequently the woods are pink – (Fr24, F1), 153
Had I not This, or This, I said (Fr828, F40), 198, 202–3, 209, 212
He fought like those Who've nought to lose – (Fr480, F23), 222n11
He fumbles at your Soul (Fr477B, F22), 6, 89–90, 99–102, 233n9
He showed me Hights I never saw (Fr346B, F16), 110, 112, 115–16, 128, 237n3, 239n11, 240n18
He was weak, and I was strong (Fr221, F9), 172
He who in Himself believes – (Fr835, F40), 208
Heart! We will forget him! (Fr64, F2), 142, 143
How happy is the little Stone (Fr1570), 197
How noteless Men and Pleiads, stand (Fr342, F16), 110, 118, 119, 128
I cannot dance opon my Toes (Fr381B, F19), 238n7
I cannot live with You – (I Fr706, F33), 21
I cautious, scanned my little life (Fr175, F8), 82, 227
I counted till they danced so (Fr45, F2), 141, 143
I dwell in Possibility – (Fr466, F22), 90, 95, 99
I felt a Funeral, in my Brain (Fr340, F16), 22, 106–10, 112, 118, 126, 128, 237n4, 242n36
I found the words to every thought (Fr436, F15), 27
I had been hungry, all the Years – (Fr439, F15), 27–28
I had not minded – Walls – (Fr554, F27), 31
I have never seen 'Volcanoes' – (Fr165, F8), 76–78, 227n2
I heard a Fly buzz – when I died – (Fr591, F26), 91
I hide myself – within my flower (Fr80, F3 and F40), 170, 196, 228n8, 249n7
I keep my pledge (Fr63, F2), 142, 143
I like a look of Agony (Fr339, F16), 79, 110, 118, 120, 121, 123, 128, 220n6, 239n11, 240n25, 241n28
I met a King this Afternoon! (Fr183, F8), 70, 227n2
I never saw a Moor (Fr800), 124
I often passed the Village (Fr41 F3), 112–14
I (Who) robbed the Woods – (Fr57, F2), 142, 143
I saw no Way – The Heavens were stitched – (Fr633, F31), 23–24

I stepped from Plank to Plank (Fr926, Set 5), 22*
I taste a liquor never brewed (Fr207, F12), 248n5
I think the Hemlock likes to stand (Fr400, F20), 220n6
I tie my Hat – I crease my Shawl (Fr522, F24), 25
I took one Draught – of Life – (Fr396, F20), 31
I was the slightest in the House (Fr473, F22), 95, 99
I would not paint – a picture (Fr348, F17), 101, 250n15
If *he dissolve* – then – there is *nothing – more* – (Fr251, F10), 184
If I can stop one Heart from breaking (Fr982, Set 7), 65*
If I could bribe them by a Rose (Fr176, F8), 82–83, 227n2
If I may have it, when it's dead (Fr431, F15), 26
If I should cease to bring a Rose (Fr53, F2), 142, 143
If the foolish call them '*flowers,*' – (Fr179, F8), 71–72, 227n2
If those I loved were lost (Fr20, F1), 164–67
If she had been the Mistletoe (Fr60, F2), 142, 143
I'll tell you how the Sun rose (Fr204, F1), 157, 244n11
I'm sorry for the Dead – Today – (Fr582, F14), 63
I'm the little "Heart's Ease"! (Fr167, F8), 227n2
In Ebon Box, when years have flown (Fr180, F8), 73, 75, 227n2
In other Motes (Fr1664), 1
It always felt to me – a wrong (Fr521, F24), 137

It did not surprise me – (Fr50, F2), 142, 143
It don't sound so terrible – quite – (Fr384, F19), 110, 237n5
It feels a shame to be Alive – (Fr524, F24), 137, 240n19
It is dead – Find it – (Fr434, F15), 26
It sifts from Leaden Sieves – (Fr291, F24), 25, 136, 195
It would have starved a Gnat – (Fr444, F21), 63
I've got an arrow here (Fr56, F2), 142
Just Once! Oh Least Request! (Fr478, F22), 233n9
Knows how to forget! (Fr391, F19), 185
Lay this Laurel on the one (Fr1428), 206
"Lethe" in my flower (Fr54, F2), 142, 143
Like Mighty Foot Lights – burned/ the Red (Fr507, F24), 136
Like some Old fashioned Miracle (Fr408, F20), 220n6
Me prove it now – Whoever doubt (Fr631, F31), 24
Midsummer, was it, when They died – (Fr822, F40), 193
Morns like these – we parted – (Fr18, F1), 153
Musicians wrestle everywhere – (Fr229, F9), 182
My Garden – like the beach (Fr469, F22), 100
My life had stood – a Loaded Gun – (Fr764, F34), 5, 57, 59–60, 62, 230n15
My period had come for Prayer – (Fr525, F28), 26
My Triumph lasted till the Drums (Fr1212, Set 8a), 241n27*
My wheel is in the dark! (Fr61, F2), 142, 143

---

\* Although the focus of this book is on the "fascicles," almost 400 pages of the Franklin Manuscript Book are devoted to representing the "sets," collections of unbound but possibly related papers which are fertile fields of studies for future scholars.

Myself was formed – a Carpenter – (Fr475, F22), 95, 99
Nature affects to be sedate (Fr1176), 228n4
Nature – sometimes sears a Sapling – (Fr457, F22), 87–89, 96, 101, 232n3, 233n9, 235n25
Nobody knows this little Rose – (Fr11, F1), 153–56, 161, 167
Not in this World to see his face – (Fr435, F15), 26
*Oh* if remembering were forgetting – (Fr9, F1), 156
Of all the Sounds dispatched abroad (Fr334, F12), 157, 244n13
Of being is a bird (Fr462, F22), 100
Of Bronze – and Blaze – (Fr319, F13), 28–29, 220n6
Of Brussels – it was not – I (Fr510, F226), 136
Of Course – I prayed (Fr581, F25), 182
Of nearness to her sundered Things (Fr337, F16), 110, 118–20, 127
On this wondrous sea (Fr3, F1), 153
One Blessing had I then the rest (Fr767, F34), 31
One Sister have I in the house (Fr5, F2), 130, 139, 141, 142–44
Once more, my now bewildered Dove (Fr65, F2), 142–44
Pain – expands the Time – (Fr833, F40), 213
Pictures [Portraits] are to daily faces (Fr174, F8), 16, 68, 73–74, 227n2
Please God [Bless God], he went as soldiers (Fr52, F2), 142, 143, 146
Presentiment – is that long shadow – on the Lawn – (Fr487, F23), 222n11
Publication – is the Auction (Fr788, F37), 8, 191, 203–6, 249n12, 250n13
Rehearsal to Ourselves (Fr664, F30), 21
Robbed by Death – but that was easy – (Fr838, F40), 193
Safe in their Alabaster Chambers – (Fr124, F6 and 10), 8, 79, 100–101, 157, 172–77, 187, 189, 228n8, 243n11
Shall I take thee, the Poet said (Fr1243), 5, 56, 226n23
She dealt her pretty words like Blades – (Fr458, F22), 90–91, 99
Show me / Eternity (Fr1658), 133
Some Work for Immortality – (Fr536, F28), 21
South winds jostle them – (Fr98, F5), 157, 244n12
That after Horror – that 'twas us – (Fr243, F11), 220n6
The Admirations – and Contempts – of time – (Fr830, F40), 193, 195, 210, 212
The Bible is an antique Volume (Fr1577), 104
The Brain – is wider than the Sky – (Fr598, F26), 35
The Definition of Beauty is (Fr797), 172
The Face I carry with me – last (Fr395, F19), 139, 142–45
The feet of people walking home (Fr16, F1 and F14), 139, 156, 161–63, 167, 228n8
The first Day's Night had come – (Fr423, F15), 23, 26
The first Day that I was a Life (Fr823, F40), 207
The Grass so little has to do (Fr379B, F19), 237n5
The Guest is gold and crimson – (Fr44, F2), 141, 143
The [maddest/ nearest] dream – recedes – unrealized – (Fr304, F14), 157, 220n6, 222n10, 244n11
The Martyr Poets – did not tell – (Fr665, F30), 240n19
The Only News I know (Fr820, F40), 26, 192, 194
The poets light but lamps (Fr930, Set 5), 250n15
The Soul's Superior instants (Fr630, F31), 24
The *Sun – just touched* the Morning (Fr251, F10), 184–85
The Sun kept stooping – stooping – low! (Fr182, F8), 70, 227n2

The Tint I cannot take – is best – (Fr696, F32), 115
The Trees like Tassels – hit – (Fr523, F24), 136
The Whole of it came not at once – (Fr485, F23), 222n11
There came a Day – at Summer's full – 157, 220, (Fr325, F13), 229n13, 244n12
There is a pain – so utter – (Fr514, F24), 230n6
There is a word (Fr42, F2), 139–41, 143
There's a certain Slant of light (Fr320, F13), 22, 28, 30
There is another sky (J2, FrA13-2), 132–33
There's something quieter than sleep (Fr62, F2), 142, 143
They shut me up in Prose (Fr445, F21), 229n12
This is my letter to the World (Fr519, F24), 25
This was a Poet (Fr446, F21), 229n12
This World is not conclusion (Fr373, F18), 241n32
Tho' I get home how late – how late – (Fr199, F10), 31
Through lane it lay – thro' bramble (Fr43, F2), 141, 143
Tie the strings to my Life, My Lord (Fr338, F16), 110, 114, 237n3
'Till Death – is narrow Loving (Fr831, F40), 210
'Tis good – the looking back on Grief – (Fr472, F22), 90
'Tis so appalling – it exhilirates (Fr341, F16), 79, 110, 120, 122, 123, 125–27, 237n3
'Tis so much joy! 'Tis so much joy! (Fr170, F8), 75–76, 227n2
'Tis Sunrise – little Maid – Hast Thou (Fr832, F40), 212
Title divine, is mine (Fr194), 23
To disappear enhances – (Fr1239, Set 10), 8, 185–87
To learn the Transport by the Pain (Fr178, F8), 70–72, 81, 227n2, 231n19

To lose One's faith – surpass (Fr632, F31), 24
To make One's Toilette – after Death (Fr471, F22), 90
To pile like Thunder to it's close (Fr1353), 239n17, 250n15
To put this World down, like a Bundle – (Fr404, F20), 59–60
To venerate the simple days (Fr55, F2), 142, 143, 148–49
'Twas just this time, last year, I died ' (Fr344, F16), 110, 111, 113, 129, 237n3
'Twas like a Maelstrom, with a notch (Fr425, F15), 23
Unfulfilled to Observation (Fr839, F40), 26, 193, 214
"Unto Me"? I do not / know you – (Fr825, F40), 210
Wait till the Majesty of Death (Fr169, F8), 74–75, 227n2
We Cover Thee – Sweet Face – (Fr461, F2), 87, 233n8
We don't cry – Tim and I (Fr231, F9), 183
We grow accustomed to the Dark – (Fr428, F15), 26
We play at Paste (Fr282), 157, 244n11
We pray – to Heaven – (Fr476, F22), 91
Wert Thou but ill – that I might show thee – (Fr821, F40), 193, 209
What Inn is this (Fr100, F5), 228n4
When I count the seeds (Fr51, F2), 142, 143
When I was small, a woman died (Fr518, F24), 137, 240n20
When we stand on the tops of Things (Fr343, F16), 110, 118, 120–21, 240n26
Who (I) robbed the Woods – (Fr57, F2), 142, 143
"Why do I love" You, Sir? (Fr459, F22), 88, 90
Wild nights! – Wild nights! (Fr269, F11), 183, 247n19
Witchcraft was hung, in History (Fr1612), 84

Without this – there is nought – (Fr464, F22), 95, 100
You constituted Time – (Fr488, F23), 222n11
You love the Lord – you cannot see – (Fr474, F22), 90

You'll know it – as you know 'tis Noon – (Fr429, F15), 27
Your Riches – taught me poverty – (Fr418, F14), 244n12

# INDEX TO LETTERS
## (INCLUDING POEMS CITED AS LETTERS)

Boston Public Library 20 to Thomas Wentworth Higginson (early June 1864), 194
L9 to Abiah Root (12 January 1846), 236n34
L22 to Austin Dickinson (17 February 1848), 236n33
L34 to George H. Gould (February 1850), 326n36
L58 to Austin Dickinson (17 October 1851), 132–33
L142 to Austin Dickinson (21 November 1853), 102
L191 to Mrs. Joseph Haven (early summer 1858), 225n16
L193 to Samuel Bowles (late August 1858?), 229n10
L233 to "Master" (about 1861), 234n19
L235 to Mrs. Samuel Bowles (about August 1861), 123
L238 to Susan Gilbert Dickinson (summer 1861), 101, 235n26
L247 to Samuel Bowles (about 11 January 1862), 243n10
L249 to Samuel Bowles (early 1862), 234n19
L255 to Louise and Frances Norcross (late March 1862), 122–23
L256 to Samuel Bowles (late March 1862), 109, 123
L260 to Thomas Wentworth Higginson (15 April 1862), 157
L261 to Thomas Wentworth Higginson (25 April 1862), 92, 157
L265 to Thomas Wentworth Higginson (7 June 1862), 157–60, 178
L290 to Thomas Wentworth Higginson (early June 1864), 92–93, 194
L293 to Lavinia Dickinson (July 1864), 234n19
L298 to Louise and Frances Norcross (1864?), 127, 194
L342a from Thomas Wentworth Higginson (16 August 1870), 101
L503 to Thomas Wentworth Higginson (June 1877), 191, 206
L749 to Thomas Niles (late April 1882), 197
L937a Helen Hunt Jackson to Emily Dickinson (5 September 1884), 229n10
L964 to an unknown correspondent (early 1885), 160–61
Prose Fragment 30 (*Letters* page 916), 217

# GENERAL INDEX

Adams, Percy C., 178–80, 262
Alcott, Bronson, 80, 253, 262
Anderson, Charles, 179, 253

Barker, Wendy, 74, 230, 253
Barrett, Faith, 110, 137, 238n6, 253
Barthes, Roland, 36
Baym, Nina, 234n23, 253, 261
Benfey, Christopher, 230n15, 253
Bennett, Paula Bernat, 4–6, 9, 68, 79, 106–29, 137, 230n15, 240n21, 241n14, 253, 261, 262, 266
Bentham, Jeremy, 92, 234n13, 253
Bergland, Renee, 121, 123, 137, 239n15, 253
Berlin, James A., 51
Bervin, Jan, 134, 135, 253
Bianchi, Martha Dickinson, 93, 123, 131, 141, 253
Bible, 97, 103–104; I Cor., 47, 116; Matt.7, 239n14
Bingham, Millicent Todd, 131, 141,
Bishop, Wendy, 176, 236n34, 253
Blake, William, 31, 132, 223n4, 256
Bogan, Louise, 67
Bonivard, François, 96–97, 234n20, 253
Bowles, Samuel, 86, 109, 152, 229n10, 231n22, 233n9, 234n19, 237n5, 243n10. See also *The Springfield Daily Republican*

Braude, Ann, 81, 232, 240n21, 253
Buescher, John B., 240n21, 254
Brown, Gillian, 249n9, 254
Browne, Francis, 239nn12,13, 254
Browning, Elizabeth Barrett, 18, 129, 222n9, 254
Browning, Robert, 6, 174, 194, 222n9, 238n10, 242n35, 264, 266
Buckingham, Willis, 171, 229n9, 230n17, 254
Budick, E. Miller, 230n15, 264
Burns, Robert, 129, 156, 254
Byron, George Gordon (Lord), 6, 96–97

Calvin, John, 116
Cameron, Sharon, xi, xiii, 2–3, 5, 12–31, 264, 266; *Lyric Time*, 12, 21. See also *Choosing Not Choosing*
Campbell, George, 50–53, 56, 62, 225n15, 226n17, 254
Capps, Jack, 222n9, 254
Chambers, William, *Cyclopedia of English Literature*, 222n9, 254
*Choosing Not Choosing* (Cameron), xiii, 2–3, 33–38, 55–62, 73–74, 99, 107–11, 115, 118, 120, 128, 134, 162, 192, 217, 219n2, 222n1, 229n9, 231n20, 237n2, 242nn1,2,3, 240n18, 242nn3,4, 243n4, 254, 266

274

Chung, Sandra, 174, 245n6, 246nn10,13,14, 254, 258
Civil War (War Between the States), 4, 6–7, 9, 74, 106–29, 136–37, 193–94, 206, 253, 254, 262, 263
Clary, Bruce, 35–37, 223nn5,7, 254
Cody, John, 74, 107, 254
Coleman, Lyman, 103, 236nn34,35
Coleridge, Samuel Taylor, 179
Copyright Laws, Publication, 8–9, 191, 200–205, 222n9, 249nn8,10, 250n13
Crumbley, Paul, xi, 4, 8, 191–215, 230n14, 238n8, 243n4, 247n17, 254, 255, 266; *Inflections of the Pen*, 237n1; *Winds of Will*, 68, 69, 107, 237n1
Curry, Samuel Silas, 238n10
Curtis, Burrill, 80, 260

Dana, Barbara, 183, 190, 255, 257, 259. See also *Wider than the Sky*
Danderand, Karen, 193, 206, 243, 255
Davis, Robert Henry, 39, 40, 43, 44fig.4, 46, 235n29, 255
Debo, Annette, 138, 255
Dickie, Margaret, 230n17, 243n5, 255
Dickinson, Austin, 7, 102, 109, 132–33, 225n16, 236n33, 243n6
Dickinson, Edward, 181, 222n9, 225n16, 236n29
*Dickinson Electronic Archives*, 245n5, 255, 263, 266, 267
Dickinson, Emily: distribution of poems (publication in her lifetime), 137, 193, 243nn8,11, 248n5, 255; education, 33, 38, 43, 50, 69, 180, 222n9, 224nn10,11,12, 225nn15, 16, 229n9, 236nn34,39, 262; *Forest Leaves*, 39, 171, 224n10; orthography, 246n11, 247n21; prosody, 4, 169–90, 245n10, 246nn10,11,12,13,14. See also Civil War; fascicles; sets; Mount Holyoke College, and biographical sources listed here: Bianchi, Gordon, Habegger, Leyda, Pollitt, Taggard, St. Armand, Sewall, Whicher

Dickinson, Lavinia, 133–32, 234n19, 244
Dickinson, Loren, 137–38
Dickinson, Martha. *See* Bianchi
Dickinson, Samuel Fowler, 137
Dickinson, Susan Gilbert, 7, 86, 101, 112, 116, 130, 131, 133, 139, 141, 144, 150–57, 161–63, 222n9, 226n25, 232n3, 233nn5,9, 236n27, 243nn6,11, 244n11, 246n2, 247n20, 263, 267
*Dickinson Unbound: Paper, Process, Poetics* (Socarides), 134, 223n8, 244, 263, 268
Diehl, Joanne Feit, 230n16, 231n19, 255
Dobson, Joanne, 81, 255
Donne, John, 92, 95, 234n18, 256

Eberwein, Jane, 75, 77, 255, 257
Eliot, T. S., 2
Emerson, Benjamin Kendall, 39, 234n19, 255
Emerson, Ralph Waldo, 14, 35, 39, 53, 54, 55, 58, 66, 80, 121, 128, 178, 229n10, 230n16, 232n16, 232n25, 241n33, 255, 256, 257
Emily Dickinson International Society, xii, 267
*Emily Dickinson's Fascicles: Meaning and Method* (Oberhaus), 2, 98, 108, 151, 197, 208, 232n5, 233n8, 234n22, 237n1, 242n2, 247n1, 248n3, 250n16, 260
Emmons, Henry Vaughan, 232n4
England, Martha, 88
Ezell, Margaret, 36, 254

Farr, Judith, 78, 107, 117, 230n16, 231n22, 240n18, 266
fascicles: arrangement of sheets, 9; 13, 17, 66, 86, 134, 139, 166, 169; circulation, 7, 152; contextual connections, 23–85; definition, 1, 3, 108, 130, 229n10, 242nn1,2, 244n1,2; dramatic monologues, dramatic lyrics, 6, 9–11, 96, 238nn6,10, 239n11, 256;

duplicates (near repetitions) of poems 16, 68, 73, 84, 152, 161, 227n2, 228n8, 233n7; heteroglossia in, 22–27, 128, 241n33; mutilations (also crossed-out lines), 7, 148, 166, 220, 246n11; pairings of poems within, 16, 26–29, 67, 70, 73, 76–77, 111, 120, 129; paper/ sheet selection, 8–9, 13, 36–37, 40, 66, 86, 131, 142, 153, 157, 161, 166, 192, 220n4, 221nn7,8, 232n2, 244n1, 248n4; pre-fascicle worksheet, 14, 152, 156, 164, 167; sets, 14, 15, 16, 87, 134, 169–70, 172, 183, 185, 189, 191, 220n4, 233n6, 234n22, 244n1, 248n4; transmission of (stewardship of texts) 130–48; variants in, 2–3, 13–20, 31–34, 38, 40, 56–61, 63, 192, 214, 219nn2,3, 220nn6,10, 223n3, 226nn22,23, 237n2, 248n6

Faust, Drew Gilpin, 74, 266
Finnerty, Paraic, 195, 211, 238, 239n11, 256
Flynt, Maria, 103
Ford, Karen, 107, 256
Foucault, Michel, 234n13, 256
Fox sisters, 80
Fraistat, Neil, 228n8, 256
Frank, Bernard, 231
Franklin, Ralph W. 2, 7–10, 13–16, 131, 135, 148, 169–70, 183–85, 192, 219n3, 220n4, 223nn5,6, 226nn22,1, 228n8, 241n32. See also *The Manuscript Books of Emily Dickinson*
Fraser, Eric, 244n16
Friedlander, Benjamin, 111, 114, 238n6, 240n20, 249n12, 256

Gall, Sally M. *See* Rosenthal
*Gaskell's Compendium of Forms,* 189, 257
Gilbert, Thomas, 244
Goodale, Lucy, 38
Gordon, Lyndall, 130, 136, 139, 256
Gould, Rev. George Henry, 103–4, 225n16, 236nn36,37, 257
Grabher, Gudrun, xiii, 254, 255, 254
Grossman, Alan, 34, 257

Guest, J. Alfred, 102, 236n33, 257
Guthrie, James, 76, 92–94, 179, 195, 234nn14,17, 245n9, 248–49n6, 257

Habegger, Alfred, 92, 101, 102, 194–95, 230n16, 235n27, 236n36, 257
Hagenbuchle, Roland, xiii, 54, 222n20, 257, 262
Hampson, Alfred Leete, xii, 131
Hardy, Josephine, 39, 41fig.3, 257
Hardy, Thomas, 2
Hart, Ellen Louise, 4, 7–8, 67, 133, 169–90, 228n8, 244nn11,14, 245nn5,6, 252, 254, 257, 258, 263, 266–67. See also *Open Me Carefully*
Hartman, Geoffrey, 12, 258
Heaney, Seamus, 174, 268, 245n8
Heginbotham, Eleanor Elson, 4, 63–85, 87, 134, 161, 228nn6,7,8, 229n9, 230nn17,18, 258, 267. See also *Reading the Fascicles of Emily Dickinson: Dwelling in Possibilities*
Herbert, George, 18, 222n9, 266
Hewitt, Elizabeth, 244n14, 268
Higginson, Thomas Wentworth 8, 15, 18, 66, 92, 101, 131, 152, 156–57, 160–61, 178, 183, 191, 194, 206, 234n19, 243n10, 244n12, 245n5; and Mabel Loomis Todd, *Poems by Emily Dickinson,* 18, 183
Hirschhorn, Norbert and Polly Longsworth, 234n16, 258
Hitchcock, Edward, 193
Hodge, Charles, 103, 235n31, 258
Hogue, Cynhia, 110, 258
Holmes, Oliver Wendell, 80, 121
Homestead, Melissa, 200, 201, 204, 249n10, 258
Housman, A. E., 2
Howe, Julia Ward, 239n15, 241n27
Howe, Susan, xi, xiii, 217, 245n3, 246n3, 261, 258, 261, 267
Howells, William Dean, 232
Hubbard, Melanie, 4–5, 9, 33–62, 229n9, 261

Hume, David, 33
Hyde, Alan (on "property"), 249n11, 258

Jackson, Helen Hunt, 229n10, 224n1
Jackson, Virginia, 7, 67, 152, 228n6, 229n10, 242n35, 244n1, 256, 258
James, Henry, 80, 232n25
Jefferson, Thomas, 202
Johnson, Thomas S., 13, 15–18, 67, 99, 132–33, 157, 174, 178, 183, 191, 220n6, 226n25, 227n2, 234n14, 235n24, 236n24, 243n12, 244nn1,12, 245n4, 246n11, 247n21, 252
Juhasz, Suzanne, 66, 259

Keats, John, 95, 179, 234n18, 259
Kerr, Howard, 80
Kittredge, Charles Baker, 46, 48, 50, 225n14, 259

Lawton, David, 177, 259
Leyda, Jay, 12, 130, 131, 135, 139–42, 259
Lindberg-Seyersted, Brita, 174, 178, 182, 246n16, 259
Locke, John, 33, 50–55, 60, 230n17, 259
Loeffelholz, Mary, 230n17, 259
Longfellow, Henry Wadsworth, 128
Lowell, James Russell, 232n25
Lowenberg, Carlton, 226n18, 259

MacKenzie, Cynthia and Barbara Dana. See *Wider than the Sky*
MacPherson, C. B. (Locke), 202, 249n9, 259
Mandeville, Bernard, 92, 233n12
*The Manuscript Books of Emily Dickinson* (Franklin), 2, 13–15, 20, 36, 40, 56, 66, 74, 75, 85, 99, 108, 110, 130, 134, 135, 136, 138, 143, 150, 169, 223n6, 226, 227n2, 228nn7,8, 232n4, 233n7, 244nn11,12, 245nn3,4, 246n11, 247n21, 248nn4,5,6, 252, 256

Marcellin, Leigh-Anne, 111, 118, 238, 238nn6,8
Margolis, Stacy, 202, 259
*The Marriage of Emily Dickinson* (Shurr), 2, 229–30n13, 233n5, 242n2, 243n3, 253n8, 263
*Measures of Possibility: Emily Dickinson's Manuscripts* (Mitchell), 244n14, 245n3
McGann, Jerome, 36, 223, 243n3, 260
Melville, Herman, 232, 266
Messmer, Marietta, 236, 260
Michael, Ian, 42, 260
Miller, Cristanne, xiii, 107, 110, 137, 179, 180, 182, 230, 239, 245, 253, 257
Miller, Perry, 101, 235n28
Miller, Ruth. See *The Poetry of Emily Dickinson* I
Mitchell, Domhnall, 4–6, 10, 86–105, 250n13, 260, 267. See also *Measures of Possibility*
*The Modern Poetic Sequence* (Rosenthal and Gall), 2, 223n3, 230n17, 262
Morris, Leslie, 244n13
Morris, Timothy, 179, 188, 260
Mossberg, Barbara, 230
Mount Holyoke College (Seminary), vii, 38–40, 43, 51, 224, 225n16, 226n24, 257, 263
Murray, Lindley, 176, 180–85, 225, 260

Newman, Samuel P., 43, 50, 55, 225n16, 260
Niles, Thomas (Roberts Brothers), 197
Norcross, Louise and Fanny, 109, 122–23, 152–53, 194, 243–44
*Norton Anthology of American Literature*, 99, 184, 234n23, 253, 257

Oberhaus, Dorothy Huff, 2. See also *Emily Dickinson's Fascicles, Meaning and Method*
O'Keefe, Martha Lindblom, 131, 135, 261, 234n22, 247n1

*Open Me Carefully: Emily Dickinson's Intimate Letters to Susan Huntington Dickinson* (Hart and Smith), 244nn11,14, 245n2, 247n20

Panopticon, 92, 234n13, 253
Park, Edwards Amasa, 6, 43, 102–3, 235nn30,31
Parker, Richard Green, 224–25n13
Patterson, L. Ray and Stanley W. Lindberg, 249n1
Patterson, Rebecca, 130
Payson, Dunton, *Scribner Manual of Style*, 190, 261
Petrino, Elizabeth A., 243n8, 261
Phelps, Elizabeth Stuart, 239nn13,14, 256, 261
Phillips, Elizabeth, 107–9, 237n4, 238n6, 242n36, 261
Piatt, Sarah, 6, 116, 128, 239n16, 240n26, 261
Plath, Sylvia, 65, 126–27
Plumb, Albert H., 235n30
Poe, Edgar Allan, 178
*The Poetry of Emily Dickinson* (Miller), 2, 131, 229n9, 248n3, 260
Pollak, Vivian, 234n16, 237n3, 238n6, 241n33, 261
Pollitt, Josephine, 136
Porter, David, 12, 75, 106–7, 222n3, 230nn14,17, 247n18; *Early Poetry*, 12; *Modern Idiom*, 107, 223n3
Porter, Ebenezer, 174, 181–83, 246n15, 261
Pound, Ezra, 2
Price, Monroe E. and Malla Pollack, 201, 261
Pugh, Christina, 182, 245n3, 261

*Reading the Fascicles of Emily Dickinson: Dwelling in Possibilities* (Heginbotham), 87, 108, 134, 161, 162, 192, 232n1, 237n1, 242n7, 243nn2,4, 244n17
Reynolds, David, 241n34

Rice, Grantland, 262
Richards, Eliza, 137, 262
Ricks, Christopher, 19, 262
Riffaterre, Michael, 68, 227n3, 229n11, 262
Root, Abiah, 236n34
Rosenthal, M. L., 265
Rosenthal, M. L. and Sally Gall, 2. See also *The Modern Poetic Sequence*
Ross, Marlon B., 262
*Rowing in Eden* (Smith), 183, 243n6, 263

St. Armand, Barton Levi, 107, 108, 109, 117, 123, 230n14, 238n7, 239n14, 240n19, 241n30, 262
Salter, Mary Jo, 175, 262
Sanchez-Eppler, Karen, 205, 262
Schleiermacher, Friedrich, 103, 235n32, 262
Schulz, Lucy, 224n11
Sewall, Richard, 69, 101–2, 104, 136, 222, 225, 236n33, 262
Shakespeare, William, 6, 18, 81, 125, 195–96, 211, 222n9, 240, 256, 267
Shaw, Robert, 124, 262
Shelley, Percy Bysshe, 179
Sheridan, Thomas, 182, 262
Shurr, William H. See *The Marriage of Emily Dickinson*
Small, Judy Jo, 179, 263
Smith, Henry Boynton, 103, 236n33
Smith, Martha Nell, 4–6, 10, 66, 130–49, 183, 230n17, 238n6, 239n14, 240n20, 243n6, 245nn3,5, 246n11, 252, 253, 262, 263, 267. See also *Open Me Carefully*, *Rowing in Eden*
Smith and Vetter, *Electronic Archive*, 133, 252, 263
Smith, Robert McClure, 108, 263
Socarides, Alexandra, 4, 7, 10–11, 134, 150–68, 223nn6,8, 224n9, 230n17, 137n2, 243n9, 244n16, 268. See *Dickinson Unbound*
*The Springfield Daily Republican*, 154–56, 167, 243n11

Storrs, Richard Salter, 102, 263
Spenser, Edmund, 31
Spiritualist/spiritualism movement, 5, 9, 68–84, 119, 230n14, 231n23, 232n25, 239n14, 240nn21,22, 253, 254, 255, 257, 259, 260, 261, 263
Spring, Suzanne, 224n9, 263
*Springfield Daily Republican,* 154–56, 167, 243n11
Stearns, Adjutant Frazar, 6–7, 107–11, 114, 118, 122–25, 237n5, 238n7, 240n16, 241n30, 261
Storrs, Dr. Richard Salter, 102, 263

Tate, Allen, 67
Tennyson, Alfred Lord, 123, 222n9
Thoreau, Henry David, 80, 217, 230n16, 232n25, 266
Todd, Mabel Loomis, 1, 7, 18, 66, 67, 130–32, 138–42, 148, 183, 221n6, 224n10, 228n6, 229n10, 243n6, 244n1, 262. *See also* Higginson

Vaidhyanatha, Siva P., 200, 202, 263
Vetter, Lara. *See* Martha Nell Smith, *Archive*

Wadsworth, Charles, 6, 98, 101–4, 128, 230, 248, 264

Walker, John, 180, 264
Washburn, Eliza, 42, 264
Watts, Isaac, 88, 181
Webster, Noah, 180, 200
Weisbuch, Robert, 12, 255, 264
Weld, Allen, 180, 264
Werner, Marta, 153, 243n5, 245nn3,5, 263, 264
Whately, Richard, 50–55, 225n16, 226n17, 264
Whicher, George Frisbie, 102, 136, 178, 264
White, Melissa, 264
Whitman, Walt, 19, 31, 35, 128, 228n8, 229n9, 239n12, 241n33, 264
*Wider than the Sky* (MacKenzie and Dana), 190, 257
Winterson, Jeannette, 190, 257, 264
Wolff, Cynthia Griffin, 69, 107, 136, 264
Wolosky, Shira, 111, 137, 288nn6,8, 241nn27, 32, 264
Wordsworth, William, 6, 65, 94–95, 234n16, 264
Wylder, Edith, 180–183, 247nn18, 19, 264

Yeats, William Butler, 19, 265

Zepper, Wilhelm, 101, 235

www.ingramcontent.com/pod-product-compliance
Lightning Source LLC
Chambersburg PA
CBHW030108010526
44116CB00005B/154